AMERICAN ENVIRONMENTALISM

Readings in Conservation History

AMERICAN ENVIRONMENTALISM

Readings in Conservation History

Roderick Frazier Nash

University of California, Santa Barbara

McGraw-Hill Publishing Company

McGraw-Hill, Inc.
New York St. Louis San Francisco Auckland Bogotá
Caracas Lisbon London Madrid Mexico Milan
Montreal New Delhi Paris San Juan Singapore
Sydney Tokyo Toronto

AMERICAN ENVIRONMENTALISM
Readings in Conservation History

5 6 7 8 9 0 **DOH DOH** 9 4 3 2

ISBN 0-07-046059-0

This book was set in Palatino by ComCom, Inc.
The editors were Christopher J. Rogers and Tom Holton;
the designer was Katharine Urban.
R. R. Donnelley & Sons Company was printer and binder.

Library of Congress Cataloging-in-Publication Data

American environmentalism: readings in conservation history / edited
by Roderick Frazier Nash. — 3rd ed.
    p.   cm.
  Rev. ed. of: The American environment. 2d ed. c1976.
  Bibliography: p.
  ISBN 0-07-046059-0
  1. Conservation of natural resources—United States—History—
Sources.   I. Nash, Roderick.   II. Nash, Roderick. American
environment.
S930.A56   1990
333.7′2′0973—dc20
                                                              89-11115
                                                                CIP

CONTENTS

PREFACE

There is no more new frontier; we have got to make it here.

—The Eagles (1976)

The first edition of *American Environmentalism* appeared in 1968 when "ecology," "pollution" and "environment" were rapidly becoming household words in the United States. The second edition of 1976 gave me an opportunity to consider the flowering of conservation—redubbed "environmentalism"—and its substantial impact on attitude and policy. The environmental movement went into at least partial eclipse in the late 1970s. Ronald Reagan and his first Secretary of the Interior, James Watt, personified impatience with restraint on individual aggrandizement. But adversity toughened American environmentalism. Conservation displayed new maturity in the 1980s, flexing surprisingly strong economic, political, legal, and technological muscles. The movement also spawned a radical edge premised on the conviction that nature had rights that mankind must respect.

This third edition offers an opportunity to display these recent trends and suggest future directions. In addition, I have dropped some of the less successful selections from the earlier versions and added a few new readings. Some are secondary analyses, but for the most part I have preferred to let the leaders of American conservation describe their own ends and means. The introductions to the several parts are freshly written and the environmental chronology and bibliography updated.

Fittingly this third edition of *American Environmentalism* is published in 1990, the centennial of the official ending of the American frontier. Americans have now lived for a century without the far and undeveloped horizons that gave rise to the myth of inexhaustibility. As the Eagles, a popular California band of the 1970s, put it: "There is no more new frontier; we have got to make it here." Doing this entails accepting the inevitable limits that a finite environment—the spaceship earth—imposes on all forms of growth. To disregard this truth is to function like the cell that grows so prolifically that it destroys its environment—and, inevitably, itself—with its own ironic success. We use the term "cancer" to describe such unrestrained parts of a living community. But most thoughtful citizens now accept the fact that protection of a livable environment over the long run (indeed as long as we wish to remain alive on earth) must be the top priority of our species. And we do act for ourselves alone. The fate of the earth and its community of life is literally in our hands. As the new technologically equipped, nuclear-powered gods, we must encourage god-like responsibility for our only home. Environmentalism is one of the most encouraging signs that the self-restraint essential to this task is possible.

In preparing this review of the highlights of American conservation I have benefited repeatedly from the reactions of the thousands of students who have, since 1970, passed through Environmental Studies 11 and my upper-division courses in environmental history at the University of California, Santa Barbara. My sincere appreciation goes to the following reviewers for their many valuable comments and suggestions: Samuel Hays, University of Pittsburgh; Mark Lytle, Bard College; Edward Schriver, University of Maine—Orono; Richard Smith; and William Steiver, Clemson University. J. Baird Callicott also lent valued suggestions. Finally, I must acknowledge the assistance of my friend Richard B. Smith, a career employee of the National Park Service, who has helped me understand how a book such as this can assist conservation professionals as well as academicians.

Roderick Frazier Nash

AN AMERICAN ENVIRONMENTAL CHRONOLOGY

1626	Plymouth Colony passes ordinances regulating the cutting and sale of timber on colony lands.
1634	Plymouth prohibits the setting of forest fires.
1639	Newport, Rhode Island, prohibits deer hunting for six months.
1681	William Penn, proprietor of Pennsylvania, decrees that for every five acres of land cleared, one must be left forested.
1691	British colonial policy provides for reserving large trees, suitable for masts, in New England by marking them with a "broad arrow."
1710	Massachusetts protects waterfowl in coastal regions.
1711	The White Pine Act of Parliament extends protection of trees suitable for masts.
1718	Massachusetts prohibits deer hunting for four years.
1739	Connecticut creates an annual closed season for deer.
1772	New York creates a closed season on quail and partridge.
1804–06	Meriwether Lewis and William Clark lead the first American transcontinental exploration.
1828–31	First experiment in federal forest management with live oaks on Santa Rosa Peninsula, Florida.
1832	George Catlin proposes a national park.
1849	U.S. Department of the Interior established.
1858	Mount Vernon purchased as a historical site.
1864	Yosemite Valley, California, reserved as a state park.

1864   George Perkins Marsh publishes *Man and Nature.*

1869   John Wesley Powell descends the Colorado River through the Grand Canyon.

1871   U.S. Fish Commission created.

1872   Arbor Day designated as April 10 as a result of the efforts of J. Sterling Morton; currently celebrated last Friday in April.

1872   Yellowstone National Park established.

1875   American Forestry Association organized.

1876   Appalachian Mountain Club organized.

1878   John Wesley Powell publishes *Report on the Lands of the Arid Region of the United States.*

1879   U.S. Geological Survey established.

1881   Division of Forestry created in the Department of Agriculture as a fact-finding agency.

1882   American Forestry Congress organized.

1885   New York, in cooperation with Ontario, creates the Niagara Reservation, protecting the Falls.

1885   New York establishes the Adirondack Forest Preserve (later Adirondack State Park).

1885   Predecessor of the U.S. Biological Survey created in the Department of Agriculture as the Division of Economic Ornithology and Mammalogy.

1885   Boone and Crockett Club founded.

1886   New York Audubon Society organized.

1886   Bernhard E. Fernow assumes direction of an expanded Division of Forestry.

1890   U.S. Census announces the end of the frontier as a definable line.

1890   Yosemite National Park established.

1891   Forest Reserve Act permits the president to establish forest reserves (later national forests) on the public domain.

1891   National Irrigation Congress organized.

1892   Sierra Club founded.

1895   American Scenic and Historic Preservation Society founded.

1897	Forest Management Act defines purpose of the forest reserves.
1898	First college-level work in forestry offered at Cornell.
1898	Gifford Pinchot named head of the Division of Forestry.
1899	River and Harbor Act establishes the first legal basis for banning pollution of navigable waterways.
1900	Society of American Foresters founded.
1900	Lacey Act makes interstate shipment of game killed in violation of state laws a federal offense.
1902	Reclamation (Newlands) Act establishes Bureau of Reclamation in the Department of the Interior and launches a federal reclamation program.
1905	National Audubon Society formed.
1905	Forest reserves transferred from the Department of the Interior to the Forest Service within Department of Agriculture.
1906	Antiquities Act permits reservation of areas of scientific or historical interest on federal land as national monuments.
1907	Inland Waterways Commission established.
1908	Grand Canyon of the Colorado made a national monument.
1908	Theodore Roosevelt hosts a conference of governors at the White House on the subject of conservation.
1908	National Conservation Commission appointed to inventory resources.
1909	North American Conservation Conference held in Washington.
1909	National Conservation Association organized as a private group to replace the National Conservation Commission.
1910	The Forest Products Laboratory established by the Forest Service in Madison, Wisconsin.
1910	The Ballinger-Pinchot controversy disrupts the conservation movement.
1911	American Game Protective and Propagation Association founded.

1911	Weeks Act, permitting purchase of forested land at headwaters of navigable streams for inclusion in the national forest system, makes possible the establishment of national forests in the East.
1913	Hetch Hetchy Valley in Yosemite National Park granted to San Francisco for a reservoir after prolonged controversy.
1916	National Park Service Act.
1918	Migratory Bird Treaty Act implements 1916 treaty with Canada to restrict hunting of migratory species.
1918	Save-the-Redwoods-League founded.
1920	Mineral Leasing Act regulates mining on federal lands.
1920	Federal Water Power Act gives the Federal Power Commission authority to issue licenses for hydropower development.
1922	Izaak Walton League organized.
1924	Oil Pollution Control Act.
1924	Teapot Dome scandal.
1924	The Forest Service designates first extensive wilderness area in the Gila National Forest, New Mexico.
1924	The first National Conference on Outdoor Recreation held in Washington, D.C.
1924	Clarke-McNary Act extends federal ability to buy lands for inclusion in the National Forest system and provides for private, state, and federal cooperation in forest management.
1926	Restoration of Williamsburg, Virginia, begun.
1928	Boulder Canyon Project (Hoover Dam) authorized.
1928	McSweeney-McNary Act authorizes a broad program of federal forestry research.
1933	Civilian Conservation Corps established.
1933	Tennessee Valley Authority created.
1933	Franklin D. Roosevelt creates the Soil Erosion Service as an emergency measure.
1934	Taylor Grazing Act provides for retention and federal regulation of use of unreserved public domain.
1935	Soil Conservation Act extends federal involvement in

erosion control and establishes the Soil Conservation Service in the Department of Agriculture.

1935   Wilderness Society founded.

1936   National Wildlife Federation, with 4.6 million members by the 1980s, founded.

1936   Omnibus Flood Control Act establishes a national flood prevention policy under the U.S. Army Corps of Engineers and the Department of Agriculture.

1937   Federal Aid in Wildlife Restoration (Pittman-Robertson) Act makes federal funds available to states for wildlife protection and propagation.

1939   Forest Service "U" regulations extend the policy of wilderness preservation in the national forests.

1940   The creation of the U.S. Fish and Wildlife Service consolidates federal protection and propagation activities.

1944   Soil Conservation Society of America founded.

1946   U.S. Bureau of Land Management established to consolidate the administration of the public domain.

1948   Federal Water Pollution Control Law enacted to regulate waste disposal.

1948   Donora, Pennsylvania, experiences severe air pollution; twenty die and 14,000 become ill.

1949   The first Sierra Club Biennial Wilderness Conference held.

1949   Congress charters the National Trust for Historic Preservation.

1949   Aldo Leopold's *A Sand County Almanac* published posthumously.

1952   London's "Killer Smog" leaves 4,000 dead in a weekend and leads to effective air pollution regulations.

1956   Mission 66 launched as a ten-year improvement program for the national parks.

1956   Echo Park Dam, scheduled for construction in Dinosaur National Monument, deleted from the Upper Colorado River Storage Project, marking a major victory for wilderness preservation and the National Park system.

1956   Water Pollution Control Act provides federal grants for water treatment plants.

1958   Congress appoints the Outdoor Recreation Resources Review Commission to study and report on the nation's future needs.

1960   The Multiple Use–Sustained Yield Act defines the purpose of the national forests to admit nonmaterial benefits.

1962   President John F. Kennedy and Secretary of the Interior Stewart Udall host a White House Conference on Conservation.

1962   Rachel Carson publishes *Silent Spring*.

1963   Clean Air Act authorizes federal hearings and legal actions.

1963   The Bureau of Outdoor Recreation established within the Department of the Interior to coordinate federal efforts.

1964   Wilderness Act establishes the National Wilderness Preservation System.

1964   Canyonlands National Park established.

1965   Land and Water Conservation Fund Act makes money available for local, state, and federal acquisition and development of park land and open space.

1965   Storm King (Scenic Hudson) case admits scenic and recreational criteria in legal actions.

1965   Lyndon B. Johnson hosts a White House Conference on Natural Beauty.

1966   National Historic Preservation Act passed.

1966   Endangered Species Act begins federal involvement in habitat protection and rare species identification.

1967   Environmental Defense Fund established.

1968   Paul Ehrlich publishes *The Population Bomb*.

1968   National Wild and Scenic Rivers Act and National Trails System Act passed.

1968   Grand Canyon Dams defeated.

1968   First manned flight to circle the moon produces dramatic photographs of "spaceship earth."

1968   Redwoods National Park established.

1969   Santa Barbara, California, oil spill dramatizes the problem of pollution.

1969   Friends of the Earth founded by David R. Brower after his ouster from the Sierra Club.

1969   Greenpeace organized.

1970   National Environmental Policy Act signed January 1.

1970   Natural Resources Defense Council founded.

1970   Zero Population Growth founded by Paul Ehrlich and others.

1970   Resource Recovery Act (Solid Waste Disposal Act).

1970   Clean Air Act amends and strengthens 1963 measure.

1970   First "Earth Day" celebrated April 22.

1970   National Oceanic and Atmospheric Administration created October 3.

1970   Environmental Protection Agency (EPA) created December 2.

1970   Environmental Education Act endeavors to promote environmental awareness in the schools.

1971   Calvert Cliffs Decision by U.S. Court of Appeals mandates environmental impact decisions for federal projects affecting the ecosystem.

1971   Barry Commoner publishes *The Closing Circle.*

1971   Congress abandons support of the supersonic transport aircraft.

1971   Alaska Native Claims Settlement Act authorizes federal nomination of "national interest lands" for permanent protection.

1972   League of Conservation Voters organized.

1972   Federal Water Pollution Control Act (Clean Water Act).

1972   Federal Environmental Pesticide Control Act.

1972   Ocean Dumping Act.

1972   Coastal Zone Management Act empowers states to lead in planning and regulation.

1972   United Nations Conference on the Human Environment held in Stockholm.

1972   The Club of Rome's publication of *The Limits of Growth* triggers worldwide debate.

1973   E. F. Schumacher publishes *Small IS Beautiful.*

1973   Walt Disney Enterprises abandons plans for a ski resort in Mineral King Valley, California, after a 1972 Supreme Court decision affirms the legal standing of the Sierra Club in the case.

1973   Endangered Species Act expands federal involvement in resisting species extinction.

1973   Congress authorizes construction of an 800-mile oil pipeline across Alaska to Prudhoe Bay.

1974   Safe Drinking Water Act.

1976   Federal Land Policy and Management Act formalizes multiple-use administration of public lands under control of Bureau of Land Management.

1976   Resource Conservation and Recovery Act promotes recycling of solid wastes.

1976   Toxic Substances Control Act.

1977   Clean Air Act amendments.

1977   Federal Water Pollution Control Act amendments.

1977   Surface Mining Control and Reclamation Act.

1978   National Energy Act.

1978   Love Canal near the Niagara River, New York, revealed to be the site of buried chemical wastes endangering the health of local residents.

1979   Three Mile Island (Pennsylvania) nuclear generating plant narrowly avoids meltdown and widespread radioactive pollution.

1980   Comprehensive Environmental Response, Compensation and Liability Act establishes the "superfund" for toxic waste abatement.

1980   Alaska National Interest Lands Conservation Act protects 104 million acres including 56 million acres in the National Wilderness Preservation System.

1980   *Global 2000 Report to the President* released.

1980   Fish and Wildlife Conservation Act protects nongame species.

1981	Earth First! organized; lists 12,000 members by 1988.
1981	Anne Gorsuch resigns as head of the Environmental Protection Administration after revelations of mismanagement.
1983	Sierra Club lists 350,000 members.
1983	James G. Watt resigns as Secretary of the Interior under mounting public criticism for antienvironmental policies.
1986	The Chernobyl (Russia) disaster pollutes large areas of northern Europe and further damages the reputation of the nuclear power industry in the United States.
1986	Superfund reauthorized (see 1980).
1986	Federal water pollution control programs reauthorized.
1987	The United States joins other industrialized nations in signing a protocol designed to protect the ultraviolet-shielding ozone layer.
1988	Drought conditions attributed to the "greenhouse effect" alarm Americans about global climate change.
1989	Massive oil spill in Prince William Sound, Alaska, arouses national indignation.

THE POTENTIAL OF ENVIRONMENTAL HISTORY

To the rapid traveler the number of elms in a town is the measure of its civility.

—*Henry David Thoreau*

Look out the nearest window and consider the environment. (If there isn't a window in sight that too is revealing about attitude toward nature.) What you see is synthetic: a human creation. The tree or patch of grass is there, in other words, either because humans put it there or because they allowed it to remain. Is what you see designed by people—farmed, landscaped, or constructed—or could you call it a wilderness? Are there offshore oil wells in your ocean view? What about habitat for other species that share the planet? And what of the built environment? Is it constructed with aesthetic considerations, historical values, and a distinctive regional or national style in mind?

The point is that at the end of the twentieth century any landscape is an artifact, something made by human beings. Its condition, rightly interpreted, reveals a society's culture and traditions as directly as does a novel or a newspaper or a code of laws. We live in a humanized habitat. The wild world is in rapid retreat before an increasingly powerful technological juggernaut. The frontier is a fading memory. In the last two centuries people have taken over from natural forces the role of primary shaper of the environment. Even the "natural," or unaltered, parts of the planet are increasingly the result of human choice. Wilderness remains because we allow it to exist—in national parks and preservation systems.

As a consequence the environment, natural as well as developed, should be understood as a historical document. The chainsaw and the bulldozer make a record that the historian can read just like the printed word. So would nuclear bombs if anyone were still around to do the reading. Environment making is an ongoing process. Earlier generations created what we see today and our choices, recorded on the land, are creating tomorrow's environment. So nature is not only a document revealing past thought and action but also a slate upon which the present outlines the kind of world it bequeaths to the future.

These assumptions ring particularly true for Americans. Almost uniquely among modern peoples, the emigrants who settled the New World had the opportunity and the responsibility to write a record of their values on the land. Little was inherited but wilderness. The native people that the colonists found had, for the most part, chosen to make a minimal impact on the continent. Asians and Europeans of the same era, by way of contrast, had no alternative but to live in a physical setting shaped by thousands of years of human occupancy. There was no blank slate, no *tabula rasa*. The Old World landscape could not as easily express a people's preferences. Americans, on the other hand, formed their environment as they formed their nation. The process continues today, most notably in the last frontiers such as the southwestern deserts and Alaska. Attitudes toward the past, contemporary tastes, and ideals for the future combine to influence nature. Consider also that "writing" with axes, rifles, and bulldozers is not limited to the literate. Libraries and archives contain a relatively thin historical record compared to condition of the land. Nowhere else have the American people collectively left more evidence about their changing priorities. There are, in sum, few richer lodes than environmental history from which to mine an understanding of American civilization.

Environmental history is a relatively new field whose growth occurred simultaneously with that of the environmental movement in the 1960s. To be sure older scholars such as Frederick Jackson Turner [*The Frontier in American History* (1920)] and Walter Prescott Webb [*The Great Plains* (1931); *The Great Frontier* (1952)] offered valuable insights into the ways the American environment influenced, indeed determined, the nation's thought and culture. This environmental determinism came under fire in the work of James Malin [*The Grassland of North America* (1947)], who perhaps tipped the balance too far in the opposite direction—toward the way American thought and policy influenced the environment. Modern environmental history begins with the assumption that what should be studied, in Richard White's words, are the "reciprocal influences of environmental change, social change and political action."* In other words, land shaped people but at the same time people shaped land. The process continued in a historical minuet of overlapping causation.

Nature, then, both reflects and influences American values. This means that the environmental historian must work not only with the conventional tools of intellectual, political, and social history but also with the biological and physical sciences—particularly ecology and geography. They also borrow data and methods from psychologists, anthropologists, and scholars of literature, art, and religion. Moreover, reality is not only what is real. As Henry Nash Smith's *Virgin Land: The American West as Symbol and Myth* (1950) reminds us, symbolism and mythology play a major role in conditioning how we feel about and act toward our environment. The use of these diverse disciplines makes environmental history both exciting and difficult. Its practitioners cast their net over such a wide range of subjects that they might be thought of as ecologists of the academic community. But their task is greater than the ecologists' whose concern is with the way existing systems of living and nonliving components function together. The environmental historian is interested in this too but with the addition of another dimension: the past. He or she wants to know how past ecosystems (including, of course, the thought and behavior of *Homo sapiens*) influenced subsequent ones. Environmental history might be thought of as ecology in three dimensions.

Donald Worster has cautioned against the "tendency to identify environmental history with the history of environmentalism."** The point is well taken if environmental history is to realize its fullest potential. Nonetheless, much of the following collection of readings will be concerned with the major personalities, ideas, issues, and policies in the American conservation (and, later, environmental) movement. But the study of what a society chooses to conserve and why and how it chooses to do it is an essential ingredient of environmental

*Richard White, "Historiographical Essay—American Environmental History: The Development of a New Historical Field," *Pacific Historical Review,* 54 (August 1985), 318. White's essay is well worth examination by those desiring an introduction into the essential literature and methods of the field. The bibliography, following the last selection, describes other methodological literature.

**Donald Worster, "World Without Borders: The Internationalizing of Environmental History," in Kendall E. Bailes, ed., *Environmental History: Critical Issues in Comparative Perspective* (Lanham, MD: University Presses of America, 1985), 664.

history. Conservation history, moreover, offers important insights into the national identity and purpose as well as into a people's aesthetic, religious, and ethical convictions. These are what shape the environment; and the shape of the environment, in turn, gives rise to new ideas and policies.

The history of American environmentalism can be brought to bear on some of the basic issues in American life. It is, for example, one of the best places to examine the tensions between individual freedom and social purpose. Enlightened use of the land demands a limitation on the action of a landowner because the easiest and most lucrative methods of exploiting a resource are seldom in the best long-term interests of the nation and the ecosystem as a whole. But in a society that covets individualism and free enterprise, especially as it concerns the land, how can conservation principles be instituted? The profit motive and so-called privatization of resources have been advocated but without signal success. Nature does not as yet exert much influence on the bottom line. The tragedy of the unregulated commons* is that it invites a competitive free-for-all and bonanza economics.

Legal coercion is difficult since it means interfering with a person's relationship to his or her property. Telling an individual, or a corporation, how to manage his or her land is close enough to telling people how to furnish their houses as to make most Americans uneasy. Consequently, conservationists have argued that some kinds of property are less private than others: specifically, those everyone shares—like the environment. What one does inside one's home is truly private, but when individual action affects resources that other people and other species depend upon for survival, individual rights must be redefined. Yet the assumption that the land I purchase is "mine," to do with as I please, has proven hard to shake.

Faced with this problem, conservation leaders have frequently supported public or social ownership of the environment: the national park idea, for example, and federal control of dams on major rivers. They have also endeavored to secure the voluntary cooperation of landowners and the sympathy of the citizenry on the basis of patriotism, long-term prosperity, national strength, democracy, and efficiency. Such human benefits, it is argued, are worth the extra cost and effort of enlightened custodianship of the land and its resources.

---

*Garrett Hardin coined the phrase and discussed the concept in "The Tragedy of the Commons," *Science*, **162** (December 13, 1968), 1243–1248.

But this line of reasoning evades the idea that the integrity, stability, and health of the environment is a desirable end in itself—human interests aside. The relatively small but increasing number of American environmentalists who have taken this position sometimes say that nature has rights that humans should respect as part of an extended code of ethics. The same restraints that, at least in theory, prevent individuals from robbing or killing their human neighbors should work to protect forests, streams, and endangered species. This issue inevitably leads to fundamental questions about the character and content of the American liberal ideology. Some have gone so far as to argue that natural rights should extend to encompass the rights of nature. The environment then becomes the latest in a series of oppressed and exploited minorities deserving liberation. From this perspective the conservation impulse represents an exploration of the limits of American liberalism.

The relationship between experts and the people in a republican form of government is another central concern in the history of American environmentalism. Frequently planners and scientists know what to do to protect the environment (for example, by limiting human population growth) but persuading the people to apply this knowledge is difficult. It is the horse-and-water problem in classic form. How does the expert convince the nonspecialist to safeguard a vital resource? In a totalitarian political system this is relatively easy: the king simply decrees that his royal forests will *not* be clear-cut or his stags exterminated. But democratic assumptions and institutions complicate the matter. So does the persistent anti-intellectualism of American civilization. When it comes to land use decisions, common sense is difficult to displace as the source of authority. Significantly, the greatest gains for conservation have occurred when the urge for reform prompted the common people to accept the leadership of strong executives such as Theodore and Franklin Delano Roosevelt. With advocates of weaker central government in power environmentalism has faltered, as the presidency of Ronald Reagan attested.

Environmental policy must frequently be hacked out of a thicket of contending and often contradictory interests. The public interest is not monolithic. There are often several "publics." In the West, municipalities, agri-business, hydropower interests, and river runners vie for the same basic resource: fresh, flowing water. So too do beaver and trout. Who speaks for their interests in the formulation of environmental policy? And once a course of action is set, there is no assurance, given the vagaries of public favor in a democracy, that it will be sustained.

American environmental history has direct relevance in cracking one of the traditional chestnuts in American historiography: the significance of the frontier, abundance, and opportunity in the national experience. Conservation may be interpreted as an effort to extend abundance and opportunity. So in a sense the conservation and environmental movements became the new American frontier. They assumed the role of open space and far horizons. Clearly the desire for an easy way to full stomachs and bank accounts is not the only relevant factor here. At stake, many believe, is the perpetuation of ideas essential to the American character: democracy, individualism, independence, and self-reliance. The nation's youth and confidence were being conserved along with natural resources. Nor can we discount as a factor in American environmentalism, particularly the movement to preserve wilderness and national parks, the vague feeling that there was something special about the New World environment worth protecting—a certain freshness, a chance for a new start that fired messianic dreams. American pride and identity are more closely connected with the history of environmentalism than appears at first glance.

Another way environmental history illuminates basic issues in the American experience is its ability to focus and give substance to the chronic controversy between utilitarian and aesthetic interests. Obviously a particular natural object, such as a tree, can be claimed by both camps—as lumber or as scenery. The same is true of a canyon that could be dammed for use as a reservoir or preserved as wilderness. The fact that neither tree nor canyon can satisfy both demands simultaneously has given rise to strident altercations. In the context of allocating resources Americans have been confronted with basic questions of value and ultimately with choices about the nature of their civilization. Frequently the issue reduces to the question of whether the nation, with its well-known material abilities and appetites, also possesses an aesthetic and spiritual sense. In the first edition of *Wilderness and the American Mind* (1967) I made much of the distinction between utilitarian-minded "conservationists" and what I termed "preservationists." But new scholarship, particularly Samuel P. Hays's *Beauty, Health and Permanence: Environmental Politics in the United States, 1955–1985* (1987), suggests that this dichotomy is too simple. Many recent environmental controversies cannot be understood as opposing those who would leave nature alone against those who would control natural processes.

Even the most ardent preservationists now recognize that a managed wilderness is not a contradiction in terms. The ecological component of American conservation combines preservationist ends with the managerial means so prized by the old utilitarian conservationists. And the new biocentrists and "deep ecologists" break from all the old categories in contending that all human interests—aesthetic as well as utilitarian—must take a back seat to the ideal of a healthy ecosystem. Nature, they say, really does bat last!

Two pitfalls are commonly encountered in the teaching and writing of environmental history. The first, as noted, is to speak of "conservation" and "environmentalism" as if it denoted a single school of thought. In fact, as some of the statements in the selections will suggest, conflicts among conservationists are as frequent and bitter as those between them and the parties they seek to restrain and reform. The second mistake is to approach the history of American relations to the natural world with a Manichean orientation—the bad guys (frontiersmen, pioneers, and exploiters of the virgin land) versus the good ones (those who tried to protect nature). Such a representation unjustly uses the emotions of the present to describe the actions of the past. It fails to employ historical sympathy to understand the past in its own terms. Neither the pioneers nor most subsequent resource developers considered themselves unthinking spoilers or were regarded as such by their contemporaries. Instead, they acted in a manner consistent with their environmental circumstances and intellectual heritage. When the forest seemed limitless, cut-out-and-get-out became the accepted style of lumbering. The fact that Alaska is presently 98 percent wilderness generates sympathy for development among Alaskans. Certainly early Americans made mistakes in treating their environment, but they became understood as such only with the passage of time. Rather than shaking moralistic fingers at pioneers, environmental historians would do better to attempt to understand why people acted as they did toward nature. There is no imperative that makes environmental historians environmental advocates. Advocacy can take the form of simply recording the past as a warning to the present.

Environmental history has the potential for displaying the successes and failures of our custodianship of the land in such a way that the present can benefit from the experience of the past. Anyone professionally concerned with resource policy or, as a citizen, interested in advancing an environmental cause can benefit from knowing the problems his or her predecessors faced and how they formulated ideas for reform, secured the public approval necessary for their institution-alization, and evaluated their effects. Moreover, in attempting to advance conservation policies today it is important to know something of the national taste in environment. One of the best places to acquire such information is from an examination of how it was formed.

PART ONE

THE CONSERVATION IMPULSE, BEGINNINGS–1878

The land was ours before we were the land's.

—*Robert Frost*

The North American environment was hardly virgin land when the first Europeans arrived. Thousands of years of occupation by Native Americans (lost white explorers initially called them "Indians") produced some environmental impact. But the Native Americans felt themselves part of nature and revered the environment that sustained them. For them, the land was literally "sacred," and their modifications were relatively slight.

But the next wave of immigrants, who came from Europe, held quite different views about the natural world. Steeped in the Judeo-Christian tradition, they understood nature to be a gift of God for the satisfaction of mankind's material desires. Genesis 1:28 commanded the first couple to "subdue" the earth and have "dominion . . . over every living thing that moveth upon the earth." Modern Christians would reinterpret this commandment (see Selection 42), but for most of American history Christianity provided the intellectual lubrication for environmental exploitation. So did the idea of civilization as a beneficient process that necessitated the control and substantial modification of the environment. Clearing the land of trees and ridding it of supposedly dangerous wild animals (including Indians) were the most obvious consequences of this attitude. Science and technology facilitated the process. Pioneers literally worshipped the rifle, axe, and barbed wire fence and later, dams, bulldozers, and nuclear energy. In their eyes these were the agents of progress.

The capitalistic free enterprise system turned the environment of the New World into a huge marketplace. Nature ceased being a community to which humans belonged and became a commodity or "resource" from which they could profit. Whereas subsistance users, such as the Native Americans, took only what they needed to support their lives, the capitalists' profit motive knew no boundaries. One could never be too rich! Moreover, white culture believed that nature (the land) could be owned—literally bought and sold. Of all the Europeans' ways, the Indians found this the most incomprehensible.

The assumption that the natural bounty of North America was inexhaustible colored every early American attitude toward the environment and loaded the deck against conservation. A scarcity of natural resources? Absurd! Over the next ridge was a cornucopia of wood, water, soil, and game. This next-ridge syndrome, coupled with the rapid pace of westward expansion, made a mockery of sustainability. Environmental problems were solved in early American history not by environmental conservation but by finding new environments. (Some contemporary attitudes toward space exploration suggest this attitude has not disappeared.) For a while, to be sure, inexhaustibility was not merely a myth. The New World *was* spacious and abundant beyond the wildest fantasies of land-starved Europeans. Up until the late-nineteenth century, Americans experienced a population density inconducive to the conservation idea.

But even as they became a "people of plenty," in historian David Potter's words, Americans engaged in what might be called deficit environmental financing of their affluence. As later generations assessed the debts they inherited and paid the price for earlier thoughtlessness, conservation made more sense. The closing of the frontier in 1890 was an important symbol of this change. Seventeen years later the chief of the U.S. Forest Service, Gifford Pinchot, would coin the word *conservation* (see Selection 11). Concern about the environment, however, had already existed in scattered corners of the American mind for several generations. The first American "conservationists" (to use the word anachronistically) had in common a willingness to challenge the dominant conception of the land's purpose and to expose inexhaustibility as a myth. They were also prepared to question the dogma of free enterprise, which balked at the prospect of government regulation in society's interest. Finally, a few of the conservation pioneers made so bold as to suggest that growth and quantity were not the only possible criteria for progress and for happiness. The kind of life lived amid abundance, they implied, also had its claims and sometimes, as in the case of parks, demanded that limits be set to civilization's expansion.

1

Native Americans Define the Natural Community

Black Elk (1931)

There are good reasons for regarding Indians as the first American environmentalists. Centuries before the birth of the science of ecology, they understood nature as a community to which humans as well as every other living thing belonged and on which they depended. Granted that Indians modified their environment (by deliberate forest and grassland burning, for example) and, of course, they hunted, gathered, fished, and trapped. But they appear to have respected the limits of their environment and, consequently, the need to restrain human impact.

Black Elk, a Sioux from the northern Great Plains, was born in 1863 just as advancing white civilization dealt the final, crushing blows to the world the Indians knew. As a young man in the 1880s, he watched the near extermination of the buffalo by profit-crazed white hunters. In 1931 he gave this statement of his beliefs to anthropologist John G. Neihardt. A close reading reveals the philosophical basis for Black Elk's reverence for the earth and its life community.

My friend, I am going to tell you the story of my life. . . .

It is the story of all life that is holy and is good to tell, and of us two-leggeds sharing in it with the four-leggeds and the wings of the air and all green things; for these are children of one mother and their father is one Spirit. . . .

So I know that it is a good thing I am going to do; and because

John G. Neihardt, *Black Elk Speaks: Being the Life Story of a Holy Man of the Ogalala Sioux* (Lincoln, NE: University of Nebraska Press, 1961), 1–3, 198–200, 203–204, 217–218. Reprinted from *Black Elk Speaks,* by John G. Neihardt, by permission of the University of Nebraska Press. Copyright 1932, 1959, 1961, 1975 by the John G. Neihardt Trust.

no good thing can be done by any man alone, I will first make an offering and send a voice to the Spirit of the World, that it may help me to be true. See, I fill this sacred pipe with the bark of the red willow; but before we smoke it, you must see how it is made and what it means. These four ribbons hanging here on the stem are the four quarters of the universe. The black one is for the west where the thunder beings live to send us rain; the white one for the north, whence comes the great white cleansing wind; the red one for the east, whence springs the light and where the morning star lives to give men wisdom; the yellow for the south, whence come the summer and the power to grow.

But these four spirits are only one Spirit after all, and this eagle feather here is for that One, which is like a father, and also it is for the thoughts of men that should rise high as eagles do. Is not the sky a father and the earth a mother, and are not all living things with feet or wings or roots their children? And this hide upon the mouthpiece here, which should be bison hide, is for the earth, from whence we came and at whose breast we suck as babies all our lives, along with all the animals and birds and trees and grasses. And because it means all this, and more than any man can understand, the pipe is holy. . . .

. . . You have noticed that everything an Indian does is in a circle, and that is because the Power of the World always works in circles, and everything tries to be round. In the old days when we were a strong and happy people, all our power came to us from the sacred hoop of the nation, and so long as the hoop was unbroken, the people flourished. The flowering tree was the living center of the hoop, and the circle of the four quarters nourished it. The east gave peace and light, the south gave warmth, the west gave rain, and the north with its cold and mighty wind gave strength and endurance. This knowledge came to us from the outer world with our religion. Everything the Power of the World does is done in a circle. The sky is round, and I have heard that the earth is round like a ball, and so are all the stars. The wind, in its greatest power, whirls. Birds make their nests in circles, for theirs is the same religion as ours. The sun comes forth and goes down again in a circle. The moon does the same, and both are round. Even the seasons form a great circle in their changing, and always come back again to where they were. The life of a man is a circle from childhood to childhood, and so it is in everything where power moves. Our tepees were round like the nests of birds, and these were always set in a circle, the nation's hoop, a nest of many nests, where the Great Spirit meant for us to hatch our children.

But the Wasichus* have put us in these square boxes. Our power is gone and we are dying, for the power is not in us any more. You can look at our boys and see how it is with us. When we were living by the power of the circle in the way we should, boys were men at twelve or thirteen years of age. But now it takes them very much longer to mature. . . .

You want to know why we always go from left to right like that. I can tell you something of the reason, but not all. Think of this: Is not the south the source of life, and does not the flowering stick truly come from there? And does not man advance from there toward the setting sun of his life? Then does he not approach the colder north where the white hairs are? And does he not then arrive, if he lives, at the source of light and understanding, which is the east? Then does he not return to where he began, to his second childhood, there to give back his life to all life, and his flesh to the earth whence it came? The more you think about this, the more meaning you will see in it. . . .

. . . It was in the summer of my twentieth year (1883) that I performed the ceremony of the elk. That fall, they say, the last of the bison herds was slaughtered by the Wasichus. I can remember when the bison were so many that they could not be counted, but more and more Wasichus came to kill them until there were only heaps of bones scattered where they used to be. The Wasichus did not kill them to eat; they killed them for the metal that makes them crazy, and they took only the hides to sell. Sometimes they did not even take the hides, only the tongues; and I have heard that fire-boats came down the Missouri River loaded with dried bison tongues. You can see that the men who did this were crazy. Sometimes they did not even take the tongues; they just killed and killed because they liked to do that. When we hunted bison, we killed only what we needed. And when there was nothing left but heaps of bones, the Wasichus came and gathered up even the bones and sold them.

All our people now were settling down in square gray houses,

---

*Black Elk's name for white people, Americans. The houses they obliged Indians to occupy on the reservations were square. [Ed.]

scattered here and there across this hungry land, and around them the Wasichus had drawn a line* to keep them in. The nation's hoop was broken, and there was no center any longer for the flowering tree. The people were in despair. They seemed heavy to me, heavy and dark; so heavy that it seemed they could not be lifted; so dark that they could not be made to see any more. Hunger was among us often now, for much of what the Great Father in Washington sent us must have been stolen by Wasichus who were crazy to get money. There were many lies, but we could not eat them. The forked tongue made promises.

I kept on curing the sick for three years more, and many came to me and were made over; but when I thought of my great vision, which was to save the nation's hoop and make the holy tree to bloom in the center of it, I felt like crying, for the sacred hoop was broken and scattered.

*Black Elk is referring to the Indian reservation system. [Ed.]

2

The Human Factor in Environmental Change

William Cronon (1983)

William Cronon's interest is in the history of the environment rather than in the history of environmentalism. He blends the skills of a historian with the sensitivity to biological process of an ecologist. In the book from which this selection is taken Cronon begins to explore the meaning of environmental change in the region Europeans called New England. His account necessarily begins with the effect of the Indian occupants, but it recognizes that the white people's fenced fields, domesticated animals, and concept of land ownership brought radically different influences to the ecosystem. Cronon's conception of nature as part of human history and of humans as natural beings opens exciting new doors for understanding the ongoing mutual interaction of people and environment.

THE VIEW FROM WALDEN

On the morning of January 24, 1855, Henry David Thoreau sat down with his journal to consider the ways in which his Concord home had been altered by more than two centuries of European settlement. He had recently read the book *New England's Prospect,* in which the English traveler William Wood recounted his 1633 voyage to southern New England and described for English readers the landscape he had found there. Now Thoreau sought to annotate the ways in which Wood's Massachusetts was different from his own. The changes seemed sweeping indeed.

He began with the wild meadow grasses, which appeared, he

William Cronon, *Changes in the Land: Indians, Colonists and the Ecology of New England* (New York: Hill & Wang, 1983), 1–15. Reprinted by permission of Hill and Wang, a division of Farrar, Straus & Giroux, Inc. Footnotes in the original have been omitted.

wrote, "to have grown more rankly in those days." If Wood's descriptions were accurate, the strawberries too had been larger and more abundant "before they were so cornered up by cultivation." Some of them had been as much as two inches around, and were so numerous that one could gather half a bushel in a forenoon. Equally abundant were gooseberries, raspberries, and especially currants, which, Thoreau mused, "so many old writers speak of, but so few moderns find wild."

New England forests had been much more extensive and their trees larger in 1633. On the coast, where Indian settlement had been greatest, the woods had presented a more open and parklike appearance to the first English settlers, without the underbrush and coppice growth so common in nineteenth-century Concord. To see such a forest nowadays, Thoreau wrote, it was necessary to make an expedition to "the sample still left in Maine." As nearly as he could tell, oaks, firs, plums, and tulip trees were all less numerous than they had been in Wood's day.

But if the forest was much reduced from its former state, most of its tree species nevertheless remained. This was more than could be said for many of its animal inhabitants. Thoreau's list of those that were now absent was stark: "bear, moose, deer, porcupines, 'the grim-fac'd Ounce, and rav'nous howling Wolf,' and beaver. Martens." Not only the mammals of the land were gone; the sea and air also seemed more empty. Bass had once been caught two or three thousand at a time. The progeny of the alewives had been "almost incredible." Neither was now present in such abundance. Of the birds, Thoreau wrote: "Eagles are probably less common; pigeons of course . . . heath cocks all gone . . . and turkeys . . . Probably more owls then, and cormorants, etc., etc., sea-fowl generally . . . and swans." To Wood's statement that one could purchase a fresh-killed swan for dinner at the price of six shillings, Thoreau could only write in wonderment, "Think of that!"

There is a certain plaintiveness in this catalog of Thoreau's, a romantic's lament for the pristine world of an earlier and now lost time. The myth of a fallen humanity in a fallen world is never far beneath the surface in Thoreau's writing, and nowhere is this more visible than in his descriptions of past landscapes. A year after his encounter with William Wood's New England of 1633, he returned to its lessons in more explicitly moral language. "When I consider," he wrote, "that the nobler animals have been exterminated here,—the cougar, panther, lynx, wolverene, wolf, bear, moose, deer, the beaver, the turkey, etc., etc.,—I cannot but feel as if I lived in a tamed, and, as it were, emasculated country." Seen in this way, a changed land-scape meant a loss of wildness and virility that was ultimately spiritual in its import, a sign of declension in both nature and humanity. "Is it not," Thoreau asked, "a maimed and imperfect nature that I am con-versant with?"

It is important that we answer this question of Thoreau's care-fully: how did the "nature" of New England change with the coming of the Europeans, and can we reasonably speak of its changes in terms of maiming and imperfection? There is nothing new to the observation that European settlement transformed the American landscape. Long before Thoreau, naturalists and historians alike were commenting on the process which was converting a "wilderness" into a land of Euro-pean agricultural settlement. Whether they wrote of Indians, the fur trade, the forest, or the farm, colonial authors were constantly aware that fundamental alterations of the ecological fabric were taking place around them. . . .

For the most part, unlike Thoreau, they did so approvingly. As early as 1653, the historian Edward Johnson could count it as one of God's providences that a "remote, rocky, barren, bushy, wildwoody wilderness" had been transformed in a generation into "a second Eng-land for fertilness." In this vision, the transformation of wilderness betokened the planting of a garden, not the fall from one; any change in the New England environment was divinely ordained and wholly positive. By the end of the eighteenth century, the metaphors for environmental change had become more humanistic than providential, but were no less enthusiastic about the progress such change repre-sented. In a passage partially anticipating Frederick Jackson Turner's frontier thesis, for instance, Benjamin Rush described a regular se-quence for clearing the forest and civilizing the wilderness. . . . The shape of the landscape was a visible confirmation of the state of human society. Both underwent an evolutionary development from savagery to civilization.

Whether interpreted as declension or progress, the shift from Thoreau's forest of "nobler animals" to Rush's fields and pastures of prosperous farmers signaled a genuinely transformed countryside, one whose changes were intimately bound to the human history which had taken place in its midst. The replacement of Indians by predomi-nantly European populations in New England was as much an ecologi-cal as a cultural revolution, and the human side of that revolution cannot be fully understood until it is embedded in the ecological one.

Doing so requires a history, not only of human actors, conflicts, and economies, but of ecosystems as well.

How might we construct such an ecological history? The types of evidence which can be used to evaluate ecological change before 1800 are not uniformly reliable, and some are of a sort not ordinarily used by historians. It is therefore important to reflect on how they should best be criticized and used. The descriptions of travelers and early naturalists, for instance, provide observations of what New England looked like in the early days of European settlement, and how it had changed by the end of the eighteenth century. As such, they provide the backbone of this study. But to use them properly requires that we evaluate each traveler's skills as a naturalist, something for which there is often only the evidence of his or her writings. Moreover, we can only guess at how ideological commitments such as Thoreau's or Rush's colored the ways they saw the landscape. How much did William Wood's evident wish to promote the Massachusetts Bay Colony lead him to idealize its environment? To what extent did the anonymous author of *American Husbandry* shape his critique of American agriculture to serve his purpose of preserving colonial attachments to Britain? Even if we can remove most of these ideological biases to discover what it was a traveler actually saw, we must still acknowledge that each traveler visited only a tiny fraction of the region. As Timothy Dwight once remarked, "Your travelers seize on a single person, or a solitary fact, and make them the representatives of a whole community and a general custom." We are always faced with the problem of generalizing from a *local* description to a *regional* landscape, but our understanding of modern ecosystems can be of great help in doing so.

A second fund of data resides in various colonial town, court, and legislative records, although here the evidence of ecological change can sometimes be tantalizingly elliptical. We cannot always know with certainty whether a governmental action anticipated or reacted to a change in the environment. When a law was passed protecting trees on a town commons, for example, did this mean that a timber shortage existed? Or was the town merely responding with prudent foresight to the experience of other localities? If a shortage existed, how severe was it? Was it limited only to certain species of trees? And so on. Only by looking at the overall pattern of legal activity can we render a reasonable judgment on such questions. These problems notwithstanding, town and colony records address almost the entire range of ecological changes in colonial New England: deforestation, the keeping of livestock, conflicts between Indians and colonists over property boundaries, the extermination of predators such as wolves, and similar matters. Deeds and surveyor records can be used statistically to estimate the composition of early forests, and are usually more accurate than travelers' accounts even though subject to sampling errors.

Then there are the less orthodox sorts of evidence which historians borrow from other disciplines and have less experience in criticizing. Relict stands of old-growth timber, such as the Cathedral Pines near Cornwall, Connecticut, can suggest what earlier forests may have looked like. The relict stands which exist today, however, are by no means identical to most of the forests which existed in colonial times, so that the record of earlier forests must be sought in less visible places. Ecologists have done very creative detective work in analyzing tree rings, charcoal deposits, rotting trunks, and overturned stumps to determine the history of several New England woodlands. The fossil pollen in pond and bog sediments is a reliable but fuzzy indicator of the changing species composition of surrounding vegetation; despite problems in determining the absolute age of such pollen, it supplies some of the most reliable evidence for reconstructing past forests. In addition, a wide variety of archaeological evidence can be used to assess past environments, particularly the changing relations of human inhabitants to them.

Finally, there are those awkward situations in which an ecological change which undoubtedly must have been occurring in the colonial period has left little or no historical evidence at all. These include microscopic changes in soil fauna and flora, soil compaction, [and] changes in the transpiration rates of forests. . . .

Although caution is required in handling all these various forms of evidence (and nonevidence), together they provide a remarkably full portrait of ecological change in colonial New England. But they also raise intriguing questions, questions which are both empirical and theoretical. . . .

This brings us to the heart of the theoretical difficulties involved in doing ecological history. When one asks how much an ecosystem has been changed by human influence, the inevitable next question must be: "changed in relation to what?" There is no simple answer to this. Before we can analyze the ways people alter their environments, we must first consider how those environments change in the absence of human activity, and that in turn requires us to reflect on what we mean by an ecological "community." Ecology as a biological science has had to deal with this problem from its outset. The first generation of academic ecologists, led by Frederic Clements, defined the communities they studied literally as superorganisms which experienced birth, growth, maturity, and sometimes death much as individual plants and animals did. Under this model, the central dynamic of community change could be expressed in the concept of "succession." Depending on its region, a biotic community might begin as a pond, which was then gradually transformed by its own internal dynamics into a marsh, a meadow, a forest of pioneer trees, and finally to a forest of dominant trees. This last stage was assumed to be stable and was known as the "climax," a more or less permanent community which would reproduce itself indefinitely if left undisturbed. Its equilibrium state defined the mature forest "organism," so that all members of the community could be interpreted as functioning to maintain the stability of the whole. Here was an apparently objective point of reference: any actual community could be compared with the theoretical climax, and differences between them could then usually be attributed to "disturbance." Often the source of disturbance was human, implying that humanity was somehow outside of the ideal climax community.

This functionalist emphasis on equilibrium and climax had important consequences, for it tended to remove ecological communities from history. If all ecological change was either self-equilibrating (moving toward climax) or nonexistent (remaining in the static condition of climax), then history was more or less absent except in the very long time frame of climatic change or Darwinian evolution. The result was a paradox. Ecologists trying to define climax and succession for a region like New England were faced with an environment massively altered by human beings, yet their research program demanded that they determine what that environment would have been like without a human presence. By peeling away the corrupting influences of man and woman, they could discover the original ideal community of the climax. One detects here a certain resemblance to Thoreau's reading of William Wood: historical change was defined as an aberration rather than the norm.

. . . [In time] ecologists began to express a stronger interest in the effects of human beings on their environment. What investigators had earlier seen as an inconvenient block to the discovery of ideal climax communities could become an object of research in its own right. But accepting the effects of human beings was only part of this shift toward a more historical ecology. Just as ecosystems have been changed by the historical activities of human beings, so too have they had their own less-recorded history: forests have been transformed by disease, drought, and fire, species have become extinct, and landscapes have been drastically altered by climatic change without any human intervention at all. As we shall see, the period of human occupation in postglacial New England has seen environmental changes on an enormous scale, many of them wholly apart from human influence. There has been no timeless wilderness in a state of perfect changelessness, no climax forest in permanent stasis.

But admitting that ecosystems have histories of their own still leaves us with the problem of how to view the people who inhabit them. Are human beings inside or outside their systems? In trying to answer this question, appeal is too often made to the myth of a golden age, as Thoreau sometimes seemed inclined to do. If the nature of Concord in the 1850s—a nature which many Americans now romanticize as the idyllic world of Thoreau's own Walden—was as "maimed" and "imperfect" as he said, what are we to make of the wholeness and perfection which he thought preceded it? It is tempting to believe that when the Europeans arrived in the New World they confronted Virgin Land, the Forest Primeval, a wilderness which had existed for eons uninfluenced by human hands. Nothing could be further from the truth. In Francis Jennings's telling phrase, the land was less virgin than it was widowed. Indians had lived on the continent for thousands of years, and had to a significant extent modified its environment to their purposes. The destruction of Indian communities in fact brought some of the most important ecological changes which followed the Europeans' arrival in America. The choice is not between two landscapes, one with and one without a human influence; it is between two human ways of living, two ways of belonging to an ecosystem. . . .

All human groups consciously change their environments to some extent—one might even argue that this, in combination with language, is the crucial trait distinguishing people from other animals—and the best measure of a culture's ecological stability may well be how successfully its environmental changes maintain its ability to reproduce itself. But if we avoid assumptions about environmental equilibrium, the *instability* of human relations with the environment can be used to explain both cultural and ecological transformations. An ecological history begins by assuming a dynamic and changing relationship between environment and culture, one as apt to produce contradictions as continuities. Moreover, it assumes that the interactions of the two are dialectical. Environment may initially shape the range of choices available to a people at a given moment, but then culture reshapes environment in responding to those choices. The reshaped environment presents a new set of possibilities for cultural reproduction, thus setting up a new cycle of mutual determination. Changes in the way people create and re-create their livelihood must be analyzed in terms of changes not only in their *social* relations but in their *ecological* ones as well. . . .

In colonial New England, two sets of human communities which were also two sets of ecological relationships confronted each other, one Indian and one European. They rapidly came to inhabit a single world, but in the process the landscape of New England was so transformed that the Indians' earlier way of interacting with their environment became impossible. The task before us is not only to describe the ecological changes that took place in New England but to determine what it was about Indians and colonists—in their relations both to nature and to each other—that brought those changes about. Only thus can we understand why the Indian landscape of precolonial times had become the much altered place Thoreau described in the nineteenth century.

The view from Walden in reality contained far more than Thoreau saw that January morning in 1855. . . . We may or may not finally agree with Thoreau in regretting the changes which European settlers wrought in the New World, but we can never share his certainty about the possibility of knowing an entire heaven and an entire earth. Human and natural worlds are too entangled for us, and our historical landscape does not allow us to guess what the "entire poem" of which he spoke might look like. To search for that poem would in fact be a mistake. Our project must be to locate a nature which is within rather than without history, for only by so doing can we find human communities which are inside rather than outside nature.

3

Frontiersmen and the American Environment

Wilbur Jacobs (1978)

Extending the analysis of William Cronon (Selection 2) to the whole continent, Wilbur Jacobs, a distinguished western historian who has been president of the American Environmental History Association, writes a devastating critique of the pioneer treatment of North America. Jacobs understands that we are the heirs not only of an ecosystem shaped by frontiersmen but of their ideas as well. Environmental responsibility, he suggests, requires not only a knowledge of history but also the capacity to transcend many frontier assumptions. The statements of and about the first American conservationists, which follow this selection, document the beginnings of this process of questioning and reconstruction.

I believe environmental themes deserve more attention in American history than they have hitherto received. Environmental history can be a window to a clearer image of the past and can offer us unique perspectives on generally accepted historical concepts of unlimited growth, frontier expansionism, and the rapid use of nonrenewable natural resources. . . .

. . . Indians were . . . America's first ecologists. Through their burning practices, their patterns of subsistence (by growing, for instance, beans and corn together to preserve the richness of the soil), by creating various hunting preserves for beaver and other animals, and by developing special religious attitudes, Indians preserved a wilderness ecological balance wheel. Even the intensive farming of the

Wilbur R. Jacobs, "The Great Despoilation: Environmental Themes in American Frontier History," *Pacific Historical Review*, **47** (1978), 1, 5–11, 24–26. Copyright 1978 by the Pacific Coast Branch, American Historical Association. Reprinted by permission. Footnotes in the original have been omitted.

Iroquois, without chemical fertilizers and pesticides, protected the ecology of the northeastern forest.

Victor Shelford, in his excellent book on the ecology of North America, argues convincingly that prehistoric America was divided into a number of distinct biotic provinces. In each, Indians, as well as plants, animals, insects, and other forms of life, were integral parts of an ecological niche. Modern Americans, Shelford maintains, have altered or destroyed ninety-eight percent of these original North American ecosystems. Indian people, on the other hand, had lived within them for centuries by developing a land ethic tuned to the carrying capacity of each ecozone. Indians today know these facts, though they are couched in a different kind of language, handed down through centuries by oral recall. As one of the most recent Indian spokesmen, Vine Deloria, Jr., a Sioux, recently wrote, "The land-use philosophy of Indians is so utterly simple that it seems stupid to repeat it: man must live with other forms of life on the land and not destroy it."

. . . There are other environmental changes in our history that illustrate my thesis that Europeans and, later, Americans set new forces in motion which altered the face of the land. I refer, for instance, to the tidal wave of settlement that in one generation occupied most of the territories of the Louisiana Purchase and substituted domestic hoofed animals (cattle, horses, hogs, sheep, and goats) for millions of wild hoofed animals (bison, deer of various kinds, including elk, moose, antelope, and wild sheep and goats). One authority estimates that 100,000,000 wild hoofed animals originally occupied North America, and certainly a large portion of that number were part of the organic ecological circle of the Louisiana land. This environmental event that swiftly transformed the natural world of a vast area is hardly mentioned in our general histories, save an occasional word of indignation over indiscriminate slaughter of plains buffalo. The very magnitude of this environmental change, including the dispossession of the Indians, boggles the mind. . . .

To detect the themes and patterns of this environmental shift, we can turn to eyewitnesses who tell us much about how and why changes persisted. Early Virginia accounts help us to understand the gradual environmental modifications that took place in the colonial south. In particular, Robert Beverley, early eighteenth-century planter, gives us clues. The soil was so rich, Beverley tells us, that all kinds of crops flourished, but tobacco was favored from the beginning because "it promised the most immediate gain," which, in turn, caused planters to "overstock the market." His fellow Virginians, Beverley complained, "spunge upon the Blessings of a warm Sun and a fruitful soil . . . gathering in the Bounties of the Earth." What Beverley so clearly observed, the extraordinary exploitation of the soil by southern planters, was echoed in the writings of a series of eminent Virginians, including George Washington, Patrick Henry, and Thomas Jefferson. Washington complained that his fields were running into gullies. Henry is credited with the statement, "he is the greatest patriot, *who stops the most gullies."* Though the planters experimented with clover, contour planting, and other devices, soil erosion and depletion persisted. This subject is a constant theme in American agricultural history.

While the farming practices in the middle colonies placed less emphasis upon cash crops which exhausted the soil, there is historical evidence of wasteful consumption everywhere in these colonies. Peter Kalm, a Swedish scientist touring this part of colonial America in the 1750s, was surprised at the destructive habit of settlers who cleared the land, used it for crops, then for pasture, and later moved on to repeat the process in new land. Another traveler observed that in New Jersey in the 1790s there was "stupid indifference" to the land. The Americans, he said, "in order to save themselves the work of shaking or pulling off the nuts, they find it simpler to cut the tree and gather the nuts from it, as it lies on the ground." Forests were regarded as "troublesome growths." A European visitor was astounded to see his landlord casually cut down "thirty two young cedars to make a hog pen."

Another side of the penetration of the wilderness is given by Cadwallader Colden, colonial New York scientist and early ethnohistorian. According to Colden and other sources collaborating his statements, the entire beaver population of what is now the state of New York, then the Iroquois country, was exterminated in the 1640s as a result of the Anglo-Dutch fur traders operating out of Albany. Only some thirty years after Henry Hudson had explored the wilderness river that bears his name, beaver, one of the most beneficial animals in the North American ecological balance, had become a victim of the assault on wildlife. The attack on beaver was persistent and far-reaching, culminating in its extermination in many areas of the Far West. . . .

In colonial New England there are reliable accounts of Puritan assaults upon forests, wildlife, and the soil. Carried on almost like the wars against the Indians, the war against the land resulted in cutting down the big trees, killing much of the furbearing animal population, and exhausting the light cover of topsoil. As one midwestern critic

educated - but no sense

alleged, New Englanders were much like their soil, intensely cultivated, but only six inches deep; they left a trail of abandoned farms and old stone fences enclosing former fields and pastures.

Despite this midwestern criticism, the evidence shows that each of the New England colonies, almost from the very beginning, did have an environmental awareness which is evident in statutes providing for protection of natural resources in the immediate neighborhood of settlements. Statutes, for instance, restricted the unlimited range of livestock, especially hogs, which invaded common pastures and corn-fields. Streams were protected from overfishing, forests from overcutting, all of which was a part of a scheme for social control that governed the life style of entire colonies, including even rebellious Rhode Island. Although some regulations were designed to prevent nearby forests from being cut so that inhabitants would not have to go great distances for firewood, we can discern here, I believe, a respect for the land. . . .

Jeremy Belknap, writing in 1792 of his beloved New Hampshire, goes so far as to tell us that the good life was living in harmony with nature, though he stresses a man-controlled environment. As he phrased it, "Were I to form a picture of a happy society, it would be a town consisting of a due mixture of hills, valleys, and streams of water. The land well fenced and cultivated. . . ." In his good land he sees the need for a good inn, a "practical preacher," a schoolmaster, and a "musical society," but he stresses that the society should be mostly "husbandmen." When all these elements are combined in a beautiful natural setting, one finds, he writes, a situation "most favorable to social happiness of any which the world can afford."

Thomas Jefferson, of course, developed a similar agrarian theme in his *Notes on Virginia.* While he took great pride in the American environment, celebrating its vastness and the superior nature of its denizens to those found elsewhere (noting, for example, "that the reindeer [of the Old World] could walk under the belly of our moose"), he believed that the land should not be left to the Indians. Benefits should come to the white farmers who subdue the land. He, indeed, called for immediate population growth, predicting, as did his friend Benjamin Franklin, that the American population would grow exponentially. "The present desire of America," he wrote, "is to produce rapid population by as great importation of foreigners as possible." He went so far as to assert that "our rapid multiplication will . . . cover the whole northern, if not the southern continent."

In Belknap as well as in Jefferson we see clearly a pride in the

American landscape as the nation expands and utilizes the bounties of nature. From the birth of the republic, then, there was an ambivalence about appreciating and protecting nature or exploiting the land. Increasingly the evidence of eyewitnesses is that there was environmental distress, but this was seen as part of the penalty of progress as America moved west to occupy the wilderness. . . .

By looking back over the highlights or themes of environmental despoliation in our history, we can, I believe, agree that there are basic environmental reasons that account, at least in part, for the severity of the problems we now face. These reasons are:

(1) The competitive exploitation of furbearing animals and nonrenewable natural resources greatly exceeded the extent to which this natural wealth had to be sacrificed. And further, the assault upon the land was tied closely to the dispossession of the Indians, our first ecologists.

(2) Pioneers from earliest times wasted natural resources, but it has been the ever increasing volume of despoliation and its cumulative effects that have brought instances of permanent environmental damage.

(3) The American government has had an increasing role in the despoliation because of its links with predatory business interests and scientists, many of them associated with leading universities. In recent times we can see this trend in certain actions of such government agencies as the Department of Agriculture, the Army Corps of Engineers, and the Atomic Energy Commission.

(4) Population growth, as predicted by Jefferson, Franklin, and others, has culminated in an occupation of the land from sea to sea. This, with the new affluence, has brought a crowding of the land and tremendous strain upon resources and energy reserves. The ambivalent attitude toward growth and conservation continues, but there is evidence that the old ideal of unlimited growth should be questioned.

(5) Data from interdisciplinary research and from competent eyewitnesses show that the familiar Turnerean frontiers of first contact in the wilderness, fur trading, farming, mining, and urban settlement had reverberating environmental impacts and destructive social losses. Most of these losses were unpaid at the time and later generations are therefore obliged to accept the costs in lost capital and in environmental despoliation.

We may also conclude that environmental history . . . involves historical lessons and questions of morality. One of these questions is, should we have more respect for the land, even a land ethic? In short, an examination of historical environmental themes reveals a need for more emphasis upon new attitudes of Americans toward the environment. More stress could well be placed upon historical themes based upon a land ethic and respect for nature as opposed to the old conquistador interpretation. We can also improve our sense of identification with future generations and acknowledge the fact that environmental problems in the United States usually have world-wide repercussions. We look to the past, not to discern what must be, but to understand environmental themes which help to explain origins of ecological transformations taking place in our lifetime. We may then catch a glimpse of our newly forming frontiers which forecast the environmental future of America.

4

An Artist Proposes a National Park

George Catlin (1832)

George Catlin's frequent travels in the West for the purpose of studying and painting the American Indian gave him ample opportunity to observe the effects of an advancing civilization. In the spring of 1832, Catlin set out for the headwaters of the Missouri. In May he arrived at Fort Pierre, in present-day South Dakota, where he made these observations in his journal. They first appeared in print that winter in a New York newspaper and later as part of Catlin's North American Indians.

Catlin's plea is outstanding as the first recognition (by twenty-five years) of the fact that without formal preservation the remaining American wilderness would vanish. Although overshadowed in reputation by Henry David Thoreau (Selection 5) and John Muir (Selection 15), Catlin deserves credit for originating the national park idea. Fifty years after his journal entry Congress established a 2,000,000-acre reserve several hundred miles west of Fort Pierre, and Catlin had his "monument" in Yellowstone National Park.

When I first arrived at this place, on my way up the river, which was in the month of May, in 1832, and had taken up my lodgings in the Fur Company's Fort, . . . [I was told] that only a few days before I arrived (when an immense herd of buffaloes had showed themselves on the opposite side of the river, almost blackening the plains for a great distance), a party of five or six hundred Sioux Indians on horseback, forded the river about mid-day, and spending a few hours amongst them, recrossed the river at sun-down and came into the Fort with *fourteen hundred fresh buffalo tongues,* which were thrown down in a mass, and for which they required but a few gallons of whiskey, which was soon demolished, indulging them in a little, and harmless carouse.

George Catlin, *North American Indians: Being Letters and Notes on their Manners, Customs, and Conditions, Written during Eight Years' Travel amongst the Wildest Tribes in North America, 1832–1839,* **I,** 2 vols (London: George Catlin, 1880), 288–295.

This profligate waste of the lives of these noble and useful animals, when, from all that I could learn, not a skin or a pound of the meat (except the tongues), was brought in, fully supports me in the seemingly extravagant predictions that I have made as to their extinction, which I am certain is near at hand. . . .

From the above remarks it will be seen, that not only the red men, but red men and white, have aimed destruction at the race of these animals. . . .

Thus much I wrote of the buffaloes, and . . . of the fate that awaits them; and before I closed my book [i.e., diary or journal], I strolled out one day to the shade of a plum-tree, where I lay in the grass on a favourite bluff, and wrote thus:—

It is generally supposed, and familiarly said that a man *'falls'* into a rêverie; but I seated myself in the shade a few minutes since, resolved to *force* myself into one; and for this purpose I laid open a small pocket-map of North America, and excluding my thoughts from every other object in the world, I soon succeeded in producing the desired illusion. This little chart, over which I bent, was seen in all its parts, as nothing but the green and vivid reality. I was lifted up upon an imaginary pair of wings, which easily raised and held me floating in the open air, from whence I could behold beneath me the Pacific and the Atlantic Oceans—the great cities of the East, and the mighty rivers. I could see the blue chain of the great lakes at the North—the Rocky Mountains, and beneath them and near their base, the vast, and almost boundless plains of grass, which were speckled with the bands of grazing buffaloes!

The world turned gently around, and I examined its surface; continent after continent passed under my eye, and yet amidst them all, I saw not the vast and vivid green, that is spread like a carpet over the Western wilds of my own country. I saw not elsewhere in the world, the myriad herds of buffaloes—my eyes scanned in vain for they were not. And when I turned again to the wilds of my native land, I beheld them all in motion! For the distance of several hundreds of miles from North to South, they were wheeling about in vast columns and herds—some were scattered, and ran with furious wildness—some lay dead, and others were pawing the earth for a hiding-place—some were sinking down and dying, gushing out their life's blood in deep-drawn sighs—and others were contending in furious battle for the life they possessed, and the ground that they stood upon. They had long since assembled from the thickets, and secret haunts of the deep forest, into the midst of the treeless and bushless plains, as the place for their safety. I could see in an hundred places, amid the wheeling bands, and on their skirts and flanks, the leaping wild horse darting among them. I saw not the arrows, nor heard the twang of the sinewy bows that sent them; but I saw their victims fall!—on other steeds that rushed along their sides, I saw the glistening lances, which seemed to lay across them; their blades were blazing in the sun, till dipped in blood, and then I lost them! In other parts (and there were many), the vivid flash of *fire-arms* was seen—*their* victims fell too, and over their dead bodies hung suspended in air, little clouds of whitened smoke, from under which the flying horsemen had darted forward to mingle again with, and deal death to, the trampling throng.

. . . Hundreds and thousands were strewed upon the plains—they were flayed, and their reddened carcasses left; and about them bands of wolves, and dogs, and buzzards were seen devouring them. Contiguous, and in sight, were the distant and feeble smokes of wigwams and villages, where the skins were dragged, and dressed for white man's luxury! where they were all sold for *whiskey,* and the poor Indians lay drunk, and were crying. I cast my eyes into the towns and cities of the East, and there I beheld buffalo robes hanging at almost every door for traffic; and I saw also the curling smokes of a thousand *Stills* *—and I said, 'Oh insatiable man, is thy avarice such! wouldst thou tear the skin from the back of the last animal of this noble race, *and rob thy fellow-man of his meat, and for it give him poison!'*

Many are the rudenesses and wilds in Nature's works, which are destined to fall before the deadly axe and desolating hands of cultivating man; and so amongst her ranks of *living,* of beast and human, we often find noble stamps, or beautiful colours, to which our admiration clings; and even in the overwhelming march of civilised improvements and refinements do we love to cherish their existence, and lend our efforts to preserve them in their primitive rudeness. Such of Nature's works are always worthy of our preservation and protection; and the further we become separated (and the face of the country) from that pristine wildness and beauty, the more pleasure does the mind of enlightened man feel in recurring to those scenes, when he can have them preserved for his eyes and his mind to dwell upon.

Of such "rudenesses and wilds," Nature has nowhere presented more beautiful and lovely scenes, than those of the vast prairies of the West; and of *man* and *beast,* no nobler specimens than those who

---

*Devices for making whiskey. [Ed.]

inhabit them—the *Indian* and the *buffalo*—joint and original tenants of the soil, and fugitives together from the approach of civilised man; they have fled to the great plains of the West, and there, under an equal doom, they have taken up their *last abode,* where their race will expire, and their bones will bleach together.

It may be that *power is right,* and *voracity a virtue;* and that these people, and these noble animals, are *righteously* doomed to an issue that *will* not be averted. It can be easily proved—we have a civilised science that can easily do it, or anything else that may be required to cover the iniquities of civilised man in catering for his unholy appetites. It can be proved that the weak and ignorant have no *rights*—that there can be no virtue in darkness—that God's gifts have no meaning or merit until they are appropriated by civilised man—by him brought into the light, and converted to his use and luxury. . . .

Reader! Listen to the following calculations, and forget them not. The buffaloes (the quadrupeds from whose backs your beautiful robes were taken, and whose myriads were once spread over the whole country, from the Rocky Mountains to the Atlantic Ocean) have recently fled before the appalling appearance of civilised man, and taken up their abode and pasturage amid the almost boundless prairies of the West. An instinctive dread of their deadly foes, who made an easy prey of them whilst grazing in the forest, has led them to seek the midst of the vast and treeless plains of grass, as the spot where they would be least exposed to the assaults of their enemies; and it is exclusively in those desolate fields of silence (yet of beauty) that they are to be found—and over these vast steppes, or prairies, have they fled, like the Indian, towards the "setting sun;" until their bands have been crowded together, and their limits confined to a narrow strip of country on this side of the Rocky Mountains.

This strip of country, which extends from the province of Mexico to Lake Winnipeg on the North, is almost one entire plain of grass, which is, and ever must be, useless to cultivating man. It is here, and here chiefly, that the buffaloes dwell; and with, and hovering about them, live and flourish the tribes of Indians, whom God made for the enjoyment of that fair land and its luxuries.

It is a melancholy contemplation for one who has travelled as I have, through these realms, and seen this noble animal in all its pride and glory, to contemplate it so rapidly wasting from the world, drawing the irresistible conclusion too, which one must do, that its species is soon to be extinguished, and with it the peace and happiness (if not the actual existence) of the tribes of Indians who are joint tenants with them, in the occupancy of these vast and idle plains.

And what a splendid contemplation too, when one (who has travelled these realms, and can duly appreciate them) imagines them as they *might* in future be seen (by some great protecting policy of government) preserved in their pristine beauty and wildness, in a *magnificent park,* where the world could see for ages to come, the native Indian in his classic attire, galloping his wild horse, with sinewy bow, and shield and lance, amid the fleeting herds of elks and buffaloes. What a beautiful and thrilling specimen for America to preserve and hold up to the view of her refined citizens and the world, in future ages! A *nation's Park,* containing man and beast, in all the wild and freshness of their nature's beauty!

I would ask no other monument to my memory, nor any other enrolment of my name amongst the famous dead, than the reputation of having been the founder of such an institution.

5

The Value of Wildness

Henry David Thoreau (1851)

The ideas of Henry David Thoreau underlie many subsequent American interpreta-
tions of the significance of nature. A transcendentalist, Thoreau believed that the
natural world symbolized or reflected spiritual truth and moral law. And nature,
especially in its wilder forms, possessed a fertilizing vitality that civilized men needed
for strength and creativity. Thoreau personally found such nourishment near his
Concord, Massachusetts, home and on occasional forays into northern Maine. His
writings attempted to convince his contemporaries of their shortsightedness in prizing
only the material potential of the environment. As early as 1858 he joined Catlin
(Selection 4) in calling specifically for the preservation of wilderness in national parks.
But, like Catlin, Thoreau spoke a half-century before most Americans were prepared
to listen sympathetically to his message. Nevertheless, his philosophy survived to
become the intellectual foundation of the wilderness preservation movement and of
aesthetic conservation.

Thoreau first composed "Walking," which follows, in 1851 as a lecture for the
Concord Lyceum. It is crowded with ideas about the significance of the American
environment for patriotism, character, and culture.

I wish to speak a word for Nature, for absolute freedom and wildness,
as contrasted with a freedom and culture merely civil,—to regard man
as an inhabitant, or a part and parcel of Nature, rather than a member
of society. I wish to make an extreme statement, if so I may make an
emphatic one, for there are enough champions of civilization: the
minister and the school-committee and every one of you will take care
of that. . . .

When we walk, we naturally go to the fields and woods: what

Henry David Thoreau, "Walking," in *Excursions, The Writings of Henry David Thoreau,* **IX,**
Riverside edition, 11 vols. (Boston: Houghton Mifflin, 1893), 251, 258–260, 264–267,
275, 277–280, 292.

would become of us, if we walked only in a garden or a mall? . . . Of course it is of no use to direct our steps to the woods, if they do not carry us thither. I am alarmed when it happens that I have walked a mile into the woods bodily, without getting there in spirit. In my afternoon walk I would fain forget all my morning occupations and my obligations to society. But it sometimes happens that I cannot easily shake off the village. . . .

Nowadays almost all man's improvements, so called, as the building of houses, and the cutting down of the forest and of all large trees, simply deform the landscape, and make it more and more tame and cheap. A people who would begin by burning the fences and let the forest stand! . . .

I can easily walk ten, fifteen, twenty, any number of miles, commencing at my own door, without going by any house, without crossing a road except where the fox and the mink do: first along by the river, and then the brook, and then the meadow and the woodside. There are square miles in my vicinity which have no inhabitant. From many a hill I can see civilization and the abodes of man afar. The farmers and their works are scarcely more obvious than woodchucks and their burrows. Man and his affairs, church and state and school, trade and commerce, and manufactures and agriculture, even politics, the most alarming of them all,—I am pleased to see how little space they occupy in the landscape. . . .

At present, in this vicinity, the best part of the land is not private property; the landscape is not owned, and the walker enjoys comparative freedom. But possibly the day will come when it will be partitioned off into so-called pleasure-grounds, in which a few will take a narrow and exclusive pleasure only,—when fences shall be multiplied, and man-traps and other engines invented to confine men to the *public* road, and walking over the surface of God's earth shall be construed to mean trespassing on some gentleman's grounds. . . .

What is it that makes it so hard sometimes to determine whither we will walk? I believe that there is a subtle magnetism in Nature, which, if we unconsciously yield to it, will direct us aright. It is not indifferent to us which way we walk. There is a right way; but we are very liable from heedlessness and stupidity to take the wrong one. We would fain take that walk, never yet taken by us through this actual world, which is perfectly symbolical of the path which we love to travel in the interior and ideal world; and sometimes, no doubt, we find it difficult to choose our direction, because it does not yet exist distinctly in our idea.

When I go out of the house for a walk, uncertain as yet whither I will bend my steps, and submit myself to my instinct to decide for me, I find, strange and whimsical as it may seem, that I finally and inevitably settle southwest, toward some particular wood or meadow or deserted pasture or hill in that direction. My needle is slow to settle,—varies a few degrees, and does not always point due southwest, it is true, and it has good authority for this variation, but it always settles between west and south-southwest. The future lies that way to me, and the earth seems more unexhausted and richer on that side. . . . Eastward I go only by force; but westward I go free. Thither no business leads me. It is hard for me to believe that I shall find fair landscapes or sufficient wildness and freedom behind the eastern horizon. I am not excited by the prospect of a walk thither; but I believe that the forest which I see in the western horizon stretches uninterruptedly toward the setting sun, and there are no towns nor cities in it of enough consequence to disturb me. Let me live where I will, on this side is the city, on that the wilderness, and ever I am leaving the city more and more, and withdrawing into the wilderness. I should not lay so much stress on this fact, if I did not believe that something like this is the prevailing tendency of my countrymen. I must walk toward Oregon, and not toward Europe. And that way the nation is moving, and I may say that mankind progress from east to west. . . .

We go eastward to realize history and study the works of art and literature, retracing the steps of the race; we go westward as into the future, with a spirit of enterprise and adventure. The Atlantic is a Lethean stream, in our passage over which we have had an opportunity to forget the Old World and its institutions. . . .

The West of which I speak is but another name for the Wild; and what I have been preparing to say is, that in Wildness is the preservation of the World. Every tree sends its fibres forth in search of the Wild. The cities import it at any price. Men plough and sail for it. From the forest and wilderness come the tonics and barks which brace mankind. Our ancestors were savages. The story of Romulus and Remus being suckled by a wolf is not a meaningless fable. The founders of every state which has risen to eminence have drawn their nourishment and vigor from a similar wild source. It was because the children of the Empire were not suckled by the wolf that they were conquered and displaced by the children of the northern forests who were.

I believe in the forest, and in the meadow, and in the night in which the corn grows. We require an infusion of hemlock-spruce or arbor vitæ in our tea. . . .

I would not have every man nor every part of a man cultivated, any more than I would have every acre of earth cultivated: part will be tillage, but the greater part will be meadow and forest, not only serving an immediate use, but preparing a mould against a distant future, by the annual decay of the vegetation which it supports. . . .

Ben Jonson exclaims,—

How near to good is what is fair!

So I would say,—

How near to good is what is *wild!*

Life consists with wildness. The most alive is the wildest. Not yet subdued to man, its presence refreshes him. One who pressed forward incessantly and never rested from his labors, who grew fast and made infinite demands on life, would always find himself in a new country or wilderness, and surrounded by the raw material of life. He would be climbing over the prostrate stems of primitive forest-trees.

Hope and the future for me are not in lawns and cultivated fields, not in towns and cities, but in the impervious and quaking swamps. . . . I derive more of my subsistence from the swamps which surround my native town than from the cultivated gardens in the village. . . .

My spirits infallibly rise in proportion to the outward dreariness. Give me the ocean, the desert, or the wilderness! . . . A town is saved, not more by the righteous men in it than by the woods and swamps that surround it. A township where one primitive forest waves above while another primitive forest rots below,—such a town is fitted to raise not only corn and potatoes, but poets and philosophers for the coming ages. In such a soil grew Homer and Confucius and the rest, and out of such a wilderness comes the Reformer eating locusts and wild honey.

6

Human Responsibility for the Land

George Perkins Marsh (1864)

For most of his history man simply accepted the environment into which he was born as a fact of life—a given. George Perkins Marsh, a Vermonter whose varied career included extensive travel in Europe and the Near East, was one of the first Americans to understand that the condition of the land was as much a product of man as of nature. In Man and Nature *Marsh contended that man's power to transform the natural world should entail a commensurate sense of responsibility. That it did not, he warned, constituted one of the gravest threats to the welfare, indeed the survival, of civilization. Focusing most of his book on the disastrous consequences of deforestation for water supply, Marsh pointed to empires whose declines paralleled that of their woodlands. His examples were so dramatic and his argument for remedial action so persuasive that* Man and Nature *exerted a profound influence on the beginnings of American conservation. Marsh's concept of "geographical regeneration," presented here, was a harbinger of regional reclamation efforts such as that involving the Tennessee Valley in the 1930s.*

The object of the present volume is: to indicate the character and, approximately, the extent of the changes produced by human action in the physical conditions of the globe we inhabit; to point out the dangers of imprudence and the necessity of caution in all operations which, on a large scale, interfere with the spontaneous arrangements of the organic or the inorganic world; to suggest the possibility and the importance of the restoration of disturbed harmonies and the material improvement of waste and exhausted regions; and, incidentally, to illustrate the doctrine, that man is, in both kind and degree, a power

George P. Marsh, *Man and Nature; or, Physical Geography as Modified by Human Action* (New York: Charles Scribner, 1864), [iii], 35–41, 45–47, 328–329. Marsh's footnotes have been omitted.

of a higher order than any of the other forms of animated life, which, like him, are nourished at the table of bounteous nature. . . .

Man has too long forgotten that the earth was given to him for usufruct alone, not for consumption, still less for profligate waste. Nature has provided against the absolute destruction of any of her elementary matter, the raw material of her works; the thunderbolt and the tornado, the most convulsive throes of even the volcano and the earthquake, being only phenomena of decomposition and recomposition. But she has left it within the power of man irreparably to derange the combinations of inorganic matter and of organic life, which through the night of æons she had been proportioning and balancing, to prepare the earth for his habitation, when, in the fulness of time, his Creator should call him forth to enter into its possession.

. . . Man is everywhere a disturbing agent. Wherever he plants his foot, the harmonies of nature are turned to discords. The proportions and accommodations which insured the stability of existing arrangements are overthrown. Indigenous vegetable and animal species are extirpated, and supplanted by others of foreign origin, spontaneous production is forbidden or restricted, and the face of the earth is either laid bare or covered with a new and reluctant growth of vegetable forms, and with alien tribes of animal life. These intentional changes and substitutions constituted, indeed, great revolutions; but vast as is their magnitude and importance, they are . . . insignificant in comparison with the contingent and unsought results which have flowed from them.

The fact that, of all organic beings, man alone is to be regarded as essentially a destructive power, and that he wields energies to resist which, nature—that nature whom all material life and all inorganic substance obey—is wholly impotent, tends to prove that, though living in physical nature, he is not of her, that he is of more exalted parentage, and belongs to a higher order of existences than those born of her womb and submissive to her dictates.

There are, indeed, brute destroyers, beasts and birds and insects of prey—all animal life feeds upon, and, of course, destroys other life,—but this destruction is balanced by compensations. It is, in fact, the very means by which the existence of one tribe of animals or of vegetables is secured against being smothered by the encroachments of another; and the reproductive powers of species, which serve as the food of others, are always proportioned to the demand they are destined to supply. Man pursues his victims with reckless destructiveness;

and, while the sacrifice of life by the lower animals is limited by the cravings of appetite, he unsparingly persecutes, even to extirpation, thousands of organic forms which he cannot consume.

The earth was not, in its natural condition, completely adapted to the use of man, but only to the sustenance of wild animals and wild vegetation. . . .

. . . [But men] cannot subsist and rise to the full development of their higher properties, unless brute and unconscious nature be effectually combated, and, in a great degree, vanquished by human art. Hence, a certain measure of transformation of terrestrial surface, of suppression of natural, and stimulation of artificially modified productivity becomes necessary. This measure man has unfortunately exceeded. He has felled the forests whose network of fibrous roots bound the mould to the rocky skeleton of the earth; but had he allowed here and there a belt of woodland to reproduce itself by spontaneous propagation, most of the mischiefs which his reckless destruction of the natural protection of the soil has occasioned would have been averted. He has broken up the mountain reservoirs, the percolation of whose waters through unseen channels supplied the fountains that refreshed his cattle and fertilized his fields; but he has neglected to maintain the cisterns and the canals of irrigation which a wise antiquity had constructed to neutralize the consequences of its own imprudence. While he has torn the thin glebe [i.e., soil] which confined the light earth of extensive plains, and has destroyed the fringe of semi-aquatic plants which skirted the coast and checked the drifting of the sea sand, he has failed to prevent the spreading of the dunes by clothing them with artificially propagated vegetation. He has ruthlessly warred on all the tribes of animated nature whose spoil he could convert to his own uses, and he has not protected the birds which prey on the insects most destructive to his own harvests.

Purely untutored humanity, it is true, interferes comparatively little with the arrangements of nature, and the destructive agency of man becomes more and more energetic and unsparing as he advances in civilization, until the impoverishment, with which his exhaustion of the natural resources of the soil is threatening him, at last awakens him to the necessity of preserving what is left, if not of restoring what has been wantonly wasted. The wandering savage grows no cultivated vegetable, fells no forest, and extirpates no useful plant, no noxious weed. If his skill in the chase enables him to entrap numbers of the animals on which he feeds, he compensates this loss by destroying also the lion, the tiger, the wolf, the otter, the seal, and the eagle, thus indirectly protecting the feebler quadrupeds and fish and fowls, which would otherwise become the booty of beasts and birds of prey. But with stationary life, or rather with the pastoral state, man at once commences an almost indiscriminate warfare upon all the forms of animal and vegetable existence around him, and as he advances in civilization, he gradually eradicates or transforms every spontaneous product of the soil he occupies. . . .

It is, on the one hand, rash and unphilosophical to attempt to set limits to the ultimate power of man over inorganic nature, and it is unprofitable, on the other, to speculate on what may be accomplished by the discovery of now unknown and unimagined natural forces, or even by the invention of new arts and new processes. But since we have seen aerostation, the motive power of elastic vapors, the wonders of modern telegraphy, the destructive explosiveness of gunpowder, and even of a substance so harmless, unresisting, and inert as cotton, nothing in the way of mechanical achievement seems impossible, and it is hard to restrain the imagination from wandering forward a couple of generations to an epoch when our descendants shall have advanced as far beyond us in physical conquest, as we have marched beyond the trophies erected by our grandfathers.

I must therefore be understood to man only, that no agencies now known to man and directed by him seem adequate to the reducing of great Alpine precipices to such slopes as would enable them to support a vegetable clothing, or to the covering of large extents of denuded rock with earth, and planting upon them a forest growth. But among the mysteries which science is yet to reveal, there may be still undiscovered methods of accomplishing even grander wonders than these. Mechanical philosophers have suggested the possibility of accumulating and treasuring up for human use some of the greater natural forces, which the action of the elements puts forth with such astonishing energy. Could we gather, and bind, and make subservient to our control, the power which a West Indian hurricane exerts through a small area in one continuous blast, or the momentum expended by the waves, in a tempestuous winter, upon the breakwater at Cherbourg [France], or the lifting power of the tide, for a month, at the head of the Bay of Fundy, or the pressure of a square mile of sea water at the depth of five thousand fathoms, or a moment of the might of an earthquake or a volcano, our age . . . might hope to scarp the rugged walls of the Alps and Pyrenees . . . , robe them once more in a vegetation as rich as that of their pristine woods, and turn their wasting torrents into refreshing streams.

Could this old world, which man has overthrown, be rebuilded, could human cunning rescue its wasted hillsides and its deserted plains from solitude or mere nomad occupation, from barrenness, from nakedness, and from insalubrity, and restore the ancient fertility and healthfulness . . . , the thronging millions of Europe might still find room on the Eastern continent, and the main current of emigration be turned toward the rising instead of the setting sun.

But changes like these must await great political and moral revolutions in the governments and peoples by whom those regions are now possessed, a command of pecuniary and of mechanical means not at present enjoyed by those nations, and a more advanced and generally diffused knowledge of the processes by which the amelioration of soil and climate is possible, than now anywhere exists. Until such circumstances shall conspire to favor the work of geographical regeneration, the countries I have mentioned . . . will continue to sink into yet deeper desolation. . . .

All human institutions, associate arrangements, modes of life, have their characteristic imperfections. The natural, perhaps the necessary defect of ours, is their instability, their want of fixedness, not in form only, but even in spirit. The face of physical nature in the United States shares this incessant fluctuation, and the landscape is as variable as the habits of the population. It is time for some abatement in the restless love of change which characterizes us, and makes us almost a nomad rather than a sedentary people. We have now felled forest enough everywhere, in many districts far too much. Let us restore this one element of material life to its normal proportions, and devise means for maintaining the permanence of its relations to the fields, the meadows, and the pastures, to the rain and the dews of heaven, to the springs and rivulets with which it waters the earth. The establishment of an approximately fixed ratio between the two most broadly characterized distinctions of rural surface—woodland and plough land— would involve a certain persistence of character in all the branches of industry, all the occupations and habits of life, which depend upon or are immediately connected with either, without implying a rigidity that should exclude flexibility of accommodation to the many changes of external circumstance which human wisdom can neither prevent nor foresee, and would thus help us to become, more emphatically, a well-ordered and stable commonwealth, and, not less conspicuously, a people of progress.

7

The Value and Care of Parks

Frederick Law Olmsted (1865)

As Frederick Law Olmsted realizes here, the preservation of natural scenery in the form of public parks was an American innovation in keeping with the best of the nation's ideals. Olmsted himself took a leading role in formulating and instituting the park concept. One of the first professional landscape architects in the United States, Olmsted was primarily responsible for translating the State of New York's 1853 authorization for a "public place" in New York City into Central Park. In 1863 Olmsted interrupted his distinguished career as a consultant on parks and city planning in the East to spend three years in California. His acquaintance with Yosemite Valley began with a visit in the summer of 1864. The following September Olmsted received an appointment as a commissioner to manage the valley that had been granted by Congress to the State of California the previous June "for public use, resort, and recreation." Sensing at once the significance of the grant, Olmsted made the following report on August 8, 1865, with the purpose of showing Yosemite's values and suggesting principles for its management. So novel and altruistic were his ideas, however, that they found little favor with California's politicians and entrepreneurs, and late in 1865 Olmsted returned to his career in the East. Yet he did not forget Yosemite; twenty-five years later another champion of the valley, John Muir (Selection 15), secured Olmsted's assistance in a successful campaign to establish Yosemite National Park.

It is the will of the nation as embodied in the act of Congress [of June 30, 1864, granting Yosemite Valley to California as a public park] that this scenery shall never be private property, but that like certain defensive points upon our coast it shall be held solely for public purposes.

Frederick Law Olmsted, "The Yosemite Valley and the Mariposa Big Trees," *Landscape Architecture*, **XLIII** (1952), 17, 20–23. Copyright by the American Society of Landscape Architects. Reprinted by permission.

Two classes of considerations may be assumed to have influenced the action of Congress. The first and less important is the direct and obvious pecuniary advantage which comes to a commonwealth from the fact that it possesses objects which cannot be taken out of its domain, that are attractive to travellers and the enjoyment of which is open to all.

To illustrate this it is simply necessary to refer to certain cantons of the Republic of Switzerland, a commonwealth of the most industrious and frugal people in Europe. The results of all the ingenuity and labor of this people applied to the resources of wealth which they hold in common with the people of other lands which have become of insignificant value compared with that which they derive from the price which travellers gladly pay for being allowed to share with them the enjoyment of the natural scenery of their mountains. These travellers alone have caused hundreds of the best inns in the world to be established and maintained among them, have given the farmers their best and almost the only market they have for their surplus products, have spread a network of railroads and superb carriage roads, steamboat routes and telegraphic lines over the country, have contributed directly and indirectly for many years the larger part of the state revenue and all this without the exportation or abstraction from the country of any thing of the slightest value to the people. . . .

A more important class of considerations, however, remains to be stated. There are considerations of a political duty of grave importance to which seldom if ever before has proper respect been paid by any government in the world but the grounds of which rest on the same eternal base of equity and benevolence with all other duties of republican government. It is the main duty of government, if it is not the sole duty of government, to provide means of protection for all its citizens in the pursuit of happiness against the obstacles, otherwise insurmountable, which the selfishness of individuals or combinations of individuals is liable to interpose to that pursuit.

It is a scientific fact that the occasional contemplation of natural scenes of an impressive character, particularly if this contemplation occurs in connection with relief from ordinary cares, change of air and change of habits, is favorable to the health and vigor of men and especially to the health and vigor of their intellect beyond any other conditions which can be offered them, that it not only gives pleasure for the time being but increases the subsequent capacity for happiness and the means of securing happiness. The want of such occasional recreation where men and women are habitually pressed by their business or household cares often results in a class of disorders the characteristic quality of which is mental disability, sometimes taking the severe forms of softening of the brain, paralysis, palsy, monomania, or insanity, but more frequently of mental and nervous excitability, moroseness, melancholy or irascibility, incapacitating the subject for the proper exercise of the intellectual and moral forces.

It is well established that where circumstances favor the use of such means of recreation as have been indicated, the reverse of this is true. For instance, it is a universal custom with the heads of the important departments of the British government to spend a certain period of every year on their parks and shooting grounds or in travelling among the Alps or other mountain regions. This custom is followed by the leading lawyers, bankers, merchants and the wealthy classes generally of the empire, among whom the average period of active business life is much greater than with the most nearly corresponding classes in our own or any other country where the same practice is not equally well established. . . .

If we analyze the operation of scenes of beauty upon the mind, and consider the intimate relation of the mind upon the nervous system and the whole physical economy, the action and reaction which constantly occur between bodily and mental conditions, the reinvigoration which results from such scenes is readily comprehended. Few persons can see such scenery as that of the Yosemite and not be impressed by it in some slight degree. All not alike, all not perhaps consciously, and amongst all who are consciously impressed by it, few can give the least expression to that of which they are conscious. But there can be no doubt that all have this susceptibility, though with some it is much more dull and confused than with others.

The power of scenery to affect men is, in a large way, proportionate to the degree of their civilization and the degree in which their taste has been cultivated. Among a thousand savages there will be a much smaller number who will show the least sign of being so affected than among a thousand persons taken from a civilized community. This is only one of the many channels in which a similar distinction between civilized and savage men is to be generally observed. The whole body of the susceptibilities of civilized men and with their susceptibilities their powers, are on the whole enlarged.

But as with the bodily powers, if one group of muscles is developed by exercise exclusively, and all others neglected, the result is general feebleness, so it is with the mental faculties. And men who exercise those faculties or susceptibilities of the mind which are called in play by beautiful scenery so little that they seem to be inert with them, are either in a diseased condition from excessive devotion of the mind to a limited range of interests, or their whole minds are in a savage state; that is, a state of low development. The latter class need to be drawn out generally; the former need relief from their habitual matters of interest and to be drawn out in those parts of their mental nature which have been habitually left idle and inert.

But there is a special reason why the reinvigoration of those parts which are stirred into conscious activity by natural scenery is more effective upon the general development and health than that of any other, which is this: The severe and excessive exercise of the mind which leads to the greatest fatigue and is the most wearing upon the whole constitution is almost entirely caused by application to the removal of something to be apprehended in the future, or to interests beyond those of the moment, or of the individual; to the laying up of wealth, to the preparation of something, to accomplishing something in the mind of another, and especially to small and petty details which are uninteresting in themselves and which engage the attention at all only because of the bearing they have on some general end of more importance which is seen ahead.

In the interest which natural scenery inspires there is the strongest contrast to this. It is for itself and at the moment it is enjoyed. The attention is aroused and the mind occupied without purpose, without a continuation of the common process of relating the present action, thought or perception to some future end. There is little else that has this quality so purely. There are few enjoyments with which regard for something outside and beyond the enjoyment of the moment can ordinarily be so little mixed. The pleasures of the table are irresistibly associated with the care of hunger and the repair of the bodily waste. In all social pleasures and all pleasures which are usually enjoyed in association with the social pleasures, the care for the opinion of others, or the good of others largely mingles. In the pleasures of literature, the laying up of ideas and self-improvement are purposes which cannot be kept out of view.

This, however, is in very slight degree, if at all, the case with the enjoyment of the emotions caused by natural scenery. It therefore results that the enjoyment of scenery employs the mind without fatigue and yet exercises it; tranquillizes it and yet enlivens it; and thus, through the influence of the mind over the body, gives the effect of refreshing rest and reinvigoration to the whole system.

Men who are rich enough and who are sufficiently free from

anxiety with regard to their wealth can and do provide places of this
needed recreation for themselves. They have done so from the earliest
the history of the world, for the great men of the
Persians and the Hebrews, had their rural retreats, as
ious as those of the aristocracy of Europe at present.
islands of Great Britain and Ireland more than one
parks and notable grounds devoted to luxury and
value of these grounds amounts to many millions of
ost of their annual maintenance is greater than that
chools; their only advantage to the commonwealth is
h the recreation they afford their owners (except as
spitality to others) and these owners with their fami-
than one in six thousand of the whole population. The
e choicest natural scenes in the country and the means
onnected with them is thus a monopoly, in a very
r, of a very few, very rich people. The great mass of
ng those to whom it would be of the greatest benefit,
m it. In the nature of the case private parks can never
mass of the people in any country nor by any considera-
en of the rich, except by the favor of a few, and in
dependence on them.

Thus without means are taken by government to withhold them
from the grasp of individuals, all places favorable in scenery to the
recreation of the mind and body will be closed against the great body
of the people. For the same reason that the water of rivers should be
guarded against private appropriation and the use of it for the purpose
of navigation and otherwise protected against obstruction, portions of
natural scenery may therefore properly be guarded and cared for by
government. To simply reserve them from monopoly by individuals,
however, it will be obvious, is not all that is necessary. It is necessary
that they should be laid open to the use of the body of the people.

The establishment by government of great public grounds for the
free enjoyment of the people under certain circumstances, is thus
justified and enforced as a political duty.

Such a provision, however, having regard to the whole people of
a state, has never before been made and the reason it has not is evident.

It has always been the conviction of the governing classes of the
old world that it is necessary that the large mass of all human communities should spend their lives in almost constant labor and that the
power of enjoying beauty either of nature or of art in any high degree,
requires a cultivation of certain faculties, which is impossible to these

humble toilers. Hence it is thought better, so far as the recreations of the masses of a nation receive attention from their rulers, to provide artificial pleasure for them, such as theatres, parades, and promenades where they will be amused by the equipages of the rich and the animation of crowds.

It is unquestionably true that excessive and persistent devotion to sordid interests cramps and distorts the power of appreciating natural beauty and destroys the love of it which the Almighty has implanted in every human being, and which is so intimately and mysteriously associated with the moral perceptions and intuition, but it is not true that exemption from toil, much leisure, much study, much wealth, are necessary to the exercise of the esthetic and contemplative faculties. It is the folly of laws which have permitted and favored the monopoly by privileged classes of many of the means supplied in nature for the gratification, exercise and education of the esthetic faculties that has caused the appearance of dullness and weakness and disease of these faculties in the mass of the subjects of kings. And it is against the limitation of the means of such education to the rich that the wise legislation of free governments must be directed. . . .

It was in accordance with these views of the destiny of the New World and the duty of the republican government that Congress enacted that the Yosemite should be held, guarded and managed for the free use of the whole body of the people forever. . . .

The main duty with which the Commissioners [appointed to manage Yosemite Valley as a park] should be charged should be to give every advantage practicable to the mass of the people to benefit by that which is peculiar to this ground and which has caused Congress to treat it differently from other parts of the public domain. This peculiarity consists wholly in its natural scenery.

The first point to be kept in mind then is the preservation and maintenance as exactly as is possible of the natural scenery; the restriction, that is to say, within the narrowest limits consistent with the necessary accommodation of visitors, of all artificial constructions and the prevention of all constructions markedly inharmonious with the scenery or which would unnecessarily obscure, distort or detract from the dignity of the scenery.

Second: it is important that it should be remembered that in permitting the sacrifice of anything that would be of the slightest value to future visitors to the convenience, bad taste, playfulness, carelessness, or wanton destructiveness of present visitors, we probably yield in each case the interest of uncounted millions to the selfishness of a few individuals. . . .

At some time, therefore, laws to prevent an unjust use by individuals, of that which is not individual but public property must be made and rigidly enforced. . . .

It should, then, be made the duty of the Commission to prevent a wanton or careless disregard on the part of anyone entering the Yosemite or the Grove, of the rights of posterity as well as of contemporary visitors, and the Commission should be clothed with proper authority and given the necessary means for this purpose.

This duty of preservation is the first which falls upon the state under the Act of Congress, because the millions who are hereafter to benefit by the Act have the largest interest in it, and the largest interest should be first and most strenuously guarded.

8

The Sportsman Factor in Early Conservation

John F. Reiger (1986)

Until John Reiger's findings were published, hunters had not been given much credit as protectors of nature. Indeed, it was commonplace to see them as part of the problem. But Reiger distinguishes between the kind of commercial or "meat" hunter who decimated American wildlife and the sportsman who respected it and desired its perpetuation in a natural habitat. He shows that the typical sportsman was a member of the upper social and economic class. For him, wildlife did not represent meat in the pot so much as one of the amenities whose presence enhanced the quality of American life. Understandably, sport hunters favored the establishment of federal land reserves such as national forests, and the most enlightened even understood the crucial role in sustaining game populations of wildlife refuges and national parks where hunting was prohibited.

Ever since the first decade of the twentieth century when President Theodore Roosevelt and his Chief Forester, Gifford Pinchot, made "conservation" a household word, the term has received a variety of definitions, and every group from the Sierra Club to the Army Corps of Engineers has claimed to be its one true representative. During the latter 1960s, the public discovered the word "ecology" and began to use it as if it were a more fashionable version of the older term. Though both words entered the American vocabulary in the late nineteenth century and are now used interchangeably—even by some historians—they have in reality very different meanings.

As a discipline, ecology is "the study of the interrelationships of

John F. Reiger, *American Sportsmen and the Origins of Conservation* (Norman: University of Oklahoma Press, 1986), 19–23, 25–28, 48–49. Copyright 1986 by the University of Oklahoma Press. Used by permission. Footnotes in the original have been omitted.

organisms to one another and to the environment." Because this book deals with the nineteenth century, its human subjects cannot be called "ecologists." Even though many of them possessed an ecological orientation—perceiving the interrelatedness of wildlife and their habitats—they studied organisms (like birds) *or* environments (like forests) but rarely both simultaneously. Not until the twentieth century did ecology become a recognized science in the United States.

"Conservationist," not "ecologist," is the more precise term for the American pioneer of environmental concern. Long before 1907—when Gifford Pinchot claims to have been the first to perceive the interrelationship of all resource use—an influential segment of the American population had come to understand that renewable resources like wildlife and forests could be exploited indefinitely as long as a certain amount of "capital" was maintained. Even nonrenewable resources like coal and oil could be made to last infinitely longer if managed on an efficient basis. Historically, conservation has not been a science like ecology but a reform movement using political and legal methods to obtain what Theodore Roosevelt called "wise use" of resources.

The confusion between ecology and conservation is only one of many ambiguities surrounding the origins of American concern for the environment. There is, in fact, no aspect of United States history more in need of revision than the historiography of conservation.

One of the most important misconceptions is that no conservation movement existed until the twentieth century. Despite the publication of a number of books and essays purporting to treat the "origins" of the crusade, environmental historians invariably begin their works at the close of the nineteenth century, with perhaps a passing nod to a few "prophets" like George Perkins Marsh and John Wesley Powell. Conversely, this volume commences several decades earlier and shows that the movement originated in the 1870s. The work ends in 1901, when most historians of conservation are just "getting into" their studies. The first years of the present century have been chosen as the closing period because with the ascendancy of Theodore Roosevelt to the Presidency, a movement that began a generation before flowered into a fully developed federal program of resource management.

Another of the widely believed myths of conservation historiography is the result . . . of historians examining only the most available sources. Accepting at face value the political rhetoric of the Roosevelt administration, scholars through the 1950s pictured conservation as a movement of "the people" against the monopolistic control of resources by "special interests." According to this thesis, conservation was an integral part of the early twentieth-century reform movement known as "progressivism."

The problems with this interpretation are immense. First is the fundamental question of whether there was really a progressive *movement* at all, or simply a myriad of different reform impulses later unified by historians under one all-encompassing label.

Even if we accept the existence of progressivism, another impasse materializes when we try to bring conservation within its fold. Though historians of progressivism and conservation have described them as middle-class movements, this study will show that conservation, at least, began as an upper-class effort. . . .

American sportsmen, those who hunted and fished for pleasure rather than commerce or necessity, were the real spearhead of conservation. . . .

With the establishment in the early 1870s of national newspapers like *American Sportsman, Forest and Stream,* and *Field and Stream,* outdoorsmen acquired a means of communicating with each other, and a rapid growth of group identity was the result. Increasingly, gunners and anglers looked upon themselves as members of a fraternity with a well-defined code of conduct and thinking. In order to obtain membership in this order of "true sportsmen," one had to practice proper etiquette in the field, give game a sporting chance, and possess an aesthetic appreciation of the whole context of sport that included a commitment to its perpetuation.

The most obvious manifestation of the new self-awareness was the rapid growth of sportsmen's clubs and associations. While a desire for comradery was the underlying reason for their creation, one need only look at the names and constitutions of these organizations to understand that subjects like "game protection" and "fish culture" were important concerns of the members.

This early emphasis on the preservation and management of wildlife contains key implications for the historiography of conservation. Accepting the opinions expressed by Roosevelt and Pinchot in their autobiographies, historians have concluded that concern for the forests was the genesis of American conservation. Yet this work will show that the first challenge to the myth of inexhaustibility that succeeded in arousing a substantial segment of the public was not the dwindling forests, but the disappearance, in region after region, of game fishes, birds, and mammals. . . .

Regardless of which of the three main areas of early conservation we pick—wildlife, timberlands, or national parks—sportsmen led the way. During the 1870s and '80s, local and state associations forced one legislature after another to pass laws limiting and regulating the take of wildlife by market men and sportsmen alike. And in this same period, outdoor journals, particularly *Forest and Stream,* anticipated the later muckrakers in exposing the federal government's shameful neglect of Yellowstone National Park, the nation's first such preserve.

Finally, in 1887, Theodore Roosevelt, George Bird Grinnell, and other prominent sportsmen founded the Boone and Crockett Club named after two of America's most famous hunters. Though almost ignored by professional historians, it—and not the Sierra Club—was the first private organization to deal effectively with conservation issues of national scope. The Boone and Crockett played an all-important role in the creation and administration of the first national parks, forest reserves, and wildlife refuges. . . .

The reasons behind [the] . . . welcome reception [of nature protection] can be found in the new attitudes arising in the 1860s regarding hunting and fishing. Before the Civil War, most Americans viewed these activities as acceptable only when necessary or helpful to the maintenance of a livelihood; one pursued game because he depended on it for food or pecuniary profit. If hunting and fishing were spoken of as "sports" at all, they were usually lumped together with diversions typified by chance and a purse, like horse racing, boxing, and cock fighting. An individual who acquired a taste for either to the point of practicing it as sport often found his "practical" neighbors regarding him as frivolous or worse. As the editor of one of the later outdoor journals put it, "a man who went 'gunnin or fishin' lost caste among respectable people just about in the same way that one did who got drunk."

Not all Americans, however, regarded these activities in utilitarian or economic terms. For a minority who looked to the British Isles for their example, "correct" hunting and fishing increasingly became a chief means of distinguishing the "gentleman" in a postwar America best known for its Philistinism and commercialism. Across the Atlantic, the accepted ways of taking game were the products of traditions stretching back *at least* to the time of Izaak Walton in the seventeenth century. Whether fly-fishing for trout in an English stream or grouse shooting on a Scottish moor, an aristocrat took his sport seriously. To be fully accepted by his peers, he had to have a knowledge of the quarry and its habitat; a familiarity with the rods, guns, or dogs necessary to its pursuit; a skill to cast or shoot with precision and coolness that often takes years to acquire; and most of all, a "social sense" of the do's and don'ts involved.

This last ingredient might be called the "code of the sportsman," and it was particularly important to nobility. Typical was Henry William Herbert, the English aristocrat who immigrated to America in 1831. A friend once said of him: "Like all true sportsmen, while fond of following the game in season with gun, dog and rod, he was a bitter and unrelenting enemy to all poachers and pot-hunters."

. . . [I]t was "Frank Forester"—as Herbert called himself—who . . . became the model for the rising generation of American sportsmen.

. . . [He] also lamented the commercial destruction of wildlife and habitat and demanded that sportsmen join together to preserve their recreation. The notion that there was only one correct way to take game and that all other methods were "common," or even immoral, was a potential reservoir of reform that would play a key role in the making of the conservation movement.

What late nineteenth-century sportsmen and their journals had to fight was nothing less than the national myth of progress. An incredible rapidity of physical change, probably unexcelled in world history, was already the single most dramatic fact of the American experience. This impermanence had long been glorified as the essence of "progress"—that indefinable but inevitable something which was the trademark of the United States. In the words of one observer of the 1830s, "Americans *love* their country, not . . . *as it is,* but *as it will be.* . . . They live in the future, and *make* their country as they go on." The truth of those statements is shown by the fact that from 1607 to 1907—scarcely more than four lifetimes by present expectations—America would be changed from a couple of wilderness settlements into the most powerful nation on earth.

By the 1870s the country was well on its way to achieving that 1907 status. In fact, no period of American history, except perhaps our own, saw more physical change than the last generation of the nineteenth century. Rapid industrialization and urbanization, development of mass-production techniques and communication systems, and the building of a national railroad system all combined to effect speedy and dramatic alterations of the natural environment.

Particularly disconcerting to sportsmen were the obvious changes in what were once thought to be inexhaustible wildlife populations. Previously undeveloped regions, teeming with animals, birds, and fish, were made readily accessible to all, and improved guns, ammunition, and fishing gear, which the average man could afford, were produced in huge quantities. Hunting and fishing now became not only more practical, but also more profitable.

... The taste buds of the American people also had to be satisfied, because it was now fashionable to eat wild game like canvasback duck and black bass. Though long in existence, the commercial hunter and fisherman were entering their "golden era." They killed big game for hides, waterfowl for flesh, wading birds for plumage, and ocean fishes for oil and fertilizer. Quick money, sometimes large amounts, could be made by men like the plume hunters who shot the snowy egret almost into extinction.

What is ironic about this dismal situation is that the same economic developments that made wildlife more accessible to the market hunter and fisherman also brought it closer to the sportsman. Indeed, a major reason for the rapid increase in the ranks of the latter group was because of improvements in transportation and equipment. An outdoorsman could now travel to his hunting and fishing spots in greater comfort and enjoy better sport when he arrived—that is, if market men had not already preceded him.

From the time of . . . Frank Forester in the 1850s, sportsmen continually complained of arriving on their favorite grounds only to find that all game had been killed or driven out by commercial hunters and fishermen. Until sportsmen finally defeated the market men in the first quarter of this century and closed off the sale of game for all except some food fishes, this controversy between the two groups frequently approached a state of war. There were, in fact, some fatalities as a result of the conflict. Sportsmen of the late nineteenth century would be little less than flabbergasted to discover that historians of today lump them together with commercial gunners and fishermen.

With the appearance of national periodicals like *American Sportsman* (1871), *Forest and Stream* (1873), *Field and Stream* (1874), and *American Angler* (1881), a new impetus was given to the sportsmen's struggle against commercial exploitation of wildlife. While the nation as a whole remained indifferent, these journals, in issue after issue, poured forth a steady stream of propaganda against the market men. Besides enumerating specific offenses, the main technique used was to teach the American public the ethics and responsibilities of sportsmanship. . . .

. . . The point is that hunting or fishing for pleasure was almost universal among early environmentalists; men like John Muir . . . , who never seem[s] to have had any interest in these activities or . . . [was]

even hostile to them, are clearly the exception. For most, the pursuit of wildlife seems to have provided that crucial first contact with the natural world that spawned a commitment to its perpetuation. Instead of ignoring sportsmen, or treating them with contempt, scholars might do better to acknowledge and investigate the role played by sport in motivating environmental reforms and achievements. The only result can be a fuller, truer picture of the history of American conservation.

9

The Beginnings of Federal Concern

Carl Schurz (1877)

Before 1890, Secretary of the Interior Carl Schurz stands as one of the few exceptions to the rule of federal indifference to forest conservation. A German immigrant, Schurz was familiar with the methods of scientific forestry then practiced in Europe. During his tenure as Secretary (1877–1881), he repeatedly called for the reservation and rational management of America's forests. At the time his pleas made little impression on a government dedicated to protecting the freedom of private enterprise, but Schurz persisted. The germ of the national forest idea appears in the following in an excerpt from his annual report for 1877. Not until March 3, 1891, however, did Congress pass an act permitting the president to create "forest reserves" by withdrawing land from the public domain. Significantly, the prime mover behind the Forest Reserve Act was another German immigrant and head of the federal Division of Forestry from 1886 to 1898, Bernhard E. Fernow.

Sir: I have the honor to submit the following summary of the operations of this department during the past year, together with such suggestions as seem to me worthy of consideration. . . .

The subject of the extensive depredations committed upon the timber on the public lands of the United States has largely engaged the attention of this department. That question presents itself in a twofold aspect: as a question of law and as a question of public economy. As to the first point, little need be said. That the law prohibits the taking of timber by unauthorized persons from the public lands of the United States, is a universally known fact. That the laws are made to be executed, ought to be a universally accepted doctrine. That the government is in duty bound to act upon that doctrine, needs no argument. There may be circumstances under which the rigorous execution

Annual Report of the Secretary of the Interior on the Operations of the Department for the Fiscal Year Ended June 30, 1877 (Washington, DC: U.S. Government Printing Office, 1877), [iii], xv–xx.

of a law may be difficult or inconvenient, or obnoxious to public sentiment, or working particular hardship; in such cases it is the business of the legislative power to adapt the law to such circumstances. It is the business of the Executive to enforce the law as it stands.

As to the second point, the statements made by the Commissioner of the General Land Office, in his report, show the quantity of timber taken from the public lands without authority of law to have been of enormous extent. It probably far exceeds in reality any estimates made upon the data before us. It appears, from authentic information before this department, that in many instances the depredations have been carried on in the way of organized and systematic enterprise, not only to furnish timber, lumber, and fire-wood for the home market, but, on a large scale, for commercial exportation to foreign countries.

The rapidity with which this country is being stripped of its forests must alarm every thinking man. It has been estimated by good authority that, if we go on at the present rate, the supply of timber in the United States will, in less than twenty years, fall considerably short of our home necessities. How disastrously the destruction of the forests of a country affects the regularity of the water supply in its rivers necessary for navigation, increases the frequency of freshets and inundations, dries up springs, and transforms fertile agricultural districts into barren wastes, is a matter of universal experience the world over. It is the highest time that we should turn our earnest attention to this subject, which so seriously concerns our national prosperity.

The government cannot prevent the cutting of timber on land owned by private citizens. It is only to be hoped that private owners will grow more careful of their timber as it rises in value. But the government can do two things: 1. It can take determined and, as I think, effectual measures to arrest the stealing of timber from public lands on a large scale, which is always attended with the most reckless waste; and, 2. It can preserve the forests still in its possession by keeping them under its control, and by so regulating the cutting and sale of timber on its lands as to secure the renewal of the forest by natural growth and the careful preservation of the young timber. . . .

. . . I have reason to believe that the measures taken by the department have already stopped the depredations on the public lands to a very great extent, and that, if continued, they will entirely arrest the evil. A comparatively small number of watchful and energetic agents will suffice to prevent in future, not, indeed, the stealing of single trees here and there, but at least depredations on a large scale.

To this end, however, it is necessary that Congress, by an appropriation for this purpose, to be immediately available, enable this department to keep the agents in the field, and also to provide a more speedy and effective system for the seizure and sale of logs, lumber, or turpentine, cut or manufactured from timber on the public lands, than is now provided by existing laws. . . .

. . . Nowhere is a wasteful destruction of the forests fraught with more dangerous results than in mountainous regions. The timber grows mostly on the mountain sides, and when these mountain sides are once stripped bare, the rain will soon wash all the earth necessary for the growth of trees from the slopes down into the valleys, and the renewal of the forests will be rendered impossible forever; the rivulets and water-courses, which flow with regularity while the forest stands, are dried up for the greater part of the year, and transformed into raging torrents by heavy rains and by the melting of the snow, inundating the valleys below, covering them with gravel and loose rock swept down from the mountain-sides, and gradually rendering them unfit for agriculture, and, finally, for the habitation of men. Proper measures for the preservation of the forest in the mountainous regions of the country appear, therefore, of especially imperative necessity. The experience of parts of Asia, and of some of the most civilized countries in Europe, is so terribly instructive in these respects that we have no excuse if we do not take timely warning.

To avert such evil results, I would suggest the following preventive and remedial measures: All timber-lands still belonging to the United States should be withdrawn from the operation of the preemption and homestead laws, as well as the location of the various kinds of scrip.

Timber-lands fit for agricultural purposes should be sold, if sold at all, only for cash, and so graded in price as to make the purchaser pay for the value of the timber on the land. This will be apt to make the settler careful and provident in the disposition he makes of the timber.

A sufficient number of government agents should be provided for to protect the timber on public lands from depredation, and to institute to this end the necessary proceedings against depredators by seizures and by criminal as well as civil action.

Such agents should also be authorized and instructed . . . to sell for the United States, in order to satisfy the current local demand, timber from the public lands under proper regulations, and in doing so especially to see to it that no large areas be entirely stripped of their timber, so as not to prevent the natural renewal of the forest. . . .

The extensive as well as wanton destruction of the timber upon the public lands by the willful or negligent and careless setting of fires calls for earnest attention. While in several, if not all, of the States such acts are made highly penal offenses by statute, yet no law of the United States provides specifically for their punishment when committed upon the public lands, nor for a recovery of the damages thereby sustained. I would therefore recommend the passage of a law prescribing a severe penalty for the willful, negligent, or careless setting of fires upon the public lands of the United States, principally valuable for the timber thereon, and also providing for the recovery of all damages thereby sustained.

While such measures might be provided for by law without unnecessary delay, I would also suggest that the President be authorized to appoint a commission, composed of qualified persons, to study the laws and practices adopted in other countries for the preservation and cultivation of forests, and to report to Congress a plan for the same object applicable to our circumstances.

I am so deeply impressed with the importance of this subject, that I venture to predict, the Congress making efficient laws for the preservation of our forests will be ranked by future generations in this country among its greatest benefactors.

10

The Reclamation Idea

John Wesley Powell (1878)

John Wesley Powell's insights into the geography of the Far West laid the basis for federal involvement in reclamation. A one-armed veteran of the Civil War, Powell led the first descent of the Colorado River in 1869. Powell continued to study the southwest and published his observations as a government document in 1878 under the title Report on the Lands of the Arid Region of the United States. *His findings destroyed several American myths by revealing the area as neither agrarian paradise nor desert but rather as adaptable to a limited amount of cultivation provided that the federal government supported extensive irrigation projects. Powell's comparative pessimism about the West's ability to support agriculture and his sugges-tion that the government take an active role in its economy did not find a warm reception in many circles. But his enthusiastic advocacy of irrigation from the position, after 1881, of Director of the U.S. Geological Survey inspired younger men like WJ McGee (Selection 12) and Frederick H. Newell to press forward. In 1902, the year Powell died, Congress passed the Reclamation Act, which institutionalized many of his recommendations and laid the basis for the Bureau of Reclamation.*

The eastern portion of the United States is supplied with abundant rainfall for agricultural purposes, receiving the necessary amount from the evaporation of the Atlantic Ocean and the Gulf of Mexico; but westward the amount of aqueous precipitation diminishes in a general way until at last a region is reached where the climate is so arid that agriculture is not successful without irrigation. This Arid Region be-gins about midway in the Great Plains and extends across the Rocky Mountains to the Pacific Ocean. . . . Experience teaches that it is not wise to depend upon rainfall where the amount is less than 20 inches

John Wesley Powell, *Report on the Lands of the Arid Region of the United States,* U.S. House of Representatives, Executive Document 73, 45th Congress, 2nd Session (Washington, DC: U.S. Government Printing Office, April 3, 1878), **viii,** [1]–3, 5–10; 19–22.

annually, if this amount is somewhat evenly distributed throughout the year; but if the rainfall is unevenly distributed, so that "rainy seasons" are produced, the question whether agriculture is possible without irrigation depends upon the time of the "rainy season" and the amount of its rainfall. Any unequal distribution of rain through the year, though the inequality be so slight as not to produce "rainy seasons," affects agriculture either favorably or unfavorably. If the spring and summer precipitation exceeds that of the fall and winter, a smaller amount of annual rain may be sufficient; but if the rainfall during the season of growing crops is less than the average of the same length of time during the remainder of the year, a greater amount of annual precipitation is necessary. In some localities in the western portion of the United States this unequal distribution of rainfall through the seasons affects agriculture favorably, and this is true immediately west of the northern portion of the line of 20 inches of rainfall, which extends along the plains from our northern to our southern boundary. . . .

The limit of successful agriculture without irrigation has been set at 20 inches, that the extent of the Arid Region should by no means be exaggerated; but at 20 inches agriculture will not be uniformly successful from season to season. Many droughts will occur; many seasons in a long series will be fruitless; and it may be doubted whether, on the whole, agriculture will prove remunerative. On this point it is impossible to speak with certainty. A larger experience than the history of agriculture in the western portion of the United States affords is necessary to a final determination of the question. . . .

The Arid Region is the great Rocky Mountain Region of the United States, and it embraces something more than four-tenths of the whole country excluding Alaska. . . .

Within the Arid Region only a small portion of the country is irrigable. These irrigable tracts are lowlands lying along the streams. On the mountains and high plateaus forests are found at elevations so great that frequent summer frosts forbid the cultivation of the soil. Here are the natural timber lands of the Arid Region—an upper region set apart by nature for the growth of timber necessary to the mining, manufacturing, and agricultural industries of the country. Between the low irrigable lands and the elevated forest lands there are valleys, mesas, hills, and mountain slopes bearing grasses of greater or less value for pasturage purposes.

Then, in discussing the lands of the Arid Region, three great classes are recognized—the irrigable lands below, the forest lands above, and the pasturage lands between. . . .

In Utah Territory agriculture is dependent upon irrigation. . . . In order to determine the amount of irrigable land in Utah it was necessary to determine the areas to which the larger streams can be taken by proper engineering skill, and the amount which the smaller streams can serve. In the latter case it was necessary to determine first the amount of land which a given amount or unit of water would supply, and then the volume of water running in the streams; the product of these factors giving the extent of the irrigable lands. A continuous flow of one cubic foot of water per second was taken as the unit, and after careful consideration it was assumed that this unit of water will serve from 80 to 100 acres of land. . . .

Having determined from the operations of irrigation that one cubic foot per second of water will irrigate from 80 to 100 acres of land when the greatest economy is used, and having determined the volume of water or number of cubic feet per second flowing in the several streams of Utah by the most thorough methods available under the circumstances, it appears that within the territory, excluding a small portion in the southeastern corner where the survey has not yet been completed, the amount of land which it is possible to redeem by this method is about 2,262 square miles, or 1,447,920 acres. . . . Excluding that small portion of the territory in the southeast corner not embraced in the map, Utah has an area of 80,000 square miles, of which 2,262 square miles are irrigable. That is, 2.8 per cent of the lands under consideration can be cultivated by utilizing all the available streams during the irrigating season. . . .

This statement of the facts relating to the irrigable lands of Utah will serve to give a clearer conception of the extent and condition of the irrigable lands throughout the Arid Region. Such as can be redeemed are scattered along the water courses, and are in general the lowest lands of the several districts to which they belong. In some of the states and territories the percentage of irrigable land is less than in Utah, in others greater, and it is probable that the percentage in the entire region is somewhat greater than in the territory which we have considered.

. . . [I]t will be interesting to consider certain questions relating to the economy and practicability of distributing the waters over the lands to be redeemed.

There are two considerations that make irrigation attractive to the agriculturist. Crops thus cultivated are not subject to the vicissitudes of rainfall; the farmer fears no droughts; his labors are seldom interrupted and his crops rarely injured by storms. This immunity from drought and storm renders agricultural operations much more certain than in regions of greater humidity. Again, the water comes down from the mountains and plateaus freighted with fertilizing materials derived from the decaying vegetation and soils of the upper regions, which are spread by the flowing water over the cultivated lands. It is probable that the benefits derived from this source alone will be full compensation for the cost of the process. Hitherto these benefits have not been fully realized, from the fact that the methods employed have been more or less crude. When the flow of water over the land is too great or too rapid the fertilizing elements borne in the waters are carried past the fields, and a washing is produced which deprives the lands irrigated of their most valuable elements, and little streams cut the fields with channels injurious in diverse ways. Experience corrects these errors, and the irrigator soon learns to flood his lands gently, evenly, and economically. It may be anticipated that all the lands redeemed by irrigation in the Arid Region will be highly cultivated and abundantly productive, and agriculture will be but slightly subject to the vicissitudes of scant and excessive rainfall.

A stranger entering this Arid Region is apt to conclude that the soils are sterile, because of their chemical composition, but experience demonstrates the fact that all the soils are suitable for agricultural purposes when properly supplied with water. It is true that some of the soils are overcharged with alkaline materials, but these can in time be "washed out." Altogether the fact suggests that far too much attention has heretofore been paid to the chemical constitution of soils and too little to those physical conditions by which moisture and air are supplied to the roots of the growing plants. . . .

The irrigable lands and timber lands constitute but a small fraction of the Arid Region. Between the lowlands on the one hand and the highlands on the other is found a great body of valley, mesa, hill, and low mountain lands. To what extent, and under what conditions can they be utilized? Usually they bear a scanty growth of grasses. These grasses are nutritious and valuable both for summer and winter pasturage. Their value depends upon peculiar climatic conditions; the grasses grow to a great extent in scattered bunches, and mature seeds in larger proportion perhaps than the grasses of the more humid regions. In general the winter aridity is so great that the grasses when touched by the frosts are not washed down by the rains and snows to decay on the moist soil, but stand firmly on the ground all winter long and "cure," forming a *quasi* uncut hay. Thus the grass lands are of value both in summer and winter. In a broad way, the greater or lesser abundance of the grasses is dependent on latitude and altitude; the higher the latitude the better are the grasses, and they improve as the altitude increases. In very low altitudes and latitudes the grasses are so scant as to be of no value; here the true deserts are found. These conditions obtain in southern California, southern Nevada, southern Arizona, and southern New Mexico, where broad reaches of land are naked of vegetation, but in ascending to the higher lands the grass steadily improves. Northward the deserts soon disappear, and the grass becomes more and more luxuriant to our northern boundary. In addition to the desert lands mentioned, other large deductions must be made from the area of the pasturage lands. There are many districts in which the "country rock" is composed of incoherent sands and clays; sometimes sediments of ancient Tertiary lakes; elsewhere sediments of more ancient Cretaceous seas. In these districts perennial or intermittent streams have carved deep waterways, and the steep hills are ever washed naked by fierce but infrequent storms, as the incoherent rocks are unable to withstand the beating of the rain. These districts are known as the *mauvaises terres* or bad lands of the Rocky Mountain Region. In other areas the streams have carved labyrinths of deep gorges and the waters flow at great depths below the general surface. The lands between the streams are beset with towering cliffs, and the landscape is an expanse of naked rock. . . .

After making all the deductions, there yet remain vast areas of valuable pasturage land bearing nutritious but scanty grass. The lands along the creeks and rivers have been relegated to that class which has been described as irrigable, hence the lands under consideration are away from the permanent streams. No rivers sweep over them and no creeks meander among their hills. . . .

The grass is so scanty that the herdsman must have a large area for the support of his stock. In general a quarter section of land alone is of no value to him; the pasturage it affords is entirely inadequate to the wants of a herd that the poorest man needs for his support.

Four square miles may be considered as the minimum amount necessary for a pasturage farm, and a still greater amount is necessary for the larger part of the lands; that is, pasturage farms, to be of any practicable value, must be of at least 2,560 acres, and in many districts they must be much larger. . . .

. . . [T]he arid lands, so far as they can be redeemed by irrigation, will perennially yield bountiful crops, as the means for their redemption involves their constant fertilization.

To a great extent, the redemption of all these lands will require extensive and comprehensive plans, for the execution of which aggregated capital or coöperative labor will be necessary. Here, individual farmers, being poor men, cannot undertake the task. For its accomplishment a wise prevision, embodied in carefully considered legislation, is necessary.

PART TWO

THE PROGRESSIVE CONSERVATION CRUSADE, 1901–1910

Conservation means the greatest good to the greatest number for the longest time.

—*Gifford Pinchot*

The first national explosion of concern about conservation—indeed the coining of the term itself—occurred during the Progressive era in the early-twentieth century. Within the space of a few years *conservation* acquired the status of a household word. For the first time in American history resource management became a national priority. Forests and wildlife continued to command attention, but water was a new focal point. Progressive conservationists dreamed of controlling rivers with dams and contemplated "reclaiming" land for civilized purposes by draining swamps and irrigating deserts. The Reclamation Act of 1902 created a mechanism for putting the proceeds from the sale of western lands to use in federal irrigation projects. Within five years the Bureau of Reclamation had twenty-five projects underway. They became showcases of the capabilities of government planners and engineers and paved the way for really comprehensive regional planning efforts such as those that would transform the Tennessee, Colorado, and Columbia watersheds in the next generation.

Conservation became entangled in national politics when President William Howard Taft failed to sustain his predecessor's, Theodore Roosevelt's, zeal for natural resource protection. Gifford Pinchot, Roosevelt's friend and chief of the U.S. Forest Service, clashed with Taft's Secretary of the Interior, Richard A. Ballinger. At issue was the acquisition of valuable public lands by big business. The so-called Ballinger-Pinchot controversy led to Pinchot's dismissal in 1910 and to a schism in the Republican party. The election of 1912 found Roosevelt and Taft splitting the Republican vote and Woodrow Wilson winning the presidency for the Democrats. World War I temporarily eclipsed conservation, but the Progressives had discovered the political potency of the human nature issue.

One way to understand the sudden emergence of Progressive conservation is in terms of its historical context. By the first decade of the twentieth century, Americans were ready to be concerned about their environment. A national mood or temper existed that had been absent, with a few exceptions, a generation before. Its dominant characteristic was anxiety over change in the American environment. The change involved industrialization, urbanization, and a growing population, but it can be expressed most succinctly as the ending of the frontier. The Census of 1890 simply announced this fact. Three years later Frederick Jackson Turner wrote *The Significance of the Frontier in American History,* and a vague uneasiness over the prospect of a frontierless America became widespread. The frontier had been almost synonymous with the abundance, opportunity, and distinctiveness of the New World. For two and a half centuries its presence largely explained America's remarkable material growth as well as many characteristics of her people. As a consequence, few could regard its passing without regret.

One result was a general tendency to look favorably on conservation. It would extend the remaining abundance, preserve the environmental qualities of the nation's youth, and assuage anxiety over population growth and industrial expansion. Conservation, to be sure, was not the only beneficiary of American uneasiness. Imperialism and the movement for immigration restriction, for instance, also reflected turn-of-the-century anxieties. But conservation had special appeal because it directly attacked the problem, which was, at root, environmental. Conservation would *be,* in a sense, the new frontier, keeping the nation young, vigorous, prosperous, democratic, replete with opportunity for the individual, and because of its relation to nature, wholesome and moral. These had once been the frontier's functions. For a civilization that had begun to notice its first gray hairs, conservation was welcome tonic, for the land as well as for the minds of its inhabitants. There were several other factors that figured in the growth and character of conservation before World War I. One was the existence in the United States of a technological capacity capable of at least entertaining the large-scale ideas for environmental engineering that Progressive conservationists put forward. In addition, the national indignation growing since the 1870s at concentrated wealth and the monopoly of natural resources conditioned some Americans to accept the ideology of conservation. And the movement would have taken a different, and probably a less potent, form had it not coincided with the widespread acceptance of the philosophy that the central government should be strong and willing to use its strength in the public interest. Along with the passing of the era of easy resources, such developments conditioned the Progressive era to give conservation a high priority.

11

The Birth of "Conservation"

Gifford Pinchot (1947, 1910)

In the public estimation at least, the man most closely associated with conservation in the United States is Gifford Pinchot. And while in the autobiographical account that follows, Pinchot may have exaggerated his personal role in originating the movement, no one did more to publicize it during the Progressive era. Graduating from Yale in 1889, Pinchot became the first American to choose forestry as a career. George Perkins Marsh's book (Selection 6) admittedly influenced his decision as did a love of the outdoors, especially fishing, and a taste for innovation. Since professional training in forestry was unavailable in the United States and the Pinchot family had ample means, Gifford enrolled at the French Forest School in Nancy. Returning fired with enthusiasm for the idea of managing forests as a crop, Pinchot quickly capitalized on his virtually unique skills. Through Frederick Law Olmsted (Selection 7), he obtained an appointment as forester on George W. Vanderbilt's North Carolina estate, Biltmore. In 1898 Pinchot became chief of the federal Forestry Division (later renamed the U.S. Forest Service and given control of the national forests). A personal friend of Theodore Roosevelt and a masterful publicist, Pinchot was the driving force behind the Progressive conservation movement, the origin of which he describes here. Pinchot's philosophy of resource management, characterized by utilitarianism and a democratic orientation, is represented in the next two parts of this selection.

[Early in 1905] there were three separate Government organizations which dealt with mineral resources, four or five concerned with streams, half a dozen with authority over forests, and a dozen or so with supervision over wild life, soils, soil erosion, and other questions of the land.

It was a mess, a mess which could be cured only by realizing that these unrelated and overlapping bureaus were all tied up together, like

From *Breaking New Ground* by Gifford Pinchot. Copyright 1947 by Harcourt Brace Jovanovich Inc., pp. 320–326. Reprinted with permission.

the people in a town. The one and only way to bring order out of this chaos was to supply a common ground on which each could take its proper place, and do its proper work, in co-operation with all the rest.

It had never occurred to us that we were all parts one of another. And the fact that the Federal Government had taken up the protection of the various natural resources individually and at intervals during more than half a century doubtless confirmed our bureaucratic nationalism. . . .

It was my great good luck that I had more to do with the work of more bureaus than any other man in Washington. This was partly because the Forest Service was dealing not only with trees but with public lands, mining, agriculture, irrigation, stream flow, soil erosion, fish, game, animal industry, and a host of other matters with which other bureaus also were concerned. The main reason, however, was that much of T.R.'s [Theodore Roosevelt's] business with the natural resources bureaus was conducted through me.

It was therefore the most natural thing in the world that the relations of forests, waters, lands, and minerals, each to each, should be brought strongly to my mind. But for a long time my mind stopped there. Then at last I woke up. And this is how it happened:

In the gathering gloom of an expiring day, in the moody month of February [1907] . . . a solitary horseman might have been observed pursuing his silent way above a precipitous gorge in the vicinity of the capital city of America. Or so an early Victorian three-volume novelist might have expressed it.

In plain words, a man by the name of Pinchot was riding a horse by the name of Jim on the Ridge Road in Rock Creek Park near Washington. And while he rode, he thought. He was a forester, and he was taking his problems with him, on that winter's day . . . when he meant to leave them behind.

The forest and its relation to streams and inland navigation, to water power and flood control; to the soil and its erosion; to coal and oil and other minerals; to fish and game; and many another possible use or waste of natural resources—these questions would not let him be. What had all these to do with Forestry? And what had Forestry to do with them?

Here were not isolated and separate problems. My work had brought me into touch with all of them. But what was the basic link between them?

Suddenly the idea flashed through my head that there was a unity in this complication—that the relation of one resource to another was not the end of the story. Here were no longer a lot of different, independent, and often antagonistic questions, each on its own separate little island, as we had been in the habit of thinking. In place of them, here was one single question with many parts. Seen in this new light, all these separate questions fitted into and made up the one great central problem of the use of the earth for the good of man.

To me it was a good deal like coming out of a dark tunnel. I had been seeing one spot of light ahead. Here, all of a sudden, was a whole landscape. Or it was like lifting the curtain on a great new stage.

There was too much of it for me to take it all in at once. As always, my mind worked slowly. From the first I thought I had stumbled on something really worth while, but that day in Rock Creek Park I was far from grasping the full reach and swing of the new idea.

It took time for me to appreciate that here were the makings of a new policy, not merely nationwide but world-wide in its scope—fundamentally important because it involved not only the welfare but the very existence of men on the earth. I did see, however, that something ought to be done about it. . . .

. . . It was [WJ] McGee* who grasped [the new idea] best. He sensed its full implication even more quickly than I had done, and saw its future more clearly.

McGee became the scientific brains of the new movement. With his wide general knowledge and highly original mind we developed, as I never could have done alone, the breadth and depth of meaning which lay in the new idea. McGee had constructive imagination.

It was McGee, for example, who defined the new policy as the use of the natural resources for the greatest good of the greatest number for the longest time. It was McGee who made me see, at long last and after much argument, that monopoly of natural resources was only less dangerous to the public welfare than their actual destruction.

Very soon after my own mind was clear enough to state my proposition with confidence, I took it to T.R. And T.R., as I expected, understood, accepted, and adopted it without the smallest hesitation. It was directly in line with everything he had been thinking and doing. It became the heart of his Administration.

Launching the Conservation movement was the most significant achievement of the T.R. Administration, as he himself believed. It

*See Selection 12.

seems altogether probable that it will also be the achievement for which he will be longest and most gratefully remembered.

Having just been born, the new arrival was still without a name. There had to be a name to call it by before we could even attempt to make it known, much less give it a permanent place in the public mind. What should we call it?

Both Overton* and I knew that large organized areas of Government forest lands in British India were named Conservancies, and for the foresters in charge of them Conservators. After many other suggestions and long discussions, either Price or I (I'm not sure which and it doesn't matter) proposed that we apply a new meaning to a word already in the dictionary, and christen the new policy Conservation.

During one of our rides I put that name up to T.R., and he approved it instantly. So the child was named, and that bridge was behind us.

Today,** when it would be hard to find an intelligent man in the United States who hasn't at least some conception of what Conservation means, it seems incredible that the very word, in the sense in which we use it now, was unknown less than forty years ago.

*Overton Price was an associate of Pinchot in the Forest Service
**Pinchot was writing in 1946. [Ed.]

. . . The principles which govern the conservation movement, like all great and effective things, are simple and easily understood. . . .

The first great fact about conservation is that it stands for development. There has been a fundamental misconception that conservation means nothing but the husbanding of resources for future generations. There could be no more serious mistake. Conservation does mean provision for the future, but it means also and first of all the recognition of the right of the present generation to the fullest necessary use of all the resources with which this country is so abundantly blessed. Conservation demands the welfare of this generation first, and afterward the welfare of the generations to follow.

The first principle of conservation is development, the use of the natural resources now existing on this continent for the benefit of the

From Gifford Pinchot, *The Fight for Conservation* (Garden City, NY: Harcourt, Brace, 1910), 42–50.

people who live here now. There may be just as much waste in neglecting the development and use of certain natural resources as there is in their destruction. We have a limited supply of coal, and only a limited supply. Whether it is to last for a hundred or a hundred and fifty or a thousand years, the coal is limited in amount, unless through geological changes which we shall not live to see, there will never be any more of it than there is now. But coal is in a sense the vital essence of our civilization. If it can be preserved, if the life of the mines can be extended, if by preventing waste there can be more coal left in this country after we of this generation have made every needed use of this source of power, then we shall have deserved well of our descendants.

Conservation stands emphatically for the development and use of water-power now, without delay. It stands for the immediate construction of navigable waterways under a broad and comprehensive plan as assistants to the railroads. More coal and more iron are required to move a ton of freight by rail than by water, three to one. In every case and in every direction the conservation movement has development for its first principle, and at the very beginning of its work. The development of our natural resources and the fullest use of them for the present generation is the first duty of this generation. . . .

In the second place conservation stands for the prevention of waste. There has come gradually in this country an understanding that waste is not a good thing and that the attack on waste is an industrial necessity. I recall very well indeed how, in the early days of forest fires, they were considered simply and solely as acts of God, against which any opposition was hopeless and any attempt to control them not merely hopeless but childish. It was assumed that they came in the natural order of things, as inevitably as the seasons or the rising and setting of the sun. Today we understand that forest fires are wholly within the control of men. So we are coming in like manner to understand that the prevention of waste in all other directions is a simple matter of good business. The first duty of the human race is to control the earth it lives upon.

We are in a position more and more completely to say how far the waste and destruction of natural resources are to be allowed to go on and where they are to stop. It is curious that the effort to stop waste, like the effort to stop forest fires, has often been considered as a matter controlled wholly by economic law. I think there could be no greater mistake. Forest fires were allowed to burn long after the people had means to stop them. The idea that men were helpless in the face of them held long after the time had passed when the means of control were fully within our reach. It was the old story that "as a man thinketh, so is he"; we came to see that we could stop forest fires, and we found that the means had long been at hand. When at length we came to see that the control of logging in certain directions was profitable, we found it had long been possible. In all these matters of waste of natural resources, the education of the people to understand that they can stop the leakage comes before the actual stopping and after the means of stopping it have long been ready at our hands.

In addition to the principles of development and preservation of our resources there is a third principle. It is this: The natural resources must be developed and preserved for the benefit of the many, and not merely for the profit of a few. We are coming to understand in this country that public action for public benefit has a very much wider field to cover and a much larger part to play than was the case when there were resources enough for every one, and before certain constitutional provisions had given so tremendously strong a position to vested rights and property in general.

. . . [B]y reason of the XIVth amendment to the Constitution, property rights in the United States occupy a stronger position than in any other country in the civilized world. It becomes then a matter of multiplied importance, since property rights once granted are so strongly entrenched, to see that they shall be so granted that the people shall get their fair share of the benefit which comes from the development of the resources which belong to us all. The time to do that is now. By so doing we shall avoid the difficulties and conflicts which will surely arise if we allow vested rights to accrue outside the possibility of governmental and popular control.

The conservation idea covers a wider range than the field of natural resources alone. Conservation means the greatest good to the greatest number for the longest time. One of its great contributions is just this, that it has added to the worn and well-known phrase, "the greatest good to the greatest number," the additional words "for the longest time," thus recognizing that this nation of ours must be made to endure as the best possible home for all its people.

Conservation advocates the use of foresight, prudence, thrift, and intelligence in dealing with public matters, for the same reasons and in the same way that we each use foresight, prudence, thrift, and intelligence in dealing with our own private affairs. It proclaims the right and duty of the people to act for the benefit of the people. Conservation demands the application of common sense to the common problems for the common good.

The principles of conservation thus described—development, preservation, the common good—have a general application which is growing rapidly wider. The development of resources and the prevention of waste and loss, the protection of the public interests, by foresight, prudence, and the ordinary business and home-making virtues, all these apply to other things as well as to the natural resources. There is, in fact, no interest of the people to which the principles of conservation do not apply.

The conservation point of view is valuable in the education of our people as well as in forestry; it applies to the body politic as well as to the earth and its minerals. A municipal franchise is as properly within its sphere as a franchise for water-power. The same point of view governs in both. It applies as much to the subject of good roads as to waterways, and the training of our people in citizenship is as germane to it as the productiveness of the earth. The application of common-sense to any problem for the Nation's good will lead directly to national efficiency wherever applied. In other words, and that is the burden of the message, we are coming to see the logical and inevitable outcome that these principles, which arose in forestry and have their bloom in the conservation of natural resources, will have their fruit in the increase and promotion of national efficiency along other lines of national life.

The outgrowth of conservation, the inevitable result, is national efficiency. In the great commercial struggle between nations which is eventually to determine the welfare of all, national efficiency will be the deciding factor. So from every point of view conservation is a good thing for the American people.

12

The Conservation Mentality

WJ McGee (1910)

In the previous document Gifford Pinchot singled out the versatile, self-taught scientist William John (he insisted on "WJ," without punctuation) McGee as "the scientific brains" of the conservation movement. McGee's crusading zeal, exemplified in this selection, was typical of Progressive conservationists. His involvement in federal resource work began in 1878 when John Wesley Powell (Selection 10) invited him to join the U.S. Geological Survey. Powell's philosophy of scientifically studying and developing resources captured McGee's imagination as did the democratic reform endeavors of Lester Frank Ward and Henry George. Late in 1906 at a meeting of the Lakes-to-the-Gulf Deep Waterway Association and several months before Pinchot "discovered" conservation, McGee glimpsed the possibility of comprehensive and systematic management of the environment in the public interest. He thereafter worked closely with Pinchot in persuading President Theodore Roosevelt to appoint the Inland Waterways Commission (March 14, 1907), which launched the Progressive conservation crusade.

. . . [America's Founding Fathers] saw Land as the sole natural resource of the country, so the succeeding generations remained indifferent to the values residing in the minerals below and the forests above. . . . Herein lay what now seems the most serious error in the world's greatest Republic. Monarchs are accustomed to retaining royal or imperial rights in the forests and minerals, and these eventually inure to the benefit of their people; ecclesiastic institutions allied with monarchial rule have commonly held rein over rarer resources until they were reclaimed by the growing generations of men; but through a lamentable lack of foresight our Republic hasted to give away, under

WJ McGee, "The Conservation of Natural Resources," *Proceedings of the Mississippi Valley Historical Association,* **III** (1909–1910), 365–367, 371, 376–379.

the guise of land to live on, values far greater than the land itself—and this policy continued for generations. . . .

The policy of free giving grew into thoughtless habit, and this into a craze which spread apace. . . . States and cities followed the national lead, and all manner of franchises—rights of way, water rights, and the rest—were given for long terms or in perpetuity to all comers, generally without money and without price. In all the world's history no other such saturnalia of squandering the sources of permanent prosperity was ever witnessed! In the material aspect, our individual liberty became collective license, and our legislative and administrative prodigality grew into national profligacy; the balance between impulse and responsibility was lost, the future of the People and Nation was forgotten, and the very name of posterity was made a by-word by men in high places; and worst of all the very profligacies came to be venerated as law and even crystallized foolishly in decisions or more questionably in enactments—and for long there were none to stand in the way of the growing avalanche of extravagance. The waste was always wildest in the West, for as settlement followed the sun new resources were discovered or came into being through natural growth. . . .

. . . [T]he free gift of these resources . . . opened the way to monopoly, and the resources passed under monopolistic control with a rapidity never before seen in all the world's history; and it is hardly too much to say that the Nation has become one of the Captains of Industry first, and one of the People and their chosen representatives only second. With the free gift, under the title of land, of resources far exceeding the land in value, the aspiration of the Fathers for a land of free families failed; for the mineral-bearing and wood-bearing lands were devoted to mining and milling and manufacturing instead of homes, and the People became in large measure industrial dependents rather than free citizens. . . .

Done in a few lines, the history of the country and its resources . . . [has been one of] wealth beyond the visions of avarice and power above the dreams of tyranny . . . [coming] to the few—at vast cost to the just patrimony of the multitude—while much of the substance of the Nation has been wasted and many of the People have passed under the domination of the beneficiaries of Privilege. Ample resources indeed remain—enough to insure the perpetuity of the People—but the question also remains whether these shall be held and used by the People, whose travail gave them value and whose rights therein are inalienable and indefeasible under the Declaration of Independence and the Constitution, or whether they shall go chiefly into the hands of the self-chosen and self-anointed few, largely to forge new shackles for the wrists and ankles of the many! This problem of history is not one of passion or for reckless action. The simple facts are that the inequities arose chiefly in the confusion of other resources with Land, and that the inequalities in opportunity due to this confusion have arisen so insidiously as to escape notice. Yet the question remains: How may American freemen proceed decently and in order to reclaim their own?

. . . [Gifford] Pinchot and [James R.] Garfield* especially, and [Theodore] Roosevelt in his turn, sought to counteract the tendency toward wholesale alienation of the public lands for the benefit of the corporation and the oppression or suppression of the settler; and in the end their efforts resulted in what is now known as the Conservation Movement. . . .

On its face the Conservation Movement is material—ultra-material. . . . Yet in truth there has never been in all human history a popular movement more firmly grounded in ethics, in the eternal equities, in the divinity of human rights! Whether we rise into the spiritual empyrean or cling more closely to the essence of humanity, we find our loftiest ideals made real in the Cult of Conservation. . . .

. . . What *right* has any citizen of a free country, whatever his foresight and shrewdness, to seize on sources of life for his own behoof that are the common heritage of all; what *right* has legislature or court to help in the seizure; and striking still more deeply, what *right* has any generation to wholly consume, much less to waste, those sources of life without which the children or the children's children must starve or freeze? These are among the questions arising among intelligent minds in every part of this country, and giving form to a national feeling which is gradually rising to a new plane of equity. The questions will not down. Nay, like Banquo's ghost they tarry, and haunt, and search! How shall they find answer? The ethical doctrine of Conservation answers: by a nobler patriotism, under which citizen-electors will cleave more strongly to their birthright of independence and strive more vigorously for purity of the ballot, for rightness in laws, for cleanness in courts, and for forthrightness in administration; by a higher honesty of purpose between man and man; by a warmer charity, under which the good of all will more fairly merge with the good of each; by a stronger family sense, tend-

*Secretary of the Interior from 1907 to 1909. [Ed.]

ing toward a realization of the rights of the unborn; by deeper probity, maturing in the realizing sense that each holder of the sources of life is but a trustee for his nominal possessions, and is responsible to all men and for all time for making the best use of them in the common interest; and by a livelier humanity, in which each will feel that he lives not for himself alone but as a part of a common life for a common world and for the common good. . . . Whatever its material manifestations, every revolution is first and foremost a revolution in thought and in spirit. . . . [The last of humanity's great revolutions] was inspired in the New World by the new realization that all men are equally entitled to life, liberty, and the pursuit of happiness. . . . Still the hope of the Fathers for a freehold citizenry joined in equitable and indissoluble Union is not fully attained. The American Revolution was fought for Liberty; the American Constitution was framed for Equality; yet that third of the trinity of human impulses without which Union is not made perfect—Fraternity—has not been established: full brotherhood among men and generations has not yet come. The duty of the Fathers was done well according to their lights; but some new light has come out of the West where their sons have striven against Nature's forces no less fiercely than the Fathers against foreign dominion. So it would seem to remain for Conservation to perfect the concept and the movement started among the Colonists one hundred and forty years ago—to round out the American Revolution by framing a clearer Bill of Rights. Whatever others there may be, surely these are inherent and indefeasible:—

1. The equal Rights of all men to opportunity.
2. The equal Rights of the People in and to resources rendered valuable by their own natural growth and orderly development.
3. The equal Rights of present and future generations in and to the resources of the country.
4. The equal Rights (and full responsibilities) of all citizens to provide for the perpetuity of families and States and the Union of States.

The keynote of all these is Fraternity. They look to the greatest good for the greatest number and for the longest time; they are essential to perfect union among men and States; and until they are secured to us we may hardly feel assured that government of the People, by the People, and for the People shall not perish from the earth.

13

Publicizing Conservation at the White House

Theodore Roosevelt (1908)

The year 1908 marked the zenith of Progressive conservation. On February 26 the Inland Waterways Commission submitted its comprehensive plan for multipurpose river development. At President Theodore Roosevelt's invitation, a thousand national leaders, including the state governors, met from May 13 to 15 for a conference on conservation. Gifford Pinchot organized the dramatic gathering at the White House to publicize the new concept of resource management and, with the assistance of WJ McGee, wrote most of the key speeches. The conference sparkled with enthusiasm and high ideals. Words, however, were the principal result of the conference. The National Conservation Commission, appointed by Roosevelt as a result of the conference, suffered from vagueness of purpose and foundered on the shoals of congressional parsimony. The Inland Waterways Commission also perished from want of appropriations. And, after a North American conservation conference in February 1909, the international movement bogged down when President William Howard Taft scotched plans for a world conference the following September. Still, Pinchot insisted, the 1908 conference was "a turning point in human history." Roosevelt opened with the following words:

Governors of the several States; and Gentlemen:

I welcome you to this Conference at the White House. You have come hither at my request, so that we may join together to consider the question of the conservation and use of the great fundamental sources of wealth of this Nation.

So vital is this question, that for the first time in our history the chief executive officers of the States separately, and of the States

Theodore Roosevelt, "Opening Address by the President," in Newton C. Blanchard, ed., *Proceedings of a Conference of Governors in the White House,* (Washington, DC: U.S. Government Printing Office, 1909), 3, 5–10, 12.

together forming the Nation, have met to consider it. It is the chief material question that confronts us, second only—and second always—to the great fundamental questions of morality. [Applause]*

With the governors come men from each State chosen for their special acquaintance with the terms of the problem that is before us. Among them are experts in natural resources and representatives of national organizations concerned in the development and use of these resources; the Senators and Representatives in Congress; the Supreme Court, the Cabinet, and the Inland Waterways Commission have likewise been invited to the Conference, which is therefore national in a peculiar sense.

This Conference on the conservation of natural resources is in effect a meeting of the representatives of all the people of the United States called to consider the weightiest problem now before the Nation; and the occasion for the meeting lies in the fact that the natural resources of our country are in danger of exhaustion if we permit the old wasteful methods of exploiting them longer to continue.

With the rise of peoples from savagery to civilization, and with the consequent growth in the extent and variety of the needs of the average man, there comes a steadily increasing growth of the amount demanded by this average man from the actual resources of the country. And yet, rather curiously, at the same time that there comes that increase in what the average man demands from the resources, he is apt to grow to lose the sense of his dependence upon nature. He lives in big cities. He deals in industries that do not bring him in close touch with nature. He does not realize the demands he is making upon nature. . . .

In [George] Washington's time anthracite coal was known only as a useless black stone; and the great fields of bituminous coal were undiscovered. As steam was unknown, the use of coal for power production was undreamed of. Water was practically the only source of power, save the labor of men and animals; and this power was used only in the most primitive fashion. But a few small iron deposits had been found in this country, and the use of iron by our countrymen was very small. Wood was practically the only fuel, and what lumber was sawed was consumed locally, while the forests were regarded chiefly

---

*This and subsequent indications of audience reaction were inserted by WJ McGee, the recording secretary. [Ed.]

as obstructions to settlement and cultivation. The man who cut down a tree was held to have conferred a service upon his fellows.

Such was the degree of progress to which civilized mankind had attained when this nation began its career. It is almost impossible for us in this day to realize how little our Revolutionary ancestors knew of the great store of natural resources whose discovery and use have been such vital factors in the growth and greatness of this Nation, and how little they required to take from this store in order to satisfy their needs.

Since then our knowledge and use of the resources of the present territory of the United States have increased a hundred-fold. Indeed, the growth of this Nation by leaps and bounds makes one of the most striking and important chapters in the history of the world. Its growth has been due to the rapid development, and alas that it should be said! to the rapid destruction, of our natural resources. Nature has supplied to us in the United States, and still supplies to us, more kinds of resources in a more lavish degree than has ever been the case at any other time or with any other people. Our position in the world has been attained by the extent and thoroughness of the control we have achieved over nature; but we are more, and not less, dependent upon what she furnishes than at any previous time of history since the days of primitive man. . . .

. . . The wise use of all of our natural resources, which are our national resources as well, is the great material question of today. I have asked you to come together now because the enormous consumption of these resources, and the threat of imminent exhaustion of some of them, due to reckless and wasteful use, . . . calls for common effort, common action.

We want to take action that will prevent the advent of a woodless age, and defer as long as possible the advent of an ironless age. [Applause] . . .

A great many of these things are truisms. Much of what I say is so familiar to us that it seems commonplace to repeat it; but familiar though it is, I do not think as a nation we understand what its real bearing is. It is so familiar that we disregard it. [Applause]

The steadily increasing drain on these natural resources has promoted to an extraordinary degree the complexity of our industrial and social life. Moreover, this unexampled development has had a determining effect upon the character and opinions of our people. The demand for efficiency in the great task has given us vigor, effectiveness, decision, and power, and a capacity for achievement which in its own lines has never yet been matched. [Applause] . . .

. . . [I]t is safe to say that the prosperity of our people depends directly on the energy and intelligence with which our natural resources are used. It is equally clear that these resources are the final basis of national power and perpetuity. Finally, it is ominously evident that these resources are in the course of rapid exhaustion.

This Nation began with the belief that its landed possessions were illimitable and capable of supporting all the people who might care to make our country their home; but already the limit of unsettled land is in sight, and indeed but little land fitted for agriculture now remains unoccupied save what can be reclaimed by irrigation and drainage—a subject with which this Conference is partly to deal. We began with an unapproached heritage of forests; more than half of the timber is gone. We began with coal fields more extensive than those of any other nation and with iron ores regarded as inexhaustible, and many experts now declare that the end of both iron and coal is in sight. . . .

. . . [W]e began with soils of unexampled fertility, and we have so impoverished them by injudicious use and by failing to check erosion that their crop-producing power is diminishing instead of increasing. In a word, we have thoughtlessly, and to a large degree unnecessarily, diminished the resources upon which not only our prosperity but the prosperity of our children and our children's children must always depend.

We have become great in a material sense because of the lavish use of our resources, and we have just reason to be proud of our growth. But the time has come to inquire seriously what will happen when our forests are gone, when the coal, the iron, the oil, and the gas are exhausted, when the soils shall have been still further impoverished and washed into the streams, polluting the rivers, denuding the fields, and obstructing navigation. These questions do not relate only to the next century or to the next generation. One distinguishing characteristic of really civilized men is foresight; we have to, as a nation, exercise foresight for this nation in the future; and if we do not exercise that foresight, dark will be the future! [Applause] We should exercise foresight now, as the ordinarily prudent man exercises foresight in conserving and wisely using the property which contains the assurance of well-being for himself and his children. We want to see a man own his farm rather than rent it, because we want to see it an object to him to transfer it in better order to his children. We want to see him exercise forethought for the next generation. We need to exercise it in some fashion ourselves as a nation for the next generation.

The natural resources I have enumerated can be divided into two sharply distinguished classes accordingly as they are or are not capable of renewal. Mines if used must necessarily be exhausted. The minerals do not and can not renew themselves. Therefore in dealing with the coal, the oil, the gas, the iron, the metals generally, all that we can do is to try to see that they are wisely used. The exhaustion is certain to come in time. We can trust that it will be deferred long enough to enable the extraordinarily inventive genius of our people to devise means and methods for more or less adequately replacing what is lost; but the exhaustion is sure to come.

The second class of resources consists of those which can not only be used in such manner as to leave them undiminished for our children, but can actually be improved by wise use. The soil, the forests, the waterways come in this category. Every one knows that a really good farmer leaves his farm more valuable at the end of his life than it was when he first took hold of it. So with the waterways. So with the forests. In dealing with mineral resources, man is able to improve on nature only by putting the resources to a beneficial use which in the end exhausts them; but in dealing with the soil and its products man can improve on nature by compelling the resources to renew and even reconstruct themselves in such manner as to serve increasingly beneficial uses—while the living waters can be so controlled as to multiply their benefits.

Neither the primitive man nor the pioneer was aware of any duty to posterity in dealing with the renewable resources. When the American settler felled the forests, he felt that there was plenty of forest left for the sons who came after him. When he exhausted the soil of his farm, he felt that his son could go West and take up another. The Kentuckian or the Ohioan felled the forest and expected his son to move west and fell other forests on the banks of the Mississippi; the Georgian exhausted his farm and moved into Alabama or to the mouth of the Yazoo to take another. So it was with his immediate successors. When the soil-wash from the farmer's field choked the neighboring river, the only thought was to use the railway rather than the boats to move produce and supplies. That was so up to the generation that preceded ours.

Now all this is changed. On the average the son of the farmer of today must make his living on his father's farm. There is no difficulty in doing this if the father will exercise wisdom. No wise use of a farm exhausts its fertility. So with the forests. We are over the verge of a timber famine in this country, and it is unpardonable for the Nation or the States to permit any further cutting of our timber save in accordance with a system which will provide that the next generation shall see the timber increased instead of diminished. [Applause]

Just let me interject one word as to a particular type of folly of which it ought not to be necessary to speak. We stop wasteful cutting of timber; that of course makes a slight shortage at the moment. To avoid that slight shortage at the moment, there are certain people so foolish that they will incur absolute shortage in the future, and they are willing to stop all attempts to conserve the forests, because of course by wastefully using them at the moment we can for a year or two provide against any lack of wood. That is like providing for the farmer's family to live sumptuously on the flesh of the milch cow. [Laughter] Any farmer can live pretty well for a year if he is content not to live at all the year after. [Laughter and applause] . . .

We are coming to recognize as never before the right of the Nation to guard its own future in the essential matter of natural resources. In the past we have admitted the right of the individual to injure the future of the Republic for his own present profit. In fact there has been a good deal of a demand for unrestricted individualism, for the right of the individual to injure the future of all of us for his own temporary and immediate profit. The time has come for a change. As a people we have the right and the duty, second to none other but the right and duty of obeying the moral law, of requiring and doing justice, to protect ourselves and our children against the wasteful development of our natural resources, whether that waste is caused by the actual destruction of such resources or by making them impossible of development hereafter. . . .

Finally, let us remember that the conservation of our natural resources, though the gravest problem of today, is yet but part of another and greater problem to which this Nation is not yet awake, but to which it will awake in time, and with which it must hereafter grapple if it is to live—the problem of national efficiency, the patriotic duty of insuring the safety and continuance of the Nation. [Applause] When the People of the United States consciously undertake to raise themselves as citizens, and the Nation and the States in their several spheres, to the highest pitch of excellence in private, State, and national life, and to do this because it is the first of all the duties of true patriotism, then and not till then the future of this Nation, in quality and in time, will be assured. [Great applause]

14

Aesthetics and Conservation

Robert Underwood Johnson (1910)

Formal, dapper Robert Underwood Johnson represents perfectly the class of genteel Americans for whom conservation meant something quite different than it did for Pinchot and his colleagues. Johnson felt that in their obsession for efficient use of the environment, the national conservation leaders slighted natural beauty. In his opinion conservationists were little better than the exploiters they purported to replace: both gave precedence to the material, as opposed to the spiritual, values of nature. From his editor's desk at Century, *Johnson lashed out repeatedly at the preoccupation of his countrymen with the main chance. In 1890 he played a leading role in securing congressional approval of the act creating Yosemite National Park. Thereafter Johnson championed the national parks as the embodiment of an enlightened approach to nature. The national forests, on the other hand, seemed hopelessly utilitarian in their acceptance of lumbering, grazing, and mining. Understandably Johnson clashed with Pinchot on this issue, a personal break that symbolized the larger schism in American conservation between the wise users and the preservationists that persists to this day.*

Although the declaration of the first White House Conference of Governors included a record of their agreement "that the beauty, healthfulness, and habitability of our country should be preserved and increased," it is much to be regretted that the official leaders of the conservation movement—than which nothing is more important to the country—have never shown a cordial, much less an aggressive, interest in safeguarding our great scenery, or in promoting, in general, this part of their admirable program. When the Appalachian Park reserve was first proposed, a prominent member of Congress embodied his objection to it by saying bluntly, "We are not buying scenery." To meet this criticism, the friends of the bill, instead of boldly insisting

[Robert Underwood Johnson], "The Neglect of Beauty in the Conservation Movement," *Century,* **LXXIX** (1910), 637–638.

upon the value of great scenery, chose to lay stress exclusively upon the material and economic side of the whole movement. The fact is, there is no more popular and effective trumpet-call for the conservation movement than the appeal to the love of beautiful natural scenery. In this matter the idealists are more practical than the materialists, whose mistake is that they never capitalize sentiment. A money valuation of the uses of our great natural scenery, attracting, as it does, a vast number of summer sojourners and the traveling public in general, would make an astonishing showing.

It could easily be proved that the fear of offending the "hard-headed" and "practical" man by such an appeal is without foundation. The first thing that a man does after he obtains a competence is to invest his money in some form of beauty, and it is in the interest of good citizenship that he should have a plot of ground to be proud of. He settles in some town, suburb, or other region mainly because it is beautiful, and he is all the happier if his home can command an attractive natural view. As he grows richer, this desire for beautiful things, and particularly for a beautiful country-place, becomes more dominant, and it is to such a feeling that we owe the development of our sea-coast and hilltops into regions of resort for health and recreation. The American still apostrophizes his country with the lines:

> I love thy rocks and rills,
> Thy woods and templed hills,

and he is not willing that this sentiment shall be changed to read:

> I love thy stocks and mills,
> Thy goods and crumpled bills.

It must always be held as a blot upon the lustrous record of the Roosevelt Administration in conservation matters that, in deference to the false sense of what is practical, and, moreover, by a strained construction of law, it gave away a large part of the people's greatest national park for a city's reservoir, confessedly without the slightest inquiry as to the necessity of doing so.* The contention that in fact this necessity does not exist was confirmed when the leader of the scheme

---

*Actually, the grant of Yosemite National Park's Hetch Hetchy Valley to San Francisco for municipal water supply and hydropower was not made until 1913. [Ed.]

acknowledged before the Senate Committee on the Public Lands that San Francisco, without invading the Park, could get an abundant water-supply from a number of other regions by the simple, though sometimes inconvenient, process of paying for it!

The time has come when, if much of what has been gained by the reservation of our great natural monuments is not to be lost, the public must make known its wishes to Congress. The scheme for the dismemberment of the Yosemite National Park, which a year ago was temporarily checked, is to be pushed during the present session. In this contest the recent visit of President Taft to the Yosemite and that of the Secretary of the Interior* to the Hetch-Hetchy will strengthen the defenders of the latter valley, for no one can view the phenomenal beauty of these Sierra gorges without feeling a solemn responsibility for its preservation. Even the San Francisco promoters of the destructive scheme threw up their hands in admiration as they caught sight of the Hetch-Hetchy, and confessed that "something was to be said for the esthetes, after all." And yet they profess to believe that water is "running to waste" if it be simply looked at! And this is said of streams which, after they have been looked at, may be utilized for the irrigation of the great San Joaquin lowlands.

Movements to safeguard Niagara and the Hudson are also impending, and in this connection we respectfully commend to Senators and Representatives, as well as to the members of the New York legislature, these judicious words of Governor [Charles Evans] Hughes, spoken at the dedication of the Palisades Interstate Park:

> Of what avail would be the material benefits of gainful occupation, what would be the promise of prosperous communities, with wealth of products and freedom of exchange, were it not for the opportunities to cultivate the love of the beautiful? The preservation of the scenery of the Hudson is the highest duty with respect to this river imposed upon those who are the trustees of its manifold benefits. It is fortunate that means have already been taken to protect this escarpment, which is one of its finest features. The two States have joined in measures for this purpose. I hope this is only the beginning of efforts which may jointly be made by these two commonwealths to safeguard the highlands and waters, in which they are both deeply inter-

*Richard A. Ballinger. [Ed.]

ested. The entire watershed which lies to the north should be conserved, and a policy should be instituted for such joint control as would secure adequate protection.

But it is not merely the colossal beauty of the Sierra, Niagara, and the Hudson that should be preserved and enhanced, but the beauty of city, town, and hamlet. What is needed is the inculcation, by every agency, of *beauty as a principle,* that life may be made happier and more elevating for all the generations who shall follow us, and who will love their country more devotedly the more lovable it is made.

15

A Voice for Wilderness

John Muir (1901, 1912)

The preservation of wilderness was a favorite cause of aesthetic conservationists like Robert Underwood Johnson (Selection 14) and John Muir. A Scot by birth, Muir grew up on the central Wisconsin frontier in the 1850s, but unlike most pioneers he formed a love of wilderness that ultimately led him to a lifetime spent close to California's Sierra. By the turn of the century Muir had become the nation's foremost publicizer of the value of wilderness and, as a founder and first president of the Sierra Club in 1892, a strong force for its protection. Transcendentalism, gleaned from Ralph Waldo Emerson and Henry David Thoreau (Selection 5), shaped his philosophy: undisturbed nature was a "window opening into heaven, a mirror reflecting the Creator." It followed that protecting wilderness was almost an act of worship. In his declining years Muir threw himself into the battle to save Yosemite National Park's wild Hetch Hetchy Valley from alteration by a dam. His failure in this cause was a bitter disappointment and probably hastened his death in 1914, but Muir's efforts did much to call into being a potent national sentiment for preserving wilderness.

The tendency nowadays to wander in wilderness is delightful to see. Thousands of tired, nerve-shaken, over-civilized people are beginning to find out that going to the mountains is going home; that wildness is a necessity; and that mountain parks and reservations are useful not only as fountains of timber and irrigating rivers, but as fountains of life. Awakening from the stupefying effects of the vice of over-industry and the deadly apathy of luxury, they are trying as best they can to mix and enrich their own little ongoings with those of Nature, and to get rid of rust and disease. Briskly venturing and roaming, some are washing off sins and cobweb cares of the devil's spinning in all-day storms on mountains; sauntering in rosiny pinewoods or in gentian meadows, brushing through chaparral, bending down and parting

John Muir, *Our National Parks* (Boston: Houghton Mifflin, 1901), 1–3.

sweet, flowery sprays; tracing rivers to their sources, getting in touch with the nerves of Mother Earth; jumping from rock to rock, feeling the life of them, learning the songs of them, panting in whole-souled exercise, and rejoicing in deep, long-drawn breaths of pure wildness. This is fine and natural and full of promise. So also is the growing interest in the care and preservation of forests and wild places in general, and in the half wild parks and gardens of towns. Even the scenery habit in its most artificial forms, mixed with spectacles, silliness, and kodaks; its devotees arrayed more gorgeously than scarlet tanagers, frightening the wild game with red umbrellas,—even this is encouraging, and may well be regarded as a hopeful sign of the times.

All the Western mountains are still rich in wildness, and by means of good roads are being brought nearer civilization every year.* To the sane and free it will hardly seem necessary to cross the continent in search of wild beauty, however easy the way, for they find it in abundance wherever they chance to be. Like Thoreau they see forests in orchards and patches of huckleberry brush, and oceans in ponds and drops of dew. Few in these hot, dim, strenuous times are quite sane or free; choked with care like clocks full of dust, laboriously doing so much good and making so much money,—or so little,—they are no longer good for themselves. . . .

---

*At this time (1901) Muir did not foresee the fact that for later preservationists roads and cars would be a major threat. [Ed.]

. . . Hetch Hetchy Valley, far from being a plain, common, rock-bound meadow, as many who have not seen it seem to suppose, is a grand landscape garden, one of Nature's rarest and most precious mountain temples. As in Yosemite, the sublime rocks of its walls seem to glow with life, whether leaning back in repose or standing erect in thoughtful attitudes, giving welcome to storms and calms alike, their brows in the sky, their feet set in the groves and gay flowery meadows, while birds, bees, and butterflies help the river and waterfalls to stir all the air into music—things frail and fleeting and types of permanence meeting here and blending, just as they do in Yosemite, to draw her lovers into close and confiding communion with her.

Sad to say, this most precious and sublime feature of the Yosemite National Park, one of the greatest of all our natural resources for the

John Muir, *The Yosemite* (New York: Century, 1912), 255–257, 260–262.

uplifting joy and peace and health of the people, is in danger of being dammed and made into a reservoir to help supply San Francisco with water and light, thus flooding it from wall to wall and burying its gardens and groves one or two hundred feet deep. This grossly destructive commercial scheme has long been planned and urged (though water as pure and abundant can be got from sources outside of the people's park, in a dozen different places), because of the comparative cheapness of the dam and of the territory which it is sought to divert from the great uses to which it was dedicated in the Act of 1890 establishing the Yosemite National Park.

The making of gardens and parks goes on with civilization all over the world, and they increase both in size and number as their value is recognized. Everybody needs beauty as well as bread, places to play in and pray in, where Nature may heal and cheer and give strength to body and soul alike. This natural beauty-hunger is made manifest in the little window-sill gardens of the poor, though perhaps only a geranium slip in a broken cup, as well as in the carefully tended rose and lily gardens of the rich, the thousands of spacious city parks and botanical gardens, and in our magnificent National parks—the Yellowstone, Yosemite, Sequoia, etc.—Nature's sublime wonderlands, the admiration and joy of the world. Nevertheless, like anything else worth while, from the very beginning, however well guarded, they have always been subject to attack by despoiling gain-seekers and mischief-makers of every degree from Satan to Senators, eagerly trying to make everything immediately and selfishly commercial, with schemes disguised in smug-smiling philanthropy, industriously, sham-piously crying, "Conservation, conservation, panutilization," that man and beast may be fed and the dear Nation made great. Thus long ago a few enterprising merchants utilized the Jerusalem temple as a place of business instead of a place of prayer, changing money, buying and selling cattle and sheep and doves; and earlier still, the first forest reservation, including only one tree, was likewise despoiled. Ever since the establishment of the Yosemite National Park, strife has been going on around its borders and I suppose this will go on as part of the universal battle between right and wrong, however much its boundaries may be shorn, or its wild beauty destroyed. . . .

That any one would try to destroy [Hetch Hetchy Valley) seems incredible; but sad experience shows that there are people good enough and bad enough for anything. The proponents of the dam scheme bring forward a lot of bad arguments to prove that the only righteous thing to do with the people's parks is to destroy them bit by bit as they are able. Their arguments are curiously like those of the devil, devised for the destruction of the first garden. . . .

These temple destroyers, devotees of ravaging commercialism, seem to have a perfect contempt for Nature, and, instead of lifting their eyes to the God of the mountains, lift them to the Almighty Dollar.

Dam Hetch Hetchy! As well dam for water-tanks the people's cathedrals and churches, for no holier temple has ever been consecrated by the heart of man.

16

Conservation as Democracy

J. Leonard Bates (1957)

In the next selections three historians analyze the Progressive conservation movement. J. Leonard Bates feels that the desire to implement democracy best explains the motives of the conservationists. His people-versus-the-interests interpretation fits neatly into the traditional understanding of progressivism as a whole. The previous selections from Gifford Pinchot and WJ McGee suggest the type of evidence on which Bates rests his conclusions.

Samuel P. Hays (Selection 17), on the other hand, argues that conservation had its origin in a passion for scientific management and efficiency among a relatively small group of planners and technicians. Far from opposing big business, conservation leaders tried to apply its methods to natural resource problems. While Hays's view seems quite different from that of Bates, it must be remembered that Hays has reference to the personal motives of the conservationists while Bates's points might be construed as applying to the public conception of the movement and to the explanations used to secure general support. Undoubtedly both the scientific and the democratic interpretations explain important parts of the motivation of Progressive conservation.

Roderick Nash (Selection 18) contends that changes in American attitude toward nature in the late-nineteenth and early-twentieth centuries created a climate of opinion favorable to conservation. While directed at the rise of the sentiment for preserving wilderness conditions, the essay can be used to understand one reason for the national concern over the exhaustion of natural resources.

Historians of modern reform have given scant attention to a rationale of conservation or to conservation as a democratic movement. In fact the program associated with Theodore Roosevelt and Gifford Pinchot

J. Leonard Bates, "Fulfilling American Democracy: The Conservation Movement, 1907–1921," *Mississippi Valley Historical Review,* XLIV (1957), 29–31, 38, 42, 47–48, 53–54, 57. Footnotes in the original have been omitted. Copyright Organization of American Historians, 1957.

is occasionally disparaged as largely sound and fury. Doubtless the ambiguity and complexity of "conservation" have tended to obscure its democratic implications. Then too, this policy was both a product of and a stimulant to the larger, so-called Progressive Movement; it shared in certain weaknesses of this epoch of reform and has shared in the criticism. The usual interpretation today is that the Progressive Movement was essentially an uprising of the middle class, protesting against monopoly and boss control of politics, stressing heavily the virtues of competition, freedom, and morality. With respect to conservation this view leads to the criticism that there existed a fundamental inconsistency between the ideas of protecting natural resources and the dominant beliefs in individualism and competition with the resultant low prices, heavy consumption, and waste. . . .

The organized conservationists were concerned more with economic justice and democracy in the handling of resources than with mere prevention of waste. One aspect of the matter was the price and income situation, the actual monetary rewards from the marvelous wealth of this land. Conservationists believed that somehow the common heritage, the socially created resources and institutions, had passed into the hands of vested interests and that the benefits were siphoned into the hands of a few. There were several ways in which this situation might be remedied, as they saw it: first, to hold on to the remaining public lands, at least temporarily, preventing further monopolization; second, to attempt to give the people a fuller share of opportunities and profits; and finally, in that period of low income to keep prices proportionately low. . . .

The conservationists' approach was broad. They believed in government studies and safeguards for the preservation of irreplaceable resources such as petroleum; they recognized and struggled with problems which remain today only partially solved. They understood the need for federal leadership in an organic structure based on the unity of nature itself. . . . They made mistakes, of course. Like most progressives, they concluded easily that the opposition on a particular issue consisted of "robber barons," conspirators, and frauds. . . .

The developing rationale of the conservationists is of the utmost importance in explaining their conduct and influence. By no means were they all alike, but people such as Roosevelt, Pinchot, and La Follette believed that a larger amount of governmental interference and regulation in the public interest was required. They were especially concerned about the remaining public lands, which, according to principles grounded in the Homestead and other acts, belonged to all.

Millions of acres had been given away or sold to corporate interests for a trifling price or had been actually stolen. This record of carelessness and exploitation could not be expunged. However, to conserve and use wisely that which remained, to show that civilized man could profit from mistakes of the past, to democratize the handling of a common heritage, would be a genuine consolation. A crisis, they felt, existed. Such an attitude was a compound of idealism, passion, and sober analysis. These men realized that American society in the twentieth century must be increasingly one of cooperative and collective gains.

As progressives they agreed passionately on the need for honesty and a social conscience in the administration of resources. . . . Conservationists were convinced that hostility toward materialism and toward money men and special interests usually was warranted, that history afforded ample justification for suspicion. If nothing else united the conservationists, there was this hatred of the boodler, the rank materialist, the exploiter.

Pinchot and his group therefore believed in using the authority of federal and state government to compel conservation practices ("socialization of management"), even aiming to do this on *private* forest lands. . . .

. . . In [Robert] La Follette's opinion there had been only one great issue in all of history: a struggle "between labor and those who would control, through slavery in one form or another, the laborers." Uppermost in his consideration, therefore, was justice for the exploited. With respect to public resources in general, he argued that there must be a policy of continuing public ownership, of leasing where possible, of price controls, and a degree of government operation depending upon the monopoly situation. Basic raw materials, even though privately owned, must sell at a reasonable price and if they did not he advocated government appropriation. Quite early he had called for leasing rather than selling government properties, and in the conservation fight of the late [Woodrow] Wilson years [1916–1920] he stressed a leasing system for coal and oil and other nonmetalliferous minerals but not without adequate safeguards for democratic development and prevention of waste. He believed, for example, that evidence of collusive bargaining and fixing of prices among the lessees should warrant government cancellation of the lease. . . . The passage of the Water Power Act and the Mineral Leasing Act of 1920 inaugurated a new policy of continuing public ownership and federal trusteeship in which conservation and the national interest seemed to be the winners.

. . . Pinchot declared that the major portion of the Roosevelt program had now been achieved. . . . Undoubtedly [conservationists] had won something of a victory and the way had been prepared for a larger federal role in the future.

. . . [T]he conservation policy contained an inner vitality that could not be obscured or destroyed. Here was an effort to implement democracy for twentieth-century America, to stop the stealing and exploitation, to inspire high standards of government, to preserve the beauty of mountain and stream, to distribute more equitably the profits of this economy. From McGee, to Pinchot and La Follette, to George Norris and Harold Ickes, to Wayne Morse and Lister Hill—there has burned a democratic zeal, a social faith. The faith was genuine; the propaganda effective. Though a careful evaluation of the impact upon this country remains to be made, it is difficult to escape the conclusion that a fighting band of conservationists has made the United States much richer in material wealth and in the democratic spirit and faith of its people.

17

Conservation as Efficiency

Samuel P. Hays (1959)

Conservation neither arose from a broad popular outcry, nor centered its fire primarily upon the private corporation. . . . In fact, it becomes clear that one must discard completely the struggle against corporations as the setting in which to understand conservation history, and permit an entirely new frame of reference to arise from the evidence itself.

Conservation, above all, was a scientific movement, and its role in history arises from the implications of science and technology in modern society. Conservation leaders sprang from such fields as hydrology, forestry, agrostology, geology, and anthropology. Vigorously active in professional circles in the national capital, these leaders brought the ideals and practices of their crafts into federal resource policy. Loyalty to these professional ideals, not close association with the grass-roots public, set the tone of the Theodore Roosevelt conservation movement. Its essence was rational planning to promote efficient development and use of all natural resources. The idea of efficiency drew these federal scientists from one resource task to another, from specific programs to comprehensive concepts. It molded the policies which they proposed, their administrative techniques, and their relations with Congress and the public. It is from the vantage point of applied science, rather than of democratic protest, that one must understand the historic role of the conservation movement.

The new realms of science and technology, appearing to open up unlimited opportunities for human achievement, filled conservation leaders with intense optimism. They emphasized expansion, not retrenchment; possibilities, not limitations. True, they expressed some fear that diminishing resources would create critical shortages in the

Samuel P. Hays, *Conservation and the Gospel of Efficiency: The Progressive Conservation Movement, 1890–1920* (Cambridge, MA: Harvard University Press, 1959), 1–4, 265–266. Copyright 1987 by Samuel P. Hays. Reprinted by permission. Footnotes in the original have been omitted.

future. But they were not Malthusian prophets of despair and gloom. The popular view that in a fit of pessimism they withdrew vast areas of the public lands from present use for future development does not stand examination. In fact, they bitterly opposed those who sought to withdraw resources from commercial development. They displayed that deep sense of hope which pervaded all those at the turn of the century for whom science and technology were revealing visions of an abundant future.

The political implications of conservation . . . grew out of the political implications of applied science rather than from conflict over the distribution of wealth. Who should decide the course of resource development? Who should determine the goals and methods of federal resource programs? The correct answer to these questions lay at the heart of the conservation idea. Since resource matters were basically technical in nature, conservationists argued, technicians, rather than legislators, should deal with them. Foresters should determine the desirable annual timber cut; hydraulic engineers should establish the feasible extent of multiple-purpose river development and the specific location of reservoirs; agronomists should decide which forage areas could remain open for grazing without undue damage to water supplies. Conflicts between competing resource users, especially, should not be dealt with through the normal processes of politics. Pressure group action, logrolling in Congress, or partisan debate could not guarantee rational and scientific decisions. Amid such jockeying for advantage with the resulting compromise, concern for efficiency would disappear. Conservationists envisaged, even though they did not realize their aims, a political system guided by the ideal of efficiency and dominated by the technicians who could best determine how to achieve it.

This phase of conservation requires special examination because of its long neglect by historians. Instead of probing the political implications of the technological spirit, they have repeated the political mythology of the "people versus the interests" as the setting for the struggle over resource policy. This myopia has stemmed in part from the disinterestedness of the historian and the social scientist. Often accepting implicitly the political assumptions of elitism, rarely having an axe of personal interest to grind, and invariably sympathetic with the movement, conservation historians have considered their view to be in the public interest. Yet, analysis from outside such a limited perspective reveals the difficulty of equating the particular views of a few scientific leaders with an objective "public interest." Those views did not receive wide acceptance; they did not arise out of widely held assumptions and values. They came from a limited group of people, with a particular set of goals, who played a special role in society. Their definition of the "public interest" might well, and did, clash with other competing definitions. The historian, therefore, cannot understand conservation leaders simply as defenders of the "people." Instead, he must examine the experiences and goals peculiar to them; he must describe their role within a specific sociological context. . . .

The broader significance of the conservation movement stemmed from the role it played in the transformation of a decentralized, non-technical, loosely organized society, where waste and inefficiency ran rampant, into a highly organized, technical, and centrally planned and directed social organization which could meet a complex world with efficiency and purpose. This spirit of efficiency appeared in many realms of American life, in the professional engineering societies, among forward-looking industrial management leaders, and in municipal government reform, as well as in the resource management concepts of Theodore Roosevelt. The possibilities of applying scientific and technical principles to resource development fired federal officials with enthusiasm for the future and imbued all in the conservation movement with a kindred spirit. These goals required public management, of the nation's streams because private enterprise could not afford to undertake it, of the Western lands to adjust one resource use to another. They also required new administrative methods, utilizing to the fullest extent the latest scientific knowledge and expert, disinterested personnel. This was the gospel of efficiency—efficiency which could be realized only through planning, foresight, and conscious purpose.

The lack of direction in American development appalled Roosevelt and his advisers. They rebelled against a belief in the automatic beneficence of unrestricted economic competition, which, they believed, created only waste, exploitation, and unproductive economic rivalry. To replace competition with economic planning, these new efficiency experts argued, would not only arrest the damage of the past, but could also create new heights of prosperity and material abundance for the future. The conservation movement did not involve a reaction against large-scale corporate business, but, in fact, shared its views in a mutual revulsion against unrestrained competition and undirected economic development. Both groups placed a premium on large-scale capital organization, technology, and industry-wide cooperation and planning to abolish the uncertainties and waste of competitive resource use.

18

Conservation as Anxiety

Roderick Frazier Nash (1966)

On the morning of August 10, 1913, the Boston *Post* headlined its lead story: Naked He Plunges into Maine Woods to Live Alone Two Months. The following article told how six days previously a husky, part-time illustrator in his mid-forties named Joseph Knowles had disrobed in a cold drizzle at the edge of a lake in northeastern Maine, smoked a final cigarette, shaken hands around a group of sportsmen and reporters, and trudged off into the wilderness. There was even a photograph of an unclothed Knowles, discreetly shielded by underbrush, waving farewell to civilization. The *Post* explained that Knowles had gone into the woods to be a primitive man for sixty days. He took no equipment of any kind and promised to remain completely isolated, living off the land "as Adam lived."

For the next two months Joe Knowles was the talk of Boston. He provided information about his experiment with periodic dispatches written with charcoal on birchbark. These reports, printed in the *Post*, revealed to an astonished and delighted public that Knowles was succeeding in his planned reversion to the primitive. Using heat from the friction of two sticks, he obtained fire. Clothing came from woven strips of bark. Knowles' first few meals consisted of berries, but he soon varied his diet with trout, partridge and even venison. On August 24 a frontpage banner in the *Post* announced that Knowles had lured a bear into a pit, killed it with a club and fashioned a coat from its skin. By this time newspapers throughout the East and as far away as Kansas City were featuring the story.

When on October 4, 1913 a disheveled but healthy Knowles finally emerged from the Maine woods extolling the values of a primitive way of life, he was swept up in a wave of public enthusiasm. His triumphant return to Boston included stops at Augusta, Lewiston and

Roderick Frazier Nash, "The American Cult of the Primitive," *American Quarterly*, **XVIII** (1966), 517–522, 524–525, 534–537. Reprinted by permission of the publisher. Copyright 1966 by the Trustees of the University of Pennsylvania. Footnotes in the original have been omitted.

Portland with speeches before throngs of eight to ten thousand people. The cheers persisted in spite of a fine of $205 which an unyielding Maine Fish and Game Commission imposed on Knowles for killing a bear out of season. But Maine's welcome paled next to Boston's. The city had not had a hero like "the modern primitive man" in a generation. On October 9 a huge crowd jammed North Station to meet Knowles' train and shouted itself hoarse when he appeared. Thousands more lined the streets through which his motorcade passed. Still clad in the bearskin, Knowles went to Boston Common, where an estimated twenty thousand persons waited. His speech was disappointingly brief, but the gathering thrilled at the way he leaped onto the podium with "the quick, graceful movements of a tiger."

In the next few days Knowles even upstaged an exciting World Series. At Harvard physicians reported on the excellence of his physical condition, and there were numerous banquets and interviews, including one with the governor of Massachusetts. Publishers besieged him for the rights to a book version of his experience which, as *Alone in the Wilderness,* sold 300,000 copies, and he toured the vaudeville circuit with top billing. The *Post* published full-page color reproductions of Joe's paintings of wild animals, pointing out that they were suitable for framing and "just the thing to hang in your den." Even when the *Post*'s rival newspaper presented substantial evidence that Knowles was a fraud whose wilderness saga had actually occurred in a secret, snug cabin* a vociferous denial arose in reply. Quite a few Americans in 1913 seemed to *want* to believe in the authenticity of the "Nature Man." In fact, the celebration of Joe Knowles was just a single and rather grotesque manifestation of popular interest in the primitive both in man (the savage) and nature (wilderness). Increasingly in evidence after 1890, this enthusiasm attained the dimensions of a national cult in the first years of the present century.

The most significant fact about the Joe Knowles craze was that it occurred at all. One hundred or even fifty years earlier anyone undertaking such an intentional reversion to the primitive would have been thought demented. Apart from a few artists and writers, Americans before Knowles' generation regarded the wild as something alien and

---

*After his venture in Maine, Knowles tried to repeat his stunt in California and, with a female companion, in New York but without success. Nor did his plan materialize for a wilderness colony where Americans could live close to nature. Ultimately, Knowles retired to an isolated shack on the coast of Washington. He died on October 21, 1942. [Ed.]

hostile. Their energies were largely directed to conquering wilderness and destroying savages in the name of progress, religion and, indeed, survival. The pioneers and their chroniclers frequently employed a military metaphor in discussing the advance of civilization: wild country was an "enemy" which had to be "vanquished" and "subdued" by a "pioneer army." Achievement was defined as winning this battle against the wild. With a ponderous regularity the reminiscences of frontiersmen dwelt on the beneficent effects of the civilizing process. The "unbroken and trackless wilderness" was "reclaimed" by being "transformed into fruitful farms and filled with flourishing cities" which was "always for the better." Others simply said that the wilderness had been made to blossom like a rose. Along with most of his countrymen, the American pioneer looked forward to a future in which Indians had all been made "good" and the wilderness fructified in the manner of a garden.

During his visit to the United States in 1831 Alexis de Tocqueville observed this aversion to the primitive. The young Frenchman made a special journey to Michigan to satisfy a romantic urge to see wilderness. But when he revealed his desire for a pleasure excursion into the back-country, the frontiersmen thought him mad. It required considerable persuasion on Tocqueville's part to convince them that his interests lay in things other than lumbering or land speculation. He concluded that "living in the wilds, [the pioneer] only prizes the works of man." The settler's eyes were "fixed upon another sight . . . : the . . . march across these wilds, draining swamps, turning the course of rivers, peopling solitudes, and subduing nature." To Tocqueville this was evidence that those farthest removed from the wild valued it the most. He knew his own attraction to wilderness was largely the result of his being a European.

By the late nineteenth century sufficient change had occurred in the conditions of life and thought in the United States to make it possible for increasing numbers of Americans to appreciate Tocqueville's attitude toward the primitive. Civilization had indeed subdued the continent. Labor-saving agricultural machinery and a burgeoning industry coupled with a surge in population turned the American focus from country to city. The census of 1890 gave only statistical confirmation to what most Americans knew first-hand: the frontier was moribund and wilderness no longer dominant. From the perspective of city streets and comfortable homes wildness inspired quite different attitudes than it did when observed from a frontiersman's clearing. No longer did the primeval forest and the Indian have to be battled in hand-to-hand combat. Men might respond to wilderness as vacationers rather than conquerors. Specifically, the solitude and hardship that had intimidated many a pioneer often proved magnetically attractive to his city-dwelling grandchild.

Indicative of the change was the way the new urban environment acquired many of the repugnant connotations of wilderness. By the 1890's cities were frequently regarded with a hostility once reserved for wild forests. In 1898 Robert A. Woods entitled a collection of exposures of Boston's slum conditions *The City Wilderness*. A few years later, Upton Sinclair's *The Jungle* employed a similar metaphor in describing the horrors of Chicago's stockyard. Too much civilization, not too little, seemed at the root of the nation's difficulties. The bugaboos of the time—"Wall Street," "trusts" and "invisible government"— were phenomena of the urban, industrialized East. In regard to primitive man, American opinion was also tending to reverse the flow of two and a half centuries. Increasing numbers joined Helen Hunt Jackson in sympathizing with the Indian and identifying the disease, whiskey and deception of civilization, not his savage state, as the crux of his problem.

Along with the physical change in American life went a closely related intellectual change in temper or mood. The general optimism and hope of the ante-bellum years partially yielded toward the end of the century to more sober assessments, doubts and uncertainties. Many considered the defects of their society evidence that an earlier age's bland confidence in progress was unfounded. Reasons for pessimism appeared on every hand. A flood of immigrants seemed to many to be diluting the American strain and weakening American traditions. Business values and urban living were felt to be undermining character, taste and morality. The vast size and highly organized nature of the economy and government posed obstacles to the effectiveness of the individual. Instead of the millennium, "progress" appeared to have brought confusion, corruption and a debilitating overabundance. The feeling could not be downed that the United States, if not the Western world, had seen its greatest moments and was in an incipient state of decline. There existed, to be sure, a countercurrent in American thought of pride and hope, but the belief persisted that the growth and change of the past century had not been entirely for the better.

As a result of this sense of discontent with civilization, no less uncomfortable because of its vagueness, *fin de siècle* America was ripe for the appeal of the uncivilized on a broad popular basis. The cult had several facets. In the first place there was a growing tendency to associate wilderness with America's frontier and pioneer past that was thought responsible for many desirable national characteristics. Related to this was the appeal of the savage as the embodiment of virility, toughness and a fighting instinct—qualities that defined fitness in Darwinian terms. A third and quite different idea invested wilderness with an aesthetic and ethical value and emphasized the opportunity it afforded for genteel contemplation and worship. Finally, defense of the primitive attracted many Americans as a means of protesting the commercialism and sordidness they observed in their country. . . .

Wilderness preservation was [one] response to the disappearance of the American frontier. The idea of giving large tracts of wild country legal protection had its roots before mid-century, but it was not until 1872 that the first reservation was established. In that year an act of Congress designated three thousand square miles in northwestern Wyoming as Yellowstone National Park. It was the world's first instance of large-scale protection of wilderness in the public interest. But in the 1870's there was no recognition that wilderness had in fact been preserved. Emphasis, rather, was placed on the park's importance in making available Yellowstone's geysers and hot springs as tourist attractions. The original rationale for the second preservation milestone, the establishment of a state forest reservation in New York's Adirondack region in 1885, was similarly unrelated to wilderness. In this case powerful commercial lobbies favored protection because they feared that if the northern forests were cut, water levels in the Erie Canal and Hudson River would fall too low for navigation.

By the 1890's, however, Americans were beginning to attach a new significance to both the Yellowstone and Adirondack reservations. Recognition grew that protecting wilderness had been their most important accomplishment. In 1892 a Congressional defender of the first national park stressed its value as a place where his countrymen could "see primeval nature, simple and pure." Two years later the revisers of New York's Constitution inserted a special provision defining the primary purpose of the Adirondack State Park as protecting a primitive environment. The changed attitude was also apparent in 1890 when the creation of Yosemite National Park was supported with the argument that it would be "a noble mark for the . . . lover of wilderness."

For Theodore Roosevelt the idea of preserving wild country in order to retain a remnant of the frontier was a primary consideration. Immensely influential in such matters, Roosevelt did much to bring wilderness into national prominence. He visited Yellowstone in 1903 and praised it as a region in which "bits of the old wilderness scenery and the old wilderness life are to be kept unspoiled for the benefit of our children's children." According to Roosevelt, modern Americans should covet such reservoirs of wildness because "as our civilization grows older and more complex, we need a greater and not a lesser development of the fundamental frontier virtues." The price, he believed, for forgetting the nation's frontier past would be degeneracy and the loss of messianic idealism. Roosevelt personally led the way in seeking the wild. Fresh out of Harvard, he spent considerable time in the 1880's on a ranch in the Dakota Territories exulting in the pioneer's life. He even had himself photographed posing fiercely in a buckskin hunting suit. A great many Americans must have shared their President's concern about the vanishing wilderness because the preservation movement gained wide support in the second decade of the twentieth century. . . .

For . . . most advocates of wilderness, the controversy over Yosemite National Park's wild and isolated Hetch Hetchy Valley was climactic. The struggle began early in the twentieth century when San Francisco, facing a shortage of fresh water, asked the federal government for permission to dam the Tuolumne River at the end of the high-walled Hetch Hetchy Valley. The Department of the Interior turned to Congress for a decision, and in the ensuing national debate the preservationists saw an opportunity to extend their case from a defense of wilderness to a full-scale critique of their society. Robert Underwood Johnson opened the fusillade when he wrote in *Century* in 1908 that San Francisco's supporters were people who had not advanced beyond the "pseudo-'practical' stage." Their presence, he added, "is one of the retarding influences of American civilization and brings us back to the materialistic declaration that 'Good is only good to eat.' " Later that year at a Congressional hearing on the Hetch Hetchy question, Johnson explained that he was defending wilderness "in the name of all lovers of beauty . . . against the materialistic idea that there must be something wrong about a man who finds one of the highest uses of nature in the fact that it is made to be looked at." Such an argument was intended to embarrass San Francisco's proponents as much as to defend Hetch Hetchy. Paradoxically, according to Johnson, appreciation of the primitive was an indicator of superior cultivation.

Others took up Johnson's theme with even more pointed reference to America's shortcomings. One man, who had camped in Hetch Hetchy, angrily demanded of the House of Representatives' Committee on the Public Lands: "is it never ceasing; is there nothing to be held sacred by this nation; is it to be dollars only; are we to be cramped in soul and mind by the lust after filthy lucre only; shall we be left some of the more glorious places?" Another letter of protest concluded: "may we live down our national reputation for commercialism." At the Senate hearings in 1909 Henry E. Gregory of the American Scenic and Historic Preservation Society appeared in person and spoke of the need to counteract "business and utilitarian motives." He pointed out that a primitive area like Hetch Hetchy had more than monetary value "as an educator of the people and as a restorer and liberator of the spirit enslaved by Mammon." . . .

Because of the more general enthusiasm for the primitive that existed at the time, the preservationists' arguments for Hetch Hetchy found a receptive audience and national concern for the Valley developed at once. After the first set of Congressional hearings, the reservoir bill was killed, according to the House report, by "an exceedingly widespread, earnest, and vigorous protest voiced by scientists, naturalists, mountain climbers, travelers, and others in person, by letters and telegrams, and in newspaper and magazine articles." Resistance gathered momentum in 1913 when another bill granting the Valley to San Francisco was introduced into the Sixty-third Congress. Robert Underwood Johnson and his National Committee for the Preservation of the Yosemite National Park sent protest literature to 1,418 newspapers and published two pamphlets on its own. The public responded, and Hetch Hetchy became a *cause célèbre.* Hundreds of newspapers throughout the country carried editorials on the question, and all but a few West Coast papers took the side of wilderness. Leading magazines, including *Outlook, Nation, Independent* and *Collier's* as well as Johnson's *Century,* published articles protesting the reservoir. A mass meeting on behalf of the Valley took place at the Museum of Natural History in New York City. Meanwhile, mail poured into the offices of Congressmen. Late in November Senator Reed Smoot of Utah estimated he had received five thousand letters opposing the bill while President Woodrow Wilson was besieged with requests that he defend the national park.

In spite of what seemed to be overwhelming national sentiment in favor of keeping Hetch Hetchy wild, the reservoir bill had effective lobbyists in Washington and appeared to have administration backing. After close votes in both houses, Wilson signed it into law December 19, 1913. The only comfort for the preservationists was the thought that on behalf of wilderness "the conscience of the whole country has been aroused from sleep." . . .

Near the close of the Senate debate on Hetch Hetchy, James A. Reed of Missouri arose to confess his incredulity at the entire controversy. How could it be, he wondered, that over such a trivial matter as the future of a piece of wilderness "the Senate goes into profound debate, the country is thrown into a condition of hysteria." Observing that the intensity of resistance to the dam increased with the distance from Yosemite, he remarked that "when we get as far east as New England the opposition has become a frenzy." In Senator Reed's opinion this was clearly "much ado about little." He might have said the same thing about the enthusiastic reception of Joe Knowles, which occurred simultaneously with the climax of the Hetch Hetchy issue. . . . But the point, as Reed himself suggested, was that a great many of his contemporaries *did* regard the primitive as worth getting excited about. The cult, to be sure, was not overwhelming nor was the popularity of primitivism the only manifestation of discontent. In a complex age it was but a single current of thought. Even in the minds of those who championed wilderness, pride in the accomplishments of American civilization and a belief in the virtues of further development of natural resources persisted. Yet by the twentieth century's second decade something of a divide had been passed. Sufficient misgivings about the effects of civilization had arisen to encourage a favorable opinion of the primitive that contrasted sharply with earlier American attitudes.

PART THREE

CONSERVING RESOURCES AND ENVIRONMENTAL QUALITY, 1921–1965

Many hard lessons have taught us the human waste that results from lack of planning.

—*Franklin D. Roosevelt*

Progressive conservation produced considerably more smoke than fire. There were urgent calls to action, grandiose plans, and elaborate conferences but relatively little help for the land. Public opinion, however, had been aroused, and after World War I the American conservation movement resumed. Some of the shrillness disappeared. Conservationists spent more time in action, less in rhetoric and scolding. They talked less about "running out" of resources and more about managing them intelligently. The people-versus-plutocrats approach gave way to acceptance of the idea that the condition of the environment was a product of American civilization as a whole. Responsibility for land health fell on the entire nation, and it responded with more comprehensive programs than those of the Progressive years.

After 1920, conservation benefited from several new approaches and circumstances. The conservationists' understanding of the interrelation of resource problems was greater than that of the Progressives. The Pinchot school of forest management, for instance, scoffed at the "sentimentalists" who extolled the recreational values of the national forests. But the next generation of foresters gradually recognized the importance of woodland for both lumber and pleasure and adjusted Forest Service policy to accommodate both demands. In the early 1920s the Forest Service, partially in an effort to prevent the ambitious National Park Service from acquiring some of its land, began to stress recreation and scenery as forest products. This unprecedented departure from the utilitarian line even extended to keeping portions of the national forests undeveloped for their value as wilderness. Similarly, reclamationists started to publicize the boating and fishing potential of reservoirs. The continued growth of federal power and responsibility, particularly under President Franklin D. Roosevelt, had a profound impact on conservation. State and private efforts were not discouraged, but increasingly Americans recognized that managing the environment was a task requiring a degree of planning, power, and money that only the national government could command.

Since World War II, the driving force in the American conservation movement has come increasingly from the quest for environmental quality. At first, to be sure, the familiar theme of providing for man's material needs was much in evidence. Books like Fairfield Osborn's *Our Plundered Planet* (1948) and William Vogt's *Road to Survival* (1948) (Selection 26) grimly raised the old Malthusian specter of population outreaching the world's productive ability. They contended that birth control, the prevention of needless waste, and the development of new processes of providing food were essential for the survival of the race. From this perspective, conservation was the means of maintaining the physical bases of life. Indeed, this had been the movement's main rationale at the time of its inception.

But the idea of protecting the environment for its nonmaterial values also had a long, if less potent, history in American thought. And by the 1960s, this concept challenged utilitarianism as the central purpose of conservation. Continued improvements in technology, for one thing, eased fears of overpopulation and resource exhaustion. More importantly, many Americans were coming to realize that an environment conducive to survival—even to affluence—was not enough. They demanded that the land had to do more than just keep people alive. Solitude, scenery, and recreational opportunity were vitally important as well. The environment was to be groomed for human pleasure as well as sustenance. For example, Robert Marshall's 1930 plea for wilderness preservation (Selection 25) made increasing sense. In 1960, Wallace Stegner (Selection 28) made a modern case for wildness, and four years later Congress created the National Wilderness Preservation System, the first instance of specific, legal protection of wild country in the world. In 1949, the ecologist-philosopher Aldo Leopold (Selection 27) went further still, proposing a "land ethic" that made human interest (material as well as aesthetic and spiritual) less important than the health and integrity of what was beginning to be called the "ecosystem." Although poorly understood at the time of its articulation, Leopold's philosophy would come to play an important role in shaping the ideology of American environmentalism after 1965.

19

Conservation in the 1920s

Donald C. Swain (1963)

For an overview of conservation history in the two decades after the Progressive period, we turn in the next selection to the account of historian Donald C. Swain. Clearly, Franklin D. Roosevelt's convictions about the desirability of positive federal action on behalf of the public welfare were more conducive to conservation than the individualistic, free-enterprise philosophies of his three predecessors in the White House. But, as Swain demonstrates, it would be a mistake to discount the 1920s, and especially the Hoover administration, as a time of conservation progress.

The personalities and political philosophies of three Republican Presidents influenced federal resource programs during the 1920s. Executive preference in matters of policy created a milieu of voluntarism, "organized coöperation," and decentralization in which the federal conservation agencies often found it advantageous to soft pedal resource regulation and to emphasize service functions. Warren G. Harding and Calvin Coolidge, while paying scant attention to conservation policy, tended to inhibit positive federal conservation activity. Herbert Hoover, on the other hand, demonstrated throughout the 1920s an active and constructive interest in promoting national conservation programs.

Riding to office on a wave of reaction against wartime restrictions, Harding understood little of the necessity for conserving natural resources. In his view, the conservation issue was unimportant. He stood for rapid resource development within an unfettered private enterprise system. . . . The Teapot Dome scandal,* eventuating from the Presi-

Donald C. Swain, *Federal Conservation Policy, 1921–1933,* University of California Publications in History, **LXXVI** (Berkeley, CA, 1963), 160–170. Footnotes in the original have been omitted. Reprinted by permission of the University of California Press.

*In 1924 a congressional investigation revealed that two years previously Secretary of the Interior Albert B. Fall had illegally leased rich oil reserves near Teapot Dome,

dent's own lack of interest in resource administration, is the best example. Without vigorous executive support, the conservation bureaus had to fall back on voluntary programs designed, in general, to appease industrial and commercial interests.

Succeeding to the presidency in 1923, Calvin Coolidge interested himself primarily in trimming the federal budget while largely ignoring natural resources. The era of executive laxity continued. . . . [Coolidge] had almost no aptitude for the subtleties of conservation policy. And his failure to grasp the long-range implications of resource problems might have proved disastrous. It was monumental naïveté, for example, to compare Muscle Shoals* in value to a "first class battleship." With evident pride, he considered himself a "practical" man. But his emphasis on economy in governmental expenditures was impractical in the long run. Among other things it severely hampered the federal conservation program. . . . Although the New Englander promoted coöperative policies in forestry, wildlife, and recreation, his only important influence on conservation came as a result of his insistence on decentralization. He wanted the states to discharge their public functions "so faithfully that instead of an extension on the part of the Federal Government there can be a contraction." When translated into action at the bureau level, this dictum meant less power for the federal conservation agencies, who were expected to stimulate state supervision of resources whenever possible.

Herbert Hoover, in contrast to his immediate predecessors, was a key conservation figure. As Secretary of Commerce, he exerted a large influence in the affairs of both the Harding and Coolidge administrations, demonstrating his personal interest in resource policy-making. From his cabinet office in Washington he crusaded for such conservation causes as the regulation of Alaskan salmon fisheries, the control of water pollution, the establishment of fish nurseries, construction of a St. Lawrence waterway, the improvement of inland navigation, and the authorization of the Boulder Canyon project.** Once in the White House, he concentrated on flood control, waterways development, and

---

Wyoming, to private interests in return for financial considerations. Fall was eventually jailed. [Ed.]

*A key site for the Tennessee Valley Authority's plan for regional reconstruction: see Selection 20. [Ed.]

**Hoover Dam. [Ed.]

oil conservation. That he was a sincere conservationist is beyond question. The methods by which he chose to implement his conservation ideas remained open to criticism. Believing wholeheartedly that natural resources should not be plundered in the name of individualism, he was nevertheless an individualist. How to reconcile his conservation thinking with his individualistic philosophy, therefore, became his personal dilemma. His attempts to solve that dilemma resulted in vigorous programs to reduce waste, to promote coöperation, and to decentralize conservation controls.

Hoover's campaigns against waste and, conversely, for efficiency developed into one of the highlights of the early 1920s. He plugged incessantly for progressive industrial technology and increased scientific research, enlarging the scientific work of the Department of Commerce as a public example. He formed trade associations and arranged voluntary industrial liaisons in which he preached national efficiency at every opportunity. His ideas unquestionably influenced his contemporaries. And the logic of his position led him into conservation. Yet, in regard to the elimination of waste, one may legitimately inquire whether Hoover's primary concern was to conserve natural resources or to stimulate ever greater production. With some inconsistency, both considerations figured prominently in his thinking. Frequently the latter seemed to be the more important.

His quest for efficiency, moreover, led him into the difficult area of governmental reorganization. Attacking the multidepartmental conservation set-up of the federal government, he called for a unification of conservation bureaucracy. He suggested that Congress establish a new organization, grouping resource agencies according to their major purposes. Yet he confined his interest in reorganization almost entirely to administration and methodology. To him, it seemed, conservation results loomed less important than conservation organization. Still, his strong belief in organizational continuity motivated him to appoint the heads of scientific bureaus exclusively from within the bureaus themselves, a policy which had important implications for the federal conservation program.

Hoover championed voluntarism as the method by which the federal government could achieve regulatory results without circumscribing the individual rights. Styling his approach as "Organized Coöperation," he sought to persuade states and individuals to coöperate with the federal government in order to reach certain goals. Even before he became President, his ideas about coöperation permeated the federal establishment. The Forest Service, the Bureau of Fisheries, the Army Engineers, the Biological Survey, the Bureau of Mines, and the Geological Survey all resorted to policies of coöperation during the 'twenties. Later, when Hoover became Chief Executive, he sought assiduously to avoid federal regulation. . . . But on the whole, coöperative tactics failed in the face of strong opposition from resource users. By the time of the New Deal, the policy of coöperation stood generally discredited. Because of his commitment to rugged individualism, Hoover never fully realized the significance to conservation of strong and direct government regulation.

Another characteristic Hoover response during the 1920s was decentralization. Influenced here more than elsewhere by the Republican Party, he consistently advocated states rights and state responsibilities. . . . Hoover's penchant for decentralized organization had a direct effect on his conservation thinking. It caused him to attempt a bold new policy toward the public domain, the range lands of which stood in need of attention.

The arid and semiarid lands of the West, comprising nearly one-third of the total area of the United States, form a valuable natural range for domestic livestock. By the decade of the 'twenties the federal government, true to its easy land policy, had sold the best sections of this vast domain to private individuals and landholding corporations. The government still owned more than 186,000,000 acres of range land, a fact which made it the largest landlord in the West. Despite their lack of title to the land, ranchers and stockmen had become accustomed to free use of these publicly owned areas. Occasionally they claimed exclusive jurisdiction over certain pastures. The trouble was that while supplementary forage on the public domain often became essential to successful grazing operations, the stockmen overused the range. They had little real chance to preserve natural vegetation because the competitive race for free forage forced them to put cattle onto the ranges too early in the spring and encouraged a continual overgrazing. After a time the native grasses tended to disappear, replaced by less desirable varieties or by total barrenness. The Forest Service had brought range lands within the national forests under regulation, but grazers still abused and exploited the unregulated public domain. After conservation organizations made repeated attempts to institute a grazing permit system for the public lands without success, Hoover decided to attack this persistent problem. . . .

As was his custom, he proposed a joint commission to study the problem. The governors agreed to coöperate, and Congress authorized the commission in April, 1930. Chaired by James R. Garfield, Secretary of the Interior under Theodore Roosevelt, and including William B. Greeley, former Forester, the Committee on the Conservation and Administration of the Public Domain commanded respect. Its report of early 1931 reflected Hoover's great influence. It proposed to place the unreserved and unappropriated public domain under responsible administration "for the conservation and beneficial use of its resources." The federal government, it suggested, should maintain jurisdiction over all reclamation projects, national forests, national parks and monuments, wildlife refuges, and any area important to the national defense. The remaining public holdings, valuable primarily as range land, were to be granted to the states. . . . The committee recommended, finally, that the national government pass title to public mineral lands to the states, with the reservation that federal agencies continue to hold the mineral rights. Supported fiercely by the Hoover administration, these proposals nevertheless had no chance of legislative enactment. A sincere attempt to bring effective regulation to the public domain, the plan satisfied too few people.

Conservationists disapproved of Hoover's suggestions for two main reasons. The Roosevelt-Pinchot faction would not sanction the reversal of a principle for which they had fought so hard—federal regulation of the resources of the public domain. Other conservation advocates believed the states incapable of coping with such a large regulatory problem. In the final analysis, the states themselves had little to gain by the committee's proposals. Regulating the public ranges would be a colossal headache, and state governments did not want title to mineral lands so long as the mineral rights resided in the federal government.

In spite of the failure of Hoover's plan for the public domain, his efforts produced a significant negative result. By offering the public lands to the states, and having the states reject the offer, the federal government freed itself to proceed with its own methods of regulation. The states-rights argument, which recurred periodically during grazing and mineral controversies, lost its validity. With the states refusing to act, the federal government had no alternative but to assume responsibility for grazing regulation. The quibbling over methods of range administration had not ended, but the argument over jurisdiction ceased. In 1934 the Taylor Grazing Act—although less than ideal legislation—at last brought conservation regulation to the public ranges of the West.

Hoover's emphasis on decentralization disappointed many conservationists who had hoped for a resurgence of strong and direct federal conservation participation. The old Progressive conservationists, still greatly influenced by Gifford Pinchot, were particularly disenchanted with Hoover.

> Instead of being inspired, [Herbert A. Smith wrote] as I had hoped and believed, by a perception of the immense gains to the public welfare that might be realized by applying science, expert knowledge, the engineer's viewpoint, and the principles of business efficiency to the task of making government serve the multitudinous and complex requirements of a highly organized modern world, I believe he [Hoover] draws back in apprehension of what looks to him like an eventual Frankenstein.

During the era of Hoover's national prominence a curious ambivalence characterized his thinking about natural resources. A convert to the conservation philosophy, he was plagued by personal inconsistencies. He announced early in his administration that "conservation of natural resources is a fixed policy of the government," but he refused to pursue certain conservation projects because he objected to their political or economic implications. He became a pioneer advocate of watershed planning, yet he vehemently rejected the idea of comprehensive federal development of Muscle Shoals. He proposed to bring the public domain under regulation, but the method he chose foredoomed his plan to failure. Although he realized fully the imperative of restricting the national production of petroleum, he stubbornly eschewed direct federal intervention. Torn between conservation considerations and strict individualism, he could not bring himself to compromise his individualistic philosophy. He was thus less effective in implementing his conservation plans than he himself had hoped to be. As the first conservationist President since Theodore Roosevelt, Hoover had aroused expectations among conservation partisans. He failed to fulfill their high hopes. His primary contribution, achieved in spite of a severe economic depression, was to rekindle national interest in the orderly development of natural resources. During his administration the era of executive laxity ended. In his hands, the presidency once more became a constructive force in the campaign to conserve public resources. Hoover prepared the way for some of the dramatic conservation successes of Franklin Roosevelt by renewing the image of the President as a conservation leader. . . .

Science had become increasingly important in the federal establishment during the 'twenties. Following the budgetary cut-backs of the post-World War I years, Congress showed a willingness to underwrite federal research programs on a greatly expanded basis. Influenced by the example of private industry, the lawmakers found scientific research increasingly respectable.

By the end of Hoover's administration federally supported scientific and technologic research had become more important than ever before. Capitalizing on the generosity of Congress, the conservation bureaus accumulated a large amount of valuable resource data. Soil erosion research progressed so rapidly, for example, that by 1933 Hugh Bennett had the scientific information on which to build his Soil Conservation Service. The Bureau of Fisheries, undertaking a wide range of scientific projects, greatly enlarged its knowledge of the life habits of fishes and made significant advances in the study of fish diseases. The Bureau of Mines perfected important new techniques of mineral extraction and refining, achieving striking technological successes. The Forest Service officially embraced science as the essential preliminary to policy-making. Its nation-wide timber survey, its forest products research, and its studies of forest management improved prospects for increased timber production and decreased timber waste. Even the Army Engineers rose to scientific heights with their excellent investigations of American river basins. By 1933 the federal conservation bureaus had collected the body of data which served as the scientific basis for New Deal resource planning. During the late 1920s government scientists were able to institutionalize a powerful reliance on scientific research. The example of the conservation agencies added impetus to the trend which, in the 1930s, saw research itself win recognition as a national resource. Considerably before the second Roosevelt entered the White House, science and technology had become dominant in resource decisions at the bureau level.

The acceptance of the principle of multiple-purpose resource planning went hand in hand with increased federal reliance on science. The logical use of resource data was developmental planning. As the prestige of research agencies mounted, and as research findings proved more and more valuable in conserving resources, Congress began to lean in the direction of the multiple-purpose approach. In matters of water development, the idea of watershed or river basin planning gained surprisingly wide acceptance. In agriculture, forestry, and soil conservation the concept of planned land utilization became progressively more important. By the time of the New Deal, resource planning had clearly become respectable. Agriculturists had already begun to think in terms of removing farmers from submarginal lands by a "resettlement" process. Congress had already committed itself to the multiple-purpose development of the Muscle Shoals region. Consequently, the Resettlement Administration and the Tennessee Valley Authority followed naturally from pressures which began building before the advent of the New Deal.

The aesthetic conservationists, whom Pinchot had deplored as "nature lovers," gained both strength and prestige during the 1920s. As the National Park Service coalesced and expanded, it furnished the organizational focus for an aesthetic renaissance and for a resurgence of preservationism. Long ignored in national conservation policy, wildlife protection and the preservation of natural beauty became popular causes. Challenging the utilitarians openly and aggressively, aesthetic conservationists forced their powerful opponents to recognize the desirability of protecting certain forms of animal life and to acknowledge the necessity for preserving unique areas of natural beauty. On the rise throughout the decade, "nature lovers" won equality within conservation ranks and received important support at the federal level.

In spite of occasional lapses in federal leadership, the 1920s were productive years in the conservation of natural resources. Stimulated by a heterogeneous group of conservationists, politicians, and resource administrators, the federal government led the way to important conservation achievement. Nation-wide forest fire protection became a reality. Federal soil conservation work began. The Boulder Canyon project, first federally sponsored large-scale multiple-purpose river basin development, won authorization. Giant flood control programs for the Mississippi Valley and other rivers took form. An integrated system of inland waterways intersected the great central section of the United States. The generation of hydroelectric power for the first time received careful consideration in resource planning. A network of migratory bird sanctuaries materialized. The national parks became a great American institution, preserving magnificent natural scenes for the edification of future generations. Left without a dynamic national conservation leader throughout most of the 'twenties, the conservation bureaus carried on unobtrusively and, in general, effectively. They laid foundations for subsequent New Deal conservation achievements.

Congress, too, chartered an independent course. Moving largely against the wishes of the Republican chief executives, the federal legislature had by 1933 anticipated the direction of much New Deal conservation policy. Contrary to widely held opinion, the national conservation program did not deteriorate in the 1920s. It expanded and matured.

20

The Tennessee Valley Authority

David Lilienthal (1944)

At Muscle Shoals, Alabama, the Tennessee River used to plunge through a major rapid. During World War I the government made plans to harness its power. Funds ran out, however, before the work was finished. In 1921 Henry Ford offered to purchase the uncompleted project. Sensing that acquisition by Ford would eliminate the possibility of a multipurpose, public development of the Tennessee watershed, Senator George W. Norris of Nebraska headed the successful fight to block the sale. But Norris could not persuade the Republican administrations of the 1920s to undertake something that seemed socialistic to them. Yet in 1928 the giant Boulder (later Hoover) Dam on the lower Colorado River was authorized and a more favorable political climate was created for federal resource development. On May 18, 1933, President Franklin D. Roosevelt signed Norris's bill establishing the Tennessee Valley Authority, and in the next decade New Deal planners and engineers constructed in the valley the kind of project about which Progressive conservationists had dreamed. The environment of an entire region was reconstructed as a unit in the public interest, and TVA became a byword for regional planning throughout the world.

David Lilienthal was one of the initial directors of TVA. His statement following captures the enthusiasm and confidence that caught up many of those associated with the project. But conservation on this scale involved many difficult problems. The answers Lilienthal gives must not be accepted uncritically. Needing special scrutiny is his contention that federal experts can institute their plans without coercing the people involved.

A new chapter in American public policy was written when Congress in May of 1933 passed the law creating the TVA. For the first time since the trees fell before the settlers' ax, America set out to command nature not by defying her, as in that wasteful past, but by understanding and acting upon her first law—the oneness of men and natural resources, the unity that binds together land, streams, forests, minerals, farming, industry, mankind. . . .

The message of President Roosevelt urging approval of the Norris bill (which became a law with his signature on May 18, 1933) boldly proposed a new and fundamental change in the development of our country's resources. The words of the President's message were not only eloquent; there was in them a creativeness and an insight born of his New York State experience in establishing regional planning as a political reality. That understanding was matured at his Georgia home, in long days of thinking of the problems of the South and its relation to the whole nation.

> It is clear [the message read] that the Muscle Shoals development is but a small part of the potential public usefulness of the entire Tennessee River. Such use, if envisioned in its entirety, transcends mere power development: it enters the wide fields of flood control, soil erosion, afforestation, elimination from agricultural use of marginal lands, and distribution and diversification of industry. In short, this power development of war days leads logically to national planning for a complete river watershed involving many states and the future lives and welfare of millions. It touches and gives life to all forms of human concerns.

The President then suggested

> legislation to create a Tennessee Valley Authority—a corporation clothed with the power of government but possessed of the flexibility and initiative of a private enterprise. It should be charged with the broadest duty of planning for the proper use, conservation, and development of the natural resources of the Tennessee River drainage basin and its adjoining territory for the general social and economic welfare of the Nation. This authority should also be clothed with the necessary power to carry these plans into effect. Its duty should be the rehabilitation of the Muscle Shoals development and the co-ordination of it with the wider plan.
> Many hard lessons have taught us the human waste that results from lack of planning. Here and there a few wise cities and counties have looked ahead and planned. But our Nation has

"just grown." It is time to extend planning to a wider field, in
this instance comprehending in one great project many States
directly concerned with the basin of one of our greatest rivers.

The TVA Act was nothing inadvertent or impromptu. It was
rather the deliberate and well-considered creation of a new national
policy. For the first time in the history of the nation, the resources of
a river were not only to be "envisioned in their entirety"; they were
to be developed *in that unity with which nature herself regards her resources*—
the waters, the land, and the forests together, a "seamless web" . . .
of which one strand cannot be touched without affecting every other
strand for good or ill.

Under this new policy, the opportunity of creating wealth for the
people from the resources of their valley was to be faced as a single
problem. To help integrate the many parts of that problem into a
unified whole was to be the responsibility of one agency. The development of the Tennessee Valley's resources was not to be dissected into
separate bits that would fit into the jurisdictional pigeon holes into
which the instrumentalities of government had by custom become
divided. It was not conceded that at the hour of Creation the Lord had
divided and classified natural resources to conform to the organization
chart of the federal government. The particular and limited concerns
of private individuals or agencies in the development of this or that
resource were disregarded and rejected in favor of the principle of
unity. What God had made one, man was to develop as one.

"Envisioned in its entirety" this river, like every river in the
world, had many potential assets. It could yield hydro-electric power
for the comfort of the people in their homes, could promote prosperity
on their farms and foster the development of industry. But the same
river by the very same dams, if they were wisely designed, could be
made to provide a channel for navigation. The river could also be made
to provide fun for fishermen and fish for food, pleasure from boating
and swimming, a water supply for homes and factories. But the river
also presented an account of liabilities. It threatened the welfare of the
people by its recurrent floods; pollution from industrial wastes and
public sewage diminished its value as a source of water supply and for
recreation; its current carried to the sea the soil of the hills and fields
to be lost there to men forever.

To a single agency, the TVA, the planning for the greatest sum
total of these potentialities of the river for good and evil were en-
trusted. But the river was to be seen as part of the larger pattern of the

region, one asset of the many that in nature are interwoven: the land, the minerals, the waters, the forests—and all of these as one—in their relation to the lives of the valley's people. It was the total benefit to all that was to be the common goal and the new agency's responsibility.

That is not the way public resource development had heretofore been undertaken in this country. Congress in creating TVA broke with the past. No single agency had in this way ever been assigned the unitary task of developing a river so as to release the total benefit from its waters for the people. . . . And through the long years there has been a continuing disregard of nature's truth: that in any valley of the world what happens on the *river* is largely determined by what happens on the *land*—by the kind of crops that farmers plant and harvest, by the type of machines they use, by the number of trees they cut down. The full benefits of stream and of soil cannot be realized by the people if the water and the land are not developed in harmony. . . .

The farmers' new pastures and meadows themselves are reservoirs. If the changed farming practices now in use on many tens of thousands of Tennessee Valley farms were applied to all the agricultural area of our watershed (as some day I am confident they will be), the soil might absorb as much as a quarter of the customary 23-inch surface run-off of rain each year.

This is of course nothing new, nothing discovered by the TVA. That a river could offer many benefits and a variety of hazards, that its improvement through engineering structures is inseparable from the development and use of the land of the watershed, has been recognized for many years by scientists and engineers. For over a generation a distinguished line of conservationists had seen this truth and written and spoken of it with great force; not the least among these were President Theodore Roosevelt and Gifford Pinchot. And as a matter of fact almost any farmer, standing in his barn door while he watches a torrential rain beat upon his land and fill his creek, could see that much. The point is that knowledge of this inseparability of land and streams has only once, here on this river, been carried into our national *action*. And though the force of example has compelled the formation of interagency committees in some river basins to carry on conversations about "co-ordination," it is still true that on every other watershed Congress continues to turn our rivers over to engineers of one agency to develop while farm experts of other bureaus or agencies concern themselves with the land. Thus far it is only in the Valley of the Tennessee that Congress has directed that these resources be dealt with as a whole, not separately. . . .

The TVA's collaboration with business and industry is based upon the use of technical skills in the public interest, the skills of public and private experts. . . . One of the tasks of the administrator or executive in public or private affairs who is committed to democratic principles is to devise ways of bringing modern science and technical skills to the hand of the layman. And this is what TVA's work at the grass roots seeks to bring about. If the technical knowledge can be made to serve the individual in the daily decisions of his life, if it can be made to serve the common purpose of improving opportunity for human beings, that is an achievement of democracy in modern form and application.

This will require some drastic changes in the prevailing relations between experts and the people, both in industry and in government.

First of all, the experts and the people must be brought together. The technicians should live where the people they serve live. There are important exceptions, in highly specialized fields, but they do not affect the principle. An expert ought not to be remote from the problems the people face, and, although physical proximity will not guarantee closeness to the people, it will encourage it, whereas physical remoteness in distance definitely encourages, if it does not actually insure, remoteness in spirit and understanding, particularly in our country of vast area and great diversity in regional customs and natural conditions. . . .

The experts who live with the people's problems are better able to learn of the people's aspirations, what it is that the people want and what they would want if they had available a knowledge of the alternatives from which they could make a choice. The people will not trust the experts and give them their confidence until they are persuaded that technicians in business as well as in government service are not setting up their own standards of what is "good for people." If technicians, by living with people, come to understand what the people want rather than what the experts want, then people will more and more repose confidence in them and their counsel, protect them from partisan and political attacks, and even help them further their specialized professional and scientific interests.

And the physical presence of the expert, the fact that he has elected to live with the people and their problems, to share their physical and social circumstances, will be accepted by laymen as one kind of proof of the sincere devotion of the expert to the improvement of the everyday living of the people, rather than to his own specialized interests and concerns. The technician, whether he be a forester, a social welfare worker, a manager, a financial or farm or mineral expert, has no more excuse to pursue his expertness simply for the pleasure its refinements give him or to increase his own or his profession's repute, than a physician at the bedside or a general in the field would be justified in following a particular course for comparable reasons of a personal or professional character.

Technicians must learn that explaining "why" to the people is generally as important (in the terms in which I am speaking) as "what" is done. To induce the action of laymen, which is the only way resource development is possible, "why" is almost always the key. Experts and managers at central business or government headquarters, isolated and remote, tend to become impatient of making explanations to the people. From impatience it is a short step to a feeling of superiority, and then to irresponsibility or dictation. And irresponsibility or dictation to the people, whether by experts or politicians or business managers or public administrators, is a denial of democracy.

Effective planners must understand and believe in people. The average man is constantly in the mind of the effective planning expert. Planners, whether they are technicians or administrators, must recognize that they are not dealing with philosophical abstractions, or mere statistics or engineering data or legal principles, and that planning is not an end in itself.

In the last analysis, in democratic planning it is human beings we are concerned with. Unless plans show an understanding and recognition of the aspirations of men and women, they will fail. Those who lack human understanding and cannot share the emotions of men can hardly forward the objectives of realistic planning. . . . And it is because of this same conviction that the TVA has never attempted by arbitrary action to "eliminate" or to force reform upon those factors or institutions in the valley's life which are vigorously antagonistic to a plan for unified development. . . .

In the TVA the merging of planning and responsibility for the carrying out of those plans forces our technicians to make them a part of the main stream of living in the region or community; this is what breathes into plans the breath of life. For in the Tennessee Valley the expert cannot escape from the consequences of his planning, as he can and usually does where it is divorced from execution. This has a profound effect on the experts themselves. Where planning is conceived of in this way, the necessity that experts should be close to the problems with which they are dealing is evident.

In this one of the thousand valleys of the earth the physical setting of men's living has improved. Each day the change becomes more pronounced. The river is productive, the land more secure and fruitful, the forests are returning, factories and workshops and new houses and electric lines have put a different face upon the Tennessee Valley.

Is this really genuine improvement? Has it enhanced the quality of human existence? Are men's lives richer, fuller, more "human" as a result of such changes in our physical surroundings? To most people, I am sure, the answer is in the clear affirmative. But, in appraising the meaning of this valley's experience, the doubts on this score can by no means be ignored, nor dealt with out of hand; people not only raise such questions but answer them differently from the way most of us would answer them.

There are those who believe that material progress does not and cannot produce good, and may indeed stand as a barrier to it. To those, and there are many who hold such belief, mechanical progress, technology, the machine, far from improving the lot of men are actually seen as a source of debasement and condemned as "materialism."

The whole theme and thesis of this book challenges these ideas and the philosophy upon which they rest. I do not, of course, believe that when men change their physical environment they are inevitably happier or better. The machine that frees a man's back of drudgery does not thereby make his spirit free. Technology has made us more productive, but it does not necessarily enrich our lives. Engineers can build us great dams, but only great people make a valley great. There is no technology of goodness. Men must make themselves spiritually free.

But because these changes in physical environment in the valley do not in and of themselves make men happier, more generous, kinder, it does not follow that they have no relation to our spiritual life.

We have a choice. There is the important fact. Men are not powerless; they have it in their hands to use the machine to augment the dignity of human existence. True, they may have so long denied themselves the use of that power to decide, which is theirs, may so long have meekly accepted the dictation of bosses of one stripe or another or the ministrations of benevolent nursemaids, that the muscles of democratic choice have atrophied. But that strength is always latent; history has shown how quickly it revives. How we shall *use* physical betterment—that decision is ours to make. We are not carried irresistibly by forces beyond our control, whether they are given some mystic term or described as the "laws of economics." We are not inert objects on a wave of the future. . . .

Whether happiness or unhappiness, freedom or slavery, in short whether good or evil results from an improved environment depends largely upon how the change has been brought about, upon the methods by which the physical results have been reached, and in what spirit and for what purpose the fruits of that change are used. Because a higher standard of living, a greater productiveness and a command over nature are not good in and of themselves does not mean that we cannot make good of them, that they cannot be a source of inner strength.

. . . In this one valley (in some ways the world in microcosm) it has been demonstrated that methods can be developed—methods I have described as grass-roots democracy—which do create an opportunity for greater happiness and deeper experience, for freedom, in the very course of technical progress. Indeed this valley even in the brief span of a decade, supports a conviction that when the use of technology has a moral purpose and when its methods are thoroughly democratic, far from forcing the surrender of individual freedom and the things of the spirit to the machine, the machine can be made to promote those very ends. . . .

We have a long way yet to go in the valley. There are many factories yet to be built, in an area with such great potential wealth and with less than its economic share of the nation's industry and manufacturing. There are many new jobs to be created by the laboratories and businessmen out of the region's dormant resources. There are millions of acres yet to be restored to full productiveness. . . . There are more trees to plant, houses, schools, roads, and hospitals to build. Many new skills have been learned—among farmers, industrial workers in the new factories, the tens of thousands of men and women who have added to their skills in the course of their work for the TVA—but lack of training is still a heavy handicap to be overcome. The task is barely begun—but the Tennessee Valley is certainly on its way.

Democracy is on the march in this valley. Not only because of the physical changes or the figures of increased income and economic activity. My faith in this as a region with a great future is built most of all upon the great capacities and the spirit of the people. . . .

Here in the valley where I have been writing this statement of faith, the people know the job of our time can be done, for they have read the signs and reaped the first token harvest. They know it can be done, not only *for* the people but *by* the people.

21

Soil

Hugh Hammond Bennett (1939)

Soil was the first natural resource in North America to experience the effects of exploitation. Fields "wore out" while still being cleared of trees and stumps. But, with the exception of a few enlightened landowners like Thomas Jefferson, Americans remained unconcerned. Couldn't fresh land be found over the next ridge to the west? Hugh H. Bennett, the father of soil conservation, was one of the first to realize that even if it could it was inviting national disaster to permit the agricultural capacity of the older regions to be destroyed. The son of a North Carolina farmer, Bennett made an early acquaintance with exhausted and eroded land. In 1903 he joined the federal Bureau of Soils and started an investigation of soil conditions in the South. For the next quarter century Bennett crusaded for soil conservation without much success. But in the late 1920s, largely in response to Bennett's incessant urgings, the federal government instituted a program of erosion research. As the Great Depression staggered the country, Bennett continued to press for action and received important assistance from the spectacular dust storms of the early 1930s that darkened skies across half the nation. His efforts were rewarded in 1933 when the Civilian Conservation Corps (Selection 22) made erosion control one of its primary tasks. The establishment of the U.S. Soil Conservation Service in 1935 marked a major victory. With Bennett at its head, the service quickly launched several hundred demonstration projects and encouraged the states to form soil conservation districts.

In fifteen decades, Americans have transformed a wilderness into a mighty nation. In all the history of the world, no people ever built so fast and yet so well. This will be a land of liberty, they said in the beginning, and as they hacked the forest, drove their ploughshares deep into the earth, and spread their herds across the ranges, they sang

From *Soil Conservation* by Hugh Hammond Bennett, pp. v–vii, 1–3, 5–6, 8–9, 11–15. Copyright 1939 by McGraw-Hill, Inc., New York. Used by permission of McGraw-Hill Book Company.

of the land of the free that they were making. All that they finally built upon this continent is founded in that faith—that here there would be opportunity and independence and security for any man.

Those things are the power and the hope of this democracy. And they have sprung, very largely, from the goodness of our land, its capacity to produce rewardingly. Yet with astonishing improvidence, Americans have plundered the resource that made it possible to realize their dream.

Moving across this country in the greatest march of occupation ever known, they have exploited and abused this soil. As a result, our vital land supply has been steadily sapped by the heavy drain of soil erosion.

Since the first crude plow uprooted the first square foot of sod, and since man's axe first bit into virgin forest, erosion of the soil has been a problem. It is as old as history. Down through the ages it has influenced the lives of men and the destinies of nations and civilizations. In the United States today, no problem is more urgent.

Millions of acres of our land are ruined, other millions of acres already have been harmed. And not mere soil is going down the slopes, down the rivers, down to the wastes of the oceans. Opportunity, security, the chance for a man to make a living from the land—these are going too. It is to preserve them—to sustain a rewarding rural life as a bulwark of this nation, that we must defend the soil.

This nation is still producing bountiful crops. But many thousands of farmers already feel the pinch of erosion. Tens of thousands of them are finding it increasingly difficult to eke out a living on eroded land almost regardless of agricultural prices.

In other words, even in this young nation, pressure on the land already has become acute in many localities. Many areas have been damaged to such an extent by erosion that not enough productive soil is left for the present population. In Puerto Rico, portions of the Southern Piedmont, and the Rio Grande Valley, for example, erosion already has crowded many people off the land and brought others to the level of precarious subsistence farming. Some of this land can be stabilized, and some severely impoverished areas can be improved, but many land users must seek better soil elsewhere if they are to remain in the business of farming or ranching. Today the nation has an abundance of land, but not enough *good* land. Probably, if there had not been so much good land in the beginning, there would not have developed the early idea that the productive soil of America was limitless and inexhaustible. This erroneous appraisal of the land resource, passed along as a tradition, accounts for much of our costly steep-land tillage, overgrazing, and failure to defend vulnerable soil from the ravage of erosion. . . .

A permanent agriculture, then, is possible, even where the land is highly vulnerable to erosion, when people are willing to pay the price of protecting it. Where the price has not been paid, civilizations have disintegrated and disappeared. If necessary for survival, the American people undoubtedly would bench-terrace all their tilled land, as did the Incas, but it would be done at an undreamed of cost. Fortunately, American agriculture is now in a stage where heavy costs may be avoided by consistently working with, rather than against, natural forces, and by provident action based on a thorough diagnosis of the present problems of land use.

All our experience has demonstrated that erosion can be controlled in a practical way. The need is for forthright, determined, nation-wide action. Today's necessity for public action is the outgrowth of yesterday's failure to look more carefully to our land. Foresight in the last century, during our march of agricultural occupation, would have produced a different result. Today we are simply retracing our steps across this land in a march of agricultural conservation. "Soil Conservation" is primarily concerned with this second march. . . .

The earliest settlers arriving on the North American continent found a land richly endowed by nature and virtually unexploited by man. . . .

Into this virgin land the eager colonists entered with energy and enthusiasm. They began a transformation of the earth's surface that is probably without parallel in the history of the world. The occupation of the continent was accomplished not through steady infiltration of population into undeveloped regions but rather through a remarkably rapid advance over a wide front by farmers, stockmen, prospectors, miners, trappers, loggers, explorers, and adventurers. Along the line of advance, there was little thought of conservation or of depleting resources. With a country of immense potential wealth beckoning for development, it is small wonder that the emphasis lay, unconsciously, on speedy exploitation. . . .

Both the march of land occupation and the ensuing national development were accompanied . . . by a prodigious wastage of the resources with which nature originally stocked the land. The white inhabitants of this country, in their "conquest of the wilderness" and their "subjugation of the West," piled up a record of heedless destruction that nearly staggers the imagination. Slopes once clothed with mighty forests now lie bare and stark. Formerly rich lands are riddled with gullies. Level plains country that once supported lush stands of native "short" grasses is overgrown with weeds or covered with shifting sands left in the wake of dust storms.

What caused this tragic transformation? What happened to the bountiful land that inspired early explorers to enthusiastic comment and rhapsodic description? The answer lies largely in a false philosophy of plenty, a myth of inexhaustibility, which prevailed generally for many years and persists, in some quarters, even at the present time.

Yet in the time of our forefathers this was a normal, perhaps an inevitable, reaction to environmental conditions. Nearly everywhere the early settlers faced rich farm and grazing lands . . . which stretched away as far as the eye could see. There was every reason to conclude that the agricultural domain was limitless and inexhaustible. Free land extended to the far horizons . . . [and consequently] much of the land was abused, mined, and ravaged. In the turmoil of national growth, abundant resources were reduced to a state of impoverishment or near-extinction. Buffaloes were slaughtered by the thousands, merely for their hides. Trappers took their harvest of pelts without restriction or restraint. Protective forests were cut from sloping hillsides and entire watersheds; immense areas of grassland were broken or bared by the onrushing settlers with their plows and their livestock. Minerals were extracted, and their wealth dissipated in a surge of exploitation.

The story of the passenger pigeon is characteristic. The last of these birds died in a Cincinnati zoo in September, 1914. Ornithologists say that once this species was one of the most abundant game birds ever known in any country. Their flights frequently darkened the skies; the branches of trees are said to have been broken off by the very weight of their numbers settling to roost. Yet within a few generations, the legions of this species have been effaced from the earth. Should man dwell upon this planet for millions of years, he would never behold another passenger pigeon.

In like manner, other valuable resources have been exhausted and continue to be exhausted. What the final result will be in terms of the national economy no one can predict with accuracy. One fact, however, is eminently clear. The potential wealth and living standard of this nation, or of any nation, depend ultimately on its store of natural resources. If, through carelessness and neglect, these resources are wasted beyond a certain point, the whole structure of national achievement must be impaired.

Out of the long list of nature's gifts to man, none is perhaps so utterly essential to human life as soil. And topsoil is the most vital part of soil (made up of topsoil plus the layers beneath). Lying at an average depth of about 7 or 8 inches over the face of the land, this upper layer of the soil is the principal feeding zone of the plants, which provide food for human or livestock consumption, fiber for clothing, and timber for shelter. Soil constitutes the physical basis of our agricultural enterprise; it is a *sine qua non* in the production of practically all food (except fish), of all fiber (without exception), and of all wood (without exception). Under many conditions, however, it is the most unstable of all major natural resources. . . .

Where the land surface is bared of protective vegetation—as it must be under cultivation—the soil is exposed directly to the abrasive action of the elements. Transposition processes of an extremely rapid order are set in motion. Stripped of the protective cover that normally anchors soil to the landscape, this indispensable material frequently is moved a thousand times faster than under natural conditions. This accelerated phenomenon of soil removal is known as *soil erosion.* Unless steps are taken to check its progress, it becomes the most potent single factor in the deterioration of productive land. . . .

Conservative estimates indicate that the annual monetary cost of erosion in the United States amounts to at least $400,000,000 in terms of lost productivity alone. This loss already totals probably not less than $10,000,000,000; and unless erosion is effectively curbed, the probable future costs will be equally gigantic. . . . To this would have to be added huge losses due to (1) clogging of great reservoirs and shoaling of stream channels with the sedimentary products of erosion; (2) the abandonment of irrigated areas dependent on reservoirs; (3) the virtual abandonment of large agricultural sections; (4) the economic devastation of large western areas dependent on grazing; and (5) the disintegration of rural communities and transfer of large farm populations to relief rolls or to new means of livelihood. . . .

. . . The plain truth is that Americans, as a people, have never learned to love the land and to regard it as an enduring resource. They have seen it only as a field for exploitation and a source of immediate financial return. In the days of expanding frontier it was customary, when land was washed, cropped, or grazed to a condition of impoverishment, to pull up stakes and move on to fresher fields and greener pastures. Today such easy migration is no longer possible. The country has expanded to the full limits of its boundaries, and erosion is causing a progressive shrinkage of the tillable area. The early frontier psychology of land treatment must be abandoned once and for all. In its place a new frontier has appeared. A restricted area of land—an indispensable area, subject to still further restriction by the inroads of uncontrolled erosion—has taken the place of a former abundance of land. Now, man must move rapidly over this diminishing area in order to clear away not trees or prairie grasses but old methods of wasteful land use and substitute therefore new methods of conservation that will provide security for the soil and for those living by the soil.

Conservation of the soil, in a national sense, requires the adoption of sound land-use principles and practices by agriculture as a whole. The attainment of this objective involves the widespread use of physical measures of land defense and the adjustment of certain economic and social forces tending to encourage exploitation of the soil. . . .

The responsibility for such a national program falls upon both the nation and the individual. National responsibility involves the protection of society's interest in a natural resource of vital importance to the whole people. Government functions properly in discharging this responsibility. Equally strong, however, is the interest of the individual in the land that he owns. National action may be led and aided by government, but the soil must be conserved ultimately by those who till the land and live by its products. Without a widespread recognition of this latter responsibility, any governmental program of soil conservation must be doomed to eventual futility and failure.

22

The Civilian Conservation Corps

Franklin D. Roosevelt (1933); Robert Fechner (1936)

The Great Depression seemed to awaken Americans to the need for more effort in maintaining the physical basis of prosperity. Not since 1908 had conservation been as important a public issue as it was in the early New Deal. Within two months at the beginning of Franklin D. Roosevelt's first administration in 1933, Congress passed two of the best-known laws in American conservation history, creating the Civilian Conservation Corps and the Tennessee Valley Authority (Selection 20). Designed to engage unemployed young men in productive work and to revive local economies, the CCC also reflected national determination to repair some of the damage three centuries of exploitation and neglect had wrought on the American environment. Organized in several thousand "camps," the two million participants in the CCC between 1933 and 1942 engaged in a host of activities on behalf of the land. Moreover, the widespread, nonpartisan sympathy they generated helped create a lasting mood favorable to conservation. In the documents that follow President Roosevelt calls upon Congress to establish the CCC in 1933 and Robert Fechner, CCC director, discusses the accomplishments of his organization after three years.

The White House, *March 21, 1933*

To the Congress: It is essential to our recovery program that measures immediately be enacted aimed at unemployment relief. . . .

. . . I propose to create a civilian conservation corps to be used in simple work, not interfering with normal employment, and confining itself to forestry, the prevention of soil erosion, flood control and similar projects. I call your attention to the fact that this type of work is of definite, practical value, not only through the prevention of great present financial loss, but also as a means of creating future national

Edgar B. Nixon, ed., *Franklin D. Roosevelt and Conservation, 1911–1945,* I (2 vols., New York, 1957), 143–144, 591–593. Reprinted by permission of National Archives and Records Service, Franklin D. Roosevelt Library.

wealth. This is brought home by the news we are receiving today of vast damage caused by floods on the Ohio and other rivers.

Control and direction of such work can be carried on by existing machinery of the departments of Labor, Agriculture, War and Interior.

I estimate that 250,000 men can be given temporary employment by early summer if you give me authority to proceed within the next two weeks.

I ask no new funds at this time. The use of unobligated funds, now appropriated for public works, will be sufficient for several months.

This enterprise is an established part of our national policy. It will conserve our precious natural resources. It will pay dividends to the present and future generations. It will make improvements in national and state domains which have been largely forgotten in the past few years of industrial development.

More important, however, than the material gains will be the moral and spiritual value of such work. The overwhelming majority of unemployed Americans, who are now walking the streets and receiving private or public relief, would infinitely prefer to work. We can take a vast army of these unemployed out into healthful surroundings. We can eliminate to some extent at least the threat that enforced idleness brings to spiritual and moral stability. It is not a panacea for all the unemployment but it is an essential step in this emergency. I ask its adoption.

Washington, D.C., *October 24, 1936*

Dear Mr. President: I am sure you will be interested in the results of a recent survey undertaken at my request by the Department of Agriculture and the Department of the Interior to determine the future work opportunities available in our forests, parks, and on other lands for a permanent Civilian Conservation Corps. These departments have reported, following an extensive inquiry covering all sections of the nation, that there is sufficient urgently needed conservation work still to be done to furnish profitable employment for a Civilian Conservation Corps of between 300,000 and 350,000 for many years to come. The departments advised me that notwithstanding the tremendous amount of reforestation, erosion control, and other conservation work accomplished by the CCC during the last three and a half years, much work remains to be completed before our forests, parks, agricultural lands, and grazing areas will have been afforded adequate protection and development.

The survey indicated that the annual work load ahead for a permanent CCC will increase rather than diminish during the next few years. This will be due largely to the gradual increase in national forest holdings, the acquisition of new forest lands by the states . . . the expansion of state-owned parks, a growing appreciation of the need for erosion control operations on agricultural lands, and an expanded demand for CCC manpower on flood control projects, for wildlife conservation and in the rehabilitation of grazing lands, irrigation systems and drainage projects. Available and planned work for the next several years, as set forth in the survey, may be broadly divided into such classifications as forestry, park development, erosion control, stream, pond and lake improvement, flood control, water conservation, range development, reclamation, wildlife protection, rehabilitation of drainage projects and other types of projects having as their objective the further preservation, improvement and increase in our natural resources.

Our records show that during the last few years the Civilian Conservation Corps has launched the nation on its first broad-gage and effective conservation program. The Civilian Conservation Corps has added enormous tangible values to the country's physical resources through the construction of roads, communication lines and fire detection facilities; through control of insect and disease pests, fire and rodents that injure and destroy natural resources on federal, state and privately owned lands; through the development of new recreational opportunities; through protection of forests, watersheds, agricultural lands and communities against flood and soil erosion; through projects conserving water and improving land drainage; through the protection and increased propagation of game animals and birds; through the planting of nearly one billion trees; through improving range conditions for livestock; through aid to land reclamation projects; through physical improvements to Indian, military and naval reservations; and through many other types of projects of public interest and utility which are noncompetitive with private industry.

The reports from cooperating federal and state agencies indicate that probably the CCC's greatest contribution to conservation has come in the nation-wide defense of our forests and parks from such destructive enemies as forest fires, insects and tree attacking diseases and the protection of agricultural lands from soil wastage due to water and wind erosion. . . .

The past three and one-half years have shown that the continuance of the CCC will be of permanent value to the nation. Public attention has been focused on the need for all types of conservation. The need has long been recognized by conservationists, but now with floods, dust storms and widespread erosion, public insistence on corrective conservation measures is much more widespread. This is particularly true, due to the fact that the effectiveness of corrective measures has been repeatedly demonstrated by CCC accomplishments. A permanent work force, which can carry out the programs of the various agencies interested in the wise use of natural resources, will enable the United States to obtain greater benefits from our heritage of natural resources which has depreciated through carelessness and misuse.

As long as there are young men eager to work, yet idle through no fault of their own, the CCC can continue to be an effective part of our national policy.

I am calling the past record of the CCC, as well as the survey showing future work possibilities for such an organization, to your attention at this time because I desire to express my conviction that steps may well be taken to make the CCC a permanent organization. I, therefore, recommend that this program of conservation work among men and natural resources be adopted as a permanent part of our national governmental activities, the size and extent of the work to be governed by the dual factors of employment conditions among young men and the urgency of the conservation work to be accomplished.

23

From Conservation to Environmentalism

Samuel P. Hays (1987)

Samuel P. Hays's earlier book (Selection 17) interpreted the conservation movement of the Progressive era. Here he turns to the transition from "conservation" concerns to those that could be called "environmental." His focus is on the years immediately after World War II, and his analysis informs many of the selections in this part as well as the next one. For example, the two selections that follow contain the ideas of people who could be thought of as harbingers of the perspective Hays describes.

Accounts of the rise of environmentalism frequently have emphasized its roots in the conservation movement of the early twentieth century. But environmental differed markedly from conservation affairs. The conservation movement was an effort on the part of leaders in science, technology, and government to bring about more efficient development of physical resources. The environmental movement, on the other hand, was far more widespread and popular, involving public values that stressed the quality of human experience and hence of the human environment. Conservation was an aspect of the history of production that stressed efficiency, whereas environment was a part of the history of consumption that stressed new aspects of the American standard of living.

Environmental objectives arose out of deep-seated changes in preferences and values associated with the massive social and economic transformation in the decades after 1945. Conservation had

Samuel P. Hays, *Beauty, Health and Permanence: Environmental Politics in the United States, 1955–1985,* (Cambridge: Cambridge University Press, 1987), 13–15, 17–24, 26–28, 34–35. Reprinted by permission of Cambridge University Press. Footnotes in the original have been omitted.

stirred technical and political leaders and then worked its way down from the top of the political order, but environmental concerns arose later from a broader base and worked their way from the middle levels of society outward, constantly to press upon a reluctant leadership. Many of the tendencies in efficient management of material resources originating in the conservation era came into sharp conflict with newer environmental objectives. The two sets of values were continually at loggerheads. . . .

The first clear notion about conservation as more efficient resource use developed in connection with water in the West. As settlement proceeded, water limited farming and urban development. It was not so much that water was scarce as that rainfall came unevenly throughout the year and winter snow melted quickly in the spring. Such patterns did not conform to the seasonal uses of agriculture on the more sustained needs of city dwellers.

How to conserve water? The initial thought was to construct reservoirs to hold rain and snowmelt for use later in the year. Cities began to build storage for urban water supply much as in the East. But for irrigated farmland larger engineering works were needed. The Newlands Act, which Congress passed in 1902, provided for a reclamation fund from the proceeds of the sale of western public lands that would finance irrigation works. By World War II vast projects included plans for a series of dams on the Missouri and the Colorado as well as other western rivers.

Schemes to conserve water for irrigation soon came to encompass more extensive notions about the construction of large engineering works to control the flow of entire river basins. Hydroelectric power was built into irrigation dams, fulfilling two purposes at once. In the East the idea arose that floods could be controlled by means of reservoirs to hold back the flow of snowmelt or excessive rainfall; the water could then be released later when river levels had subsided. The flow could also facilitate navigation. By 1926 Congress had granted the U.S. Army Corps of Engineers, which had long been responsible for navigation works, authority to conduct full-scale studies for flood-control projects throughout the nation, and by the 1930s that agency was ready to proceed with construction. The most ambitious example of "multipurpose" river development was the Tennessee Valley Authority, established in 1933, which constructed engineering works to control the entire flow of the Tennessee and Cumberland rivers.

The spirit of intensive management, born in these projects, was extended to rivers in other sections of the nation. As projects of lesser cost and scale were completed, the agencies moved on to those of greater and more extensive water transfer. Although the initial projects emphasized the main stems of the larger rivers, the drive to control water expanded steadily into the headwaters to include the flow of entire river basins. By the end of World War II, multipurpose river development was extending its influence to wider and wider realms of action. And it ran headlong into conflict with newer environmental interests that began to emphasize the importance of free-flowing streams unmodified by large engineering structures. . . .

The spirit of large-scale management for efficient resource development also pervaded the early forestry movement. Concern for the depletion of the nation's wood supplies grew steadily in the last quarter of the nineteenth century. Cutover lands in the East, which took on the appearance of wastelands, deeply influenced public opinion. And their social impact was massive. Towns, jobs, and governments based on the lumber industry boomed, but when the supply of timber was gone they collapsed. Local governments found their tax base depleted as lands were abandoned and became tax delinquent. All this provided fertile ground for the concept of a balance between cutting and growth that would provide a continuous supply of timber and a reliable foundation for local economies. . . .

The major theme of forest management was "scientific forestry." This involved reforestation of cutover lands, protection from fire, and a balance of annual cut with annual growth, to produce a continuous supply of wood—known as sustained-yield forest management. Over the years foresters improved techniques for measuring yield and cut and for controlling both through a regulatory process that shaped more precisely the flow of growth and harvest.

The economic value of wood production was emphasized above all else. . . . This spirit continued over the years through the more intensive application of science, technology, and capital to the production of more wood per acre. But this direction also ran counter to new values that were emerging in the American public as the meaning of forestland began to change. Forests were increasingly viewed as environments, aesthetic resources that provided amenities and enhanced daily life, rather than as simply sources of commodities. . . .

Water and forest conservation emerged in the late nineteenth century and evolved steadily throughout the first half of the twentieth, but interest in soil conservation developed at a later time. In the 1920s a number of writers warned of the severe long-term problems confronting the nation because of the persistent erosion of productive croplands. Soil that had taken thousands of years to build up now was being lost by destructive farming practices. The future food supply was seriously threatened. . . .

In the 1950s soil conservation took a new twist and emphasized the enhancement of land for greater productivity. Cooperating farm districts were given funds to construct reservoirs on smaller upland streams to provide benefits similar to those of large reservoirs built by the Corps of Engineers. Channelization was promoted: the straightening of streams either to enhance flow through flood-prone areas or to drain swampland so as to make it available for sustained farming.

These new turns in policy shifted the SCS [Soil Conservation Service] program from preventing soil erosion to developing farmland and related water resources, and helped to identify the spirit of the SCS as part of earlier water and forest conservation—efficiency in resource production. The new policies also triggered extensive conflicts with emerging environmental concerns. Those who considered streams valuable for their biological merits and the aesthetic experience they offered, rather than for development, found the SCS watershed program as much a threat to their objectives as were the projects of the Corps of Engineers. The new departure set the stage for a series of new confrontations between the older conservation movement and newer environmental objectives. . . .

If game and fish management was a matter of maintaining a balance between supply and demand, the growing demand for recreational opportunities would make the prime objective an increase in supply. Populations of wild animals such as the white-tailed deer and the wild turkey were restored above their former numbers. . . .

In these programs wildlife was seen as a commodity. This view brought the wildlife conservation movement into close harmony with water-, forest-, and soil-conservation efforts in a common interest to use science and technology under centralized direction for natural resource management. Yet the concern for game and fish habitat also led to conflicts with water, forest, and soil conservation. Dam construction and channelization destroyed habitat; many forest practices that placed primary emphasis on wood production reduced the extent and quality of habitat; intensive farming destroyed areas available for wildlife. The stress on habitat also brought those interested in fish and game into closer cooperation with a new breed of wildlife enthusiasts who emphasized appreciation of wildlife rather than hunting and fishing. Hence the wildlife movement arose out of a conservation background but also played an integral role in newer environmental affairs. . . .

In conservation, forests and waters were closely linked. As soil conservation and game management developed they became allied with both water and forest conservation in a shared set of attitudes. Together they emphasized the scientific management of physical commodities and brought together technical specialists for a common purpose. Departments of state government dealing with such affairs were commonly called departments of natural resources. And professional training at academic institutions evolved from an initial interest in forestry to a larger set of natural resource or conservation matters.

The management of natural resources often displayed a close kinship with the entire movement for scientific management that evolved in the twentieth century and pervaded both industry and government. It emphasized large-scale systems of organization and control and increasing output through more intensive input. Professional expertise played an important role in all four facets of conservation, with strong links among them and a sense of kinship with the wider community of technical professions as a whole. Their self-respect came to be firmly connected to the desire to maintain high professional standards in resource management.

Equally important was the evolution of a common political outlook among resource specialists that professionals should be left free from "political influence" to determine how resources should be managed and for what purpose. This shared sense of professionalism was itself a political stance, an assertion that those with special training and expertise should determine the course of affairs. From the management of commodity resources in water, forests, soils, and wildlife emerged not just a sense of direction that stressed maximum output of physical resources but also a view about who should make decisions and how they should be made.

The coming conflicts between conservation and environment were rooted in different objectives: efficiency in the development of material commodities or amenities to enhance the quality of life. In these earlier years the national-parks movement and leaders such as John Muir had provided important beginnings for the latter. After World War II extensive changes in human values gave these intangible natural values far greater influence. To them now was added the growing view that air and water, as well as land, constituted a valuable human environment.

The early conservation movement had generated the first stages in shaping a "commons," a public domain of public ownership for public use and the public ownership of fish and wildlife as resources not subject to private appropriation. This sense of jointly held resources became extended in the later years to the concept of air, land, and water as an environment. Their significance as common resources shifted from a primary focus on commodities to become also meaningful as amenities that could enhance the quality of life. . . .

The most widespread source of emerging environmental interest was the search for a better life associated with home, community, and leisure. A new emphasis on smaller families developed, allowing parents to invest their limited time and income in fewer children. Child rearing was now oriented toward a more extended period of childhood in order to nurture abilities. Parents sought to provide creative-arts instructions, summer camps, and family vacations so as to foster self-development. Within this context the phrase "environmental quality" would have considerable personal meaning.

It also had meaning for place of residence. Millions of urban Americans desired to live on the fringe of the city where life was less congested, the air cleaner, noise reduced, and there was less concentrated waste from manifold human activities. In the nineteenth century only the well-to-do could afford to live some distance from work. . . .

There was also the desire to obtain private lands in the countryside so as to enjoy nature not found in the city. In the 1960s and 1970s the market for vacation homesites boomed. Newspaper advertisements abounded with phrases that signaled the important values: "by a sparkling stream," "abundant wildlife," "near the edge of a forest road," "200 feet of lakefront," "on the edge of a state forest."

This pursuit of natural values by city dwellers led to a remarkable turnabout in the attitudes of Americans toward natural environments. These had long been thought of as unused wastelands that could be made valuable only if developed. But after World War II many such areas came to be thought of as valuable only if left in their natural condition. Forested land, once thought of by many as dark, forbidding, and sinister, a place to be avoided because of the dangers lurking within, now was highly esteemed.

Wetlands, formerly known as swamplands, fit only for draining so that they could become productive agricultural land, were valued as natural systems, undisturbed and undeveloped. Similar positive attitudes were expressed for the prairies of the Midwest, the swamps of the South, and the pine barrens of the East. For many years wild animals had been seen as a threat to farmers and others. Little concern had been shown for the sharp decline even in the deer population, let alone among the bear and bobcat. Yet by the 1960s and 1970s predators, as well as deer, small mammals, and wild turkey, had assumed a positive image for many Americans, and special measures were adopted to protect them and increase their numbers.

Close on the heels of these changes in attitude were new views about western deserts. The desert had long been thought of as a forbidding land where human habitation was impossible and travel was dangerous. . . . But by the late 1970s this had changed. The increased popularity of nature photography had brought home the desert to the American people as a place of wonder and beauty. By 1976 western deserts had been explored and identified by many Americans as lands that should be protected in their natural condition.

Ecological objectives—an emphasis on the workings of natural biological and geological systems and the pressures human actions placed on them—were [also an] . . . element of environmental concern. Whereas amenities involved an aesthetic response to the environment, and environmental health concerned a choice between cleaner and dirtier technologies within the built-up environment, ecological matters dealt with imbalances between developed and natural systems that had both current and long-term implications. These questions, therefore, involved ideas about permanence.

The term "ecology" had long referred to a branch of biology that emphasized study of the interaction of living organisms with their physical and biological environment. Popular ecology in the 1960s and 1970s went beyond that scientific meaning. One heard of the impact of people on "the ecology." Professional ecologists disdained this corruption of the word as they had used it. Popular use involved both a broad meaning, the functioning of the biological and geological world, and a narrower one, the disruption of natural processes by human action, as well as the notion that the two, natural systems and human stress, needed to be brought into a better balance.

The popular ecological perspective was reflected in the ecology centers that arose in urban areas. Initially these grew out of the recycling movement—the collection of paper, glass, and tin cans for reprocessing. These centers drew together people who wished to help solve the litter problem and thus to enhance the aesthetic quality of their communities. But soon the concept of recycling seemed to spill over into larger ideas about natural cycles, a traditional ecological theme, and to human action to foster such processes. Ecology centers often expanded their activities into community organic gardens, nutrition and food for better health, and changing life-styles to reduce the human load on natural resources and natural systems.

An ecological perspective grew from the popularization of knowledge about natural processes. These were ideas significant to the study of ecology, but selected and modified by popular experience rather than as a result of formal study. An increasing number of personal or media encounters with the natural world gave rise to widely shared ideas about the functioning of biological and geological systems and the relationship of human beings to them.

Even before World War II, the problem of deer overpopulation on the north rim of the Grand Canyon, or imbalances between the numbers of deer and food in the cutover forestlands of Pennsylvania, Michigan, Wisconsin, and Minnesota, had popularized knowledge about predator-prey and food-population relationships. Overgrazing by cattle and sheep on the western range sparked discussions in the media of the problem of stress in plant communities in which, through overuse, the more vulnerable plants gave way to the hardier, reducing the variety of species. This conveyed the ideas that species diversity had evolved in the process of natural succession, that the number and diversity of species were reduced under population pressures, and that the capacity of ecological systems to sustain human use without major changes were limited.

. . . Environmental and ecological values were an integral part of the continuous search for a better standard of living. They reflected changing attitudes about what constitutes a better life. The natural and the developed became intermingled as coordinated, mutually reinforcing aspects of the quality of living.

We could place these ideas about quality of life in a historical sequence of evolving levels of consumption. A century ago most consumption involved necessities, elementary needs in the areas of food, clothing, and shelter. As real incomes rose, so did standards of living, giving rise to a new stage of consumption in the form of conveniences, those material possessions, such as the automobile and indoor plumbing, that reduced the time and energy required for daily chores. After World War II, for an increasing share of the American people, these wants had been filled; discretionary income could now be spent for other goods and services beyond necessities and conveniences.

The search for environmental quality was an integral part of this rising standard of living. Environmental values were based not on one's role as a producer of goods and services but on consumption, the quality of home and leisure. Such environmental concerns were not prevalent at earlier times. But after World War II, rising levels of living led more people to desire qualitative experiences as well as material goods in their lives. In earlier times only the well-to-do could afford a summer at the seashore or a home in the suburbs, away from daily exposure to urban air pollution and congestion. By the mid-twentieth century similar desires were expressed by an increasing number of people so that the search for amenities became a normal expectation on the part of most Americans. . . .

Often these new qualitative consumer demands could be provided by the private market. One could buy a house in more pleasant surroundings, in the suburban fringe or the countryside. But many such amenities could not be purchased. The air surrounding the city was common property, incapable of being carved into pieces that could be bought and sold. The same was true for the water environment. Since the private economy could not supply these environmental amenities, there was increasing demand that public and private nonprofit institutions do so.

. . . The focus was on changing life-styles, those qualitative concerns associated with increased leisure time and a greater ability to use leisure time creatively and enjoyably.

24

The Planned Landscape

Benton MacKaye (1928)

Benton MacKaye took a leading role in refining the methods and the goals of American conservation in the direction of environmental quality. He was one of the first environmental engineers, a man who sensed that not just natural resources but the whole environment could be planned and managed in society's best interests. MacKaye's reading of Henry David Thoreau (Selection 5) and his acquaintance with the ideas of Aldo Leopold (Selection 27) and Lewis Mumford, a historian of the city, alerted him to the limitations of urbanization in the United States. His home in Shirley Center, Massachusetts, offered an excellent vantage point from which to observe the spread of megalopolis. In 1921 Mackaye published "An Appalachian Trail: A Project in Regional Planning" in the Journal of the American Institute of Architects. *He thought of the trail not just as a footpath along the crest of the mountains from Maine to Georgia but also as a kind of "indigenous" or natural alternative to the civilized environment. During the 1930s the TVA utilized Mac-Kaye's talents as a regional planner, but he still found time to help found the Wilderness Society in 1935.*

It takes more than towns and railroads and corn fields to make a nation and a pleasant land to live in. These are enough for the "material fact," but not for the "spiritual form." They are enough for a mechanical state of "civilization," but not for a living "culture." Man needs more than this to cover God's green earth if he would be a *soul.* He needs just one thing further. He needs it in his home and dooryard; he needs it within his community; he needs it throughout his country and his planet. It is the right kind of *environment.*

Benton MacKaye, *The New Exploration: A Philosophy of Regional Planning* (New York: Harcourt, Brace and Co., 1928), 29–30, 45, 50–51, 169–170, 178–181, 226–228. Reprinted by permission of the author.

Environment is to the would-be cultured man what air is to the animal—it is the breath of life. So far as outward matters go, environment is the basic ingredient of living as air is of existence.

Here, then, we have the fields of the old exploration and the new: the outward needs of man engaged merely in a material struggle, and those of cultured man. Pioneer man needs land as the tangible source of bodily existence; he needs the flow of waters to make that source effective; but above all, he needs air as the constant source and revivifier of his activity. Cultured man needs land and developed natural resources as the tangible source of bodily existence; he needs the flow of commodities to make that source effective; but first of all he needs a harmonious and related environment as the source of his true living.

These three needs of cultured man make three corresponding problems:

a. The conservation of natural resources.

b. The control of commodity-flow.

c. The development of environment.

The visualization of the potential workings of these three processes constitutes the new exploration—and regional planning.

The essentials of the old exploration were *actualities;* the essentials of the new exploration are *potentialities.* The old exploration described *that which is,* while the new exploration projects *that which can be.* The first was based on descriptive science; the second is based on applied science. The one was a recording of actual facts and of nature's laws; the other is a charting of possible facts lying within those laws. . . .

. . . The fundamental problem of regional engineering, comes down to the control and guidance of industrial migration, and control in such wise as to secure the objectives cited regarding resources, commodities, and environment. In this way may a *single engineering* achieve its application, and attain its final goal—"the making of the mold in which future generations shall live."

What approaches offer themselves in the stupendous task of charging the wilderness of civilization and creating the mold for a genuine culture? Well, they are legion, and a few illustrations have been given from present-day engineering practice. But there seem to be two major approaches to the subject. . . .

1. *The metropolitan world:* a framework of worldwide standardized civilization which forms itself around the traffic stream of modern industry and commerce.

2. *The indigenous world:* a quiltwork of varied cultures, each with its own environment of racial and regional setting. . . .

. . . On the Times Building [in New York City] (or on its counterpart, the Boston Custom House) we have at our feet the metropolitan world—the "passing streams of traffic" merged in conflux and pouring in from all corners of the land; and we have a glimpse only of the indigenous world—in the distant view of the Hudson Highlands (or of the summit of Mt. Monadnock [New Hampshire]). But when we go and climb this summit, then we have these "worlds" reversed: then we have at our feet the indigenous world; we have the traffic stream not in conflux or midway, but at its two extremes. We have on one hand the field or forest or resource from which the stream arises, and on the other hand we have the home community to which the stream is destined. But we have in this view a *glimpse* only of the metropolitan world—in the distant view of the factory chimney, the screaming locomotive, or the Boston Custom House. . . .

The indigenous world may be said to be *composed* of natural resources, and these may be divided into three great classes:

1. Material resources (soils, forests, metallic ores).
2. Energy resources (the mechanical energy resident in falling water, coal seams, and other natural elements).
3. Psychologic resources (the human psychologic energy, or happiness, resident in a natural setting or environment).

The term "natural resources," as we have used it in previous chapters, has referred to material resources and mechanical energy alone. These resources have been compared with the geographic element of "land": they form the tangible source of man's existence. The psychologic resources (environment) have been compared with the geographic element of "air." Environment, the contours of the landscape, the arrangement of its vegetation, the visible marks of man's efforts in clearings and fences and farms and gardens and cities as well as in wild forests and mountain areas—environment, in one or all of its many forms, is the pervasive source of man's true living. Raw material and mechanical energy relate to the means of life: environment, whether in natural or in humanized forms, relates to the objectives of life. Man (and civilization), considered as a "material fact," is concerned with the means of life: man (and civilization), considered as a "spiritual form," is concerned with the objectives of life, the pursuit of a higher estate in human development. Raw material and mechanical energy form the terrestrial basis of civilization as a material fact, while environment forms the terrestrial basis of civilization as a spiritual form. . . .

. . . Through such developments as the railroad in the [eighteen] sixties, and motor transportation and electric transmission of power, since the nineties, a series of sudden jumps has taken place in this country. The leisurely growth of an American indigenous culture, which promised so much before the Civil War, has been burked, or diverted into purely metropolitan interests and concerns.

This metropolitan invasion is, I believe, in the nature of an interruption, but whether it will amount actually to this or to our permanent undoing depends on what we are going to do about it. The attitude of the regional planner, as conceived in this particular Philosophy of Regional Planning, is to view this phenomenon as an interruption, to cope with it as a distinct intruder, and to proceed with the development of the indigenous America as something belonging to the future as well as to the past. The coming of the metropolitan invasion, overnight as it were, like a flood suddenly set loose from a thousand ruptured reservoirs, may be viewed as the emergent reason, the *occasion* if you please, for the dormant but awakening movement of regional planning and the New Exploration.

The "thousand ruptured reservoirs" refer to the great metropolitan centers (or the thousand and one centers large and small) which are scattered throughout the country. . . .

The flow of metropolitanism we have compared loosely with the flow of waters—but we must now be more precise: we must compare it with the flow of *flood waters*. Metropolitan development is the result of revolution—the industrial revolution. It has come upon us, in its potent form, within a generation. And its potence lies not so much in the particular thing it is as in the *suddenness* of its appearance. This fact is critical: it is critical as to our choice of means for coping with the general problem. One set of means is required for controlling the general normal flow issuing from the upland headwaters; but a different set of means is needed for handling the flow issuing from an upland reservoir which has suddenly broken down. . . .

. . . What manner of embankments (what "dams" and what "levees") can we construct "downstream" to hold our deluge in check? . . .

If left alone, the metropolitan deluge will flow out along the main highways (and the side highways) in the fashion described in the last chapter, distributing the population in a series of continuous strings, which together would make a metropolitan cobweb of the locality. In this way the area with its several villages would become engulfed by the metropolitan flood. What are the barriers and footholds supplied by nature in this locality for narrowing and checking the full workings of this cataclysm? What topographic features are there, and what common public ground, which could be developed as a series of "embankments"?

The outstanding topographic feature consists of the range of hills and mountains encircling the locality, together with the four ridges reaching toward the central city. This could be reserved as a common public ground, serving the double purpose of a public forest and a public playground. It might be called a "wilderness area." It would form a linear area, or belt, around and through the locality, well adapted for camping and primitive travel (by foot or horseback). Overnight, week-end, and vacation trips could be made from the central city and from the adjacent villages by way of a number of varied circuits. This series of open areas and ways would form a distinct realm: it would be a primeval realm (or near-primeval)—the opposite realm from the metropolitan. These open ways (along the crestlines) mark the lines for developing the primeval environment, while the motor ways mark the lines for extending the metropolitan environment. . . .

A system of open ways of this design would form a series of breaks in the metropolitan deluge: it would divide—or tend to divide—the flood waters of metropolitanism into separate "basins" and thereby tend to avert their complete and total confluence. This it would do in two ways—physically and psychologically. . . . [Q]uite as important perhaps as [the] physical control would be the opportunity provided by the open way for carrying out in practical fashion the latent if not evident desire, within a large body of the people, for experiencing the opposite mode of life from that provided for by the channels of metropolitan civilization. The motor way marks a belt of travel devoted to establishing a certain phase of civilization: the open way reveals a belt of travel dedicated to the development of a counter phase of civilization. One opens a channel for the expansion of the "material fact": the other opens a trail for the growth of the "spiritual form." The open way, practically equipped with facilities for camping and for walking or leisurely conveyance, provides definitely for the exercise, and hence for the increased strength, of those cultural powers within human society which would develop the country for the innate ultimate purposes of true *living* and not merely for the routine of mechanical *existence*. In this way we would stimulate within the individual an inner and immediate desire for controlling an overmechanical civilization—something more potent perhaps than the control alone by outward physical means. . . . The open way flanking the motor way, even at a remote distance, if equipped for actual use as a zone of primeval sojourn and outdoor living, might form in the public consciousness a forbidding of the metropolitan flood which would be quite as effective as the occasional physical barrier across the flood's path. . . . [H]ere is a means at our disposal—sticking out of the countryside and its topography. It is a means which will prove weak or strong according as you and I—as engineers, as citizens—prove weak or strong. . . .

The forces set loose in the jungle of our present civilization may prove more fierce than any beasts found in the jungle of the continents—far more terrible than any storms encountered within uncharted seas. Here in America . . . we have an area which, potentially, is perhaps the most "volcanic" of any area on earth. It is an area laden with the ingredients of modern industry and civilization: iron, coal, timber, petroleum. It is electric with a high potential—for human happiness or human misery. The coal and iron pockets which lie beneath the surface may be the seeds of freedom or seeds of bitterness; for in them is the latent substance of distant foreign wars as well as deep domestic strife.

These forces are neither "good" nor "bad" but *so*. And they do not stand still, but flow and spread as we have told. Can we control their flow before it controls us? Can we do it *soon enough?* This is a crucial question of our day. What instructions can we issue to our modern-day explorer (whether technician or amateur) to guide him in coping with this modern-day invasion?

The new explorer, of this "volcanic" country of America, must first of all be fit for all-round action: he must combine the engineer, the artist, and the military general. It is not for him to "make the country," but it is for him to know the country and the trenchant flows that are taking place upon it. He must not scheme, he must reveal: he must reveal so well the possibilities of A, B, C, and D that when E happens he can handle it. His job is not to wage war—nor stress an argument: it is to "wage" a determined *visualization.* His attitude in this must be one not of frozen dogma or irritated tension, but of gentle and reposeful power: he must speak softly but carry a big map. He need not be a crank, he may not be a hero, but he must be a scout. . . . And our last instruction to our new explorer and frontiersman is to hold ever in sight his final goal—to reveal within our innate country, despite the fogs and chaos of cacophonous mechanization, *a land in which to live.*

25

Wilderness

Robert Marshall (1930)

Robert Marshall's passion for wild country led him to become one of the great forces in the movement for preservation of the wilderness. Subsequently, the presence of wilderness became a key component of the American definition of environmental quality. Son of the noted lawyer and philanthropist Louis Marshall and independently wealthy, Bob, as he was known, earned a Ph.D. in plant physiology and worked for the U.S. Forest Service and the Office of Indian Affairs. In the 1930s he pleaded the case for preservation before development-minded New Deal administrators and succeeded in pushing through the Forest Service "U" regulations (September 1939), which made wilderness recreation the dominant use of fourteen million acres in the western national forests. In 1935 Marshall carried out the suggestion he makes in what follows and took the lead in organizing and financing the Wilderness Society as a political pressure group. The passage of the Wilderness Act in 1964 was in large part a tribute to the effectiveness of this organization. But Marshall's untimely death in 1939 at the age of thirty-eight (his insistence on continuing strenuous backpacking against medical advice contributed to the fatal heart attack) prevented him from witnessing the culmination of the movement he had done so much to inspire. In this 1930 essay, Marshall attempts to define the values of wilderness for modern civilization.

The Lewis and Clark exploration inaugurated a century of constantly accelerating emigration into the American West such as the world had never known. Throughout this frenzied period the only serious thought ever devoted to the wilderness was how it might be demolished. To the pioneers pushing westward it was an enemy of diabolical cruelty and danger, standing as the great obstacle to industry and

Robert Marshall, "The Problem of the Wilderness," *Scientific Monthly*, **XXX** (1930), 142–143, 145–148. Copyright 1930 by the American Association for the Advancement of Science. Reprinted by permission.

development. Since these seemed to constitute the essentials for felicity, the obvious step was to excoriate the devil which interfered. And so the path of empire proceeded to substitute for the undisturbed seclusion of nature the conquering accomplishments of man. Highways wound up valleys which had known only the footsteps of the wild animals; neatly planted gardens and orchards replaced the tangled confusion of the primeval forest; factories belched up great clouds of smoke where for centuries trees had transpired toward the sky, and the ground-cover of fresh sorrel and twinflower was transformed to asphalt spotted with chewing-gum, coal dust and gasoline.

Today there remain less than twenty wilderness areas of a million acres, and annually even these shrunken remnants of an undefiled continent are being despoiled. Aldo Leopold has truly said:

> The day is almost upon us when canoe travel will consist in paddling up the noisy wake of a motor launch and portaging through the back yard of a summer cottage. When that day comes canoe travel will be dead, and dead too will be a part of our Americanism. . . . The day is almost upon us when a pack train must wind its way up a graveled highway and turn out its bell mare in the pasture of a summer hotel. When that day comes the pack train will be dead, the diamond hitch will be merely a rope and Kit Carson and Jim Bridger will be names in a history lesson.*

Within the next few years the fate of the wilderness must be decided. This is a problem to be settled by deliberate rationality and not by personal prejudice. Fundamentally, the question is one of balancing the total happiness which will be obtainable if the few undesecrated areas are perpetuated against that which will prevail if they are destroyed. For this purpose it will be necessary: first, to consider the extraordinary benefits of the wilderness; second, to enumerate the drawbacks to undeveloped areas; third, to evaluate the relative importance of these conflicting factors, and finally, to formulate a plan of action.

The benefits which accrue from the wilderness may be separated into three broad divisions: the physical, the mental and the esthetic.

*Leopold's statement appeared in "The Last Stand of the Wilderness," *American Forests and Forest Life*, **XXXI** (1925), 600–604. For Leopold see Selection 27. [Ed.]

Most obvious in the first category is the contribution which the wilderness makes to health. This involves something more than pure air and quiet, which are also attainable in almost any rural situation. But toting a fifty-pound pack over an abominable trail, snowshoeing across a blizzard-swept plateau or scaling some jagged pinnacle which juts far above timber all develop a body distinguished by a soundness, stamina and élan unknown amid normal surroundings.

More than mere heartiness is the character of physical independence which can be nurtured only away from the coddling of civilization. In a true wilderness if a person is not qualified to satisfy all the requirements of existence, then he is bound to perish. As long as we prize individuality and competence it is imperative to provide the opportunity for complete self-sufficiency. This is inconceivable under the effete superstructure of urbanity; it demands the harsh environment of untrammeled expanses.

Closely allied is the longing for physical exploration which bursts through all the chains with which society fetters it. . . . Adventure whether physical or mental, implies breaking into unpenetrated ground, venturing beyond the boundary of normal aptitude, extending oneself to the limit of capacity, courageously facing peril. Life without the chance for such exertions would be for many persons a dreary game, scarcely bearable in its horrible banality. . . .

One of the greatest advantages of the wilderness is its incentive to independent cogitation. This is partly a reflection of physical stimulation, but more inherently due to the fact that original ideas require an objectivity and perspective seldom possible in the distracting propinquity of one's fellow men. . . .

Another mental value of an opposite sort is concerned not with incitement but with repose. In a civilization which requires most lives to be passed amid inordinate dissonance, pressure and intrusion, the chance of retiring now and then to the quietude and privacy of sylvan haunts becomes for some people a psychic necessity. It is only the possibility of convalescing in the wilderness which saves them from being destroyed by the terrible neural tension of modern existence.

Finally, . . . the wilderness furnishes perhaps the best opportunity for pure esthetic enjoyment. This requires that beauty be observed as a unity and that for the brief duration of any pure esthetic experience the cognition of the observed object must completely fill the spectator's cosmos. There can be no extraneous thoughts—no question about the creator of the phenomenon, its structure, what it resembles or what vanity in the beholder it gratifies. . . . In the wilderness, with its entire freedom from the manifestations of human will, that perfect objectivity which is essential for pure esthetic rapture can probably be achieved more readily than among any other forms of beauty.

But the problem is not all one-sided. Having discussed the tremendous benefits of the wilderness, it is now proper to ponder upon the disadvantages which uninhabited territory entails.

In the first place, there is the immoderate danger that a wilderness without developments for fire protection will sooner or later go up in smoke and down in ashes.

A second drawback is concerned with the direct economic loss. By locking up wilderness areas we as much as remove from the earth all the lumber, minerals, range land, water-power and agricultural possibilities which they contain. In the face of the tremendous demand for these resources it seems unpardonable to many to render nugatory this potential material wealth.

A third difficulty inherent in undeveloped districts is that they automatically preclude the bulk of the population from enjoying them. For it is admitted that at present only a minority of the genus *Homo* cares for wilderness recreation, and only a fraction of this minority possesses the requisite virility for the indulgence of this desire. Far more people can enjoy the woods by automobile. Far more would prefer to spend their vacations in luxurious summer hotels set on well-groomed lawns than in leaky, fly-infested shelters bundled away in the brush. Why then should this majority have to give up its rights?

As a result of these last considerations the irreplaceable values of the wilderness are generally ignored, and a fatalistic attitude is adopted in regard to the ultimate disappearance of all unmolested localities. It is my contention that this outlook is entirely unjustified, and that almost all the disadvantages of the wilderness can be minimized by forethought and some compromise.

The problem of protection dictates the elimination of undeveloped areas of great fire hazard. Furthermore, certain infringements on the concept of an unsullied wilderness will be unavoidable in almost all instances. Trails, telephone lines and lookout cabins will have to be constructed, for without such precaution most forests in the west would be gutted. But even with these improvements the basic primitive quality still exists: dependence on personal effort for survival. Economic loss could be greatly reduced by reserving inaccessible and unproductive terrain. Inasmuch as most of the highly valuable lands have already been exploited, it should be easy to confine a great share of the wilderness tracts to those lofty mountain regions where the possibility of material profit is unimportant. . . . The way to meet our commercial demands is not to thwart legitimate divertisement, but to eliminate the unmitigated evils of fire and destructive logging. It is time we appreciated that the real economic problem is to see how little land need be employed for timber production, so that the remainder of the forest may be devoted to those other vital uses incompatible with industrial exploitation.

Even if there should be an underproduction of timber, it is well to recall that it is much cheaper to import lumber for industry than to export people for pastime. The freight rate from Siberia is not nearly as high as the passenger rate to Switzerland. . . .

But the automobilists argue that a wilderness domain precludes the huge majority of recreation-seekers from deriving any amusement whatever from it. This is almost as irrational as contending that because more people enjoy bathing than art exhibits therefore we should change our picture galleries into swimming pools. . . . It is of the utmost importance to concede the right of happiness also to people who find their delight in unaccustomed ways. This prerogative is valid even though its exercise may encroach slightly on the fun of the majority for there is a point where an increase in the joy of the many causes a decrease in the joy of the few out of all proportion to the gain of the former. . . .

These steps of reasoning lead up to the conclusion that the preservation of a few samples of undeveloped territory is one of the most clamant issues before us today. Just a few years more of hesitation and the only trace of that wilderness which has exerted such a fundamental influence in molding American character will lie in the musty pages of pioneer books and the mumbled memories of tottering antiquarians. To avoid this catastrophe demands immediate action. . . .

A thorough study should forthwith be undertaken to determine the probable wilderness needs of the country. Of course, no precise reckoning could be attempted but a radical calculation would be feasible. It ought to be radical for three reasons: because it is easy to convert a natural area to industrial or motor usage, impossible to do the reverse; because the population which covets wilderness recreation is rapidly enlarging and because the higher standard of living which may be anticipated should give millions the economic power to gratify what is today merely a pathetic yearning. Once the estimate is formulated, immediate steps should be taken to establish enough tracts to insure every one who hungers for it a generous opportunity of enjoying wilderness isolation.

To carry out this program it is exigent that all friends of the wilderness ideal should unite. If they do not present the urgency of their view-point the other side will certainly capture popular support. Then it will only be a few years until the last escape from society will be barricaded. If that day arrives there will be countless souls born to live in strangulation, countless human beings who will be crushed under the artificial edifice raised by man. There is just one hope of repulsing the tyrannical ambition of civilization to conquer every niche on the whole earth. That hope is the organization of spirited people who will fight for the freedom of the wilderness.

26

The Global Perspective

William Vogt (1948)

One of the intellectual consequences of World War II was new sensitivity to the global dimensions of environmental problems. The ecologists' message of interrelatedness made more sense. Local, regional, and national environments inevitably existed in the broader, planetary context. The United States was no more an environmental "island" than it was a political one.

Although George Perkins Marsh had glimpsed the concept in 1864 (Selection 6), William Vogt was the first modern writer to place American environmentalism in a world context. His exposure of the myth of inexhaustibility in a finite space transcended the American frontier and focused on the whole earth. Vogt realized the problems a rapidly growing human population posed for forests, minerals, soil, and water. Humans could not go on waging what he called a "war" against nature without ultimately defeating themselves. Ecological health was essential to a successful civilization. There was no welfare without environmental welfare.

Along with Fairfield Osborn, author of Our Plundered Planet *(1948) and the significantly titled* The Limits of the Earth *(1953), Vogt laid the groundwork of awareness that climaxed in the 1960s and 1970s with the work of Paul Ehrlich (Selections 32 and 41), Garrett Hardin (Selection 37), and the Global 2000 Study (Selection 50).*

By excessive breeding and abuse of the land mankind has backed itself into an ecological trap. By a lopsided use of applied science it has been living on promissory notes. Now, all over the world, the notes are falling due.

Payment cannot be postponed much longer. Fortunately, we still may choose between payment and utterly disastrous bankruptcy on a world scale. It will certainly be more intelligent to pull in our belts and accept a long period of austerity and rebuilding than to wait for a

William Vogt, *Road to Survival* (New York: William Sloane Associates, 1948), 284–288.

catastrophic crash of our civilization. In hard fact, we have no other choice.

When I write "we" I do not mean the other fellow. I mean every person who reads a newspaper printed on pulp from vanishing forests. I mean every man and woman who eats a meal drawn from steadily shrinking lands. Everyone who flushes a toilet, and thereby pollutes a river, wastes fertile organic matter and helps to lower a water table. Everyone who puts on a wool garment derived from overgrazed ranges that have been cut by the little hoofs and gullied by the rains, sending runoff and topsoil into the rivers downstream, flooding cities hundreds of miles away. Especially do I mean men and women in overpopulated countries who produce excessive numbers of children who, unhappily, cannot escape their fate as hostages to the forces of misery and disaster that lower upon the horizon of our future.

If we ourselves do not govern our destiny, firmly and courageously, no one is going to do it for us. To regain ecological freedom for our civilization will be a heavy task. It will frequently require arduous and uncomfortable measures. It will cost considerable sums of money. Democratic governments are not likely to set forth on such a steep and rocky path unless the people lead the way. Nations with lower educational standards than ours, nations that are technologically retarded, are still less likely to move. In our own interest we must accept the responsibility for this leadership, as we have in the spheres of economics and politics.

Drastic measures are inescapable. Above everything else, we must reorganize our thinking. If we are to escape the crash we must abandon all thought of living unto ourselves. We form an earth-company, and the lot of the Indiana farmer can no longer be isolated from that of the Bantu. This is true, not only in John Donne's mystical sense,* in the meaning of brotherhood that makes starving babies in Hindustan the concern of Americans; but in a direct, physical sense. An eroding hillside in Mexico or Yugoslavia affects the living standard and probability of survival of the American people. Irresponsible breeding makes amelioration of the condition of the Greeks—or the Italians or Indians or Chinese—difficult, if not impossible; it imposes a drain on the world's wealth, especially that of the United States, when this wealth might be used to improve living standards and survival chances

---

*Donne wrote that no man is an island. [Ed.]

for less people. We cannot escape our responsibility, since it is a responsibility to ourselves.

We must equally abandon any philosophy of "Sufficient unto the day—." We are paying for the foolishness of yesterday while we shape our own tomorrow. Today's white bread may force a break in the levees, and flood New Orleans next spring. This year's wheat from Australia's eroding slopes may flare into a Japanese war three decades hence. Comic books from the flanks of the Nevado de Toluca in 1948 may close Mexico City's factories in 1955. The freebooting, rugged individualist, whose vigor, imagination, and courage contributed so much of good to the building of our country (along with the bad), we must now recognize, where his activities destroy resources, as the Enemy of the People he has become. The exploiting lumberman of Madagascar was beheaded; we should impose at least as effective, if kinder, controls. We must develop our sense of time, and think of the availability of beefsteaks not only for this Saturday but for the Saturdays of our old age, and of our children and grandchildren's youth. The day has long since passed when a senator may callously demand, "What has posterity ever done for me?" Posterity is of our making, as is the world in which it will have to live.

Above all, we must learn to know—to feel to the core of our beings—our dependence upon the earth and the riches with which it sustains us. We can no longer believe valid our assumption that we live in independence. No longer can we rest secure in the certainty that somehow, from somewhere, our wants will be supplied. We, even we fortunate Americans, are pressing hard on our means of subsistence. Our neighbors on five continents know what it means to find their cupboards bare. There is no phase of our civilization that is not touched by wasting dearth. There is hardly an aspect of human activity, through all the complex span of our lives, that does not, in some open or occult manner, feel the chill of scarcity's damp breath.

We must—all of us, men, women, and children—reorient ourselves with relation to the world in which we live. We must learn to weigh the daily news in terms of man's subsistence. We must come to understand our past, our history, in terms of the soil and water and forests and grasses that have made it what it is. We must see the years to come in the frame that makes space and time one, that will keep us strong only as, like Antaeus, we draw our strength from the earth. Our education must be reshaped, as the story of our existence in an environment as completely subjected to physical laws as is a ball we let drop from our hands. Our philosophies must be rewritten to remove them from the domain of words and "ideas," and to plant their roots firmly in the earth. Above all, we must weigh our place in the society of nations and our future through the decades to come in the scale of our total environment.

The history of our future is already written, at least for some decades. As we are crowded together, two and a quarter billions of us, on the shrinking surface of the globe, we have set in motion historical forces that are directed by our total environment.

We might symbolize these forces by graphs. One of them is the curve of human populations that, after centuries of relative equilibrium, suddenly began to mount, and in the past fifty years has been climbing at a vertiginous rate.

The other graph is that of our resources. It represents the area and thickness of our topsoil, the abundance of our forests, available waters, life-giving grasslands, and the biophysical web that holds them together. This curve, except for local depressions, also maintained a high degree of regularity through the centuries. But it, too, has had its direction sharply diverted, especially during the past hundred and fifty years, and it is plunging downward like a rapid.

These two curves—of population and the means of survival—have long since crossed. Ever more rapidly they are drawing apart. The farther they are separated the more difficult will it be to draw them together again.

Everywhere, or nearly everywhere, about the earth we see the results of their divergence. The crumbling ruins of two wars mark their passing. The swollen bellies of hungry babies, from San Salvador to Bengal, dot the space between them. Parching fevers and racking coughs, from Osorno to Seoul, cry aloud the cleavage between these curves. The angry muttering of mobs, like the champing of jungle peccaries, is a swelling echo of their passing.

The direction of these curves and the misery they write across the earth are not likely to be changed in the proximate future. Their direction is fixed for some decades. Great masses of people have a preponderantly young population; as they come into the breeding age we must, despite all possible efforts short of generalized slaughter, expect human numbers to increase for a time. The drag imposed by ignorance, selfishness, nationalism, custom, etc., is certain to retard, by some decades, any effective or substantial improvement of resource management.

So that the people shall not delude themselves, find further frustration through quack nostrums, fight their way into blind alleys, it is imperative that this world-wide dilemma be made known to all mankind. The human race is caught in a situation as concrete as a pair of shoes two sizes too small. We must understand that, and stop blaming economic systems, the weather, bad luck, or callous saints. This is the beginning of wisdom, and the first step on the long road back.

The second step is dual—the control of populations and the restoration of resources.

Unless we take these steps and begin to swing into them soon—unless, in short, man readjusts his way of living, in its fullest sense, to the imperatives imposed by the *limited* resources of his environment—we may as well give up all hope of continuing civilized life.

27

A Land Ethic

Aldo Leopold (1949)

Prior to Aldo Leopold, American conservationists had justified their concern for nature in terms of economics or democracy or, less frequently, aesthetics and religion. The emphasis, in each case, was on human *well-being. Leopold, however, took as his axiom the right of other forms of life, and ultimately of the environment itself, to a healthy existence. The environment, Leopold pointed out, did not "belong" to man; he shared it with everything alive. But because of his power, man bore the responsibility of maintaining it in the best interests of the life community. Leopold's land ethic had scientific rather than religious or sentimental roots. He pioneered in the development of an understanding of the complex interrelationships of organisms and the environment known as the science of ecology.*

In 1909 Leopold graduated from the Yale Forest School and joined the U.S. Forest Service. Assigned to the southwest, he attracted national attention for his efforts on behalf of wildlife management and wilderness preservation. During the 1930s, as a professor at the University of Wisconsin, Leopold formulated the ideas presented here. He lost his life in 1948 while fighting a brush fire along the Wisconsin River, but his collected writings became one of the chief sources of inspiration for the new environmentalism.

When god-like Odysseus returned from the wars in Troy, he hanged all on one rope a dozen slave-girls of his household whom he suspected of misbehavior during his absence.

This hanging involved no question of propriety. The girls were property. The disposal of property was then, as now, a matter of expediency, not of right and wrong.

Concepts of right and wrong were not lacking from Odysseus'

Aldo Leopold, *A Sand County Almanac and Sketches Here and There* (New York: Oxford University Press, 1949), 201–204, 207, 209–210, 223–226. Copyright 1949 and 1977 by Oxford University Press, Inc. Reprinted by permission.

Greece: witness the fidelity of his wife through the long years before at last his black-prowed galleys clove the wine-dark seas for home. The ethical structure of that day covered wives, but had not yet been extended to human chattels. During the three thousand years which have since elapsed, ethical criteria have been extended to many fields of conduct, with corresponding shrinkages in those judged by expediency only. . . .

The first ethics dealt with the relation between individuals. . . . Later accretions dealt with the relation between the individual and society. . . .

There is as yet no ethic dealing with man's relation to land and to the animals and plants which grow upon it. Land, like Odysseus' slave-girls, is still property. The land-relation is still strictly economic, entailing privileges but not obligations.

The extension of ethics to this third element in human environment is, if I read the evidence correctly, an evolutionary possibility and an ecological necessity. It is the third step in a sequence. The first two have already been taken. Individual thinkers since the days of Ezekiel and Isaiah have asserted that the despoliation of land is not only inexpedient but wrong. Society, however, has not yet affirmed their belief. I regard the present conservation movement as the embryo of such an affirmation. . . .

All ethics so far evolved rest upon a single premise: that the individual is a member of a community of interdependent parts. His instincts prompt him to compete for his place in that community, but his ethics prompt him also to co-operate (perhaps in order that there may be a place to compete for).

The land ethic simply enlarges the boundaries of the community to include soils, waters, plants, and animals, or collectively: the land.

This sounds simple: do we not already sing our love for and obligation to the land of the free and the home of the brave? Yes, but just what and whom do we love? Certainly not the soil, which we are sending helter-skelter downriver. Certainly not the waters, which we assume have no function except to turn turbines, float barges, and carry off sewage. Certainly not the plants, of which we exterminate whole communities without batting an eye. Certainly not the animals, of which we have already extirpated many of the largest and most beautiful species. A land ethic of course cannot prevent the alteration, management, and use of these 'resources,' but it does affirm their right to continued existence, and, at least in spots, their continued existence in a natural state.

In short, a land ethic changes the role of *Homo sapiens* from conqueror of the land-community to plain member and citizen of it. It implies respect for his fellow-members, and also respect for the community as such. . . .

Conservation is a state of harmony between men and land. Despite nearly a century of propaganda, conservation still proceeds at a snail's pace; progress still consists largely of letterhead pieties and convention oratory. On the back forty we still slip two steps backward for each forward stride.

The usual answer to this dilemma is 'more conservation education.' No one will debate this, but is it certain that only the *volume* of education needs stepping up? Is something lacking in the *content* as well? . . .

. . . [T]he education actually in progress makes no mention of obligations to land over and above those dictated by self-interest. Land-use ethics are still governed wholly by economic self-interest, just as social ethics were a century ago. . . .

No important change in ethics was ever accomplished without an internal change in our intellectual emphasis, loyalties, affections, and convictions. The proof that conservation has not yet touched these foundations of conduct lies in the fact that philosophy and religion have not yet heard of it. In our attempt to make conservation easy, we have made it trivial. . . .

It is inconceivable to me that an ethical relation to land can exist without love, respect, and admiration for land, and a high regard for its value. By value, I of course mean something far broader than mere economic value; I mean value in the philosophical sense.

Perhaps the most serious obstacle impeding the evolution of a land ethic is the fact that our educational and economic system is headed away from, rather than toward, an intense consciousness of land. Your true modern is separated from the land by many middlemen, and by innumerable physical gadgets. He has no vital relation to it; to him it is the space between cities on which crops grow. Turn him loose for a day on the land, and if the spot does not happen to be a golf links or a 'scenic' area, he is bored stiff. If crops could be raised by hydroponics instead of farming, it would suit him very well. Synthetic substitutes for wood, leather, wool, and other natural land products suit him better than the originals. In short, land is something he has 'outgrown.'

Almost equally serious as an obstacle to a land ethic is the attitude of the farmer for whom the land is still an adversary, or a taskmaster that keeps him in slavery. Theoretically, the mechanization of farming ought to cut the farmer's chains, but whether it really does is debatable.

One of the requisites for an ecological comprehension of land is an understanding of ecology, and this is by no means co-extensive with 'education'; in fact, much higher education seems deliberately to avoid ecological concepts. An understanding of ecology does not necessarily originate in courses bearing ecological labels; it is quite as likely to be labeled geography, botany, agronomy, history, or economics. This is as it should be, but whatever the label, ecological training is scarce. . . .

The 'key-log' which must be moved to release the evolutionary process for an ethic is simply this: quit thinking about decent land-use as solely an economic problem. Examine each question in terms of what is ethically and esthetically right, as well as what is economically expedient. A thing is right when it tends to preserve the integrity, stability, and beauty of the biotic community. It is wrong when it tends otherwise.

It of course goes without saying that economic feasibility limits the tether of what can or cannot be done for land. It always has and it always will. The fallacy the economic determinists have tied around our collective neck, and which we now need to cast off, is the belief that economics determines *all* land-use. This is simply not true. An innumerable host of actions and attitudes, comprising perhaps the bulk of all land relations, is determined by the land-users' tastes and predilections, rather than by his purse. The bulk of all land relations hinges on investments of time, forethought, skill, and faith rather than on investments of cash. . . .

The evolution of a land ethic is an intellectual as well as emotional process. Conservation is paved with good intentions which prove to be futile, or even dangerous, because they are devoid of critical understanding either of the land, or of economic land-use. . . .

The mechanism of operation is the same for any ethic: social approbation for right actions: social disapproval for wrong actions.

By and large, our present problem is one of attitudes and implements. We are remodeling the Alhambra* with a steamshovel, and we are proud of our yardage. We shall hardly relinquish the shovel, which after all has many good points, but we are in need of gentler and more objective criteria for its successful use.

*A royal palace of great beauty in Spain. Leopold is here equating it to the natural world. [Ed.]

28

The Meaning of Wilderness for American Civilization

Wallace Stegner (1960)

The growing emphasis on quality of the environment and ecological integrity gave wilderness preservation unaccustomed influence in American conservation. On September 3, 1964, after eight years of hearings and revisions, the bill establishing the National Wilderness Preservation System became law. While failing to satisfy preservationists' demands completely, the act made most disturbances of wilderness conditions on selected federal lands illegal. Ultimately the Wilderness System could contain about 2 percent of the nation's land area.

While the wilderness bill was under congressional consideration, Wallace Stegner, novelist, university professor, and the biographer of John Wesley Powell (Selection 10), wrote eloquently about the meaning of wild country in modern American life. His statement was written for the report of the Wildland Research Center to the Outdoor Recreation Resources Review Commission, a body created by Congress in 1958 to determine the recreational needs of Americans in the years 1976 and 2000. Stegner credits David R. Brower (Selection 39) with inspiring him to write his "wilderness letter." A more recent statement of the value of wilderness may be found in Selection 40.

I should like to urge some arguments for wilderness preservation that involve recreation, as it is ordinarily conceived, hardly at all. Hunting, fishing, hiking, mountain-climbing, camping, photography, and the enjoyment of natural scenery will all, surely, figure in your report. So will the wilderness as a genetic reserve, a scientific yardstick by which we may measure the world in its natural balance against the world in its man-made imbalance. What I want to speak for is not so much the

Wallace Stegner, "The Wilderness Idea," in David Brower, ed., *Wilderness: America's Living Heritage* (San Francisco: Sierra Club, 1961), 97–102. Reprinted by permission of the publisher.

wilderness uses, valuable as those are, but the wilderness *idea,* which is a resource in itself. Being an intangible and spiritual resource, it will seem mystical to the practical-minded—but then anything that cannot be moved by a bulldozer is likely to seem mystical to them.

I want to speak for the wilderness idea as something that has helped form our character and that has certainly shaped our history as a people. It has no more to do with recreation than churches have to do with recreation, or than the strenuousness and optimism and expansiveness of what historians call the "American Dream" have to do with recreation. Nevertheless, since it is only in this recreation survey that the values of wilderness are being compiled, I hope you will permit me to insert this idea between the leaves, as it were, of the recreation report.

Something will have gone out of us as a people if we ever let the remaining wilderness be destroyed; if we permit the last virgin forests to be turned into comic books and plastic cigarette cases; if we drive the few remaining members of the wild species into zoos or to extinction; if we pollute the last clear air and dirty the last clean streams and push our paved roads through the last of the silence, so that never again will Americans be free in their own country from the noise, the exhausts, the stinks of human and automotive waste. And so that never again can we have the chance to see ourselves single, separate, vertical and individual in the world, part of the environment of trees and rocks and soil, brother to the other animals, part of the natural world and competent to belong in it. Without any remaining wilderness we are committed wholly, without chance for even momentary reflection and rest, to a headlong drive into our technological termite-life, the Brave New World of a completely man-controlled environment. We need wilderness preserved—as much of it as is still left, and as many kinds—because it was the challenge against which our character as a people was formed. The reminder and the reassurance that it is still there is good for our spiritual health even if we never once in ten years set foot in it. It is good for us when we are young, because of the incomparable sanity it can bring briefly, as vacation and rest, into our insane lives. It is important to us when we are old simply because it is there—important, that is, simply as idea.

We are a wild species, as Darwin pointed out. Nobody ever tamed or domesticated or scientifically bred us. But for at least three millennia we have been engaged in a cumulative and ambitious race to modify and gain control of our environment, and in the process we have come close to domesticating ourselves. Not many people are likely, any more, to look upon what we call "progress" as an unmixed blessing. Just as surely as it has brought us increased comfort and more material goods, it has brought us spiritual losses, and it threatens now to become the Frankenstein that will destroy us. One means of sanity is to retain a hold on the natural world, to remain, insofar as we can, good animals. Americans still have that chance, more than many peoples; for while we were demonstrating ourselves the most efficient and ruthless environment-busters in history, and slashing and burning and cutting our way through a wilderness continent, the wilderness was working on us. It remains in us as surely as Indian names remain on the land. If the abstract dream of human liberty and human dignity became, in America, something more than an abstract dream, mark it down at least partially to the fact that we were in subtle ways subdued by what we conquered.

The Connecticut Yankee, sending likely candidates from King Arthur's unjust kingdom to his Man Factory for rehabilitation, was overoptimistic, as he later admitted. These things cannot be forced, they have to grow. To make such a man, such a democrat, such a believer in human individual dignity, as Mark Twain himself, the frontier was necessary, Hannibal and the Mississippi and Virginia City, and reaching out from those the wilderness: the wilderness as opportunity and as idea, the thing that has helped to make an American different from and, until we forget it in the roar of our industrial cities, more fortunate than other men. For an American, insofar as he is new and different at all, is a civilized man who has renewed himself in the wild. The American experience has been the confrontation of old peoples and cultures by a world as new as if it had just arisen from the sea. That gave us our hope and our excitement, and the hope and excitement can be passed on to newer Americans; Americans who never saw any phase of the frontier. But only so long as we keep the remainder of our wild as a reserve and a promise—a sort of wilderness bank.

As a novelist, I may perhaps be forgiven for taking literature as a reflection, indirect but profoundly true, of our national consciousness. And our literature, as perhaps you are aware, is sick, embittered, losing its mind, losing its faith. Our novelists are the declared enemies of their society. There has hardly been a serious or important novel in this century that did not repudiate in part or in whole American technological culture for its commercialism, its vulgarity, and the way in which it has dirtied a clean continent and a clean dream. I do not expect that the preservation of our remaining wilderness is going to cure this condition. But the mere example that we can as a nation apply some other criteria than commercial and exploitative considerations would be heartening to many Americans, novelists or otherwise. We need to demonstrate our acceptance of the natural world, including ourselves; we need the spiritual refreshment that being natural can produce. And one of the best places for us to get that is in the wilderness where the fun houses, the bulldozers, and the pavements of our civilization are shut out.

Sherwood Anderson, in a letter to Waldo Frank in the 1920s, said it better than I can. 'Is it not likely that when the country was new and men were often alone in the fields and the forest they got a sense of bigness outside themselves that has now in some way been lost? . . . Mystery whispered in the grass, played in the branches of trees overhead, was caught up and blown across the American line in clouds of dust at evening on the prairies . . . I am old enough to remember tales that strengthen my belief in a deep semi-religious influence that was formerly at work among our people. The flavor of it hangs over the best work of Mark Twain . . . I can remember old fellows in my home town speaking feelingly of an evening spent on the big empty plains. It had taken the shrillness out of them. They had learned the trick of quiet. . . .'

We could learn it too, even yet; even our children and grandchildren could learn it. But only if we save, for just such absolutely nonrecreational, impractical, and mystical uses as this, all the wild that still remains to us.

It seems to me significant that the distinct downturn in our literature from hope to bitterness took place almost at the precise time when the frontier officially came to an end, in 1890, and when the American way of life had begun to turn strongly urban and industrial. The more urban it has become, and the more frantic with technological change, the sicker and more embittered our literature, and I believe our people, have become. For myself, I grew up on the empty plains of Saskatchewan and Montana and in the mountains of Utah, and I put a very high valuation on what those places gave me. And if I had not been able periodically to renew myself in the mountains and deserts of Western America I would be very nearly bughouse. Even when I can't get to the back country, the thought of the colored deserts of southern Utah, or the reassurance that there are still stretches of prairie where the world can be instantaneously perceived as disk and bowl, and where the little but intensely important human being is exposed to the five directions and the thirty-six winds, is a positive consolation. The idea alone can sustain me. But as the wilderness areas are progressively exploited or 'improved,' as the jeeps and bulldozers of uranium prospectors scar up the deserts and the roads are cut into the alpine timberlands, and as the remnants of the unspoiled and natural world are progressively eroded, every such loss is a little death in me. In us.

Nevertheless I am not moved by the argument that those wilderness areas which have already been exposed to grazing or mining are already deflowered, and so might as well be 'harvested.' For mining I cannot say much good except that its operations are generally short-lived. The extractable wealth is taken and the shafts, the tailings, and the ruins left, and in a dry country such as the American West the wounds men make in the earth do not quickly heal. Still, they are only wounds; they aren't absolutely mortal. Better a wounded wilderness than none at all. And as for grazing, if it is strictly controlled so that it does not destroy the ground cover, damage the ecology, or compete with the wildlife it is in itself nothing that need conflict with the wilderness feeling or the validity of the wilderness experience. I have known enough range cattle to recognize them as wild animals; and the people who herd them have, in the wilderness context, the dignity of rareness; they belong on the frontier, moreover, and have a look of rightness. The invasion they make on the virgin country is a sort of invasion that is as old as Neanderthal man, and they can, in moderation, even emphasize a man's feeling of belonging to the natural world. Under surveillance, they can belong; under control, they need not deface or mar. I do not believe that in wilderness areas where grazing has never been permitted, it should be permitted; but I do not believe either that an otherwise untouched wilderness should be eliminated from the preservation plan because of limited existing uses such as grazing which are in consonance with the frontier condition and image. . . .

So are great reaches of our western deserts, scarred somewhat by prospectors but otherwise open, beautiful, waiting, close to whatever God you want to see in them. Just as a sample, let me suggest the Robbers' Roost country in Wayne County, Utah, near the Capitol Reef National Monument. In that desert climate the dozer and jeep tracks will not soon melt back into the earth, but the country has a way of making the scars insignificant. It is a lovely and terrible wilderness, such a wilderness as Christ and the prophets went out into; harshly and beautifully colored, broken and worn until its bones are exposed, its great sky without a smudge or taint from Technocracy, and in hidden corners and pockets under its cliffs the sudden poetry of springs. Save a piece of country like that intact, and it does not matter in the slightest that only a few people every year will go into it. That is precisely its value. Roads would be a desecration, crowds would ruin it. But those who haven't the strength or youth to go into it and live with it can still drive up onto the shoulder of the Aquarius Plateau and simply sit and look. They can look two hundred miles, clear into Colorado; and looking down over the cliffs and canyons of the San Rafael Swell and the Robbers' Roost they can also look as deeply into themselves as anywhere I know. And if they can't even get to the places on the Aquarius where the present roads will carry them, they can simply contemplate the *idea,* take pleasure in the fact that such a timeless and uncontrolled part of earth is still there.

These are some of the things wilderness can do for us. That is the reason we need to put into effect, for its preservation, some other principle than the principles of exploitation or usefulness or even recreation. We simply need that wild country available to us, even if we never do more than drive to its edge and look in. For it can be a means of reassuring ourselves of our sanity as creatures, a part of the geography of hope.

Beautification

Lyndon B. Johnson (1965)

On February 8, 1965, President Lyndon B. Johnson sent a special message on natural beauty to the Congress of the United States that is perfectly illustrative of the thesis argued by Samuel P. Hays (Selection 23). A landmark in defining the emphasis of American conservation since World War II, it stimulated action on local, state, and federal levels. The White House Conference on Natural Beauty, which Johnson mentions in this message, met on May 24 and 25, 1965. The event resembled Theodore Roosevelt's 1908 conference (Selection 13); again the power and prestige of the executive office was used to dramatize the most pressing conservation issue of the time. But aesthetic rather than material concerns received emphasis in Johnson's "new conservation." Of course, John Muir (Selection 15) had championed natural beauty a half century earlier, but never before 1965 had it been accorded such enthusiastic official endorsement. The conference chairman Laurance S. Rockefeller, a member of a family whose philanthropy has recently done much to protect and beautify the American landscape, led a panel of experts who reported on subjects ranging from highway billboards and automobile junkyards to the underground installation of utilities. A prominent figure at the conference as well as in the national beautification movement was Mrs. Lyndon B. Johnson.

To the Congress of the United States:

For centuries Americans have drawn strength and inspiration from the beauty of our country. It would be a neglectful generation indeed, indifferent alike to the judgment of history and the command of principle, which failed to preserve and extend such a heritage for its descendants.

Yet the storm of modern change is threatening to blight and

Lyndon B. Johnson, "Natural Beauty—Message from the President of the United States," *Congressional Record,* 89th Congress, 1st Session, Vol. 111, Pt. 2 (February 8, 1965), 2085–2089.

diminish in a few decades what has been cherished and protected for generations.

A growing population is swallowing up areas of natural beauty with its demands for living space, and is placing increased demand on our overburdened areas of recreation and pleasure.

The increasing tempo of urbanization and growth is already depriving many Americans of the right to live in decent surroundings. More of our people are crowding into cities and being cut off from nature. Cities themselves reach out into the countryside, destroying streams and trees and meadows as they go. A modern highway may wipe out the equivalent of a 50-acre park with every mile. And people move out from the city to get closer to nature only to find that nature has moved farther from them.

The modern technology, which has added much to our lives can also have a darker side. Its uncontrolled waste products are menacing the world we live in, our enjoyment and our health. The air we breathe, our water, our soil, and wildlife, are being blighted by the poisons and chemicals which are the by-products of technology and industry. The skeletons of discarded cars litter the countryside. The same society which receives the rewards of technology, must, as a cooperating whole, take responsibility for control.

To deal with these new problems will require a new conservation. We must not only protect the countryside and save it from destruction, we must restore what has been destroyed and salvage the beauty and charm of our cities. Our conservation must be not just the classic conservation of protection and development, but a creative conservation of restoration and innovation. Its concern is not with nature alone, but with the total relation between man and the world around him. Its object is not just man's welfare but the dignity of man's spirit.

In this conservation the protection and enhancement of man's opportunity to be in contact with beauty must play a major role.

This means that beauty must not be just a holiday treat, but a part of our daily life. It means not just easy physical access, but equal social access for rich and poor, Negro and white, city dweller and farmer.

Beauty is not an easy thing to measure. It does not show up in the gross national product, in a weekly paycheck, or in profit-and-loss statements. But these things are not ends in themselves. They are a road to satisfaction and pleasure and the good life. Beauty makes its own direct contribution to these final ends. Therefore it is one of the most important components of our true national income, not to be left out simply because statisticians cannot calculate its worth.

And some things we do know. Association with beauty can enlarge man's imagination and revive his spirit. Ugliness can demean the people who live among it. What a citizen sees every day is his America. If it is attractive it adds to the quality of his life. If it is ugly it can degrade his existence.

Beauty has other immediate values. It adds to safety whether removing direct dangers to health or making highways less monotonous and dangerous. We also know that those who live in blighted and squalid conditions are more susceptible to anxieties and mental disease.

Ugliness is costly. It can be expensive to clean a soot-smeared building, or to build new areas of recreation when the old landscape could have been preserved far more cheaply.

Certainly no one would hazard a national definition of beauty. But we do know that nature is nearly always beautiful. We do, for the most part, know what is ugly. And we can introduce, into all our planning, our programs, our building, and our growth, a conscious and active concern for the values of beauty. If we do this then we can be successful in preserving a beautiful America. . . .

In almost every part of the country, citizens are rallying to save landmarks of beauty and history. The Government must also do its share to assist these local efforts which have an important national purpose. We will encourage and support the National Trust for Historic Preservation in the United States, chartered by Congress in 1949. I shall propose legislation to authorize supplementary grants to help local authorities acquire, develop, and manage private properties for such purposes.

The Registry of National Historic Landmarks is a fine Federal Program with virtually no Federal cost. I commend its work and the new wave of interest it has evoked in historical preservation.

Our present system of parks, seashores, and recreation areas—monuments to the dedication and labor of farsighted men—do not meet the needs of a growing population.

The full funding of the land and water conservation fund will be an important step in making this a parks-for-America decade. . . .

More than any country ours is an automobile society. For most Americans the automobile is a principal instrument of transportation, work, daily activity, recreation, and pleasure. By making our roads highways to the enjoyment of nature and beauty we can greatly enrich the life of nearly all our people in city and countryside alike.

Our task is twofold. First, to insure that roads themselves are not destructive of nature and natural beauty. Second, to make our roads ways to recreation and pleasure.

I have asked the Secretary of Commerce to take a series of steps designed to meet this objective. This includes requiring landscaping on all Federal interstate primary and urban highways, encouraging the construction of rest and recreation areas along highways, and the preservation of natural beauty adjacent to highway rights-of-way. . . .

. . . I will recommend legislation to insure effective control of billboards along our highways.

In addition, we need urgently to work toward the elimination or screening of unsightly, beauty-destroying junkyards and auto graveyards along our highways. To this end, I will also recommend necessary legislation to achieve effective control, including Federal assistance in appropriate cases where necessary.

I hope that, at all levels of government, our planners and builders will remember that highway beautification is more than a matter of planting trees or setting aside scenic areas. The roads themselves must reflect, in location and design, increased respect for the natural and social integrity and unity of the landscape and communities through which they pass.

Those who first settled this continent found much to marvel at. Nothing was a greater source of wonder and amazement than the power and majesty of American rivers. They occupy a central place in myth and legend, folklore and literature.

They were our first highways, and some remain among the most important. We have had to control their ravages, harness their power, and use their water to help make whole regions prosper.

Yet even this seemingly indestructible natural resource is in danger.

Through our pollution control programs we can do much to restore our rivers. We will continue to conserve the water and power for tomorrow's needs with well-planned reservoirs and power dams. But the time has also come to identify and preserve free flowing stretches of our great scenic rivers before growth and development make the beauty of the unspoiled waterway a memory. . . .

The forgotten outdoorsmen of today are those who like to walk, hike, ride horseback, or bicycle. For them we must have trails as well as highways. Nor should motor vehicles be permitted to tyrannize the more leisurely human traffic. . . .

As with so much of our quest for beauty and quality, each community has opportunities for action. We can and should have an abundance of trails for walking, cycling, and horseback riding, in and close to our cities. In the back country we need to copy the great Appalachian Trail in all parts of America, and to make full use of rights-of-way and other public paths.

One aspect of the advance of civilization is the evolution of responsibility for disposal of waste. Over many generations society gradually developed techniques for this purpose. State and local governments, landlords, and private citizens have been held responsible for insuring that sewage and garbage did not menace health or contaminate the environment.

In the last few decades entire new categories of waste have come to plague and menace the American scene. These are the technological wastes—the byproducts of growth, industry, agriculture, and science. We cannot wait for slow evolution over generations to deal with them. . . .

In addition to its health effects, air pollution creates filth and gloom and depreciates property values of entire neighborhoods. The White House itself is being dirtied with soot from polluted air.

Every major river system is now polluted. Waterways that were once sources of pleasure and beauty and recreation are forbidden to human contact and objectionable to sight and smell. Furthermore, this pollution is costly, requiring expensive treatment for drinking water and inhibiting the operation and growth of industry. . . .

In addition to our air and water we must, each and every day, dispose of a half billion pounds of solid waste. These wastes—from discarded cans to discarded automobiles—litter our country, harbor vermin, and menace our health. Inefficient and improper methods of disposal increase pollution of our air and streams.

Almost all these wastes and pollutions are the result of activities carried on for the benefit of man. A prime national goal must be an environment that is pleasing to the senses and healthy to live in.

Our Government is already doing much in this field. We have made significant progress. But more must be done. . . .

I intend to call a White House Conference on Natural Beauty to meet in mid-May of this year. . . .

It is my hope that this Conference will produce new ideas and approaches for enhancing the beauty of America. Its scope will not be restricted to Federal action. It will look for ways to help and encourage State and local governments, institutions and private citizens, in their own efforts. It can serve as a focal point for the large campaign of public education which is needed to alert Americans to the danger to their natural heritage and to the need for action. . . .

In my 33 years of public life I have seen the American system move to conserve the natural and human resources of our land.

TVA transformed an entire region that was "depressed." The rural electrification cooperatives brought electricity to lighten the burdens of rural America. We have seen the forests replanted by the CCC's, and watched Gifford Pinchot's sustained yield concept take hold on forest lands.

It is true that we have often been careless with our natural bounty. At times we have paid a heavy price for this neglect. But once our people were aroused to the danger, we have acted to preserve our resources for the enrichment of our country and the enjoyment of future generations.

The beauty of our land is a natural resource. Its preservation is linked to the inner prosperity of the human spirit.

The tradition of our past is equal to today's threat to that beauty. Our land will be attractive tomorrow only if we organize for action and rebuild and reclaim the beauty we inherited. Our stewardship will be judged by the foresight with which we carry out these programs. We must rescue our cities and countryside from blight with the same purpose and vigor with which, in other areas, we moved to save the forests and the soil.

PART FOUR

THE GOSPEL OF ECOLOGY, 1962–1972

*We travel together, passengers on a little spaceship, dependent
on its vulnerable reserves of air and soil; all committed for our
safety to its security and peace; preserved from annihilation only
by the care, the work, and, I will say, the love we give our
fragile craft.*

—*Adlai Stevenson*

After 1960, old-style utilitarian or resource-oriented conservation
decreased in importance relative to environmental quality.
Americans expanded their understanding of this idea to include not
only scenic and recreational amenities but also the health of the
habitat. As an indicator of this change, the term *conservation* lost
favor to *environmentalism*. *Ecology* also became a household word. Few
could define it correctly as the study of the interrelationships
between organisms and their environment, but many associated it
with sacred connotations. Indeed, at the zenith of the
environmental era in the late 1960s and early 1970s, many
subscribed to what could be called a "gospel of ecology." It
resembled, although with more intensity, the utilitarian-based
"gospel of efficiency" (Selection 17) that empowered Progressive
conservation.

One factor in the elevation of ecology to sacred status in
American thought was that broad questioning of traditional ideals
and priorities known as the "counterculture." If traditional
Americanism stressed growth, competition, and affluence, the new
one emphasized stability, community, and simplicity. But as

Samuel P. Hays has demonstrated (Selection 23), even the American establishment began to understand that human health and welfare was linked directly to the protection of nature.

Fear catalyzed modern environmentalism. It was not the old fear of running out of useful resources that inspired the utilitarian conservationists of the Progressive and New Deal years. Neither was it the fear of making the world ugly that played a major role in aesthetic conservation, preservation, and the early calls for environmental quality. The new fear developed from an understanding of ecology and centered on William Vogt's concern (Selection 26) that a careless technological civilization could impact catastrophically on the health of the entire ecosystem. Fear for the future of humanity, of course, remained, but it was now part of an uneasiness about the condition of humanity's only home. If this was still anthropocentrism, at least it recognized that the new self-interest demanded the subordination of many tenets of the old variety to the new ecological imperatives. Pollution, no matter how much the product of a productive economy, had to be abated; human beings could not continue to foul their nest with impunity.

The gospel of ecology resulted from an intellectual fusion of scientific and what might be called *theological* ecology. The logic of the scientist blended into the intuition of the poet; Western analysis to Eastern mysticism. The result was not just a new science but a civil religion that featured a holistic sense of oneness, of ecological community, that could stand the test of both fact and feeling. Another component of environmental awareness in the late 1960s was the uncertainty and awe aroused by the beginning of space exploration. Those familiar photographs of the tiny "spaceship earth" taken by the lunar orbiters in 1968 and particularly in association with the first moon walk of July 1969 did much to fuel the environmental era. It suddenly was undeniable that the earth was very small, completely finite, apparently unique, and extremely delicate. From the perspective of space, environmentalism became much more than protecting profitable resources and scenic beauty. It involved the sanctity of mankind's only home. No one said it better than Adlai Stevenson in his "spaceship earth" speech (see epigraph, p. 187) delivered in July 1965.

Riding the crest of a wave of public interest and support, conservation-turned-environmentalism attained unprecedented cultural visibility and political power as the 1960s gave way to the

1970s. The first two waves of conservation enthusiasm—those of
the Progressive era and the New Deal years—appeared minor by
comparison. Events such as the Santa Barbara, California, oil spill
of January 28, 1969, the burning of the Cuyahoga River in Ohio,
and the alleged "death" of Lake Erie made headline news.
President Richard Nixon reserved for the first day of the 1970s the
signing into law of the National Environmental Policy Act (NEPA).
It established a Council on Environmental Quality in the Executive
Office of the President, required "environmental impact
statements" for all federal expenditures, and officially recognized,
in the words of the act, the necessity of achieving "harmony
between man and his environment." Despite precedents for such
ideals in the work of George Perkins Marsh (Selection 6) and Aldo
Leopold (Selection 27), NEPA was epoch making in terms of
official recognition of ecological realities. The camp meeting
atmosphere associated with the first Earth Day, April 22, 1970,
revealed a similar recognition at a broad public level. More
important in terms of policy was the establishment on December 2,
1970, of the Environmental Protection Agency as a federal
watchdog over land and water use. The Chronology (pages xi–xix)
reveals the impressive effect of the environmental era on the
legislative and judicial processes.

30

Pesticides

Rachel Carson (1962)

In 1960 a distinguished naturalist and best-selling nature writer, Rachel Carson, published a series of articles in the New Yorker *that generated widespread discussion. The series concerned the effects of chemical insecticides on the balance of nature. Miss Carson was less concerned about the ethics of pesticides, as Aldo Leopold (Selection 27) might have been, and more about the possible consequences for man's health of unenlightened use of his ability to kill lower forms of life. Keyed to react strongly to Carson's message by the radioactive "fallout" scare that occurred simultaneously, many Americans were horrified at her revelations. But some scientists and, of course, the chemical companies that manufactured pesticides dismissed her fears as unfounded.*

The history of life on earth has been a history of interaction between living things and their surroundings. To a large extent, the physical form and the habits of the earth's vegetation and its animal life have been molded by the environment. Considering the whole span of earthly time, the opposite effect, in which life actually modifies its surroundings, has been relatively slight. Only within the moment of time represented by the present century has one species—man—acquired significant power to alter the nature of his world.

During the past quarter century this power has not only increased to one of disturbing magnitude but it has changed in character. The most alarming of all man's assaults upon the environment is the contamination of air, earth, rivers, and sea with dangerous and even lethal materials. This pollution is for the most part irrecoverable; the chain of evil it initiates not only in the world that must support life but in living tissues is for the most part irreversible. In this now universal contamination of the environment, chemicals are the sinister and little-recognized partners of radiation in changing the very nature of the world—the very nature of its life. Strontium 90, released through nuclear explosions into the air, comes to earth in rain or drifts down as fallout, lodges in soil, enters into the grass or corn or wheat grown there, and in time takes up its abode in the bones of a human being, there to remain until his death. Similarly, chemicals sprayed on croplands or forests or gardens lie long in soil, entering into living organisms, passing from one to another in a chain of poisoning and death. Or they pass mysteriously by underground streams until they emerge and, through the alchemy of air and sunlight, combine into new forms that kill vegetation, sicken cattle, and work unknown harm on those who drink from once pure wells. As Albert Schweitzer has said, "Man can hardly even recognize the devils of his own creation."

It took hundreds of millions of years to produce the life that now inhabits the earth—eons of time in which that developing and evolving and diversifying life reached a state of adjustment and balance with its surroundings. The environment, rigorously shaping and directing the life it supported, contained elements that were hostile as well as supporting. Certain rocks gave out dangerous radiation; even within the light of the sun, from which all life draws its energy, there were short-wave radiations with power to injure. Given time—time not in years but in millennia—life adjusts, and a balance has been reached. For time is the essential ingredient; but in the modern world there is no time.

The rapidity of change and the speed with which new situations are created follow the impetuous and heedless pace of man rather than the deliberate pace of nature. Radiation is no longer merely the background radiation of rocks, the bombardment of cosmic rays, the ultraviolet of the sun that have existed before there was any life on earth; radiation is now the unnatural creation of man's tampering with the atom. The chemicals to which life is asked to make its adjustment are no longer merely the calcium and silica and copper and all the rest of the minerals washed out of the rocks and carried in rivers to the sea; they are the synthetic creations of man's inventive mind, brewed in his laboratories, and having no counterparts in nature.

To adjust to these chemicals would require time on the scale that is nature's; it would require not merely the years of a man's life but the life of generations. And even this, were it by some miracle possible, would be futile, for the new chemicals come from our laboratories in an endless stream; almost five hundred annually find their way into actual use in the United States alone. The figure is staggering and its implications are not easily grasped—500 new chemicals to which the bodies of men and animals are required somehow to adapt each year, chemicals totally outside the limits of biologic experience.

Among them are many that are used in man's war against nature. Since the mid-1940's over 200 basic chemicals have been created for use in killing insects, weeds, rodents, and other organisms described in the modern vernacular as "pests"; and they are sold under several thousand different brand names.

These sprays, dusts, and aerosols are now applied almost universally to farms, gardens, forests, and homes—nonselective chemicals that have the power to kill every insect, the "good" and the "bad," to still the song of birds and the leaping of fish in the streams, to coat the leaves with a deadly film, and to linger on in soil—all this though the intended target may be only a few weeds or insects. Can anyone believe it is possible to lay down such a barrage of poisons on the surface of the earth without making it unfit for all life? They should not be called "insecticides," but "biocides."

The whole process of spraying seems caught up in an endless spiral. Since DDT was released for civilian use, a process of escalation has been going on in which ever more toxic materials must be found. This has happened because insects, in a triumphant vindication of Darwin's principle of the survival of the fittest, have evolved super races immune to the particular insecticide used, hence a deadlier one has always to be developed—and then a deadlier one than that. It has happened also because, for reasons to be described later, destructive insects often undergo a "flareback," or resurgence, after spraying, in numbers greater than before. Thus the chemical war is never won, and all life is caught in its violent crossfire.

Along with the possibility of the extinction of mankind by nuclear war, the central problem of our age has therefore become the contamination of man's total environment with such substances of incredible potential for harm—substances that accumulate in the tissues of plants and animals and even penetrate the germ cells to shatter or alter the very material of heredity upon which the shape of the future depends.

Some would-be architects of our future look toward a time when it will be possible to alter the human germ plasm by design. But we may easily be doing so now by inadvertence, for many chemicals, like radiation, bring about gene mutations. It is ironic to think that man might determine his own future by something so seemingly trivial as the choice of an insect spray.

All this has been risked—for what? Future historians may well be amazed by our distorted sense of proportion. How could intelligent beings seek to control a few unwanted species by a method that contaminated the entire environment and brought the threat of disease and death even to their own kind? Yet this is precisely what we have done. . . .

It is not my contention that chemical insecticides must never be used. I do contend that we have put poisonous and biologically potent chemicals indiscriminately into the hands of persons largely or wholly ignorant of their potentials for harm. We have subjected enormous numbers of people to contact with these poisons, without their consent and often without their knowledge. If the Bill of Rights contains no guarantee that a citizen shall be secure against lethal poisons distributed either by private individuals or by public officials, it is surely only because our forefathers, despite their considerable wisdom and foresight, could conceive of no such problem.

I contend, furthermore, that we have allowed these chemicals to be used with little or no advance investigation of their effect on soil, water, wildlife, and man himself. Future generations are unlikely to condone our lack of prudent concern for the integrity of the natural world that supports all life.

There is still very limited awareness of the nature of the threat. This is an era of specialists, each of whom sees his own problem and is unaware of or intolerant of the larger frame into which it fits. It is also an era dominated by industry, in which the right to make a dollar at whatever cost is seldom challenged. When the public protests, confronted with some obvious evidence of damaging results of pesticide applications, it is fed little tranquilizing pills of half truth. We urgently need an end to these false assurances, to the sugar coating of unpalatable facts. It is the public that is being asked to assume the risks that the insect controllers calculate. The public must decide whether it wishes to continue on the present road, and it can do so only when in full possession of the facts.

31

Pollution

President's Science Advisory Committee (1965)

The pesticide menace that Rachel Carson described (Selection 30) was only a portion of the problem that Americans of the 1960s referred to as "pollution." Indicative of the degree of national concern over pollution was the appointment of an Environmental Pollution Panel by the President's Science Advisory Committee. In 1965 the panel made a report that underlined concerns that would dominate environmental legislation for the next two decades.

The production of pollutants and an increasing need for pollution management are an inevitable concomitant of a technological society with a high standard of living. Pollution problems will increase in importance as our technology and standard of living continue to grow.

Our ancestors settled in a fair and unspoiled land, easily capable of absorbing the wastes of its animal and human populations. Nourished by the resources of this continent, the human inhabitants have multiplied greatly and have grouped themselves to form gigantic urban concentrations, in and around which are vast and productive industrial and agricultural establishments, disposed with little regard for state or municipal boundaries.

Huge quantities of diverse and novel materials are dispersed, from city and farm alike, into our air, into our waters and onto our lands. These pollutants are either unwanted by-products of our activities or spent substances which have served intended purposes. By remaining in the environment they impair our economy and the quality of our life. They can be carried long distances by air or water or on articles of commerce, threatening the health, longevity, livelihood, recreation,

Environmental Pollution Panel, President's Science Advisory Committee, *Restoring the Quality of Our Environment* (Washington, DC: U.S. Government Printing Office, 1965), 1–2, 5–7, 10–15.

cleanliness and happiness of citizens who have no direct stake in their production, but cannot escape their influence.

Pollutants have altered on a global scale the carbon dioxide content of the air and the lead concentrations in ocean waters and human populations. Pollutants have reduced the productivity of some of our finest agricultural soils, and have impaired the quality and the safety of crops raised on others. Pollutants have produced massive mortalities of fishes in rivers, lakes and estuaries and have damaged or destroyed commercial shellfish and shrimp fisheries. Pollutants have reduced valuable populations of pollinating and predatory insects, and have appeared in alarming amounts in migratory birds. Pollutants threaten the estuarine breeding grounds of valuable ocean fish; even Antarctic penguins and Arctic snowy owls carry pesticides in their bodies.

The land, water, air and living things of the United States are a heritage of the whole nation. They need to be protected for the benefit of all Americans, both now and in the future. The continued strength and welfare of our nation depend on the quantity and quality of our resources and on the quality of the environment in which our people live.

The pervasive nature of pollution, its disregard of political boundaries including state lines, the national character of the technical, economic and political problems involved, and the recognized Federal responsibilities for administering vast public lands which can be changed by pollution, for carrying out large enterprises which can produce pollutants, for preserving and improving the nation's natural resources, all make it mandatory that the Federal Government assume leadership and exert its influence in pollution abatement on a national scale. . . .

Man is but one species living in a world with numerous others; he depends on many of these others not only for his comfort and enjoyment but for his life. Plants provide the principal mechanism whereby energy from the sun can serve the earth's inhabitants. In doing so, they maintain the oxygen content of the air and furnish the basic habitat and food of animals and men. Microorganisms—bacteria, algae, fungi, and protozoa—perform a myriad of essential functions including the purification of air, soil, and water, and the recycling of nutrients. Animals serve man as great converters, changing plant-stored energy into forms of food he prefers and supplying him with a wide variety of materials: leather and furs, oils and pharmaceuticals, ivory and pearls, bristles and wool. Many insects are beneficial, some as pollinators; others as predators on harmful forms; some as makers of silk and honey.

As contributors to happiness and the quality of life, plants and animals provide opportunities for enjoyment of natural beauty, for hunting, fishing, gardening, scientific study, entertainment, and the satisfaction of our human curiosity.

In the control of pollution, plants, animals and microorganisms are directly useful in two ways: First, living things, especially microorganisms, have a capacity for absorption and decomposition of pollutants, with resulting purification of air, water and soil. Second, many species of organisms, each with its own particular range of sensitivity to each pollutant, stand as ready-made systems for environmental bioassay and monitoring, and for warnings of danger to man and his environment.

Because living things are interdependent and interacting, they form a complex, dynamic system. Tampering with this system may be desirable and necessary, as in agriculture, which involves artificial manipulation of the balances of nature on a huge scale. But such tampering often produces unexpected results, or side effects, and these are sometimes very damaging. Many of the effects of pollution fall into this category.

In small amounts, pollution can produce effects so subtle as to escape notice. Small changes in the reproductive rates of birds or fish, for example, can result from pesticide pollution at low levels, yet be very difficult to detect in nature. At high levels, damaging effects of pollution become clearly evident, as when fish are killed in large numbers or bees disappear from a locality.

Pollution affects living things in many different ways: In high concentrations, the sulfur dioxide in stack fumes kills trees and crop plants. The mixture of pollutants in urban smog damages spinach, tobacco, and other valuable plants. Domestic sewage and animal wastes can act as fertilizers, stimulating the growth of algae, but creating unfavorable conditions for game fish. Heating of rivers and lakes by return of waters used to cool industrial processes or power plants can favor some living forms and devastate others. Soils and waters can be polluted by radioactive materials derived from weapons testing, from industrial release, or from naturally contaminated fertilizers or spring waters. Once in soils or water, the radioactivity may then become concentrated in organisms. Sediments released into streams or lakes can reduce the supply of light for plants, and smother fish eggs and other useful forms.

The effects of pollution on livestock and crop plants often show up clearly because farmers quickly notice any impairment of health or yield. Effects on wild forms are much less likely to be detected and are harder to measure. Disappearance or catastrophic diminution of a wild population often occurs before the effects of a pollutant are recognized.

The effects of pollutants on living things are usually complicated and seldom well understood. Organisms are subjected to many different pollutants at the same time, pollutants that may enhance one another, partially compensate for one another, or act side by side.

Because different species react differently, and because the living world is so thoroughly interdependent, pollution produces profound indirect effects. A pesticide directed at a certain insect pest may, as a side effect, destroy a population of beneficial predator insects, so that a population of aphids that the predators had kept small suddenly multiplies and becomes highly destructive. A pollutant may fertilize a lake, creating vigorous algal growth near the surface, which shuts off the supply of sunlight from deeper-growing plants. The latter then consume the oxygen dissolved in the water, so that microscopic animals perish, and fish, depending on them for food and on dissolved oxygen for respiration, either starve or suffocate.

Pollutants tend to reduce the numbers of species, and to make the relationships of those that remain less stable. Large bodies of water, such as Lake Erie, may be depleted of many useful living forms. Pollution typically reduces the variety and abundance of wildlife serving our recreation and enjoyment.

From the economic point of view, pollution may produce serious adverse effects on living things used by man. Useful crops have been damaged by air and soil pollution, valuable commercial fisheries have been destroyed or diminished, as in the Great Lakes, Raritan Bay, and Long Island Sound, and wild populations of game fish and game birds valued for human recreation have been reduced. In a few instances, milk from herds of cattle fed on polluted forage has been so contaminated as to be unmarketable. . . .

Deliberate disposal of wastes is a more or less systematized activity. Most such wastes are not toxic, though some may carry disease. But odors, excess fertility of waters, and offenses against natural beauty are widespread. . . .

A frequently quoted estimate for the annual output of urban solid wastes, containing such things as paper, grass and brush cuttings, garbage, ashes, metal, and glass, is 1600 pounds per capita. Currently, this means 125 million tons each year, whose collection and disposal costs about 2.5 billion dollars a year. . . .

The combustion of coal, oil, and gas in our homes, vehicles, and factories results in the discharge into the air of sulfur dioxide, carbon dioxide, carbon monoxide, oxides of nitrogen, and partially burned hydrocarbons. Some of these gases, together with gasoline and natural gas vapors, undergo chemical change in air and in sunlight, and become the noxious constituents of smog; others, like carbon dioxide, are accumulating in such large quantities that they may eventually produce marked climatic change. Large amounts of lead are dispersed into the atmosphere from motor vehicle exhausts. Indeed, the pollution from internal combustion engines is so serious, and is growing so fast, that an alternative nonpolluting means of powering automobiles, buses and trucks is likely to become a national necessity. . . .

Pollution touches us all. We are at the same time pollutors and sufferers from pollution. Today, we are certain that pollution adversely affects the quality of our lives. In the future, it may affect their duration.

Present levels of pollution of air, water, soils and living organisms are for the most part below the levels that have been demonstrated to cause disease or death in people. At the same time we recognize a number of episodes where air pollution has caused deaths, where disease has been spread by water, where accidental poisonings have occurred from pesticides. The documented cases of pollution-caused injuries to plants, fish, birds and mammals are extensive and the economic loss from these injuries has been considerable. Some waters no longer support any useful fish or invertebrates. Some areas have been rendered unsuitable for useful plants. Many natural waters throughout the country are becoming continually less beautiful and less usable. Air in some of our cities is unpleasant to breathe and obscures our surroundings; our buildings are dirtied and sometimes rapidly weathered. Pollution has denied to some of our farmers the most desirable uses of parts of their lands. Prudence and self interest dictate that we exert ourselves not only to prevent further buildup of pollutants but to reduce present burdens of pollution in our air, our waters, and our land.

Arrangements to deal with pollution have grown on a piecemeal basis, with organizations, programs and legislation created when problems became evident or critical. With this background it is not surprising that current organization is a hodge-podge, with responsibilities widely separated among government agencies, and some unassigned.

Some pollutants are dealt with on the basis of the environmental medium in which they occur, for example, pollutants in air and water; others are dealt with on the basis of the kinds of effect they have, for example, toxic materials in food; some are dealt with on the basis of their sources, for example, artificially radioactive materials.

With some pollutants there is no Federal authority to act until a problem exists. Such is the case with water pollution and air pollution. With some pollutants there is no Federal authority to act at all, as is the case with pesticide residues on tobacco. With some pollution problems existing Federal authorities constrain the type of action that can be taken, as with water pollution problems that can be approached by the Corps of Engineers only through providing excess water storage for low-flow augmentation (usually a costly and inefficient process). With some pollutants such as radionuclides, extreme caution is exercised to assure that unwanted effects in the environment will be prevented; with other materials, such as pesticides, consideration of side effects has been scant in the past. . . .

Many kinds of pollution problems could be prevented by the exercise of ecological foresight. Given a reasonable knowledge of persistence, biological effect and expected initial distribution and amount, at least part of the impact on living things can be predicted. In the future, such advance evaluations will be essential.

Disposal of wastes is a requisite for domestic life, for agriculture, and for industry. Traditionally waste disposal was accomplished in the cheapest possible way, usually by dumping in the nearest stream. This tradition is no longer acceptable—we believe industrial and agricultural waste disposal must now be accomplished in such a way that pollution is avoided, and that the higher costs of such disposal should be borne by industry and agriculture, and considered as a part of the cost of operation. The pressure to pollute in the past has been an economic one; the pressure to abate must in the future also be economic.

Much can be done by enforcement of today's regulatory laws, and by modifying the administrative policy under which Federal assistance is provided. For example, pollution from farm animal wastes could be alleviated by vigorous enforcement without technological advances. The same is true of particulate materials in air and sewage effluents in water.

As a basis for pollution abatement, we need to establish environmental quality standards. Such standards imply that the community is willing to bear certain costs or to enforce these costs on others in order to maintain its surroundings at a given level of quality and utility. For each pollutant the elements that must be taken into account are: its effects; technological capabilities for its control; the costs of control; and the desired uses of the resources that pollutants may affect.

These complex problems cannot be handled without a sufficient number of trained technicians, engineers, economists, administrators and scientists, and without the requisite scientific, technical and economic knowledge. The manpower and knowledge now at hand are insufficient for the complete task, though much can be accomplished with present resources. Our government has a clear responsibility to insure that persons of ability and imagination are attracted into this broad field and trained in its intricacies, and that scientists and engineers are enabled to produce the knowledge and technology that will give the people of our country a clean, healthy, and happy environment.

32

Overpopulation

Paul Ehrlich (1968)

The Population Bomb was one of the books that exploded upon American complacency in the 1960s. Like Rachel Carson's Silent Spring of 1962 (Selection 30) it shocked readers into awareness of a problem that was already in an advanced stage of severity. Of course, writers since Thomas R. Malthus in 1798, and including William Vogt in 1948 (Selection 26), pleaded for recognition of the perils of unchecked human reproduction. But Ehrlich's book appeared in the year of the first manned mission to the moon. The dramatic photographs of a tiny spaceship earth underscored his call for public recognition of limits, and his book became a best-seller.

Ehrlich's contention that environmental degradation could be attributed to overpopulation and his predictions of famine in the very near future were criticized as overly dramatic, "doom and gloom" scare tactics. They also received a challenge from Barry Commoner (Selection 33) chiefly in his book The Closing Circle (1971). Commoner felt that technological change and industrial development were the primary causes of pollution. In fact, both positions had merit. Even Ehrlich implies at the opening of the following statement that relatively small populations with a high standard of living, such as the United States, impact the environment as much as large numbers of poverty-stricken people. The favorite way to make the point in the late 1960s was to say that one American baby would consume over its lifetime sixty times the energy and material resources as one of the babies Ehrlich encountered in India. As for the famines Ehrlich predicted, the agony of Ethiopia and the Sudan in the mid-1980s lent substance to his ideas.

The battle to feed all of humanity is over. In the 1970's the world will undergo famines—hundreds of millions of people are going to starve to death in spite of any crash programs embarked upon now. At this

Paul R. Ehrlich, *The Population Bomb* (New York: Ballantine, 1968), (ii), 15–19, 44–45. Reprinted by permission of Random House, Inc. Footnotes in the original have been omitted.

late date nothing can prevent a substantial increase in the world death rate, although many lives could be saved through dramatic programs to "stretch" the carrying capacity of the earth by increasing food production. But these programs will only provide a stay of execution unless they are accompanied by determined and successful efforts at population control. Population control is the conscious regulation of the numbers of human beings to meet the needs, not just of individual families, but of society as a whole.

Nothing could be more misleading to our children than our present affluent society. They will inherit a totally different world, a world in which the standards, politics, and economics of the 1960's are dead. As the most powerful nation in the world today, *and its largest consumer,* the United States cannot stand isolated. We are today involved in the events leading to famine; tomorrow we may be destroyed by its consequences.

Our position requires that we take immediate action at home and promote effective action worldwide. We must have population control at home, hopefully through a system of incentives and penalties, but by compulsion if voluntary methods fail. We must use our political power to push other countries into programs which combine agricultural development and population control. And while this is being done we must take action to reverse the deterioration of our environment before population pressure permanently ruins our planet. The birth rate must be brought into balance with the death rate or mankind will breed itself into oblivion. We can no longer afford merely to treat the symptoms of the cancer of population growth; the cancer itself must be cut out. Population control is the only answer. . . .

I have understood the population explosion intellectually for a long time. I came to understand it emotionally one stinking hot night in Delhi a couple of years ago. My wife and daughter and I were returning to our hotel in an ancient taxi. The seats were hopping with fleas. The only functional gear was third. As we crawled through the city, we entered a crowded slum area. The temperature was well over 100, and the air was a haze of dust and smoke. The streets seemed alive with people. People eating, people washing, people sleeping. People visiting, arguing, and screaming. People thrusting their hands through the taxi window, begging. People defecating and urinating. People clinging to buses. People herding animals. People, people, people, people. As we moved slowly through the mob, hand horn squawking, the dust, noise, heat, and cooking fires gave the scene a hellish aspect. Would we ever get to our hotel? All three of us were, frankly, frightened. It seemed that anything could happen—but, of course, nothing did. Old India hands will laugh at our reaction. We were just some overprivileged tourists, unaccustomed to the sights and sounds of India. Perhaps, but since that night I've known the *feel* of overpopulation. . . .

Americans are beginning to realize that the undeveloped countries of the world face an inevitable population-food crisis. Each year food production in undeveloped countries falls a bit further behind burgeoning population growth, and people go to bed a little bit hungrier. While there are temporary or local reversals of this trend, it now seems inevitable that it will continue to its logical conclusion: mass starvation. The rich are going to get richer, but the more numerous poor are going to get poorer. Of these poor, a minimum of three and one-half million will starve to death this year, mostly children. But this is a mere handful compared to the numbers that will be starving in a decade or so. And it is now too late to take action to save many of those people.

In a book about population there is a temptation to stun the reader with an avalanche of statistics. I'll spare you most, but not all, of that. After all, no matter how you slice it, population is a numbers game. Perhaps the best way to impress you with numbers is to tell you about the "doubling time"—the time necessary for the population to double in size.

It has been estimated that the human population of 6000 B.C. was about five million people, taking perhaps one million years to get there from two and a half million. The population did not reach 500 million until almost 8,000 years later—about 1650 A.D. This means it doubled roughly once every thousand years or so. It reached a billion people around 1850, doubling in some 200 years. It took only 80 years or so for the next doubling, as the population reached two billion around 1930. We have not completed the next doubling to four billion yet, but we now have well over three billion people. The doubling time at present seems to be about 37 years. Quite a reduction in doubling times: 1,000,000 years, 1,000 years, 200 years, 80 years, 37 years. Perhaps the meaning of a doubling time of around 37 years is best brought home by a theoretical exercise. Let's examine what might happen on the absurd assumption that the population continued to double every 37 years into the indefinite future.

If growth continued at that rate for about 900 years, there would be some 6,000,000,000,000,000 people on the face of the earth. Sixty million billion people. This is about 100 persons for each square yard of the Earth's surface, land and sea. A British physicist, J. H. Fremlin, guessed that such a multitude might be housed in a continuous 2,000-story building covering our entire planet. . . .

All of this boils down to a few elementary facts. There is not enough food today. How much there will be tomorrow is open to debate. If the optimists are correct, today's level of misery will be perpetuated for perhaps two decades into the future. If the pessimists are correct, massive famines will occur soon, possibly in the early 1970's, certainly by the early 1980's. So far most of the evidence seems to be on the side of the pessimists, and we should plan on the assumption that they are correct. After all, some two billion people aren't being properly fed in 1968!

33

Fundamental Causes of the Environmental Crisis

Barry Commoner (1970)

The gospel of ecology was part of a broader and deeper unrest in American society. The values and attitudes that lay behind environmental problems also produced social discontent and international disorder. Environmentalism of the 1960s, in fact, must be seen as drawing part of its force from a more general cultural questioning. In the following selection Barry Commoner, the biologist whose allegation that Lake Erie had "died" from pollution caused a minor sensation in 1968, draws the connections between the environmental movement and other troubling issues of the 1960s such as war, racial equality, and poverty. Behind these comments is a recurrent theme in Commoner's writing, particularly in his book The Closing Circle *(1971), concerning the need to weigh the liabilities of scientific and technological progress against their advantages.*

The sudden public concern with the environment has taken many people by surprise. After all, garbage, foul air, putrid water, and mindless noise are nothing new; the sights, smells, and sounds of pollution have become an accustomed burden of life. To be sure, the mess has worsened and spread in the last decade, but not at a rate to match the dramatic, nearly universal reaction to it that has hit the country in the past year.

Although the growing demand for action against environmental pollution is very clear, it is not so clear how the movement came about and where it is going. This is a particularly crucial time to find out. For the environmental teach-ins that are being planned on thousands of

Barry Commoner, "Beyond the Teach-In," *Saturday Review,* **LIII** (1970), 50–52, 62–64. Reprinted by permission of Omni Publications International.

campuses this month are both the chief evidence of the origins of the movement and the main force that will determine its future.

Several environmental teach-ins have already taken place, the largest of them being that of March 11–14 at the University of Michigan, where the roster of speakers and participants was dramatic evidence that the environmental movement has become a meeting place for major and divergent elements of American society.

The kick-off rally for the teach-in, attended by 15,000 enthusiastic students, was addressed by Michigan's Governor Milliken, and a number of other municipal, state, and federal officials were present—testimony to the importance government figures attach to voter interest in the environment.

Among the teach-in speakers were a variety of scientists with a professional interest in the environment: biologists, ecologists, engineers, sociologists, urban analysts, and public health experts. This reflects one of the earliest origins of the environmental movement—the work of those of us in the scientific community who, some years ago, began to detect in our own studies evidence that pollution is not only a nuisance but a threat to the health, even the survival, of mankind. . . .

Industry was represented by officers of the Detroit Edison Company, Ford Motor Company, Dow Chemical Company, and others—all industries that bear a large responsibility for serious pollution problems. The interest of these companies in public concern with the environment has become a matter of direct corporate necessity.

Labor was represented by Walter Reuther, whose union—the United Automobile Workers—opposed the construction about five years ago of Detroit Edison's Fermi reactor, located about five miles outside Detroit. Through an educational program, the UAW has developed a broad interest in environmental quality, and that consideration is now included among UAW contract demands.

That the president of the Dow Chemical Company was invited to speak at Michigan reveals another important element in the environmental movement. Dow has been, of course, a prime target of the antiwar movement; its campus recruiting program has triggered many demonstrations by student activists, who cite the hold of the military-industrial complex on U.S. policy as a reason why our social system must be radically changed. And the activists had *their* representatives on the roster of teach-in speakers—one being Murray Bookchin, an environmental analyst who takes a socio-revolutionary approach to this and other social ills. Finally, the speech that closed the teach-in was given by Richard Hatcher, mayor of Gary, Indiana, a city that suffers the specially intense environmental problems of a largely black population.

The Michigan teach-in epitomized the remarkable convergence around the environmental issue of a number of earlier, separate concerns: conservation, scientists' responsibility for the social consequences of science and technology, the consumer movement, the young generation's feeling for a more humane life-style, the businessman's worries over the impact of all of these on industrial profits, the problem of the ghetto and urban decay, the antiwar movement, and student activism against the nation's social and economic system. Somehow, the issue of environmental quality touches all these separate facets of the crisis of American society.

I can report from my own experience that there is a close link between the problem of war and the problem of the environment. My concern with the environment does not stem from my professional training: I was trained as a cellular biologist, not as an ecologist. But I also learned that science is part of society and that every scientist owes it to himself, and to the society that supports him, to be concerned with the impact of science on social problems. And it was the problem of war that first introduced me to the environmental crisis. In the 1950s, when nuclear tests first showered the world with fallout, and the Atomic Energy Commission showered the nation with assurances that radiation was "harmless," I studied, along with many other scientists, the path that fallout takes in the environment from the bomb to man. And I was shocked to learn that nuclear radiation is never harmless, to the ecosystem or to man. That is when I began to appreciate the importance of the environment to man. It was the AEC that turned me into an ecologist.

There are specific links between the environmental crisis, the evils of war in general, and the war in Vietnam in particular. One link can be seen in the economics of war and of pollution. That our industrial system is heavily sustained by the military diversion of human and natural resources from human needs has been demonstrated cogently by numerous observers; the military-industrial complex was not a myth to President Eisenhower, nor is it to the stockholders in major American industries. What is less known, but can be equally well documented, is that the profitability of most American industry and agriculture has been related significantly to their avoidance of a large cost of doing business—environmental deterioration. For example, the power industry, a major cause of urban air pollution, sells electricity to its consumers for a certain amount of money, but those same consumers pay an added cost for the environmental consequences of the power they buy—in laundry bills caused by soot, and in doctor bills (and some reduction in their life expectancy) caused by sulfur dioxide and organic air pollutants from power plants. The dollar value alone of these "social costs" of air pollution that we now know of—and many remain unknown—adds about 25 per cent to the city dweller's electric bill.

Some economists assert that the economic system could readily adjust itself to this situation by undertaking the cost of preventing pollution and adding that cost to the real price of its products. Such a readjustment would affect the cost to the consumer, not only of power but of all manufactured goods (nearly every factory pollutes the air and water), of transportation (cars, trucks, and airplanes are major polluters of air), and of food (U.S. agriculture, through its use of intensive fertilization and feedlots for fattening cattle to high-priced grades, bears a major responsibility for water pollution; organic wastes from U.S. feedlots exceed those produced by the total U.S. urban population). It may be that the economic system *can* get along without the crutch provided by the diversion of environmental costs to the people, and that it *can* get along without the crutch of military production. But thus far it hasn't, and one can at least suspect that in both cases the crutch has become a support essential to the system's stability.

Another close link between the problems of war and the environment is that both represent the inability of our technology to foresee its own inherently fatal environmental flaws. Like detergents—which, much to their developers' surprise, failed to be accommodated by natural water systems and bloomed into unsightly mounds of foam on our rivers—or the unanticipated ecological backlash of DDT, the nation's war program can be viewed as a vast technological blunder. When, in the 1950s, the Pentagon and its scientific advisers decided to hang the nation's defense on nuclear weapons, they did not know what the scientific community has since told them: It will not work; no nation can survive a nuclear war. Remember that in 1956 Eisenhower campaigned for continued nuclear tests in part because "by the most sober and responsible scientific judgment they do not imperil the health of man." Eight years later, Johnson praised the nuclear test ban treaty, because it "halted the steady, menacing increase of radioactive fallout." The Pentagon also told scientists that it would not use herbicides in Vietnam if it believed that these agents would have "long-term ecological effects" on that tortured land. Now we know from scientific evidence that mangrove areas of Vietnam will not recover from herbicide attacks for at least twenty years. Indeed, because of herbicide attacks not only on forest areas but on food crops, together with the massive assaults by more conventional weapons, the war in Vietnam represents, in my opinion, the first ecological warfare conducted by the United States since the attacks on American Indians. The technological failure of biological warfare as a suitable means of defense (for there is no way to test artificial infectious agents, much less use them, without incurring serious risks to ourselves) was recently acknowledged when the government ordered the abandonment of its entire biological warfare program.

If there is little reason to regard the environmental movement as a diversion from the antiwar movement, its relation to the racial issue is less clear. Some approaches to the environmental problem seem to run counter to the interests of the blacks. This was dramatized recently at San Jose State College, where, as a symbol of environmental rebellion, a student program was climaxed by the burial of a brand new car. The event was picketed by black students who believed the $2,500 paid for the car could have been better spent in the ghetto.

The San Jose burial reflects a personalized attack on the environmental crisis, an approach that is now fairly common among some student groups. They reason that pollution in the United States is caused by the excessive consumption of goods and resources, a favorite statistic being that the U.S. contains about 6 per cent of the world's population but consumes half of the planet's total goods and resources. Since the wastes generated by this intense consumption pollute our environment, the eco-activist is advised to "consume less." In the absence of the added statistic that in the United States the per capita consumption by blacks is much lower than that of whites, such observations are not likely to arouse the enthusiasm of blacks.

Disaffiliation of blacks from the environmental movement would be particularly unfortunate, because in many ways blacks are the special victims of pollution and have much to teach whites about survival. A white suburbanite can escape from the city's dirt, smog, carbon monoxide, lead, and noise when he goes home; the ghetto dweller not only works in a polluted environment, he lives in it. And in the ghetto he confronts added environmental problems: rats and other vermin and the danger of his children's suffering lead poisoning when they eat bits of ancient, peeling paint. To middle-class Americans, survival is not a familiar issue. They have not yet learned how to face such a soul-shaking threat, as demonstrated by the continued failure to appreciate that the existence of ready-armed nuclear weapons may bring doomsday as close as tomorrow. For blacks, the issue of survival is 200 years old. If they have not yet mastered it, they at least have had a good deal of experience that may be enormously valuable to a society that now, as a whole, must face the threat of extinction. Blacks need the environmental movement, and the movement needs the blacks.

Confusion between certain aspects of the environmental movement and other social issues is also generated by the view that the former is closely connected to the population crisis. In one sense, this belief is valid, for clearly the world population cannot continue to grow at its present rapid rate (largely in underdeveloped countries) without eventually outrunning the capacity of the planetary ecosystem to produce sufficient food to sustain it. But some environmentalists* hold that in an advanced country like the United States "the pollution problem is a consequence of population." This view leads to the idea that the environmental crisis in the U.S., which clearly calls for drastic action, can be solved only if we take strong action to stop the growth of the U.S. population.

A good deal of the confusion surrounding priorities can be cleared up by some facts. Nearly all of the stresses that have caused the environmental breakdown here—smog, detergents, insecticides, heavy use of fertilizers, radiation—began about 20 to 25 years ago. That period saw a sharp rise in the *per capita* production of pollutants. For example, between 1946 and 1966 total utilization of fertilizer increased about 700 per cent, electric power nearly 400 per cent, and pesticides more than 500 per cent. In that period the U.S. population increased by only 43 per cent. This means that the major factor responsible for increasing pollution in the U.S. since 1946 is not the increased number of people, but the intensified effects of ecologically faulty technology on the environment.

So the environmental movement—and the teach-ins that signal its emergence as a major political force—has become a meeting place for the major issues that trouble American society. This is its strength, and this is the importance of its future course.

Demands for *action* dominate the environmental movement, and

---

*Commoner is referring here to Paul Ehrlich, (Selection 32). [Ed.]

wide-ranging programs of action are being organized. Some are direct, personal efforts to clear up the environment, such as community-wide campaigns to remove the junk from a stream bed. Some are politically oriented demonstrations, such as the delivery of a mass of beer cans to the lawn of a can manufacturer's home. Petition campaigns directed at remedial legislation abound, and legislators have been busy trying to reflect in law the new desire of their constituents for a clean environment. There are strong indications that on most campuses the current teach-ins will lead to environmental action's becoming a major, continuing feature of campus life.

Of course, there are those who regard the environmental movement as only the latest in a series of ephemeral fads for political action, doomed like its predecessors—civil rights, the antiwar movement, and student power—to rise to an enthusiastic peak and fade away before the hard, intransigent realities of political life. I disagree.

That danger does exist, for there are no easy solutions to the *fundamental* problems of the environmental crisis. Some of the superficial symptoms can be attacked directly: Creeks can be cleared of junk and beer cans can be collected. But no band of activists can return a river to an unpolluted state when the polluting agent is fertilizer draining from the surrounding farmland. And if farmers were abruptly required to halt their intensive use of fertilizer, often crucial to the solvency of their operation, they would simply go out of business.

Once we look beyond its immediate accessible symptoms, the environmental crisis confronts us with very hard, inescapable choices. If we really want to cure the evil of water pollution, we will have to make drastic revisions in present waste-treatment methods, for these overfertilize the algae in the water, which soon die, reimposing on rivers and lakes the very burden of organic waste that the treatment was supposed to remove. The natural ecological system that can accommodate organic waste is not in the water, but in the soil, and no lasting solution to the deterioration of both surface waters and the soil can be achieved until organic waste is returned to the soil. For the same reason no scheme of handling garbage that fails to meet this fundamental requirement of nature can, in the long run, succeed. And since these and similar violations of the demands of the ecosystem have become embedded in our ways of productivity, any effort to change them will encounter the massive economic, social, and political forces that sustain that system. Our major technologies—power production, transport, the metal and chemical industries, and agriculture—are a threat to the ecosystems that support them and to our very lives.

Because we reckon the value of a technology by the value of its marketable products, we have neglected their cost to society—which is, potentially, extinction.

President Nixon has spoken of the need for "the total mobilization of the nation's resources" in order to pay our "debt to nature." But the resources needed to roll back pollution remain immobilized by the cost of the Vietnam war and the huge military budget, by the talent- and money-gulping space program, by the disastrous cuts in the federal budget for research support, by the reduction in funds for the cities and for education. The environmental crisis, together with all of the other evils that blight the nation—racial inequality, hunger, poverty, and war—cries out for a profound revision of our national priorities. No national problem can be solved until that is accomplished.

Confronted by the depth of this multiple crisis, it is easy to respond with a spate of studies, reports, and projections for future action. But, however essential they may be, more than plans are needed. For the grinding oppression of environmental deterioration—the blighted streets and uncollected garbage, the rats and the cockroaches, the decaying beaches and foul rivers, the choking, polluted air—degrades the hope of our citizens for the future and their will to secure it. To unwind this spiral of despair, we must take immediate steps against the symptoms as well as the fundamental disorder. Community efforts to clean up rivers and beaches, to build parks, to insist on enforcement of anti-pollution ordinances and to improve them can give tangible meaning to the spirit of environmental revival.

All of our problems seem to have a common root. Something is wrong with the way this nation uses its human and natural resources. And I believe that it is always healthy to reexamine, to test, the basic mechanism we have created to run our affairs. Those who are already convinced that our social system is in need of radical revision will welcome this opportunity to discuss the prospect. Those who are convinced that the system is fundamentally sound and can be adjusted to the new stresses should welcome this opportunity to demonstrate their conviction. Here, then, is good reason to bring the social revolutionary and the industrialist onto the same platform. Both need to face the same question: How should our society be organized to resolve the crisis of survival?

It is fitting that these issues are being called to our attention by the nation's youth—in the teach-ins and in the student movement that will surely follow them. For young people, our future generations, are the real victims of the impending environmental catastrophe. They are the first generation in human history to carry strontium 90 in their bones and DDT in their fat; their bodies will record, in time, the effects on human health of the new environmental insults. It is they who face the frightful task of seeking humane knowledge in a world that has, with cunning perversity, transformed the power knowledge generates into an instrument of catastrophe. And during the coming months, I think, our young people will demonstrate that they are, in fact, equal to this task, as their environmental teach-ins and ecological actions begin to mobilize the knowledge of our schools and universities and the civic zeal of our communities for a real attack on the environmental predicament.

We have long known that ours is a technological society, a society in which the knowledge generated by science is a chief source of wealth and power. But what the environmental crisis tells us is that the future of our society now depends on new, profoundly fundamental judgments of how this knowledge, and the power that it endows, is to be used. If power is to be derived from the will of the people, as it should be in our democracy, then the people need to have the new knowledge—about strontium 90, DDT, herbicides, smog, and all the other elements of the environmental crisis—that must be the source of the grave new judgments and sweeping programs this nation must undertake. Here, then, is an urgent task that must follow the teach-ins. Let us take our knowledge about the environmental plight to the people; let us help them learn what they need to know to decide the future course of our society.

The obligation that our technological society forces upon all of us is to discover how humanity can survive the new power engendered by science. Every major advance in man's technological competence has enforced new obligations on human society. The present age is no exception to this rule of history. We already know the enormous benefits technology can bestow, and we have begun to perceive its frightful threats.

The environmental peril now upon us is a grim challenge. It also represents a great opportunity. From it we may yet learn that the proper use of science is not to conquer nature but to live in it. We may yet learn that to save ourselves we must save the world, which is our habitat. We may yet discover how to devote the wisdom of science and the power of technology to the welfare and survival of man.

34

The State of the Environment

The Council on Environmental Quality (1970)

The Council on Environmental Quality was among the most important institutional consequences of the gospel of ecology. Established in the Executive Office of the President by the National Environmental Policy Act (January 1, 1970), the three-person council and modest supporting staff had a difficult task. The act required them to report immediately on the condition of the American environment and the effects upon it of federal, state, local, corporate, and individual actions. Undaunted, the council produced by August of its first year a book-length overview of environmental issues facing the nation. The opening chapter, reproduced in part here, was a joint effort of the council members, Russell E. Train, Robert Cahn, and Gordon J. MacDonald. Their thoughts provide a good overview of American thought at the height of the environmental era.

Historians may one day call 1970 the year of the environment. They may not be able to say that 1970 actually marked a significant change for the better in the quality of life; in the polluting and the fouling of the land, the water, and the air; or in health, working conditions, and recreational opportunity. Indeed, they are almost certain to see evidence of worsening environmental conditions in many parts of the country.

Yet 1970 marks the beginning of a new emphasis on the environment—a turning point, a year when the quality of life has become more than a phrase; environment and pollution have become everyday words; and ecology has become almost a religion to some of the young. Environmental problems, standing for many years on the threshold of national prominence, are now at the center of nationwide concern. Action to improve the environment has been launched by government

Council on Environmental Quality, *Environmental Quality: The First Annual Report of the Council on Environmental Quality* (Washington, DC: U.S. Government Printing Office, 1970), 5–18.

at all levels. And private groups, industry, and individuals have joined · the attack.

No one can say for sure just how or why the environment burst into national prominence in 1970. Certainly national concern had been mounting for a long time, and the tempo has increased greatly in the last decade.

Early environmentalists—Henry David Thoreau, George Perkins Marsh, John Muir, Gifford Pinchot, Theodore Roosevelt, Aldo Leopold—and a legion of dedicated citizens contributed to the rise in awareness. In its early days, the conservation movement aimed primarily at stemming the exploitation of natural resources and preserving wildlife and important natural areas. By the 1950's, Federal air and water pollution laws had been enacted, and the pace of environmental legislation quickened dramatically in the decade of the 1960's. Now the conservation movement has broadened to embrace concern for the totality of man's environment, focusing on pollution, population, ecology, and the urban environment.

The public has begun to realize the interrelationship of all living things—including man—with the environment. The Santa Barbara oil spill in early 1969 showed an entire nation how one accident could temporarily blight a large area. Since then, each environmental issue— the jetport project near Everglades National Park, the proposed pipeline across the Alaskan wilderness, the worsening blight of Lake Erie, the polluted beaches off New York and other cities, smog in mile-high Denver, lead in gasoline, phosphates in detergents, and DDT—flashed the sign to Americans that the problems are everywhere and affect everyone. Millions of citizens have come to realize that the interdependent web of life—man, animals, plants, earth, air, water, and sunlight—touches everyone.

A deteriorating environment has awakened a lively curiosity in Americans about exactly what is meant by an ecosystem, a biome, or the biosphere. Citizens who are now aware of environmental problems want to know the full extent of the environmental crisis and the nature of the factors that have contributed to it. They are anxious to learn what can be done to correct the mistakes that have led to the current condition of the environment. This report attempts to answer some of these questions.

Ecology is the science of the intricate web of relationships between living organisms and their living and nonliving surroundings. These interdependent living and nonliving parts make up *ecosystems*. Forests, lakes, and estuaries are examples. Larger ecosystems or combinations of ecosystems, which occur in similar climates and share a similar character and arrangement of vegetation, are *biomes*. The Arctic tundra, prairie grasslands, and the desert are examples. The earth, its surrounding envelope of life-giving water and air, and all its living things comprise the *biosphere*. Finally, man's total *environmental system* includes not only the biosphere but also his interactions with his natural and manmade surroundings.

Changes in ecosystems occur continuously. Myriad interactions take place at every moment of the day as plants and animals respond to variations in their surroundings and to each other. Evolution has produced for each species, including man, a genetic composition that limits how far that species can go in adjusting to sudden changes in its surroundings. But within these limits the several thousand species in an ecosystem, or for that matter, the millions in the biosphere, continuously adjust to outside stimuli. Since interactions are so numerous, they form long chains of reactions. Thus small changes in one part of an ecosystem are likely to be felt and compensated for eventually throughout the system.

Dramatic examples of change can be seen where man has altered the course of nature. It is vividly evident in his well-intentioned but poorly thought out tampering with river and lake ecosystems. The Aswan Dam was primarily built to generate electric power. It produced power, but it also reduced the fish population in the Mediterranean, increased the numbers of disease-bearing aquatic snails, and markedly lowered the fertility of the Nile Valley.

In the United States, the St. Lawrence Seaway has contributed significantly to the economic growth of the Great Lakes region. Yet it has done so at a high and largely unforeseen cost to the environment. The completion of the Welland Canal let the predatory sea lamprey into the Great Lakes. Trout, which had been the backbone of the lakes' fishing industry, suffered greatly from the lamprey invasion. By the mid-1950's the trout and some other large, commercial predatory fish were nearly extinct. And with their near extinction, smaller fish, especially the alewife, normally kept under control by these predators, proliferated. The aggressive alewife dominated the food supply and greatly reduced the numbers of small remaining native fish, such as the lake herring. The alewife became so numerous, in fact, that on occasion great numbers died and the dead fish along the shore caused a major public nuisance.

Man attempted to restore the ecological balance by instituting sea lamprey control in the 1950's and 1960's and by stocking the lakes

with coho salmon beginning in 1965—to replace the lost native predatory fish. Feeding on the abundant alewife, the salmon multiplied
rapidly and by 1969 had become important both as a commercial and
sport resource. Some of the salmon, however, were contaminated by
excessive concentrations of DDT and were taken off the commercial
market.

The lesson is not that such activities as the St. Lawrence Seaway
must be halted, but that the consequences of construction must be
carefully studied in advance of construction. Planners and managers
must begin to appreciate the enormous interrelated complexity of
environmental systems, weigh the tradeoffs of potential environmental harm against the benefits of construction, look at alternatives, and
incorporate environmental safeguards into the basic design of new
developments.

The stability of a particular ecosystem depends on its diversity.
The more interdependencies in an ecosystem, the greater the chances
that it will be able to compensate for changes imposed upon it. A
complex tropical forest with a rich mosaic of interdependencies possesses much more stability than the limited plant and animal life found
on the Arctic tundra, where instability triggers frequent, violent fluctuations in some animal populations, such as lemmings and foxes.
The least stable systems are the single crops—called monocultures—
created by man. A cornfield or lawn has little natural stability. If they
are not constantly and carefully cultivated, they will not remain corn-
fields or lawns but will soon be overgrown with a wide variety of
hardier plants constituting a more stable ecosystem.

The chemical elements that make up living systems also depend
on complex, diverse sources to prevent cyclic shortages or oversupply.
The oxygen cycle, which is crucial to survival, depends upon a vast
variety of green plants, notably plankton in the ocean. Similar diversity is essential for the continued functioning of the cycle by which
atmospheric nitrogen is made available to allow life to exist. This cycle
depends on a wide variety of organisms, including soil bacteria and
fungi, which are often destroyed by persistent pesticides in the soil.

Although pollution may be the most prominent and immediately
pressing environmental concern, it is only one facet of the many-sided
environmental problem. It is a highly visible, sometimes dangerous
sign of environmental deterioration. Pollution occurs when materials
accumulate where they are not wanted. Overburdened natural processes cannot quickly adjust to the heavy load of materials which man,
or sometimes nature, adds to them. Pollution threatens natural sys-

tems, human health, and esthetic sensibilities; it often represents valuable resources out of place. DDT, for instance, is a valuable weapon in combating malaria. But DDT, when out of place—for example in lakes and streams—concentrates in fish, other wildlife, and the smaller living things on which they depend.

Historically, man has assumed that the land, water, and air around him would absorb his waste products. The ocean, the atmosphere, and even the earth were viewed as receptacles of infinite capacity. It is clear now that man may be exceeding nature's capacity to assimilate his wastes.

Most pollutants eventually decompose and diffuse throughout the environment. When organic substances are discarded, they are attacked by bacteria and decompose through oxidation. They simply rot. However, some synthetic products of our advanced technology resist natural decomposition. Plastics, some cans and bottles, and various persistent pesticides fall into this category. Many of these materials are toxic, posing a serious health danger. . . .

Radioactive fallout from the air also concentrates through food chains. Arctic lichens do not take in food through their roots but instead absorb mineral nutrition from dust in the air. Radioactive fallout tends therefore to collect in the lichens and is further concentrated by grazing caribou, which eat huge quantities of lichen. Caribou meat is a major part of the Eskimo's diet. Although reconcentration of radioactive fallout at low levels has not been proved damaging to health, the effects of long-term, low-level exposure to radioactive pollutants are still not well known.

Water pollution is a problem throughout the country, but is most acute in densely settled or industrial sections. Organic wastes from municipalities and industries enter rivers, where they are attacked and broken down by organisms in the water. But in the process, oxygen in the river is used up. Nutrients from cities, industries, and farms nourish algae, which also use up oxygen when they die and decompose. And when oxygen is taken from the water, the river "dies." The oxygen is gone, the game fish disappear, plant growth rots, and the stench of decay reaches for miles.

Air pollution is now a problem in all parts of the United States and in all industrialized nations. It has been well known for some time to Los Angeles residents and visitors who have long felt the effect of highly visible and irritating smog from automobile exhaust. Now Los Angeles's local problem is becoming a regional problem, because noxious air pollution generated in the Los Angeles Basin has spread beyond the metropolitan area. This same problem, which seemed unique to Los Angeles in the 1950s is today common to major cities in the United States and abroad. Smog is but one of the many types of air pollution that plague the United States, especially its cities.

Urban land misuse is one of today's most severe environmental problems. The character of our urban areas changes rapidly. Old buildings and neighborhoods are razed and replaced by structures designed with little or no eye for their fitness to the community's needs. A jumble of suburban developments sprawls over the landscape. Furthermore, lives and property are endangered when real estate developments are built on flood plains or carved out along unstable slopes.

Unlimited access to wilderness areas may transform such areas into simply another extension of our urban, industrialized civilization. The unending summer flow of automobiles into Yosemite National Park has changed one of nature's great wilderness areas into a crowded gathering place of lessened value to its visitors. The worldwide boom in tourism, teamed with rapid and cheap transportation, threatens the very values upon which tourist attraction is based.

The proposed jetport west of Miami and north of the Everglades National Park raised a dramatic land use problem. The jetport, together with associated transportation corridors, imperiled a unique ecological preserve. Planners for the jetport had considered density of population, regional transportation needs, and a host of other related variables. But they gave slight consideration to the wildlife and recreational resources of the Everglades. The jetport could have spawned a booming residential, commercial, and industrial complex which would have diminished water quality and without question drastically altered the natural water cycle of Southern Florida. This in turn would have endangered all aquatic species and wildlife within the park and beyond.

Natural resource depletion is a particular environmental concern to a highly technological society which depends upon resources for energy, building materials, and recreation. And the methods of exploiting resources often create problems that are greater than the value of the resources themselves.

A classic case was the Federal Government's decision to permit oil drilling in California's Santa Barbara Channel. There, primary value was placed on development of the oil resources. The commercial, recreational, esthetic, and ecological values, which also are important to the residents of Santa Barbara and to the Nation, were largely ignored. The President recently proposed to the Congress that the

Federal Government cancel the 20 Federal leases seaward from the State sanctuary extending 16 miles along the Santa Barbara Channel. This is where the blowout erupted in January 1969, spreading a coat of oil across hundreds of square miles including the sanctuary. This action illustrates a commitment to use offshore lands in a balanced and responsible way.

Environmental problems seldom stem from simple causes. Rather they usually rise out of the interplay of many contributing circumstances.

Many individuals cite selfish profit seekers for environmental degradation, rather than laying much of the blame—where it belongs—to misplaced incentives in the economic system. Progress in environmental problems is impossible without a clearer understanding of how the economic system works in the environment and what alternatives are available to take away the many roadblocks to environmental quality.

Our price system fails to take into account the environmental damage that the polluter inflicts on others. Economists call these damages—which are very real—"external social costs." They reflect the ability of one entity, e.g., a company, to use water or air as a free resource for waste disposal, while others pay the cost in contaminated air or water. If there were a way to make the price structure shoulder these external costs—taxing the firm for the amount of discharge, for instance—then the price for the goods and services produced would reflect these costs. Failing this, goods whose production spawns pollution are greatly underpriced because the purchaser does not pay for pollution abatement that would prevent environmental damage. Not only does this failure encourage pollution but it warps the price structure. A price structure that took environmental degradation into account would cause a shift in prices, hence a shift in consumer preferences and, to some extent, would discourage buying pollution-producing products.

Another type of misplaced incentive lies imbedded in the tax structure. The property tax, for example, encourages architectural design that leans more to rapid amortization than to quality. It may also encourage poor land use because of the need for communities to favor industrial development and discourage property uses, such as high-density housing, which cost more in public services than they produce in property taxes. Other taxes encourage land speculation and the leap-frog development that has become the trademark of the urban-rural fringe.

Americans have placed a high priority on convenience and consumer goods. In recent times they have learned to value the convenience and comfort of modern housing, transportation, communication, and recreation above clean earth, sky, and water. A majority, like a prodigal son, have been willing to consume vast amounts of resources and energy, failing to understand how their way of life may choke off open space, forests, clean air, and clear water. It is only recently that the public has become conscious of some of the conflicts between convenience and a deteriorating environment.

In the early days of westward expansion, a period in which many national values were shaped, choices did not seem necessary. The forests, minerals, rivers, lakes, fish, and wildlife of the continent seemed inexhaustible. Today choices based on values must be made at every turn. Values can be gauged to some degree by the costs that the Nation is collectively willing to incur to protect them. Some of the costs of environmental improvements can be paid with local, State, and Federal tax money. But paying taxes and falling back on government programs is not enough. People may ultimately have to forgo some conveniences and pay higher prices for some goods and services.

Americans are just beginning to measure the magnitude of the impact of population and its distribution on their environment. The concept that population pressures are a threat to the Nation's well-being and to its environment is difficult to grasp in a country which, during its formative decades, had an ever receding western frontier. That frontier ended at the Pacific many years ago. And it is at the western end of the frontier that some of the most serious problems of population growth emerge most clearly.

California continues to lure large numbers of Americans from all over the country, in large part because of its climate and its beauty. But as the people come, the pressures of population mount. Smog, sprawl, erosion, loss of beaches, the scarring of beautiful areas, and the congestion of endless miles of freeways have caused thoughtful Californians to consider stemming the continued uncontrolled development of their State. When the Governor's Conference on California's Changing Environment met last fall, it agreed that there was now a need "to deemphasize growth as a social goal and, rather, to encourage development within an ideal and quality environment."

The magnitude of the press of population, although significant, must be put in perspective. This is a vast country, and its potential for assimilating population is impressive, although there is disagreement over what level of population would be optimum. Some authorities believe that the optimum level has already been passed, others that it has not yet been reached. More troublesome, population control strikes at deeply held religious values and at the preference of some Americans for large families.

Population density outside metropolitan areas is not high. There is a desire—indeed an almost inevitable compulsion—to concentrate population in urban areas—primarily in the coastal and Great Lakes regions. If the trend continues, 70 to 80 percent of all Americans will be concentrated in five large urban complexes by the year 2000. The pressures that cause environmental problems that the Nation now confronts—water and air pollution and inefficient land use—will only increase.

Population growth threatens the Nation's store of natural resources. Currently the United States, with about 6 percent of the world's population, uses more than 40 percent of the world's scarce or nonreplaceable resources and a like ratio of its energy output. Assuming a fixed or nearly fixed resource base, continued population growth embodies profound implications for the United States and for the world.

The major environmental problems of today began with the Industrial Revolution. Belching smoke from factory stacks and the dumping of raw industrial wastes into rivers became the readily identified, but generally ignored hallmarks of "progress" and production. They are no longer ignored, but the extraordinary growth of the American economy continues to outpace the efforts to deal with its unwanted by-products.

The growth of the economy has been marked not just by greater production but also by an accelerating pace of technological innovation. This innovation, although it has provided new solutions to environmental problems, has also created a vast range of new problems. New chemicals, new uses for metals, new means of transportation, novel consumer goods, new medical techniques, and new industrial processes all represent potential hazards to man and his surroundings. The pace of technological innovation has exceeded our scientific and regulatory ability to control its injurious side effects. The environmental problems of the future will increasingly spring from the wonders of 20th-century technology. In the future, technology assessment must be used to understand the direct and secondary impacts of technological innovation.

The extraordinary, growing mobility of the American people constitutes another profound threat to the environment—in at least three major ways. The physical movement of people crowds in on metropolitan centers and into recreation areas, parks, and wild areas. Mobility permits people to live long distances from their places of employment, stimulating ever greater urban and suburban sprawl. The machines of this mobility—particularly automobiles and aircraft—themselves generate noise, air pollution, highways, and airports—all in their way affecting the environment.

The automobile freed Americans from the central city and launched the flight to the suburbs. As a consequence, thousands of acres of undeveloped land fall prey each year to the bulldozer. More single-family, detached homes shoulder out the open spaces. Many of these developments are drab in design and wasteful of land. They denude the metropolitan area of trees and thus affect climate; they cause erosion, muddy rivers, and increase the cost of public services.

Most government agencies charged with solving environmental problems were not originally designed to deal with the severe tasks they now face. And their focus is often too narrow to cope with the broad environmental problems that cut across many jurisdictions. Agencies dealing with water pollution, for example, typically do not have jurisdiction over the geographic problem area—the watersheds. Control is split instead among sewerage districts, municipalities, and a multitude of other local institutions. To attack water pollution effectively may require establishing new river basin authorities or statewide basin agencies with the power to construct, operate, and assess for treatment facilities.

Public decisions, like private decisions, suffer from the inadequate balancing of short-run economic choices against long-term environmental protection. There is a nearly irresistible pressure on local governments to develop land in order to increase jobs and extend the tax base—even if the land is valuable open space or an irreplaceable marsh. The problem is amplified by the proliferation of agencies, all competing narrowly, without consideration of broader and often common goals. The development that generates economic benefits in a town upstream may create pollution and loss of recreation in a town downstream.

Sometimes people persist in actions which cause environmental damage because they do not know that they are causing it. Construction of dams, extensive paving of land surfaces, and filling of estuaries for industrial development have in many cases been carried out with incomplete or wrong information about the extent of the impact on the environment. Furthermore, change in the environment has often been slow and exceedingly difficult to detect, even though piecemeal changes may eventually cause irreversible harm. Widespread use of certain types of pesticides, mercury pollution, and the use of dangerous substances such as asbestos occurred without advance recognition of their potential for harm.

The impact of environmental deterioration on health is subtle, often becoming apparent only after the lapse of many years. The speed of change in a rapidly altering technological society and the complex causes of many environmental health problems produce major uncertainty about what environmental changes do to human well-being. Nevertheless, it is clear that today's environment has a large and adverse impact on the physical and emotional health of an increasing number of Americans.

Air pollution has been studied closely over the past 10 years, and its tie to emphysema and chronic bronchitis is becoming more evident. These two diseases are major causes of chronic disability, lost workdays, and mortality in industrial nations. Estimates of deaths attributable to bronchitis and emphysema are beset with doubts about cause; nevertheless, physicians have traced 18,000 more deaths in the United States to these two causes in 1966 than 10 years earlier—an increase of two and one-half times. The increase of sulfur oxides, photochemical oxidants, and carbon monoxide in the air is related to hospital admission rates and length of stay for respiratory and circulatory cases.

Whether the accumulation of radioactive fallout in body tissues will eventually produce casualties cannot be predicted now, but close surveillance is needed. Nor has a direct correlation between factors in the urban environment and major malignancies of the digestive, respiratory, and urinary tracts been established. But the frequency of these diseases is much higher in cities than in nonurban environments.

The impact of the destruction of the environment on man's perceptions and aspirations cannot be measured. Yet today citizens are seeking better environments, not only to escape pollution and deterioration but to find their place in the larger community of life. It is clear that few prefer crowding, noise, fumes, and foul water to esthetically pleasing surroundings. Objections today to offensive sights, odors, and sounds are more widespread than ever. And these mounting objections are an important indicator of what Americans are unwilling to let happen to the world about them.

The economic costs of pollution are massive—billions of dollars annually. Paint deteriorates faster, cleaning bills are higher, and air filtering systems become necessary. Direct costs to city dwellers can be measured in additional household maintenance, cleaning, and medical bills. Air pollution causes the housewife to do her laundry more often. The farmer's crop yield is reduced or destroyed. Water pollution prevents swimming, boating, fishing, and other recreational and commercial activities highly valued in today's world.

Vast natural systems may be severely damaged by the improvident intervention of man. The great Dust Bowl of the 1930's was born in the overuse of land resources. Many estuarine areas have been altered and their ecology permanently changed. On a global scale, air pollution could trigger large-scale climatic changes. Man may also be changing the forces in the atmosphere through deforestation, urban construction, and the spilling of oil on ocean waters.

In the short run, much can be done to reverse the deadly downward spiral in environmental quality. Citizens, industries, and all levels of government have already begun to act in ways which will improve environmental quality. The President's February 10 Message on the Environment spelled out some specific steps which can be taken now.

It is clear, however, that long-range environmental improvement must take into account the complex interactions of environmental processes. In the future, the effects of man's actions on complete ecosystems must be considered if environmental problems are to be solved.

Efforts to solve the problems in the past have merely tried—not very successfully—to hold the line against pollution and exploitation. Each environmental problem was treated in an ad hoc fashion, while the strong, lasting interactions between various parts of the problem were neglected. Even today most environmental problems are dealt with temporarily, incompletely, and often only after they have become critical.

The isolated response is symptomatic of the environmental crisis. Americans in the past have not adequately used existing institutions to organize knowledge about the environment and to translate it into policy and action. The environment cuts across established institutions and disciplines. Men are beginning to recognize this and to contemplate new institutions. And that is a hopeful sign.

35

The Force of Public Awareness

Ralph Nader (1970)

In 1965, lawyer Ralph Nader began his crusade against the human and environmental irresponsibility of big business with the publication of Unsafe at Any Speed. *The book's attack on General Motors was first ignored, then featured in congressional hearings, and later made the subject of litigation that Nader won. But more important for his cause, he captured the interest and admiration of millions of Americans who saw in him a countervailing force to profits at any price. By the end of the 1960s, Nader had gathered around him a group of young, tough-minded researchers and lawyers dubbed "Nader's Raiders." Some of their exposures did not concern environmental problems, but many did. Nader turned the spotlight of his criticism on pesticides, air pollution, and water pollution. His principal tactic in every instance was to alert and arouse the citizenry, who, through pressure on their government, can force reforms on even the most powerful organizations. In the arena of public opinion and as a crusader for conservation, Ralph Nader ranks with Gifford Pinchot (Selection 11) and John Muir (Selection 15). Of special interest in the following essay is Nader's eight-point program for changing the behavior of corporate America with regard to the environment.*

The modern corporation's structure, impact, and public accountability are the central issues in any program designed to curb or forestall the contamination of air, water, and soil by industrial activity. While there are other sources of pollution, such as municipalities dumping untreated or inadequately treated sewage, industrial processes and products are the chief contributors to the long-term destruction of natural resources that each year increases the risks to human health and safety.

Moreover, through active corporate citizenship, industry could

Ralph Nader, "The Profits in Pollution," *The Progressive,* **XXXIV** (1970), 19–22. Reprinted by permission from *The Progressive,* 409 East Main Street, Madison, WI 53703. Copyright 1970 by The Progressive, Inc.

soon overcome many of the obstacles in the way of curbing noncorporate pollution. The mighty automobile industry, centered around and in Detroit, never thought it part of its role to press the city of Detroit to construct a modern sewage treatment plant. The automobile moguls, whose products, according to Department of Health, Education and Welfare data, account for fifty-five to sixty per cent of the nation's air pollution, remained silent as the city's obsolete and inadequate sewage facilities dumped the wastes of millions into the Detroit River. Obviously, local boosterism does not include such elementary acts of corporate citizenship.

The toilet training of industry to keep it from further rupturing the ecosystem requires an overhaul of the internal and external levers which control corporations. There are eight areas in which policies must be changed to create the pressures needed to make corporate entities and the people who run them cease their destruction of the environment:

One—The conventional way of giving the public a share in private decisions that involve health and safety hazards is to establish mandatory standards through a public agency. But pollution control standards set by governmental agencies can fall far short of their purported objectives unless they are adequately drafted, kept up to date, vigorously enforced, and supported by sanctions when violated. Behind the adoption of such standards, there is a long administrative process, tied to a political infrastructure. The scientific-engineering-legal community has a key independent role to play in this vital and complex administrative-political process. Almost invariably, however, its talents have been retained on behalf of those to be regulated. Whether in Washington or in state capitals around the country, the experts demonstrate greater loyalty to their employers than to their professional commitments in the public interest. . . .

Two—Sanctions against polluters are feeble and out of date, and, in any case, are rarely invoked. For example, the Federal air quality act has no criminal penalties no matter how willful and enduring the violations. In New Jersey, New York, and Illinois, a seventy-one year old Federal anti-water pollution law was violated with total impunity by industry until the Justice Department moved against a few of the violators in recent months. Other violators in other states are yet to be subjected to the law's enforcement. To be effective, sanctions should come in various forms, such as non-reimbursable fines, suspensions, dechartering of corporations, required disclosure of violations in company promotional materials, and more severe criminal penalties. Sanctions, consequently, should be tailored to the seriousness and duration of the violation.

It is expressive of the anemic and nondeterrent quality of existing sanctions that offshore oil leaks contaminating beaches for months, as in Santa Barbara, brought no penalty to any official of any offending company. The major controversy in Santa Barbara was whether the company—Union Oil—or the Government or the residents would bear the costs of cleaning up the mess. And even if the company bore the costs initially, the tax laws would permit a considerable shifting of this cost onto the general taxpayer.

Three—The existing requirements for disclosure of the extent of corporate pollution are weak and flagrantly flouted. The Federal Water Pollution Control Administration (FWPCA) has been blocked since 1963 by industrial polluters (working with the Federal Bureau of the Budget) from obtaining information from these companies concerning the extent and location of discharges of pollutants into the nation's waterways. For three years, the National Industrial Waste Inventory has been held up by the Budget Bureau and its industry "advisers," who have a decisive policy role. Led by the steel, paper, and petroleum industries, corporate polluters have prevented the FWPCA from collecting specific information on what each company is putting into the water. Such information is of crucial importance to the effective administration of the water pollution law and the allocation of legal responsibility for violations. . . .

Four—Corporate investment in research and development of pollution controls is no longer a luxury to be left to the decision or initiative of a few company officers. Rather, such research and development must be required by law to include reinvestment of profits, the amount depending on the volume of pollution inflicted on the public. For example, in 1969 General Motors grossed $24 billion, yet last year spent less than $15 million on vehicle and plant pollution research and development, although its products and plants contribute some thirty-five per cent of the nation's air pollution by tonnage. A formula proportional to the size of a company and its pollution could be devised as law, with required periodic reporting of the progress of the company's research and its uses. A parallel governmental research and development program aimed at developing pollution-free product prototypes suitable for mass production, and a Federal procurement policy favoring the purchase of less-polluting products, are essential external impacts.

Five—Attention must be paid to the internal climate for free expression and due process within the corporate structure. Again and again, the internal discipline of the corporate autocracy represses the civic and professional spirit of employees who have every right to speak out or blow the whistle on their company after they have tried in vain, working from the inside, to bring about changes that will end pollution practices. Professional employees—scientists, engineers, physicians—have fewer due process safeguards than the blue collar workers in the same company protected by their union contract. . . .

Six—The corporate shareholder can act, as he rarely does, as a prod and lever for jolting corporate leaders out of their lethargy. The law and the lawyers have rigged the legal system to muffle the voice of shareholders, particularly those concerned with the broader social costs of corporate enterprise. However, for socially conscious and determined stockholders there are many functions that can be performed to help protect the public (including themselves) from industrial pollution. . . .

Seven—Natural, though perhaps unexercised, countervailing forces in the private sector can be highly influential incentives for change. For example, the United Auto Workers have announced that pollution will be an issue in the collective bargaining process with automobile company management this year; the union hopes to secure for workers the right not to work in polluting activities, or in a polluted environment. Insurance companies could become advocates for loss prevention in the environmental field when confronted with policyholder, shareholder, and citizen demonstrative action. Through their political influence, their rating function in evaluating risks and setting premium charges, and their research and development capability, insurance companies could exert a key countervailing stress on polluters. Whether they do or not will first depend on citizen groups to whip them into action.

Eight—Environmental lawsuits, long blocked by a conservative judiciary and an inflexible judicial system, now seem to be coming into their own—a classic example of how heightened public expectations, demands, and the availability of facts shape broader applications of ancient legal principles. Environmental pollution is environmental violence—to human beings and to property. The common law has long recognized such violence against the person as actionable or enjoinable. What has been lacking is sufficient evidence of harm and avoidability to persuade judges that such hitherto invisible long-range harm outweighed the economic benefits of the particular plant activity in the community.

It now appears that such lawsuits will gain greater acceptance, especially as more evidence and more willing lawyers combine to breathe contemporary reality into long-standing legal principles. An amendment to the U.S. Constitution providing citizens with basic rights to a clean environment has been proposed; similar amendments to state constitutions are being offered. Such generic provisions can only further the judicial acceptance of environmental lawsuits. Imaginative and bold legal advocacy is needed here. The *forced consumption* of industrial pollutants by 200 million Americans must lead to a recognition of legal rights in environmental control such as that which developed with civil rights for racial minorities over the last two decades.

Three additional points deserve the attention of concerned citizens:

First, a major corporate strategy in combating anti-pollution measures is to engage workers on the company side by leading them to believe that such measures would threaten their livelihood. This kind of industrial extortion in a community—especially a company town—has worked before and will again unless citizens anticipate and confront it squarely.

Second, both industry spokesmen and their governmental allies (such as the President's Science Adviser, Lee DuBridge) insist that consumers will have to pay the price of pollution control. While this point of view may be an unintended manifestation of the economy's administered price structure, it cannot go unchallenged. Pollution control must not become another lever to lift up excess profits and fuel the fires of inflation. The costs of pollution control technology should come from corporate profits which have been enhanced by the use of the public's environment as industry's private sewer. The sooner industry realizes that it must bear the costs of cleanups, the more likely it will be to employ the quickest and most efficient techniques.

Finally, those who believe deeply in a humane ecology must act in accordance with their beliefs. They must so order their consumption and disposal habits that they can, in good conscience, preach what they actually practice. In brief, they must exercise a personal discipline as they advocate the discipline of governments and corporations.

The battle of the environmentalists is to preserve the physiological integrity of people by preserving the natural integrity of land, air, and water. The planet earth is a seamless structure with a thin slice of sustaining air, water, and soil that supports almost four billion people. This thin slice belongs to all of us, and we use it and hold it in trust for future earthlings. Here we must take our stand.

36

Respect for Nature

Gary Snyder (1971)

A Pulitzer Prize-winning poet and early member of what came in the 1960s to be called the "counterculture," Snyder's experience has included logging, university study of anthropology, bohemianism in San Francisco, and an extended visit to Japan where he steeped himself in non-Western ways of thinking about the human-nature relationship. In 1969 he wrote Four Changes, *an argument for radical alterations in American thought, government, and lifestyle with the aim of making our civilization more environmentally responsible. The following, shorter essay builds on the ideas of Aldo Leopold (Selection 27) and anticipates "deep ecology" (Selection 47). Snyder believes in the ideal of natural community that includes mankind and other creatures as equal partners. He is quite serious in his proposal that the interests of nonhuman life forms be represented in human systems of government. Interestingly, a year after Snyder originally published his essay, a member of the U.S. Supreme Court came to similar conclusions (see Selection 38).*

I am a poet. My teachers are other poets, American Indians, and a few Buddhist priests in Japan. The reason I am here is because I wish to bring a voice from the wilderness, my constituency. I wish to be a spokesman for a realm that is not usually represented either in intellectual chambers or in the chambers of government.

I was climbing Glacier Peak in the Cascades of Washington several years ago, on one of the clearest days I had ever seen. When we reached the summit of Glacier Peak we could see almost to the Selkirks in Canada. We could see south far beyond the Columbia River to Mount Hood and Mount Jefferson. And, of course, we could see Mount Adams and Mount Rainier. We could see across Puget Sound

Gary Snyder, "The Wilderness," from Snyder's *Turtle Island* (New York: New Directions, 1974), 106–110. Copyright 1971 by Gary Snyder. Reprinted by permission of New Directions Publishing Corporation.

to the ranges of the Olympic Mountains. My companion, who is a poet, said: "You mean, there is a senator for all this?"

Unfortunately, there isn't a senator for all that. And I would like to think of a new definition of humanism and a new definition of democracy that would include the nonhuman, that would have representation from those spheres. This is what I think we mean by an ecological conscience.

I don't like Western culture because I think it has much in it that is inherently wrong and that is at the root of the environmental crisis that is not recent; it is very ancient; it has been building up for a millennium. There are many things in Western culture that are admirable. But a culture that alienates itself from the very ground of its own being—from the wilderness outside (that is to say, wild nature, the wild, self-contained, self-informing ecosystems) and from that other wilderness, the wilderness within—is doomed to a very destructive behavior, ultimately perhaps self-destructive behavior.

The West is not the only culture that carries these destructive seeds. China had effectively deforested itself by 1000 A.D. India had effectively deforested itself by 800 A.D. The soils of the Middle East were ruined even earlier. The forests that once covered the mountains of Yugoslavia were stripped to build the Roman fleet, and those mountains have looked like Utah ever since. The soils of southern Italy and Sicily were ruined by latifundia slave-labor farming in the Roman Empire. The soils of the Atlantic seaboard in the United States were effectively ruined before the American Revolution because of the one-crop (tobacco) farming. So the same forces have been at work in East and West.

You would not think a poet would get involved in these things. But the voice that speaks to me as a poet, what Westerners have called the Muse, is the voice of nature herself, whom the ancient poets called the great goddess, the Magna Mater. I regard that voice as a very real entity. At the root of the problem where our civilization goes wrong is the mistaken belief that nature is something less than authentic, that nature is not as alive as man is, or as intelligent, that in a sense it is dead, and that animals are of so low an order of intelligence and feeling, we need not take their feelings into account.

A line is drawn between primitive peoples and civilized peoples. I think there is a wisdom in the worldview of primitive peoples that we have to refer ourselves to, and learn from. If we are on the verge of postcivilization, then our next step must take account of the primitive worldview which has traditionally and intelligently tried to open and keep open lines of communication with the forces of nature. You cannot communicate with the forces of nature in the laboratory. One of the problems is that we simply do not know much about primitive people and primitive cultures. If we can tentatively accommodate the possibility that nature has a degree of authenticity and intelligence that requires that we look at it more sensitively, then we can move to the next step. "Intelligence" is not really the right word. The ecologist Eugene Odum uses the term "biomass."

Life-biomass, he says, is stored information; living matter is stored information in the cells and in the genes. He believes there is more information of a higher order of sophistication and complexity stored in a few square yards of forest than there is in all the libraries of mankind. Obviously, that is a different order of information. It is the information of the universe we live in. It is the information that has been flowing for millions of years. In this total information context, man may not be necessarily the highest or most interesting product.

Perhaps one of its most interesting experiments at the point of evolution, if we can talk about evolution in this way, is not man but a high degree of biological diversity and sophistication opening to more and more possibilities. Plants are at the bottom of the food chain; they do the primary energy transformation that makes all the life-forms possible. So perhaps plant-life is what the ancients meant by the great goddess. Since plants support the other life-forms, they became the "people" of the land. And the land—a country—is a region within which the interactions of water, air, and soil and the underlying geology and the overlying (maybe stratospheric) wind conditions all go to create both the microclimates and the large climactic patterns that make a whole sphere or realm of life possible. The people in that realm include animals, humans, and a variety of wild life.

What we must find a way to do, then, is incorporate the other people—what the Sioux Indians called the creeping people, and the standing people, and the flying people, and the swimming people—into the councils of government. This isn't as difficult as you might think. If we don't do it, they will revolt against us. They will submit non-negotiable demands about our stay on the earth. We are beginning to get non-negotiable demands right now from the air, the water, the soil.

I would like to expand on what I mean by representation here at the Center from these other fields, these other societies, these other communities. Ecologists talk about the ecology of oak communities, or pine communities. They *are* communities. This institute—this Center—is of the order of a kiva of elders. Its function is to maintain and transmit the lore of the tribe on the highest levels. If it were doing its job completely, it would have a cycle of ceremonies geared to the seasons, geared perhaps to the migrations of the fish and to the phases of the moon. It would be able to instruct in what rituals you follow when a child is born, when someone reaches puberty, when someone gets married, when someone dies. But, as you know, in these fragmented times, one council cannot perform all these functions at one time. Still it would be understood that a council of elders, the caretakers of the lore of the culture, would open themselves to representation from other life-forms. Historically this has been done through art. The paintings of bison and bears in the caves of southern France were of that order. The animals were speaking through the people and making their point. And when, in the dances of the Pueblo Indians and other peoples, certain individuals became seized, as it were, by the spirit of the deer, and danced as a deer would dance, or danced the dance of the corn maidens, or impersonated the squash blossom, they were no longer speaking for humanity, they were taking it on themselves to interpret, through their humanity, what these other life-forms were. That is about all we know so far concerning the possibilities of incorporating spokesmanship for the rest of life in our democratic society.

Let me describe how a friend of mine from a Rio Grande pueblo hunts. He is twenty-seven years old. The Pueblo Indians, and I think probably most of the other Indians of the Southwest, begin their hunt, first, by purifying themselves. They take emetics, a sweat bath, and perhaps avoid their wife for a few days. They also try not to think certain thoughts. They go out hunting in an attitude of humility. They make sure that they need to hunt, that they are not hunting without necessity. Then they improvise a song while they are in the mountains. They sing aloud or hum to themselves while they are walking along. It is a song to the deer, asking the deer to be willing to die for them. They usually still-hunt, taking a place alongside a trail. The feeling is that you are not hunting the deer, the deer is coming to you; you make yourself available for the deer that will present itself to you, that has given itself to you. Then you shoot it. After you shoot it, you cut the head off and place the head facing east. You sprinkle corn meal in front of the mouth of the deer, and you pray to the deer, asking it to forgive you for having killed it, to understand that we all need to eat, and to please make a good report to the other deer spirits that he has been treated well. One finds this way of handling things and animals in all primitive cultures.

37

The Debate over Growth

Garrett Hardin (1972)

Growth has been as American as apple pie. For a nation that expanded for three centuries, "growth" was so inextricably involved with "progress" as to be almost synonymous. It was a tenet of the national faith that went unquestioned. But the finitude of the earth, noted by William Vogt in 1948 (Selection 26), inevitably caught up with and destroyed the illusion of endless expansion. Clearly the advent of the space age, with its dramatic photographs and television images of a spaceship earth, hastened the new awareness. So did computer-assisted projections of growth trends. The most widely discussed of these, sponsored by the Club of Rome, bore the title The Limits of Growth *(1972). The book was not only a commentary; for many it became a historical fact with an influence on thought and feeling that added new dimensions to its scholarly format and tone. Among the many discussions of* The Limits of Growth *was a review by Garrett Hardin, a professor of human ecology at the University of California, Santa Barbara. Hardin had attracted attention in 1968 with his assertion that the environment suffered from the "tragedy of the commons" syndrome: many individuals pursuing their best interests spelled disaster for shared resources. The only way out was to cut down the number of the individuals involved. This led Hardin to the concept of "lifeboat ethics." The world, like a lifeboat, could not be overcrowded or it would sink. Some would-be occupants, even humans currently alive, must be denied a place on the boat for the good of those already aboard. Humanitarians scored Hardin for his lack of compassion and respect for human life, but he countered with the assertion that, while tough on the individual, his system was the most respectful of the long-term interests of the species.*

Hardin and other opponents of unlimited growth cheered in March 1971 when Congress refused to approve further funding for an American version of the supersonic transport (SST). For virtually the first time in its history, the nation turned its back on possible technological advancements. In 1973 E. F. Schumacher's Small Is Beautiful *provided a philosophical foundation for questioning the beneficence of*

Garrett Hardin, "We Live on a Spaceship," *Bulletin of the Atomic Scientists,* **XXIII** (1972), 23–25. Reprinted by permission of the Bulletin of the Atomic Scientists and the author. Copyright 1972 by the Educational Foundation for Nuclear Science.

growth. Several years later the State of Colorado opted not to host the 1976 Winter Olympics for fear of the consequences of growth and development in the Rocky Mountains.

The first problem of human ecology is to determine the facts: how do population, technology and environment interact? And how can we move toward the best possible arrangement of things? This is a fiendishly difficult intellectual problem.

The second problem of human ecology is no less difficult: as we reach each partial answer, how do we get the general body politic to accept the truth? In the twentieth century, Julian Huxley, Aldous Huxley, Karl Sax, William Vogt, Robert C. Cook and the Paddock brothers have each, in their time, publicized shocking and irrefutable facts. Each has had his moment of glory, and then his contribution has been drowned in the unending torrent of printed words as mankind has continued in its thoughtless way to make a shambles of the world. Paul Ehrlich is the latest to make a splash; but already his message is being suppressed. To date, all population prophets have been Cassandras: the price for their vision of the truth has been public disbelief in what they say.

Now come some more candidates for the Cassandra corps: a research group at MIT headed by Jay Forrester. By computer simulation they have produced a large number of plausible "scenarios" of the future course of population, prosperity and pollution. Their conclusions were described first in mimeographed in-house documents, then in rather weighty books put out by an obscure publisher, and in hearings before Congressional committees. With the publication of "The Limits to Growth," their findings reach a much larger audience. A financially well-endowed group called the Club of Rome has sponsored this work and bought 10,000 copies for distribution to influential business leaders, statesmen and journal editors. The book is receiving wide notice and thoughtful discussion. Perhaps this time the message will be remembered. Perhaps this time Cassandra will be believed. Let us hope so.

The message can be summarized in five words (though the authors never explicitly say as much): We live on a spaceship. All the rest is an extended gloss on this simple text. The method of elaboration is well-chosen for our day: computer read-outs. The pronouncements of computers are the magic of our time: it is well to use them. The authors are not deceived; as they state repeatedly, none of the computer outputs is a prediction. Each merely shows the interaction of the important variables on each other during the next few seconds of historic time, i.e., for roughly the next 200 years. Many different assemblages of arbitrary rate-constants are worked out, all yielding qualitatively the same picture: "The basic mode of the world system is exponential growth of population and capital, followed by collapse." The conclusion proves to be astonishingly insensitive to variation in the parameters. Collapse follows even with the most optimistic assumptions, e.g., an infinite supply of energy.

We should not be surprised at this conclusion (and we do not really need a computer to reach it). The same thing was said by Sir Geoffrey Vickers in a BBC broadcast that was published in "The Listener" for October 28, 1965. The title of this article on population could not have been more graphic: "The End of Free Fall." To anyone who has taken Physics 1A the imagery is frightening.

Picture a man who has jumped off a very high building. His falling corresponds to the growth of population, and of the gross national product. It is not in the least painful; on the contrary, the feeling is one of excitement and exhilaration. But if he is one of those oddballs who insist on looking ahead, he sees the ground approaching and realizes he really ought to do something about decelerating his rate of descent.

He could reach out and grab a cornice of the building and stop his fall. What would you think if he reacted to this suggestion in the following way? "No, I won't do it, because if I do my legs will slam against the building and that will hurt." So he continues to fall and to accelerate; consequently, by the time he's fallen another story his speed is even greater, and the pain of stopping would be still worse. This mode of thought is a trap which insures that the end, when it comes, will be devastating.

Is this a far-fetched analogy? I think not. The demographer Ansley J. Coale, belaboring the Zero Population Growth people, has pointed out that achieving ZPG instantly would produce, within a few years, an age-distribution like that of St. Petersburg, Florida. One can grant Coale's point that the thought of living in such a gerontocracy is frightening. But does that mean that we should reconcile ourselves to descending a few more stories in a state of free fall? And then more? The demographer never spells out this implication of his position; he contents himself with pointing out that stopping will be painful. Indeed it will. But not stopping will be worse.

The biological situation is, if anything, more dangerous than the physical one because of time-lags built into the system. Each child that is born threatens the world with a further increase in population about 16 years later when it becomes sexually mature. DDT (with some other pollutants) percolates its way through the ecosystem slowly and may produce the maximum kill of peregrine falcons (and perhaps harm man as well) a decade after the pollutant has been outlawed (if it ever is). Radioactive garbage may overwhelm mankind generations after it is produced as a result of "accidents." (Definition: "An accident is a low-frequency event that is certain to happen sooner or later, but I don't want to think about it.") It is not easy to feed such considerations into the computer, but it is clear that the results of doing so would be even more frightening than those graphed by Meadows, et al.

Considerations like these throw new light on the meaning of "conservatism." Usually we think of conservative action as one of no interference with current practices. Change is regarded as nonconservative action, and the old-fashioned conservative advises us to take no such positive action until we have made exhaustive studies of the phenomena involved. But when human survival is at stake, is clinging to the status quo conservative? As the theologian Harvey Cox has said: "Not to decide is to decide." To continue on our present course, while we gather more facts about DDT, atmospheric carbon dioxide, the permeability of rock salt to radioactive atoms, etc., is neither conservative nor wise. We don't have to know exactly how far away the ground is, or exactly what the value of g is, to know that we had better put brakes on our free fall. Waiting for the report of another committee is not the most conservative course to follow.

Some of the poorly educated commentators who man the mikes of TV stations and peck at the typewriters of the popular press have defended inaction in the usual way. Malthus has been buried again. (This is the 174th year in which that redoubtable economist has been interred. We may take it as certain that anyone who has to be buried 174 times cannot be wholly dead.) It is futile to cross swords with the ignorant; but better informed critics who assume that true conservatism is the defense of the status quo deserve a reply. I will deal with two such critics at some length because the way in which they badger the authors of this book throws light on the mechanisms whereby dangerous inaction is defended.

In the *Washington Post* for March 2, 1972, Allen Kneese and Ronald Ridker of Resources for the Future did their best to see to it that no one should take Meadows, et al., seriously (or become too concerned about the future). Early on, they used the time-honored reviewers' ploy of undermining confidence by pointing out errors which in fact are not crucial to the development of the argument. In the third paragraph, Kneese and Ridker say that the MIT group is mistaken in thinking that any species of whales have been hunted to extinction. This is a quibble; several species have been brought so near to extinction that they are now not worth hunting—but the animals are still killed when found. (Playing the reviewers' game, let me point out that Kneese and Ridker, in paragraph four, identify 1826 as the year of publication of Malthus' "Essay on Population." They are wrong by 28 years. So what?)

More important are the rhetorical arts the reviewers use to insure that their audience remains immobile in the face of approaching catastrophe. Consider this passage: "New discoveries and technological improvements over the past 100 years fully kept up with the demand. In other words, the effectively useful resource base has been expanding exponentially too. Although it cannot be expected to do so indefinitely, it does seem reasonable that a model explicitly based on past tendencies would incorporate this."

The "although" denigrates to second-class status the admission that follows. The essential truth becomes a truth "in passing." To appreciate the effect of this rhetorical ploy, let's return to our man in free fall. He has just passed the 30th story, counting from the top downward. We ask him how he views his prospects. Calmly he replies: "Well, the wind is rushing past me, but I've learned how to adjust to it without discomfort. Although I can't expect to do so indefinitely, still any theory about free fall must be explicitly based on this past tendency to adjust."

In a court of law, such a statement might be defended. But how long can we safely be advised by men who use an "although" clause in this way?

Further on, the reviewers point out that the authors did not—which Meadows, et al., admit—program their computer for the "social-adaptation, learning, and institution-building process," and go on to say that "One can't help but believe that this failure accounts for the fact that almost all of the scenarios considered result in collapse. This is not to assert that collapse is unlikely. . . ."

Again, we are confronted with the rhetoric of the belittling "although." And again the reviewers are on safe ground, legally speaking. At Judgment Day, if it turns out that the MIT crowd has been right, and the RFF crowd wrong, Kneese and Ridker will still get off the hook—if the Lord is a lawyer. They've hedged their bets astutely. But is such cleverness part of the great tradition of science?

There also is a paradoxical aspect to this second criticism coming from RFF. By implying that an unspecified "social-adaptation, learning, and institution-building process" will appear on the scene as a deus ex machina to save mankind, the writers in fact encourage inaction of all sorts. Their verbal tranquilizer inhibits the active search for such processes (which presumably will appear spontaneously). In contrast, the targets of their criticism, by restricting themselves to a frightening description of what will happen in the absence of such processes, actually stimulate research in social engineering.

It's curious that spokesmen for an organization named "Resources for the Future" should, in fact, throw so many roadblocks in the way of planning for the future. They sometimes seem to act as if they had a vested interest in nonaction. If they were part of the R&D arm of a great industrial concern this would be understandable, but they are not. One would hope that the millions of dollars they receive from the Ford Foundation would give them the feeling of intellectual independence that is needed to prepare for the future in the face of monumental opposition by a multitude of vested interests, both public and private. Yet I am afraid that this admirably endowed organization deserves the name I have heard the geologist Preston Cloud bestow on it—Resources for the Near Future. The label may be a bit unkind because occasionally RFNF does look beyond the near future. Not, however, in the present instance, in which Kneese and Ridker seem more interested in "putting down" their rivals in futurology at another institution than in preparing the public for change. The point of view of their criticism is a narrowly near one. Unconsciously, the critics admit as much in their closing paragraph:

> Our assessment? An interesting framework upon which to hang some types of resources and environmental research? We think so. A helpful near-term tool for strengthening and deepening our understanding of man's predicament and what to do about it? We think not.

It is doubtful if much needed light will be thrown on man's predicament by minds in which the adjective "near term" reverberates so strongly. In contrast, the authors of "The Limits to Growth" march to a different drummer. Wisely so, I think.

38

Mineral King and "Standing" for Trees

William O. Douglas (1972)

In 1965 the U.S. Forest Service, as part of its multiple-use management program, offered the Mineral King Valley of Sequoia National Forest in California's Sierra to prospective developers of ski resorts. Walt Disney Enterprises' bid for a $35 million complex was eventually accepted, but the Sierra Club, concerned with destruction of the aesthetics and ecology of the fragile valley, contested the decision. The battle for Mineral King began. The weapons were years of tedious and costly court proceedings. Many of them centered on the question of legal "standing." Disney and the Forest Service, arguing that the Sierra Club had no property in the area, challenged its right to be a participant in the proceedings. In April 1972 the U.S. Supreme Court ruled otherwise: the Sierra Club's interest in the environment was just as viable as interests of an economic nature. But one justice, William O. Douglas, led a more radical minority opinion. Influenced by Aldo Leopold (Selection 27) and more particularly by law professor Christopher Stone's 1972 essay "Should Trees Have Standing?" Douglas argued that Mineral King Valley itself *should have standing in the case. The Sierra Club should articulate the interests of nature in the government of humans. Here was a real-life application of the concept Gary Snyder (Selection 36) discussed. The Mineral King controversy was finally resolved when the Disney interests, tired of the long and costly delay, withdrew its proposal for the resort. In 1978 Congress added the valley to Sequoia National Park.*

The critical question of "standing" would be simplified and also put neatly in focus if we fashioned a federal rule that allowed environmental issues to be litigated before federal agencies or federal courts in the name of the inanimate object about to be despoiled, defaced, or invaded by roads and bulldozers and where injury is the subject of

Supreme Court of the United States, *Sierra Club* v. *Morton,* 70–34, April 19, 1972.

public outrage. Contemporary public concern for protecting nature's ecological equilibrium should lead to the conferral of standing upon environmental objects to sue for their own preservation.

Inanimate objects are sometimes parties in litigation. A ship has a legal personality, a fiction found useful for maritime purposes. The corporation sole—a creature of ecclesiastical law—is an acceptable adversary and large fortunes ride on its cases. The ordinary corporation is a "person" for purposes of the adjudicatory processes, whether it represents proprietary, spiritual, aesthetic, or charitable causes.

So it should be as respects valleys, alpine meadows, rivers, lakes, estuaries, beaches, ridges, groves of trees, swampland, or even air that feels the destructive pressures of modern technology and modern life. The river, for example, is the living symbol of all the life it sustains or nourishes—fish, aquatic insects, water ouzels, otter, fisher, deer, elk, bear, and all other animals, including man, who are dependent on it or who enjoy it for its sight, its sound, or its life. The river as plaintiff speaks for the ecological unit of life that is part of it. Those people who have a meaningful relation to that body of water—whether it be a fisherman, a canoeist, a zoologist, or a logger—must be able to speak for the values which the river represents and which are threatened with destruction.

I do not know Mineral King. I have never seen it nor travelled it, though I have seen articles describing its proposed "development." . . . The Sierra Club in its complaint alleges that "One of the principal purposes of the Sierra Club is to protect and conserve the national resources of the Sierra Nevada Mountains." The District Court held that this uncontested allegation made the Sierra Club "sufficiently aggrieved" to have "standing" to sue on behalf of Mineral King.

Mineral King is doubtless like other wonders of the Sierra Nevada such as Tuolumne Meadows and the John Muir Trail. Those who hike it, fish it, hunt it, camp in it, or frequent it, or visit it merely to sit in solitude and wonderment are legitimate spokesmen for it, whether they may be a few or many. Those who have that intimate relation with the inanimate object to be injured, polluted, or otherwise despoiled are its legitimate spokesmen. . . .

The voice of the inanimate object, therefore, should not be stilled. That does not mean that the judiciary takes over the managerial functions from the federal agency. It merely means that before these priceless bits of Americana (such as a valley, an alpine meadow, a river, or a lake) are forever lost or are so transformed as to be reduced to the eventual rubble of our urban environment, the voice of the existing beneficiaries of these environmental wonders should be heard.

Perhaps they will not win. Perhaps the bulldozers of "progress" will plow under all the aesthetic wonders of this beautiful land. That is not the present question. The sole question is, who has standing to be heard?

Those who hike the Appalachian Trail into Sunfish Pond, New Jersey, and camp or sleep there, or run the Allagash in Maine, or climb the Guadalupes in West Texas, or who canoe and portage the Quetico Superior in Minnesota, certainly should have standing to defend those natural wonders before courts or agencies, though they live 3,000 miles away. Those who merely are caught up in environmental news or propaganda and flock to defend these waters or areas may be treated differently. That is why these environmental issues should be tendered by the inanimate object itself. Then there will be assurances that all of the forms of life which it represents will stand before the court—the pileated woodpecker as well as the coyote and bear, the lemmings as well as the trout in the streams. Those inarticulate members of the ecological group cannot speak. But those people who have so frequented the place as to know its values and wonders will be able to speak for the entire ecological community.

Ecology reflects the land ethic; and Aldo Leopold wrote in *A Sand County Almanac* (1949), "The land ethic simply enlarges the boundaries of the community to include soils, waters, plants, and animals, or collectively, the land."

That, as I see it, is the issue of "standing" in the present case and controversy.

39

Friendship with the Earth

David R. Brower (1967, 1977)

With his appointment as executive director of the Sierra Club in 1952, David Brower assumed the role of one of the nation's leading evangelists of the gospel of ecology. During the next three decades the club's membership rose from 7,000 to 350,000—one indicator of the American environmental movement's coming of age. In the mid-1960s Brower led the Sierra Club in an all-out battle against the placement of two dams in Arizona's Grand Canyon. The first document following is the text of a full-page statement that Brower placed in newspapers of national visibility. It helped generate a massive expression of public outrage, and in 1968 Congress voted against the dams. But the following year Brower was ousted from his position in the Sierra Club by a segment of the board of directors that thought he had pushed environmentalism too far, too fast, and without the proper approvals. Others, to be sure, thought he had not gone far enough. These persons formed the organizing nucleus of Brower's new organization, Friends of the Earth. In 1977 Brower wrote the second document as an introduction to a Friends of the Earth publication.

History repeated itself in 1984 when Brower was dismissed by a group of disgruntled Friends of the Earth directors. Selection 44 analyzes this schism in the ranks of American environmentalists.

SHOULD WE ALSO FLOOD THE SISTINE CHAPEL SO TOURISTS CAN GET NEARER THE CEILING?

Earth began four billion years ago and Man two million. The Age of Technology, on the other hand, is hardly a hundred years old. . . .

It seems to us hasty, therefore, during this blip of time, for Man to think of directing his fascinating new tools toward altering irrevocably the forces which made him. Nonetheless, in these few brief years among four billion, wilderness has all but disappeared. And now these:

New York Times, April 16, 1967.

1) There are proposals before Congress to "improve" Grand Canyon. Two dams would back up artificial lakes into 148 miles of canyon gorge. This would benefit tourists in power boats, it is argued, who would enjoy viewing the canyon wall more closely. See headline. Submerged underneath the tourists would be part of the most revealing single page of earth's history. The lakes would be as deep as 600 feet, deeper for example than all but a handful of New York buildings are high, but in a century, silting would have replaced the water with that much mud, wall to wall.

There is no part of the wild Colorado River, the Grand Canyon's sculptor, that would not be maimed.

Tourist recreation, as a reason for the dams, is in fact an afterthought. The Bureau of Reclamation, which has backed them, has called the dams "cash registers." It expects the dams would make money by sale of commercial power.

They will not provide anyone with water.

2) In Northern California, four lumber companies have nearly completed logging the private virgin redwood forests, an operation which to give you an idea of its size, has taken fifty years.

Where nature's tallest living things have stood silently since the age of the dinosaurs, much further cutting could make creation of a redwood national park absurd.

The companies have said tourists want only enough roadside trees for the snapping of photos. They offered to spare trees for this purpose, and not much more. The result would remind you of the places on your face you missed while you were shaving.

3) And up the Hudson, there are plans for a power complex—a plant, transmission lines, and a reservoir near and on Storm King Mountain—effectively destroying one of the last wild and high and beautiful spots near New York City.

4) A proposal to flood a region in Alaska as large as Lake Erie would eliminate at once the breeding grounds of more wildlife than conservationists have preserved in history.

5) In San Francisco, real estate interests have for years been filling a bay that made the city famous, putting tract houses over the fill; and now there's a new idea—still more fill, enough for an air cargo terminal as big as Manhattan.

There exists today a mentality which can conceive such destruction, giving commerce as ample reason. For 74 years, the Sierra Club has opposed that mentality. But now, when even Grand Canyon is endangered, we are at a critical moment in time.

This generation will decide if something untrammelled and free remains, as testimony we had love for those who follow.

We have been taking ads, therefore, asking people to write their Congressmen and Senators; Secretary of the Interior Stewart Udall; The President; and to send us funds to continue the battle. Thousands have written, but meanwhile, Grand Canyon legislation still stands a chance of passage. More letters are needed and much more money, to help right the notion that Man no longer needs nature.

What kind of country do you want? What kind of world? What kind of neighborhood on a small planet? If you have asked yourself such questions, we think you will like this book. If you haven't, you need it.

The kind of country and world a growing number of people want—and indeed, the kind we all require for sheer survival—will be less populous, more decentralized, less industrial, more agrarian. Our anxiously acquisitive consumer society will give way to a more serenely thrifty conserver society, one which relies most on renewable resources and least on the irreplaceables. Recycling will be taken for granted and planned obsolescence won't. Nuclear proliferation will be viewed in retrospect as a form of temporary insanity. We will stride confidently and lightly along the soft solar energy path so ably scouted out by physicist Amory Lovins. Restless mobility will diminish; people will put down roots and recapture a sense of community. Full employment will be the norm in a sustainable, skill-intensive economy, and indoor pollution where we work, now fifty times higher than outdoors, will no longer be tolerated (and such questions as "Would you rather risk asbestos-caused cancer in five years or be unemployed for five years?" will be judged felonious). Medicine's role in curing disease will shrink as preventive medicine grows and leaves less and less disease to be cured. Corporations will no longer demand the right to dispense cancer to you, or to scrub their pollutants with your lungs. People will turn on TV less and turn on their own senses more, and

Introduction to Hugh Nash, ed., *Progress As If Survival Mattered* (San Francisco: Friends of the Earth, 1977), 7–11.

be better informed of, by, and for the natural world that made them. Parks and wilderness areas will be recognized as legal "persons," as corporations and ships already are, to ensure their permanent and productive survival. Science (and applied science, or technology) will pay more than lip service to elegant solutions; that is, solutions that achieve desired results with the utmost economy of means. (As an archetypically inelegant solution, consider the agitation for space colonization and the fascination of star wars; the truly elegant solution is not to abandon our planet, but, using appropriate technology, to make it increasingly habitable in ways acceptable to it.) Growthmania will yield to the realization that physical growth is wholesome only during immaturity, and that to continue such growth beyond that point leads to malignancy or other grim devices that keep the planet from being suffocated with a surfeit. The earth will not swarm with life, but be graced with it.

Whatever kind of country and world people decide they want, the next question is, How can they get it? Probably by gaining a new understanding of politics. Politics is democracy's way of handling public business. There is no other. We won't get the kind of country in the kind of world we want unless people take part in the public's business. Unless they embrace politics and people in politics.

Embrace politicians? Yes. Why not? Theirs is, in essence, an honorable calling. When we treat it accordingly, we will deserve politicians who honor their having been called. There is public business to be done. We need to help the men and women who have chosen to undertake it. And from time to time they need our help. The Conserver Society will encourage the Internal Revenue Service to encourage the public to participate in the public's political business.

More than four score and seven years ago Thoreau looked beyond what our fathers had brought forth on this continent and asked a transcendent question: What is the use of a house if you haven't got a tolerable planet to put it on? A growing number of people see that the planet is less and less tolerable because its beauty—and let 'beauty' epitomize all the things that make an environment excellent and the earth a rewarding place to live upon—is being lost more and more rapidly. A slowly growing number of politicians see that there will be no politics at all on a planet that becomes too degraded to support people any longer.

Suppose that one of this growing number of politicians is a presidential candidate and wants to appeal to this growing constituency, to make excellence of environmental quality in fact *the* campaign issue.

What kind of platform would such a candidate choose to run on? Or suppose a new political party arose, dedicated, as Friends of the Earth is, to natural law and order. Suppose that party dedicated itself to preserving, restoring, and equitably using the earth and its resources, mineral and living. And suppose it knew that if 'progress' continued to depend upon wiping out irreplaceable resources, such progress could not last long. Imagine, then, a party dedicating itself to timely rethinking and corrective action. What would the platform be like?

Questions like these occurred to us in 1970 and we tried our hand at a voter's guide for environmental protection. It was pretty good. . . . Early in 1976 we asked ourselves more questions, better ones, and this book is the result. We hoped at first to produce an instant book on the environmental issues of the day, a "platform book," and to challenge candidates in that election to state publicly which of our planks they could stand on and which they feared they would fall between. It is still an appealing idea. We might have helped make the earth's health more of an issue in 1976, and might have nudged some candidates toward realizing that we all needed breatheable air as much as Detroit's lagging engineers needed to build their old air-spoiling cars—perhaps even more so. And that we needed to stop nuclear proliferation, not by lecturing our neighbors, but by cutting it off at the pockets, and cutting it out of any secret desires, right here at home.

Who knows? We might conceivably have encouraged a genuine "environmental candidate" to emerge. Thanks to our sister organization, Les Amis de la Terre, this did happen in France. In the United States, candidates Jerry Brown, Jimmy Carter, and Morris Udall came close enough to keep that contingency feasible. The League of Conservation Voters, founded initially as part of Friends of the Earth and later separated for legal reasons (corporations are not supposed to contribute to political candidates), has been surprisingly successful in giving the environment political weight. So has Environmental Action's Dirty Dozen approach. But no number of preliminary successes will endure if people who know how important the environment is rest on their oars. Or let their powder get wet, or suffer from premature congratulation, or otherwise forget that most of the public must understand why, how, and when before the whole society will let a politician move to spare its environment and save itself. . . .

The basic idea, although it needed tinkering with, looked as good as ever. As intelligent tinkerers, according to Leopold's Law, we saved all the parts. We would reassemble them as something less ephemeral than a campaign document. An environmental manifesto or credo would obsolesce less. Since the natural laws upon which environmentalism is based can only be perceived, and can never be amended, we thought that a book perceiving those laws well would have lasting value. It could also serve as a yardstick against which to measure the environmental literacy and commitment of a candidate, a party, ourself, and yourself as understanding evolved. . . .

. . . The greater the number of needed causes you espouse, the greater the chance of displeasing somebody. Cheap shots are easy. You can positively oppose cancer, heart disease, multiple sclerosis, inflation, unemployment [and] forest fires . . . and never lose a vote. But if you oppose exponential economic growth, however lethal it is, you are not liked by the Conventional Wisdom set. If you take a position for or against abortion or gun control, you divide your constituency and conquer—yourself at the polls.

Conservation organizations, like candidates, have political needs to face. We are aware of the risk to FOE as we try to delineate sound environmental views of the many aspects of society we discuss here. It is perilous to take that risk but more perilous not to. We will pin our faith on your intelligence as a lay citizen who cares. Though you may not share our view in all aspects, we ask you to remember that consensus can be carried too far. It can produce not only a dull world, but also an endangered one. Opinions need to differ. As long as they do, you will know people are alive, awake, not programmed, and still in honest search of truth. And you will remain young in the important sense—still able to listen, ready to change your mind, and willing to avoid being the Practical Man whom Disraeli worried about, who could be counted upon to perpetuate the errors of his ancestors.

Let us propose a grading system. If you agree with, say, seventy-five per cent of what we propose, we'll give you a passing grade, and you can give us one. That's close enough, and qualifies you and us for working together. We probably should.

We freely concede, and think you will, that getting a world to change course will require powerful motivating forces, and we hope to discern them in time. As Dr. Daniel B. Luten (chemist, lecturer on resources, and a FOE director) has said from time to time: Too many people would rather die than change their habits. Almost all of them think the society exists to serve its economy. Too many of them mistake growth for progress. Almost no one understands the extraordinary demands as we now pass from an empty earth to a full one. We have been slow, as we look at the rising population, to ask how dense people can be. We know the planet is lone and finite and that finite things have limits. But we have preferred denying them to facing them. Or we have looked for an escape to some greener colony in space.

People who sense the humor in Dr. Luten's way of putting the vital questions can be cheered. For surely the dawn of new perceptions is breaking. We see that there are better things to do than polarize ourselves. We do not get anywhere by trading epithets, doomsayer versus doommaker, or charging each other with degrees of elitism. We wince at trying to win through intimidation even if the intimidation guidebook sells well. We do not admire the squidlike habit of squirting printer's ink and retreating into the mock security of a different murk. The fatal urge to take care of Number One, whether on one's home lot or one's hemisphere, can be diverted with patience and love, and probably no other way. Before the child in us will give up the lethal toys forged by mindless growth, that child must be offered something else, attractive as well as beneficial.

Our ultimate goal herein is to find an alternative to the most lethal of the Great Powers' toys and to what led the powers to fashion it—to find that alternative before its absence makes all our other hopes academic. Nuclear proliferation is that deadly toy. Nobody wants it. No leading power has lessened the pressure to use it. The Stockholm International Peace Research Institute has predicted that within nine years thirty-five nations will have the capability of making nuclear weapons and nuclear war will be inevitable. Garrett Hardin handles that one: Inevitable? Not if we say no. . . .

The United States, and we think only the United States, can lead the world back from the nuclear brink to which we led it, with the best of intentions, in the first place. The U.S. can do so, however, only if we step back ourselves and thus persuade other peoples we are to be believed. At this writing we are not stepping back, but rushing forward again, faster than we have been in recent years, protecting our reactor exports, which after all bring us a billion-dollars-plus a crack and let's get the business before someone else does. Nobody needs that business, and those who think they do ought to try to learn a different trade. . . .

People can bring about great changes once they construe the difficult problem to be a challenging opportunity. As an example of such public achievement, consider the National Environmental Policy Act (NEPA). It moved the United States from an old danger to a new safety. One of Mr. Nixon's good deeds was to sign the Act and name Russell Train to oversee it as the first chairman of the Council on Environmental Quality. NEPA became our finest export.

Environmental victories do not, however, stay won by themselves. They require much vigilance and renewed persuasion. The NEPA victory made many enterprising businessmen so uneasy that they set about trying to weaken it without realizing how important it will be to them in the long run if it is kept strong. . . . NEPA requires strengthening if the environment is to remain whole and productive—a requirement as real for corporations as it is for people. It will pay all segments of society well to look searchingly at the social and environmental consequences of a new proposal to alter a piece of the earth. They should also, as NEPA provides, look as hard at the consequences of a fair range of alternatives designed to serve the broad interest instead of the narrow one.

One alternative, rarely considered, can be "Thanks a lot but forget it," coupled with a list of such benefits as would derive from letting things alone—a list that can sometimes be amazingly long. Another alternative is to consider the advantages of exploiting a given resource later on, or more slowly. Alaska's oil, for instance, could be budgeted to last for the next two or three centuries instead of the next two or three decades. A nation that took from the *Mayflower* until now to get where it is should not rule out, by wiping out, the resources that could get it through another three and a half centuries. Our consideration could well extend to a far-distant future and spare our heirs the need to isolate the nuclear radioactivity generated for our convenience. If Iodine$_{129}$ had been so isolated 300 million years ago at the bottom of the Redwall Limestone formation in the Grand Canyon, it would be safe about now to let it touch living things whose genes should be left intact. It would be fair to do for our genes what our genes have done for us. That way we would not tinker with them. We would revere the miracle in them instead. . . .

The unraveling of the earth's heritage of resources can be stopped, we think. . . . People do not have to go on being profligate with resources that are not to be renewed. This is especially true about oil, the unique resource that pervades present-day thinking and that made today's industrial-age euphoria possible. They can stretch it instead, to fuel the transition to other, enduring ways of getting along with the earth. North American oil is but a small part of the recoverable oil left on earth. Although we in the United States are quite capable of using all fossil fuels before our next centennial, we have more admirable capabilities. We could drop out of the lead in the race to see who can make the earth less livable fastest. We would then have a chance of persuading Russia and Japan, or other contenders, from thinking the old race worth the trouble.

Ours was quite a binge. We were not alone in it. The earth's people can still escape the tensions that continuation of the binge will intensify, tensions that threaten the survival of all we or anyone else care about most. We cannot escape by forging on, resolutely and regardless, driven by the unmitigated inertia of outworn habits, until we have forced ourselves over the brink in the "giant step for mankind" no one needs. When you have reached the edge of an abyss . . . the only progressive move you can make is to step backward. . . . Progress, if survival matters, can then become a process that lets people find more joy at less cost to their children and to the earth.

PART FIVE

THE NEW ENVIRONMENTALISM, 1973–1990

*A third stage of environmental advocacy is emerging, one that
is not satisfied with the precast role of opponent to environmental
abuser. . . . Finding new ways to solve persistent
(environmental) problems is harder than merely opposing them.
. . . The American public does not want conflict between
improving our economic well-being and preserving our health
and natural resources.*

—Frederic D. Krupp

*We must constantly extend the community to include all. . . .
The other beings—four-legged, winged, six-legged, rooted,
flowing, etc.—have just as much right to be in that place as we
do, they are their own justification for being, they have inherent
value, value completely apart from whatever worth they have for
. . . humans.*

—Dave Foreman

The explosive force of the gospel of ecology that made
environmental protection a high priority in the late 1960s and early
1970s transformed American policy. Antipollution and
environmental protection legislation flourished. Only the opening
years of the New Deal, 1933–1936, approached this legislative
record in strength and comprehensiveness. The federal acts ranged
from broad mandates such as the National Environmental Policy
Act (1970) and the Coastal Zone Management Act (1972) to tight
regulatory controls typified by the Clean Air Act (1970), the
Federal Water Pollution Control Act (1972), and the Toxic

Substance Control Act (1976). The old nature preservation component of American conservation also received unprecedented support. The Endangered Species Act (1973) provided the strongest recognition to date of the intrinsic value and right to life of organisms threatened with extinction. In 1980 the Alaska National Interest Lands Conservation Act became the greatest single national park and wilderness protection measure in world history and will likely remain so unless international action occurs on behalf of Antarctica.

Inevitably, given the tides of historical change, the intensity of environmental concern cooled. A new wave of American materialism, conservatism, and narcissism chafed against the restraints necessary for environmental protection. Many young, ambitious, urban professionals, the so-called yuppies of the "Me Generation," refused to forgo self-interest for amorphous concepts like harmony with the earth that had been so attractive to the "hippies" of the 1960s. The oil shortages and price rises of 1974 and 1979 precipitated a rush to exploit new sources of energy offshore, in Alaska, and in western coal and oil shale deposits. Indeed by the late 1970s and early 1980s environmentalism faced an active backlash of criticism. Indicative of the new climate of opinion was the appearance of James G. Watt as President Ronald Reagan's Secretary of Interior from 1981 to 1983. Turning back the conservation clock at least a century, Watt set out to liberate American business and technology from the restraints of proenvironment policy. But, ironically, Watt actually helped environmentalism. In protest against him, membership in the nation's leading conservation organizations doubled during his tenure in office. The environmental lobby flexed new muscles at the federal level and blocked much of Watt's program. Eventually, the Secretary proved so great a political liability that even President Reagan, no friend of conservation himself, was obliged to find a replacement.

As the 1990s begin, it is clear that the strength of the American environmental movement is greater than ever before. Polls reveal overwhelming support for environmental protection even at the expense of jobs and profits. A new professionalism characterizes modern environmentalism. Environmentalists not only have learned to play the national political game more skillfully; they also use the courts with unprecedented vigor and effectiveness. Economic tools have become a standard part of the arsenal of the new environmentalist. Using benefit-cost analysis, they demonstrate that conservation pays at the bottom line. The energy industry, in particular, was revolutionized by such reasoning, with nuclear power a notable casualty. In the 1960s, "technology" was almost a dirty word in environmental circles, but the new environmentalists are adept at putting it to work for their own ends. Instead of saying "no" to proposals for technological utilization of resources, modern environmentalists strive to satisfy legitimate social needs in ways compatible with environmental protection. Wind and solar generators are examples along with pollution abatement technology. Environmental abuse has become a problem to be solved rather than an evil to be opposed. Although there was dissent on the point from the radical fringe (Selections 44–47), many environmentalists held out hope that improvement of society's standard of living and environmental protection were compatible ends. The popular phrase "sustainable development" summarized this ideal.

The new American environmentalism professed an unprecedented degree of concern with the global ecosystem. A new science of whole-earth systems used remote sensing techniques to reveal the adverse impact of technology on the life-support capabilities of the planet. There was evidence that "greenhouse gases" were enveloping the planet in a layer of insulation; the global climate was warming. Destruction of stratospheric ozone by synthetic chemicals increased the amount of cancer-causing ultraviolet radiation that reached the earth. Acid precipitation polluted fresh and salt water. Deforestation, desertification, and the loss of biodiversity on a global scale dominated conservation agendas. The greatest pollution threat of all, popularized after 1983 as "nuclear winter," remained hypothetical but only a button-push away. In short, there was no longer much doubt that an unrestrained human civilization had the capability of severely altering life on earth. No death star, but a precocious part of its own life community threatened spaceship earth.

Between 1960 and 1990, environmentalism changed from a religion to a profession. The blue-jean-and-granola style of conservation evident at the time of the first Earth Day in 1970 gave way two decades later to pin-striped suits and briefcases full of sophisticated data. Even materialistic "yuppies" began to support environmental reform on the grounds that there was no good life without a good environment. But the old fervor of the

1960s persisted in a radical wing of American environmentalism that coalesced around the concept of environmental ethics. The radical environmentalists, or self-styled "deep ecologists," deplored established or mainstream conservation as hopelessly conservative and anthropocentric. The only legitimate foundation for conservation policy, they contended, was the idea that nature had intrinsic value and, it followed, rights to exist that mankind ought to respect. Much of American conservation, even in recent years, assumed the primacy of human interests and attempted to manage the natural world on their behalf. Along with Edward Abbey and Dave Foreman (Selection 46), the radical critics of this posture simply said "Earth First!" Their goal, following Aldo Leopold (Selection 27), was to make humans members and not masters of the biotic community with full cognizance of community obligations. Ethics would replace economics, however enlightened, as the guiding philosophy for human-nature relations. If this meant sacrificing human standards of living, it was accepted by the radicals as not only prudent but morally proper.

Potentially highly divisive as Kirkpatrick Sale notes (Selection 44), the deep ecological critique of "shallow" or anthropocentric environmentalism ignored possible grounds of commonality. Both philosophies converged at the point of realization that respect for the intrinsic value of nature could also be the best long-term way to advance the most basic human interest: survival. There was no prosperity, no health, no beauty, indeed no existence, apart from the environmental context. As part of nature, the interest of mankind and nature are, ultimately, the same. Black Elk (Selection 1) and Henry David Thoreau (Selection 5) were part of a small minority that attempted to gain attention for this idea much earlier but with little success. By the 1990s, with the cold, dark cloud of nuclear war hanging over nature as well as civilization, it was finally gaining widespread credibility.

40

Wilderness Advocacy

Roderick Frazier Nash (1988)

Increasingly in today's world of accelerating technological capability and a growing appetite for natural resources, the existence of wilderness indicates the exercise of restraint. At the edge of wilderness society opts to limit its impact on the earth. For some wilderness advocates this restraint is justified by human interest in scenic beauty and outdoor recreation. But others find deeper reasons to protect the wild, and some understand wilderness preservation to be a gesture of planetary modesty. They say that wilderness recognizes the right of other forms of life to a place on spaceship earth.

The United States has led the world in the preservation of wilderness. The national park idea was an American invention and, according to Wallace Stegner (Selection 28), the best idea our civilization ever had. In 1964 the United States established a National Wilderness Preservation System—the first effort to give wilderness permanent, legal protection. The American wilderness movement owes much to John Muir (Selection 15), Robert Marshall (Selection 25), Aldo Leopold (Selection 27), and contemporary thinkers like Stegner. Here Roderick Frazier Nash, author of Wilderness and the American Mind *(1982), sets forth the most effective ways to defend wilderness. The speech was delivered at the Fourth World Wilderness Congress held in Denver in 1987.*

This is a time of irreversible decision for wilderness on earth. As a species, our kind has followed with a vengeance the advice of the Old Testament prophet and "made the crooked straight and the rough places plain." The transformation of wilderness into civilization has taken on aspects of a religion and crusade and nowhere is this more than in the United States. Presently in the 48 continuous states, excluding Alaska, the amount of protected wilderness is approximately equal to the amount of pavement: about 2 percent of the total land

Roderick Frazier Nash, "Why Wilderness?" in *For the Conservation of the Earth,* Vance Martin, ed., (Golden, CO: Fulcrum, 1988), 194–201.

mass is in each category. . . . Wilderness is indeed an endangered geographical species.

Today, not 1890, is the effectual end of the American frontier. Our generation is making the final decisions about the continuing presence of wildness in the environment. The limits of the earth are rapidly being reached, and what this means is that wilderness will no longer exist as left-over or forgotten land that nobody knows. It will either be consciously and deliberately preserved by policy and law or it will vanish. The future will hold us accountable for the quality of environment it inherits. Will we pass on an enduring legacy of wilderness or will we bequeath a totally modified earth?

Pioneering in the past involved the destruction of wilderness, and it has almost completely succeeded. Future pioneering should emphasize preservation. The mission of the new frontiersmen should be centered on restraining, not extending, civilization. The point is that we have conquered the wilderness; now we need to conquer ourselves and our appetite for growth and development. Axes and rifles, barbed wire and bulldozers were useful in a time when civilization was struggling for a foothold in the wild world. But now it is wilderness that is struggling for existence, and the need is for new tools. Research into and education about the value of wilderness are the appropriate tools for the new frontiersmen. So are institutions such as the proposed World Conservation Bank. . . .

There is substantial wilderness left on parts of the planet. The polar regions are largely wild; . . . so is the floor of the ocean and the moon. But for most of us these are not "meaningful" wildernesses. Like heaven, it is nice to know it exists, but most of us are never going to get there! More specifically, in the tropical and temperate latitudes, where most humans live, wilderness is melting away, as Bob Marshall liked to say, like a snowbank in the August sun. Extrapolating from the recent growth of science and technology, can we be certain that we will not have within our power in a few decades the ability to civilize the poles, the oceans and even the stars? The necessity, again, is for restraint. We need to understand that on a limited planet everything must have limits. This includes our numbers and our impact. It is time to understand that civilization can be ironic: some is undeniably good, but in excess it can destroy itself by its own "too much." Balance is the key. Wilderness should no longer be seen as a threat to civilization, but rather as a valuable part of a rich and full civilization—an asset and not an adversary. In time we might discover something the old-style pioneers could not have been expected to know: Wilderness is not the enemy of civilization, but a necessity if that civilization is to live up to its potential as a human habitat. . . .

Edward Abbey, the writer, says that wilderness needs no defense, only more defenders. Respectfully, I disagree. There is a pressing need for elucidation of the underlying principles and values upon which an effective defense of wilderness can be built. Such a philosophy of wilderness has been notable for its absence in the U.S. preservation movement.

We have, rather, witnessed a series of frantic, subjective and highly-emotional defenses of particular places. "Save the grizzly!" or "Save Grand Canyon!" we cry. If anyone asked, "Why?" there was a sharp intake of breath, a scowl and the reply that it was the *Grand Canyon*. But that is not enough. The questions remain: *Why* save a place like the Grand Canyon, *why* keep it wild?

The point is that wilderness appreciation has been a creed, a faith, something you felt in your bones, something that was almost sullied by analysis and explication. But that is not good enough, especially when the world's wild places are increasingly hard-pressed by demands for the expansion of civilization. There is a need for an articulation of wilderness values based on historical fact, contemporary experience and the projected future needs of human life and of all life. This is the vital philosophy of wilderness. It must lie behind the defense of particular wild places like the philosophy of human dignity lies behind defenses of human freedom. Philosophers have spent 2,500 years setting forth the liberal philosophy. So, when Thomas Jefferson wrote his famous Declaration, when Lincoln emancipated the slaves or when more recent protests of discrimination occurred, few needed to ask, "Why?" The value of liberty and equality is well defined. Not so with the value of wilderness. The appreciation of wild places and wild creatures is, after all, barely a century old.

We should pause for a moment to consider several ways *not* to defend wilderness, ways that do not make the best case for preservation. The first is *scenery*. The problem here is that wilderness is not about scenery; it is about the absence of technological civilization and its controlling influence. Now some people do find the absence of civilization "scenic," but many others find it strange, weird, harsh, frightening and decidedly unlovely. They value it not because it is beautiful but because it is wild. Basing a defense of this kind of country on scenic beauty is to leave the case open to all sorts of logical pitfalls. How, for instance, is fire to be justified as a natural part of a wilderness ecosystem? Using beauty to defend wilderness, in sum, is like saying that only beautiful people are to be accorded rights to exist. We abandoned that tactic long ago in defending human rights, and it is time to question its validity in making a case for wilderness.

Recreation is another sandy foundation for wild country because it is not wilderness dependent. . . . People can and do recreate and generally have fun outdoors in very nonwilderness settings. Camping can be had in KOA campgrounds, and excellent hunting and fishing is available in fenced and stocked compounds. We need to investigate what it is about *wilderness* recreation that is different and valuable.

A third way not to defend wilderness is *economics,* and I say this with the full realization that cost-benefit analyses and the expenditures of tourists have been used repeatedly to justify the existence of wildness. Generally, proponents of the economic argument are interested in offering a countervailing argument to the developers' calculations of the cash value of natural resources present in wilderness. The problem is that wilderness almost always loses in such figuring. Its "benefits" are invariably less than, say, that which timber or mineral extraction, or condominium building, would provide. And tourists utilizing hotels and restaurants always spend more than backpackers. Economic arguments are thus a dead end for wilderness. Moreover, there is the point that wilderness should be measured on a different scale of value, like the Parthenon or Chartres Cathedral or a beloved person. I am reminded here of an exchange I once had with a distinguished resource economist who was using the cost-benefit technique to evaluate wilderness. At the conclusion of his remarks, I simply asked him, "What's the cost-benefit ratio of your 87-year-old mother?" Affronted, the economist blustered, "Well, that's different." So, I submit, is wilderness. It's our biological and cultural mother. The point is that wilderness defenders should have the courage to not go to the economic mat with their opponents. They should remember that economists are sometimes accused of knowing the price of everything and the value of nothing.

A corollary to this reasoning is that the wilderness we have protected around the world is generally worthless land. There are few designated wildernesses in Iowa or France. We have saved places that are high, dry, cold, and remote. When an economic use is found for such a place, more likely than not, its wilderness value is forgotten. The classic instance in U.S. history is Yosemite National Park's once-spectacular Hetch Hetchy Valley. In 1913 San Francisco convinced Congress that the highest value of the region was as a municipal water reservoir and hydropower facility. It was removed from the national park and flooded, a reminder to our foreign guests that the U.S. example can demonstrate how not to care for wilderness as well as how to preserve it. The lesson is that those who lean too heavily on economic arguments for wilderness run the risk of having their leaning posts cut off at the roots.

Reviewing the liabilities of scenery, recreation, and economics as defenses of wilderness, and thinking about the reasons why we love it, I thought about an analogy. May I address the men in the audience for a moment? Isn't it true, gentlemen, that we have all been asked by a woman at one time or another (usually, it seems, late at night), "Why do you love me?" I suggest that three reasons that won't be satisfactory are scenery, recreation, and economics!

So how are we to answer the question, "Why do we love wilderness?" I will sketch, briefly, seven reasons that are wilderness-dependent, historically valid and shaped by an understanding of both the realities of wilderness and the needs of civilization. They have been refined by our best wilderness philosophers and they constitute the granite philosophical bedrock in which the case for wilderness should rest.

1. The first might be called the *scientific value.* It rests on the idea that wilderness is a reservoir of normal ecological and evolutionary processes as well as a kind of biological safe-deposit box for the many forms of life. One variation of this value is quite utilitarian and might be called the "cure-for-cancer" argument. The wild places of the world harbor species presently and potentially important to human welfare and even survival. As David Brower is fond of saying, "Wilderness holds the answers to questions we do not yet know how to ask." Norman Myers prefers the metaphor of an ark: those who protect wilderness are like Noah. They make sure that nothing is lost from the full complement of genetic raw material evolved on earth. But on a less instrumental plane, the scientific argument suggests that humans have no right to disturb the evolutionary process. We have already modified the planet enough. When it comes to the existence of species, we should be careful about playing God in Yellowstone or anywhere else. Perhaps Also Leopold put it best when he observed that the first law of successful tinkering is to save all the parts. Our own survival, and that of many other creatures, depends on wilderness environments far more than we think. And mistakes in this area are generally final. Extinction, as the Nature Conservancy likes to point out, is forever.

2. *Spiritual values* are the second important pillar in support of wilderness. For many people wilderness is as important as temple or

church. We might start with the American Indians and other aboriginal people who regarded places, not just buildings with steeples, as sacred. Commonly, these sacred spaces were in the wilderness where the messages of divine powers seemed the clearest. Later generations, pursuing answers to the weightier problems in human existence, found wilderness to have religious significance. Some worshipped nature outright, some found evidence of God in the natural world and some simply turned to wilderness as an appropriate place to pray and reflect. Henry David Thoreau and Ralph Waldo Emerson, the American Transcendentalists, certainly believed that nature was the symbol of the spiritual world. And John Muir regarded Hetch Hetchy Valley as a temple. Even Colorado's own John Denver sings about cathedral mountains. Around the world we find that the deserts and open spaces have been the source of many of the world's great faiths. Jesus was not the only religious leader to commune with deity in the wilderness.

The religious significance many find in wilderness raises the possibility of defending it on the grounds of freedom of worship. This is a basic right in U.S. culture and in many others. Even if wilderness is a church for a minority, do not they have a right to worship as they choose? Indians have been accorded this right under the Native American Religious Freedom Act of 1978. Although hitherto neglected, it could become a bulwark of non-Indian defense of wilderness.

3. Earlier I dismissed scenery as a basis for a wilderness philosophy, but there is an *aesthetic value* dependent on wild settings. The Romantic movement of the seventeenth and eighteenth centuries had a word for it: "sublimity." It involved awe in the face of large, unmodified natural forces and places such as storms, waterfalls, mountains and deserts. Some people find a beauty here that cannot be replicated in pastoral settings, cities or art museums. If the destruction of beauty is to be avoided, then wilderness should be preserved.

4. The *heritage value* of wilderness is grounded on the fact that wild country has been a major force in the shaping of character and culture. As a species, we have lived in the wilderness a thousand times longer than in civilization. In nations like the United States, Canada and Australia, wilderness has had a very recent and very strong formative influence. The U.S. historian Frederick Jackson Turner pointed to one form when he argued in 1893 that the frontier experience built respect for the individual and, later, for democratic institutions. We need wilderness, Turner implied, if we are to understand the source of freedom. Wilderness nourishes it by permitting people to be different,

to escape the controlling force of established institutions. The Puritans in Massachusetts Bay and the Mormons in Utah understood this association. So do contemporary freedom fighters who take to the hills to continue their rebellion if the hills exist. Parenthetically, the totalitarian regime that George Orwell described in his novel, *1984,* made its first concern the elimination of wilderness. Big Brother could not control thought in wild country.

Wilderness is also an historical document just as much as a collection of manuscripts or a bill of rights. Losing wilderness means losing the ability to understand our past; it is comparable to tearing pages from a book in the library. Could we go even further and say that people have a right to their heritage, their history? If so, the preservation of wilderness is incumbent on our generation.

5. Physical health is not wilderness-dependent. You can become very fit at an urban health club. But wilderness has *psychological value* based on the contrast it offers to the environments which most people occupy most of the time. When these civilized environments become repressive, to use a concept the psychologist Sigmund Freud popularized, wilderness offers a unique opportunity for psychological renewal—literally recreation. The reason is that our minds developed under wilderness conditions for millions of years. Suddenly in the last few hundred we have been propelled into a world of bewildering speed and complexity. For some people occasional relief is a vital mental necessity. They covet the chance to drop back into the older and more comfortable channels. Isn't this what Grey Owl, whose statement graces the program of this Congress, meant by offering distraught civilized humans a green leaf? He is not alone in holding that idea. Primitivists from Jean-Jacques Rousseau with his "noble savage" to Edgar Rice Burroughs and Tarzan have argued that the wild world produces a superior human being. Overcivilization is a real and growing danger. Contemporary therapy programs, such as those of Outward Bound, use the challenges of wilderness to build self-reliance and self-respect. A wilderness area may well have more psychological importance than hundreds of beds in a mental hospital.

6. Wilderness has *cultural value,* because in the words of Ralph Waldo Emerson, it permits an opportunity for an original relationship to the universe. The wild world is cultural raw material. Artists, musicians, poets and writers have turned to it repeatedly in their quest to shape a distinctive and distinguished culture. In the United States, cultural independence from the Old World did not come until writers

such as James Fenimore Cooper and painters such as Thomas Cole began to use wilderness as a setting for their work. This has been true around the world. If we preserve it, wilderness can continue to inspire cultural creativity. Without it we will be reduced to making ever-fainter copies of copies, like a Xerox machine. Indeed, wilderness seems to be associated with the very roots of the creative process. It is no accident that artists and scholars use adjectives such as "path-breaking" and "pioneering" to describe fresh work. They speak of the "frontiers" of knowledge. The unknown is the primary stimulant of discovery, and classic wilderness is the unknown. Its presence invigorates a culture, in Henry David Thoreau's terms, as fertilizer does a barren, sandy field. Perhaps this is what Thoreau had in mind when he wrote in 1851 that in wilderness is the preservation of the world.

7. The last and least anthropocentric wilderness benefit derives from the very recent idea that nonhuman life and even wild ecosystems themselves have *intrinsic value* and the right to exist. From this perspective wilderness is not *for* humans at all, and wilderness preservation testifies to the human capacity for restraint. A designated wilderness, in this sense, is a gesture of planetary modesty and a way of demonstrating that humans are members, not masters, of the community of life. In the last decade, environmental ethics and deep ecology have called attention to the idea that rights, and ethical obligations, do not end with human-to-human relationships but extend to the farthest limits of nature. Americans, especially, should not find this concept strange because the history of liberalism in the United States has been one of a selected group of white males; we now find the limits of liberalism extended to the rights of nature. In the course of this progression slavery disappeared and now the more radical environmentalists are calling for the end of *land* slavery. Wilderness is the best place to learn humility, dependency and reverence for all life.

From this nonanthropocentric point of view wilderness preservation is truly a radical act. It is indeed subversive to the forces that have accelerated modern civilization to power but now threaten its continuation: materialism, utilitarianism, growth, domination, hierarchy, exploitation. Development and the preservation of wilderness are *not* compatible. If we are going to really have enduring wilderness on earth, we must challenge the growth ethic. In a limited world everything must have limits including human population and civilization. Only cancer cells respect no limits, and in doing so they destroy their habitat and perish. Civilization has cancerous tendencies; wilderness protection is an antidote. Growth, it increasingly appears, is like a drug that can destroy the user. The antidrug slogan on the streets is, "Just say NO." It is time to apply the same logic to growth. The existence of wilderness is the surest sign that mankind has understood this truth and that he is prepared to put his own legitimate demands into ecological balance with those of his fellow travelers on spaceship earth.

41

Nuclear Winter

Paul Ehrlich (1985)

The impact of a third, nuclear world war on human beings and their civilization has been the subject of much attention. But only recently have we begun to grasp the catastrophic effect of nuclear war on nature. As Paul Ehrlich explains here, the force of the initial blast and subsequent radioactive poisoning would be only part of the problem. Smoke and dust occasioned by the bombs would cast a pall over the planet, reducing even summer temperatures to below freezing. Photosynthesis, and the life that depends upon it, would be greatly impaired. When the skies cleared, depletion of the ozone layer that buffers sunlight would mean blindness for most terrestrial beings.

Nuclear winter, as Paul Ehrlich, Carl Sagan, and their colleagues dubbed conditions following a war, could be understood as an air pollution problem of a magnitude unprecedented on earth at least during occupancy by our species. It would also represent the greatest adverse impact made by mankind on the environment. Perhaps a species capable of triggering a nuclear war deserves itself, but what are the ethical implications of our destruction of most of the life forms and natural processes of the planet?

It is a privilege, although a rather somber one, to be able to present to you the consensus of a large and distinguished group of biologists on the likely biological effects of a large-scale nuclear war. . . .

. . . The environment that will confront most human beings and other organisms after a thermonuclear holocaust will be so altered, and so malign, that extreme and widespread damage to living systems is inevitable. It is, for example, entirely possible that the biological impacts of a war, *apart* from those resulting directly from a blast, fire, and prompt radiation, could result in the end of civilization in the Northern

Paul R. Ehrlich, "The Biological Consequences of Nuclear War," in Paul R. Ehrlich, Carl Sagan, Donald Kennedy, and Walter Orr Roberts, *The Cold and the Dark: The World After Nuclear War* (New York: W. W. Norton, 1985), 43–59.

Hemisphere. Biologists can agree to that as easily as we all could agree that accidentally using cyanide instead of salt in the gravy could spoil a dinner party. . . .

Most of my focus will be on widely ignored indirect consequences for human beings of such a war that would be transmitted through effects on ecological systems. But I do not want to downplay the potential direct effects, well known as they may be, for they will be truly horrifying. Consider what recent studies indicate would happen in a large thermonuclear war, in which somewhere between 5,000 and 10,000 megatons of weapons were detonated—mostly in the Northern Hemisphere. (To put such a war in perspective, consider it *roughly* equal to the explosion of one-half to three-quarters of a million Hiroshima-sized atomic bombs, which amounts to only a portion of the current nuclear arsenals of the U.S.A. and U.S.S.R.) . . .

Blast alone, according to one estimate, would be expected to cause 750 million deaths. As many people *as existed on the planet when our nation was founded* would be vaporized, disintegrated, mashed, pulped, and smeared over the landscape by the explosive force of the bombs. Another study predicts that 1.1 *billion* people would be killed and a like number injured immediately by blast, heat, and radiation. In other words, almost *half* of the current global population—including most of the residents of the rich nations of the Northern Hemisphere—could become casualties within a few hours. . . .

. . . The fates of the 2–3 billion people who were not killed immediately—including those in nations far removed from targets—might in many ways be worse. They, of course, would suffer directly from the freezing temperatures, darkness, and midterm fallout. . . . But the most significant long-term effects would be produced indirectly by the impact of these and other factors on the environmental systems of the planet. . . .

What kinds of assaults would ecosystems be subjected to in the event of a full-scale nuclear exchange between the United States and the U.S.S.R.? . . . The two that would probably be the most important—widespread darkness and very cold continental weather. Others that would not be trivial, however, include wildfires; toxic smog (which might engulf the entire Northern Hemisphere); enrichment of sunlight (when it did penetrate) with dangerous wavelengths of ultraviolet light (UV-B) that, among other things, damages the genetic material (DNA); increased levels of nuclear radiation; acid rains; the release of poisonous chemicals into ground, surface, and onshore oceanic waters; the siltation and sewage pollution of lakes, rivers, and ocean margins; and violent storms in coastal areas. . . .

Reduced temperatures would have dramatic direct effects on animal populations, many of which would be wiped out by the unaccustomed cold. Nevertheless, the key to ecosystem effects is the impact of the war on green plants. Their activities provide what is known as *primary production*—the binding of energy (through photosynthesis) and the accumulation of nutrients that are necessary for the functioning of all biological components of natural and agricultural ecosystems. Without the photosynthetic activities of plants, virtually all animals, including human beings, would cease to exist. All flesh is truly "grass." Both cold and darkness are inimical to green plants and to photosynthesis. . . . [After a thermonuclear war] land surface temperatures away from the coasts could well be below freezing over the entire Northern Hemisphere for a year, and that near-freezing cold could afflict the Southern Hemisphere for months as well. . . .

What all this boils down to is that virtually all land plants in the Northern Hemisphere would be damaged or killed in a war that occurred just prior to or during the growing season. Most annual crops would likely be killed outright, and there would also be severe damage to many perennials if the war were to occur when they were growing actively. . . .

Cold, remember, is just *one* of the stresses to which green plants would be subjected. The blockage of sunlight that caused the cold would also reduce or terminate photosynthetic activities. This would have innumerable consequences that would cascade through food chains including those supporting human beings. Primary productivity would be reduced roughly in proportion to the amount of light reduction, even if the vegetation were not otherwise damaged. If the light level declined to 5 percent or less of normal levels—which is likely to be the case for months in the middle latitudes of the Northern Hemisphere—most plants would be unable to maintain any net growth. Thus, even if temperatures remained normal, the productivity of crops and natural ecosystems would be enormously reduced by the blocking of sunlight following a war. In combination, the cold and darkness would constitute an unprecedented catastrophe for those systems. . . .

As the cold and darkness abated, green plants would be subjected to another serious insult. Nuclear fireballs would inject large amounts of nitrogen oxides into the stratosphere. These would result in large reductions of the stratospheric ozone shield—on the order of 50 percent. Ozone normally screens out UV-B. In the weeks or months immediately following the war, the atmospheric soot and dust would prevent the increased UV-B from reaching ground level. But the ozone depletion would persist longer than the soot and dust, and, as the atmosphere cleared, organisms would be subjected to UV-B radiation levels much higher than those considered dangerous to ecosystems and human beings. . . .

Ecosystems of the Northern Hemisphere would also be subjected to much higher levels of ionizing radiation from radioactive fallout than has been previously thought. One estimate suggests that a total of about 2 million square miles downwind of the detonations would be exposed to 1,000 rems or more of radiation, mostly within 48 hours. Such levels of radiation would be lethal to all exposed people and to many other sensitive animal and plant species. . . .

Ecosystemic effects of high levels of radiation are more difficult to predict. Nonhuman organisms are differentially susceptible to radiation damage. The most vulnerable include most of the coniferous trees that form extensive forests over the cooler parts of the Northern Hemisphere. Conifers could be killed over an area making up more than 2 percent of the entire land surface of the Northern Hemisphere. This, in turn, would create conditions conducive to the development of extensive fires. . . .

This recital by no means exhausts the impacts that ecosystems would suffer. Many ecosystems, of course, would be damaged or destroyed by the blast, fires, and radiation from the thousands of nuclear weapons detonations. Oil wells, coal supplies, peat marshes, coal seams, and so on could continue to burn for months or years. Secondary wildfires, possibly covering 5 percent or more of the Northern Hemisphere's land surface, would have devastating direct effects on ecosystems—especially those not adapted to periodic fires. Multiple air bursts over California in the late summer or early fall could burn off much of the state, leading to catastrophic flooding and erosion during the next rainy season. Silting, toxic runoff, and radioactive rainout could kill much of the fauna of fresh and coastal waters. Human survivors seeking nourishment from filter-feeding shellfish such as mussels at the ocean's edge would be likely to find that they were either dead or had concentrated so much radioactivity that they would be lethal to consume. . . .

The disaster that would befall many or most of the plants of the Northern Hemisphere from the effects of a nuclear exchange would contribute to an equal or greater disaster for the higher animals. Wild herbivores and carnivores and domestic animals either would be killed outright by the cold or would starve or die of thirst because surface waters were frozen. Following a fall or winter war, many dormant animals in colder regions might survive, only to face extremely difficult conditions in a cold, dark spring and summer.

Scavengers that could withstand the projected extreme cold would likely flourish in the postwar period because of the billions of unburied human and animal bodies. Their characteristically rapid population growth rates could, after the thaw, quickly make rats, roaches, and flies the most prominent animals shortly after World War III.

Soil organisms are not directly dependent on photosynthesis and can often remain dormant for long periods. They would be relatively unaffected by the cold and the dark. But in many areas the loss of aboveground vegetation would expose the soil to severe erosion by wind and water. Soil organisms may not be terribly susceptible to the atmospheric aftereffects of nuclear war, but entire soil ecosystems are likely to be destroyed anyway. . . .

. . . [W]hat would happen to the parts of our planet that are covered with water? Aquatic organisms tend to be protected from dramatic fluctuations in air temperature by the slowness with which water changes its temperature. In general, therefore, aquatic systems should suffer somewhat less disruption than terrestrial ones. Nonetheless, many freshwater systems would freeze to considerable depths (or completely). After a nuclear war in the spring, for instance, three feet or more of ice would form on all bodies of fresh water, at least in the North Temperate Zone. This would even further reduce light levels in lakes, ponds, rivers, and streams in a darkened world. Oxygen would be depleted, and many aquatic organisms would be exterminated. Moreover, the depth of the freezing would make access to surface water by surviving people and other animals extremely difficult.

In the oceans, the darkness would inhibit photosynthesis in the tiny green plants (algae) that form the base of all significant marine food chains. The reproduction of these plants, known collectively as phytoplankton, would be slowed or stopped in many areas, and the surviving phytoplankton would be quickly eaten up by the small floating animals (zooplankton) that prey upon them. Near the ocean's surface, the productivity of phytoplankton is reduced by present levels of UV-B; so after a war, an increase in this sort of radiation would be an additional stress. In the Northern Hemisphere, marine food chains might be disrupted for long enough to cause extinction of many valuable fish species, especially after a spring or summer war.

Plausible nuclear war scenarios can be constructed that would result in the dominant atmospheric effects of darkness and cold spreading over virtually the entire planet. Under those circumstances, human survival would be largely restricted to islands and coastal areas of the Southern Hemisphere, and the human population might be reduced to prehistoric levels.

When many of us read Jonathan Schell's book, *The Fate of the Earth,* we were very much impressed by the moving way in which he presented the case, but I suspect that most biologists, like myself, thought it was a little extreme to imagine that our species might actually disappear from the face of the planet. It did not seem plausible from what we knew then.

Now, the biologists have had to consider the possibility of the spread of darkness and cold over the entire planet and throughout the Southern Hemisphere. It still seemed unlikely to them that that would immediately result in the deaths of all the people in the Southern Hemisphere. We would assume that on islands, for instance, far from sources of radioactivity and where the temperatures would be moderated by the oceans, some people would survive. Indeed, there probably would be survivors scattered throughout the Southern Hemisphere and, perhaps, even in a few places in the Northern Hemisphere.

But one has to ask about the long-term persistence of these small groups of people, or of isolated individuals. Human beings are very social animals. They are very dependent upon the social structures that they have built. They are going to face a very highly modified environment, one not only strange to them but also in some ways much more malign than people have ever faced before. The survivors will be back in a kind of hunter and gatherer stage. But hunters and gatherers in the past have always had an enormous cultural knowledge of their environments; they knew how to live off the land. But after a nuclear holocaust, people without that kind of cultural background will suddenly be trying to live in an environment that has never been experienced by people anywhere. In all likelihood, they will face a completely novel environment, unprecedented weather, and high levels of radiation. If the groups are very small, there is a possibility of inbreeding. And, of course, social and economic systems and value systems will be utterly shattered. The psychological state of the survivors is difficult to imagine.

. . . [U]nder those conditions, we could not exclude the possibility that the scattered survivors simply would not be able to rebuild their populations, that they would, over a period of decades or even centuries, fade away. In other words, we could not exclude the possibility of a full-scale nuclear war entraining the extinction of *Homo sapiens*. . . .

Let me briefly recap. A large-scale nuclear war, as far as we can see, would leave, at most, scattered survivors in the Northern Hemisphere, and those survivors would be facing extreme cold, hunger, water shortages, heavy smog, and so on, and they would be facing it all in twilight or darkness and without the support of an organized society.

The ecosystems upon which they would be extremely dependent would be severely stressed, changing in ways that we can hardly predict. Their functioning would be badly impaired. Ecologists do not know enough about these complicated systems to be able to predict their exact state after they had "recovered." Whether the biosphere would ever be restored to anything resembling that of today is entirely problematical.

42

Religion and the Environment

Wendell Berry (1979)

Wendell Berry, novelist, professor, and Kentucky farmer, emerged in the late 1970s as a foremost exponent of Christian stewardship. This doctrine implied that humans had a responsibility to God to nurture and protect the natural world that was His creation. Stewardship reversed centuries of Christian indifference, or outright hostility, to nature. By the 1980s many theologians and religious leaders had become participants in the environmental movement. Berry concentrated his work on the importance of ecologically responsible land ownership. He deplored "agribusiness" and urged the preservation and extension of family farming. His book The Unsettling of America *(1977) became a central statement in the new back-to-the-land argument of some new environmentalists. But others reasoned that since there was not enough arable land for everyone to own a farm like Berry's, it would be well to explore forms of beneficent concentration of people rather than "unsettling." Of course, the fundamental problem was overpopulation.*

My purpose here is double. I want, first, to attempt a Biblical argument for ecological and agricultural responsibility. Second, I want to examine some of the practical implications of such an argument. I am prompted to the first of these tasks partly because of its importance in our unresolved conflict about how we should use the world. That those who affirm the divinity of the Creator should come to the rescue of His creation is a logical consistency of great potential force.

The second task is obviously related to the first, but the origin of my motive here is somewhat more personal. I wish to deal directly at last with my own long-held belief that Christianity, as usually presented by its organizations, is not *earthly* enough. . . .

Wendell Berry, "The Gift of Good Land," *Sierra,* **64** (November/December 1979), 20–26. Copyright 1981 by Wendell Berry. Published by North Point Press and reprinted by permission.

Some of the reluctance to make a forthright Biblical argument against the industrial rape of the natural world seems to come from the suspicion that this rape originates with the Bible, that Christianity cannot cure what, in effect, it has caused. The best known spokesman for this view is Professor Lynn White, Jr. . . .

Professor White asserts that it is a "Christian axiom that nature has no reason for existence save to serve man." He seems to base his whole argument on one Biblical passage, Genesis 1:28, in which Adam and Eve are instructed to "subdue" the earth. "Man," says Professor White, "named all the animals, thus establishing his dominance over them." There is no doubt that Adam's superiority over the rest of Creation was represented, if not established, by this act of naming; he *was* given dominance. But that this dominance was meant to be tyrannical, or that "subdue" meant to destroy, is by no means a necessary inference. Indeed, it might be argued that the correct understanding of this "dominance" is given in Genesis 2:15, which says that Adam and Eve were put into the Garden "to dress it and to keep it."

But these early verses of Genesis can give us only limited help. The instruction in Genesis 1:28 was, after all, given to Adam and Eve in the time of their innocence, and it seems virtually certain that the word "subdue" would have had a different intent and sense for them then than it could have for them, or for us, after the Fall. . . .

I do not mean to imply that I see no involvement between that tradition and the abuse of nature. I know very well that Christians have often been not only indifferent to such abuse, but often have condoned and perpetrated it. That is not the issue. The issue is whether or not the Bible explicitly or implicitly defines a *proper* human use of Creation or the natural world. Proper use, as opposed to improper use, or abuse, is a matter of great complexity, and to find it adequately treated it is necessary to turn to a more complex story than that of Adam and Eve.

The story of the giving of the Promised Land to the Israelites is more serviceable to this issue than the story of the giving of the Garden of Eden, because the Promised Land is a divine gift to a *fallen* people. For that reason the giving is more problematical, and the receiving is more conditional and more difficult. In the Bible's long working-out of the understanding of this gift, it seems to me, we find the beginning—and, by implication, the completion too—of the definition of an ecological discipline. . . .

In token of His landlordship, God required a sabbath for the land, which was to be left fallow every seventh year; and a sabbath of sabbaths every fiftieth year, a "year of jubilee," during which not only would the fields lie fallow, but the land would be returned to its original owners, as if to free it of the taint of trade and the conceit of human ownership. But beyond their agricultural and social intent, these sabbaths ritualize an observance of the limits . . . of human control. Looking at their fallowed fields, the people are to be reminded that the land is theirs only by gift; it exists in its own right, and does not begin or end with any human purpose. . . .

. . . [T]he good land is not given as a reward. It is made clear that the people chosen for this gift do not deserve it, for they . . . have been wicked and faithless. To such a people such a gift can be given only as a moral predicament: Having failed to deserve it beforehand, they must prove worthy of it afterwards; they must use it well, or they will not continue long in it.

How are they to prove worthy?

First, they must be faithful, grateful and humble; they must remember that the land is a gift. . . .

Second, they must be neighborly. They must be just, kind to one another, generous to strangers, honest in trading. These are social virtues, yet, as they invariably do, they have ecological and agricultural implications. For the land is described as an "inheritance"; the community is understood to exist not just in space, but also in time. One lives in the neighborhood, not just of those who now live "next door," but of the dead who have bequeathed the land to the living, and of the unborn to whom the living will in turn bequeath it. The demanding fact here is that we can have no direct behavioral relation to those who are not yet alive. The only neighborly thing we can do for them is to preserve their inheritance: We must take care, among other things, of the land, which is never a possession, but an inheritance to the living, borrowed from the unborn.

And so the third thing the possessors of the land must do to be worthy of it is to practice good husbandry. The story of the Promised Land has a good deal to say on this subject. . . . Let us consider just a couple of verses (Deuteronomy 22:6–7):

> If a bird's nest chance to be before thee in the way in any tree,
> or on the ground, whether they be young ones, or eggs, and the
> dam sitting upon the young, or upon the eggs, thou shalt not
> take the dam with the young.

> But thou shalt in any wise let the dam go, and take the young
> to thee; that it may be well with thee, and that thou mayest
> prolong thy days.

This, obviously, is a perfect paradigm of ecological and agricultural discipline, in which the idea of inheritance is necessarily paramount. The inflexible rule is that the source must be preserved. You may take the young, but you must save the breeding stock. You may eat the harvest, but you must save seed, and you must preserve the fertility of the fields.

What we are talking about, of course, is an extremely elaborate understanding of charity. . . . Charity cannot be just human, any more than it can be just Jewish or just Samaritan. Once begun, wherever it begins, it cannot stop until it includes all Creation, for all creatures are parts of a whole upon which each is dependent, and it is a contradiction in terms to love your neighbor and despise the great inheritance on which all life depends. Charity even for one person does not make sense except in terms of an effort to love all Creation in response to the Creator's love for it. . . .

The Creator's love for the Creation is mysterious precisely because it does not conform to human purposes. The wild ass and the wild lilies are loved by God for their own sake; and yet they are part of a pattern that we must love because of our dependence on it. . . .

The divine mandate to use the world justly and charitably, then, defines every person's moral predicament as that of a steward. But this is hopeless and meaningless unless it produces an appropriate discipline: stewardship. And stewardship is hopeless and meaningless unless it involves long-term courage, perseverance, devotion and skill. This skill is not to be confused with any accomplishment or grace of spirit or of intellect. It has to do with everyday proprieties in the practical use and care of created things—with "right livelihood."

If "the earth is the Lord's" and we are His stewards, then obviously some livelihoods are "right" and some are not. Is there, for instance, any such thing as a Christian stripmine? A Christian atomic bomb? A Christian nuclear power plant or radioactive waste dump? . . .

. . . If we are willing to pollute the air—to harm the elegant creature known as the atmosphere—by that token we are willing to harm all creatures that breathe, ourselves and our children among them. There is no begging off or "trading off." You cannot affirm the power plant and condemn the smokestack, or affirm the smoke and condemn the cough.

That is not to suggest that we can live harmlessly, or strictly at our own expense; we depend upon other creatures and survive by their deaths. To live we must daily break the body and shed the blood of Creation. When we do this lovingly, knowingly, skillfully, reverently, it is a sacrament. When we do it greedily, clumsily, ignorantly, destructively, it is a desecration.

43

Human Responsibility for Environments beyond Earth

Gar Smith (1987)

The advent of space exploration in the 1960s forced American environmentalists to expand their horizons. The question inevitably arose: Would the new frontier be treated more responsibly than the old western one? Optimistic thinkers hoped America had learned from history; others feared a repetition of the same wasteful, disruptive, and nationalistic patterns that altered the environment in the nineteenth century. Another fascinating problem concerned the meaning of space as wilderness. Would parks and reserves be established and recreation seekers of the future plan camping trips in them? And what about the rights of extraterrestrial matter or, if encountered, life forms and ecosystems? But at least one thing was clear—the new frontier would not be developed, as was the old one, in an age before the conservation and environmental protection movements. Still undecided, however, was whether the United States and the world could transcend its 500-year-old tradition of abusing and exploiting new worlds.

For millions of years, cave dwellers, cattle herders, campers and kings have gazed into the night skies and felt the same emotions. Wonder and terror. Through the ages the great wildernesses of the planet Earth—the vast and crashing oceans, the dark and growling forests, the silent, star-filled skies—have inspired reverence and fear.

But humankind learned to build ships to ride the seas, and the forests began to fall to the axe. The forests and the seas are no longer what they once were. They have been explored, mapped and tamed. They have been conquered.

Only thirty years ago a child of Earth could look up on a dark, chill night and marvel at the mystery of the stars. But today, the night sky is no longer an inaccessible mystery. It is now the "Last Frontier," complete with "challenges" to "overcome," with "new worlds" to "conquer," with places to be "colonized." Significantly, this same vocabulary in the past justified the desecration of mountains, rivers, forests and indigenous peoples: it is the rhetoric of unregulated, exponential growth. Clearly, the same philosophy that propelled our exploitation of the planet now fuels our ambition to explore the stars.

As human civilization stands on the brink of major incursions into the reaches of "near space," it is a good time to pause and reflect on what we stand to lose if we proceed to explore, exploit and colonize space in the same manner in which we have explored, exploited and colonized our beautiful, but battered planet. . . .

Are we about to lose the planet's "last wilderness"? The question is moot. We have *already* turned large portions of the planet's last and greatest wilderness into a cosmic dump.

Since the beginning of the Space Age in the 1950s, more than 15,000 objects from Earth have accumulated in planetary orbit—spent payloads, rocket bodies, clamps, frozen human wastes, fragments from exploded satellites and lost wrenches. To date, 80 satellites are reported to have broken up in Earth orbit.

The planet is already running out of "space" for communications satellites: 139 have been sent into high-altitude orbit, and the US will reach its limit with only 37 more launches. Satellites are now jamming each others' signals, threatening what the Rand Corporation calls "catastrophic failures." The Air Force fears this orbiting Babel might interfere with its war-fighting satellites. . . .

The "Noble Quest" of space exploration recently moved columnist George Will to write: "Now we are talking about space in the language of commerce, as a realm to be exploited for material comforts on Earth." . . .

Space Services* plans to orbit a $250–500 million, 45-foot-long space factory powered by a 200-foot array of solar panels. But SSI is also the author of the most bizarre plan yet to make a killing in orbit. Working with the Celestis Group—a Florida consortium of morticians and retired Kennedy Space Center engineers—SSI plans to start charging customers up to $3,000 to rocket human remains into permanent orbit around the Earth.

---

*Space Services, Inc. of Houston, Texas, a privately-owned company. [Ed.]

Transportation Secretary Elizabeth Dole, NASA, the Defense Department and the Department of State have all given clearance for the space burial missions. The first space coffin flights are set to begin in 1987. The rocket assigned to carry the ashes of these 5,000 pioneering cadavers into 1,900-mile-high Earth orbit, is aptly named the "Conestoga."

Oxygen may be the first major commodity that scientists try to extract from the moon. Sixty percent of the lunar soils are composed of silicon-based oxides, and researchers are toying with the idea of using nuclear reactors or solar furnaces to turn moon dust into oxygen. Each 10,000 tons of lunar soil would also release a ton of hydrogen, a valuable component of water and rocket fuel as well as an essential element in many chemical manufacturing processes. Magnets could recover iron particles from moondust. The vast lunar highlands could be mined for anorthosite, which has a higher aluminum content than most terrestrial rocks. Titanium can be extracted from the soils of the lunar mares. Lunar basalt could be melted down to create molded pipes, tiles, containers and crafts.

NASA scientists predict a permanent moonbase population of 1,000 by the year 2040. Tourists could someday reach the moon, training their spacehardened video camera on the remains of the US Apollo lunar lander in the Sea of Tranquility. If there is to be a human presence on the moon, there should be a campaign to establish protected "international parks" at the Tycho, Aristarchus and Alphonsus craters, for example.

To date, human activity on the Moon has set a poor precedent for future visits. US astronauts have left Polaroid snapshots on the moon's surface. They have taken golf clubs and knocked divots of moondust into space. Astronauts aboard the Apollo 17 "moon buggy" reportedly "careened around crater rims" like joyriding teenagers and Astronaut Eugene Cernan racked up the first lunar "fender-bender" when he accidentally broke off one of the buggy's back fenders.

If there is to be a moonbase, scientists agree it should be an international base after the multinational model of Antarctica. And it should be guided by the "golden rule" of space exploration—i.e. a lunar colony should be conducted "in such a way that it reduce, not aggravate, tensions on Earth."

The next target for exploitation will be the asteroid belt. Scientists have plans to "harvest" these orbiting rocks for hydrogen, oxygen, water, platinum and nickel-iron alloys to fuel space industries. Under one plan, "mass drivers" installed on smaller asteroids could eject the waste material from mining into space, providing enough thrust to propel the asteroid into Earth orbit. This would be a delicate operation. Even the smallest of these asteroids, falling into Earth's atmosphere, could cause what one researcher warns would be "a Hiroshima-class explosion."

In his book *New Earths: Restructuring Earth and Other Planets,* James Oberg explains how "terraforming" can transform the Red Planet Mars into a habitable environment. Giant mirrors aimed at the polar ice caps would vaporize the frozen water. After the atmosphere has been sufficiently "engineered," algae and lichens would be introduced to generate oxygen.

A more immediate way to form an atmosphere, some argue, is to intentionally crash asteroids rich in water, nitrogen and carbon compounds into the surface of the Moon or Mars. By hammering at existing moons and planets with "stolen" asteroids, human space engineers could change the axis or rate-of-spin of these celestial bodies at will.

Oberg realizes technology, even in space, is a two-edged sword. "It should not be hard to imagine how the giant machines of planetary engineering can be turned into weapons," Oberg says. "Making sterile planets habitable, then, is just another side of the coin to making habitable planets (such as Earth) sterile." . . .

Existing bodies of law suggest ways to protect the "high seas" of space and the celestial islands of the cosmos. The 1967 Outer Space Treaty, for instance, includes a number of "wilderness provisions" including freedom of scientific investigation, public access, a ban on "nuclear weapons or any other weapons of mass destruction," noncontamination of celestial environments and the internationalization of space as "the province of all mankind." Article 7 of the 1979 Moon Treaty forbids "disruption of the existing balance of [the Moon's] environment." (The US has refused to ratify the Moon Treaty because of Article 11 which proclaims the satellite to be a "common heritage of mankind.")

In his book, *Third Planet Operating Instructions,* David Brower noted that the planet Earth is a self-service island. "The planet is self-maintaining, and the external fuel source will provide exactly as much energy as is needed or can be safely used." But the rational Western mind has yet to grasp the concept of limits. Faced with the incontrovertible fact that our greed for extracting resources is approaching limits, we could learn to live within the planet's laws and limits. Instead, many have turned to space as an "escape hatch," invoking a "disposable planet mentality" that argues that humanity has simply "outgrown" the planet Earth and is destined to find new nests to foul, on the Moon, on Venus, on Mars.

But as William K. Hartmann points out in *Beyond Spaceship Earth*, "The Earth turns out to be a Hawaii in a solar system full of Siberias. . . . Unlike some early frontiersmen who exhausted one farmland and moved on to the next, we will find no rational motivation for destroying the planet to which we are umbilically linked and then attempting to move on."

The proper frame of reference for Near and Outer Space, then, is not to think of it as a "High Frontier" to be expropriated for the convenience of the fittest entrepreneur. The "High Commons" of Space is the common property of all life on earth. If our common High Ground becomes too polluted with orbiting trash, radioactive debris or military weapons, our entire planet will suffer. Instead of becoming our stepping stone to the stars, the space around our planet could be transformed into a trash-strewn, radioactive shroud. The lessons learned on Earth should tell us that wildernesses of space exist not just to be "challenged"; they also need to be preserved.

The fact is, we cannot consider ourselves competent to venture into space until we have mastered the ability to survive within the limits of our own planetary ecosystem. If we are not to carry our contagions into the stars, we must first find our cures here on Earth. Before novice pilots are allowed to take off into the sky, they must first graduate from Ground School, and, from all the evidence at hand, it would appear our species has not even learned to taxi safely.

At this moment in our evolution as a species, a march to the stars would really be nothing more than fleeing our responsibilities as dwellers upon the Earth. As we prepare to face the wilderness of Space we should take care that we are not simply turning our backs on the planet Earth.

44

Schism in Environmentalism

Kirkpatrick Sale (1986)

There was a time in American environmental history when conservation groups founded in the nineteenth century such as the Sierra Club and the Audubon Society were considered radical. By the 1980s these large and successful organizations had become established and were themselves under attack by a new wave of environmental radicalism. Kirkpatrick Sale calls its ahderents new ecologists *while others prefer the adjective* deep. *The driving force of these people is their belief that nature has intrinsic value (some say "rights") equal to that of human beings. For further insight into contemporary radical environmentalism see Selections 45, 46, and 47.*

Along with Gary Snyder (Selection 36), Sale is a leading exponent of "bioregionalism." According to this philosophy, the fundamental answer to environmental problems requires a new relationship with the earth based on "living in place." Rather than modifying their environments, people, like animals and Native Americans, should adapt to them. Simplicity is the key. Bioregionalists reserve their most intense scorn for desert cities with high water consumption such as Las Vegas, Phoenix, and Los Angeles. In general, bioregionalists avoid politics, radical or conventional, in preference to creating models of human-environment relationships that might inspire others.

"The environmentalists are now entrenched. They're professionals. They're not in it for a cause—they're in it because it's a 'public interest,' highfalutin *job.* You've got a new group of professionals, bureaucratic professionals—all right, yuppies—and the idealistic ones aren't there anymore; they've gone."

Lorna Salzman, a disaffected former staff member at Friends of the

Kirkpatrick Sale, "The Forest for the Trees: Can Today's Environmentalists Tell the Difference?" *Mother Jones,* **11** (November 1986), 25–26, 28–29, 32–33, 58. Reprinted with permission from *Mother Jones* magazine. Copyright 1986 by Foundation for National Progress.

Earth and longtime political activist, leans forward to emphasize the exasperation she feels. "Just look at the boards of directors of these environmental groups, most of them anyway. They're the power elite. I'm no Marxist, but I find that class analysis can be pretty useful sometimes. And there's no way, looking at the boards of those organizations, you're going to get a populist, decentralist, bioregionalist, or radically ecological or socially ecological view." . . .

She speaks with heat, and a little anger—and it's not surprising. Her views reflect the passion of a new and growing movement that has become disenchanted with the environmental establishment and has in recent years mounted a serious and sweeping attack on it—style, substance, systems, sensibilities, and all. The attack is all the more devastating because it comes not from the plutocratic Right, where the attacks usually arise, but from within the very ranks of the environmental movement and among those who have been its most ardent champions.

The new challenge is probably no more than three or four years old, and the ranks are still only sparsely populated, but it has already caused reverberations equal to an 8.6 on the political Richter scale. Friends of the Earth, for example, was wracked this year by a bitter fight that ended with founder David Brower's being ousted from his board chairmanship and the headquarters officially moving from San Francisco to Washington, D.C. . . . The National Audubon Society and the Sierra Club have had heated disputes within their memberships, often over questions involving larger social causes like nuclear power and a weapons freeze, sometimes over such basic issues as hunting and wilderness protection. . . .

At the same time, new actionist groups like the Arizona-based Earth First! have sprung up, started by dissidents from other stuffier and tamer organizations. More than 40 local Green parties and alliances have been formed all over the country by environmentalists who regard the national organizations as uninterested in their direct regional concerns. The decade-old bioregional movement has grown to the point where it can claim some 70 groups around the country. A new spirit of defiance and urgency is abroad, as activists and theorists alike seek to propel the nation's environmental consciousness in what can only be called a more radical direction.

Things have gone so far that Michael McCloskey, an officer at the Sierra Club for more than two decades and now its chairman, was moved to send a confidential memo to his board of directors in January warning of the "new splits developing in the environmental movement. . . . New, more militant" forces are emerging, he warns, "who do not hesitate to criticize the main players such as the Sierra Club." However, he notes, their target is not just the Sierra Club. They want to change "the relationship of individuals to society and the ways in which society works."

In a sense, the current split in the environmental movement is only the latest version of a bifurcation that goes back to the 19th century. From the start there have been raw tensions and outright disputes between what are generally known as the "preservationists" and the "conservationists." The former—symbolized by John Muir, founder of the Sierra Club in 1892 and one of the most important nature philosophers America has produced—tended to favor a hands-off position, emphasizing the ethical values "of pristine wilderness in its original glory." The latter—symbolized by Gifford Pinchot, founder of the U.S. Forest Service in 1905* and friend of Teddy Roosevelt— advocated "the development and use of the earth and all its resources for the enduring good of men." Pinchot's conservationism and its concomitants—tree farming, game management, scientific agriculture, predator control, environmental manipulation, and resource development—have dominated most official thinking, much academic research, and almost all governmental actions throughout this century.

The Muir-inspired tradition, though, has always had its champions, often very eloquent ones, including in recent decades Lewis Mumford, Rachel Carson, and Joseph Wood Krutch. Among the best of them was Aldo Leopold, who, though he began as a quite conventional conservationist, came to espouse the wisdom of the preservationists. . . .

The environmental movement that swept over the 1960s was set in motion by Rachel Carson's *Silent Spring* in 1962 and accelerated by the antiestablishmentarian mood of that decade. It reflected a revival of Muir's preservationist spirit, reinforced by the new holistic insights of academic ecology and a new perception that finally the human had to be added to the endangered species list. The tide probably crested around Earth Day in 1970, but what followed was something that stayed very much in the mold of Pinchot. First came an outcry for national regulations and palliatives; second, a set of modest reformist laws from the U.S. Congress; and third, almost inevitably, a whole new

*More accurately, Pinchot had been the director of the federal division of forestry since 1898 when it received a name change. [Ed.]

industry of environmental professionals—lobbyists, lawyers, publicists, bureaucrats, and scientists. Thus was born the new form of conservationism known as "environmentalism," giving rise to the environmental establishment that has become so prominent in the last decade.

And now has come the backlash. As yet this upstart movement has no agreed-upon name, nor even much in the way of cohesion or self-identification. It is taking shape in perhaps as many as a hundred different organizations, not more than half a dozen of them national in scope. It has roots in, and derives its basic tenets from, a confounding variety of ideas and doctrines, including bioregionalism, Green politics, deep ecology, animal liberationism, ecofeminism, permaculture, steady-state economics, ecophilosophy, native spiritualism, and social ecology—and that's just for starters. It puts itself forth in everything from academic quarterlies and slick monthlies to occasional newsletters and street-corner handouts, with a few hardcover books for added respectability. Its tactics run the gamut from petitions and letter-writing campaigns to alternative assemblies and even full-scale ecological sabotage ("ecotage," as it is known in the trade).

Since the adherents of this movement have been guided primarily by the new understanding of nature provided by contemporary ecological studies, and since they are pressing their insights in innovative ways on both the political and philosophical fronts, I think it is fair to describe them as the "New Ecologists."

It is a slippery word, *ecology,* and I use it with some caution, because all too often it has lost its meaning. . . .

. . . [I]t is *not* interchangeable with *environment,* as the fashion has it. It is, first of all, an academic branch of biology, the study of organisms and their interactions *within* an environment—especially of communities of species in some particular segment or niche of that environment—and how they relate interdependently. It is by extension a description of a philosophical, and in a sense political, position that seeks not merely to study but to preserve such communities in their healthiest state. This means interpreting the concept of interdependence so that it includes, and thus limits, the activities of the human species.

What we have ultimately is a moral and ethical belief system that seeks to supplant the long-dominant Western commitment to *anthropocentrism*—the human first, and dominant—with a new appreciation of *ecocentrism*—the human as just another species in the natural web, having no special claim to the resources of the earth, certainly no claim to control or exploit them, and decidedly no right to threaten their very continuation. . . .

It is ecology in *this* sense, this profound sense, that informs—and impassions—the New Ecologists. And no wonder it is raising so many hackles. George Sessions, a professor of philosophy at Sierra College in California and a prominent academic champion of the new perspective, asserts that it "shows us that the basic assumptions upon which the modern urban-industrial edifice of Western culture rests are erroneous and highly dangerous. An ecologically harmonious social paradigm shift is going to require a *total* reorientation of the thrust of Western culture."

Given their starting point, it is little wonder that the New Ecologists are sharply critical of this country's major conservationist groups, including the National Wildlife Federation, the National Audubon Society, the Environmental Defense Fund, the National Resources Defense Council, the Wilderness Society, and the Sierra Club.

Not that they scorn everything those organizations do and say— not at all. In fact, some of the New Ecologists go out of their way to praise the work the mainstream groups have done: the breakthrough legislation, the bureaucratic battles, the stopgaps, and the holdbacks. Sessions, who is the coauthor of a book called *Deep Ecology* and likes to make deep/shallow distinctions, says, "You've got to have legal machinery, you've got to have money and lobbying—all the work the shallow environmentalists are doing. If we lost the shallow environmentalists overnight, we'd be in big trouble—these big corporations and agencies would roll over the environment in no time."

Many New Ecologists acknowledge that in the years ahead, their most likely recruits will come from among those already allied in one way or another with environmental causes, but the new movement does not mince words about what's wrong with the environmental establishment. The charges tend to cluster around four themes. . . .

1. *Environmentalists are reformist, working within "the system" in ways that ultimately reinforce it instead of seeking the thoroughgoing social and political changes that are necessary to halt massive assaults on the natural world.*

Peter Berg, for example, one of the cofounders of the Planet Drum Foundation in San Francisco and a longtime theorist of the bioregional movement, says . . . that the trouble with the "environmentalist perspective" is that it means "attempting to reform industrialism instead of aiming to replace it." He scoffs at the effort to pass bigger and better laws. . . .

. . . If the Superfund legislation comes up, for example, the only matters discussed are which sites will be cleaned up, and by how much, and when, but never why the corporations produced—and continue to produce—the poisons in the first place. . . .

2. *Environmentalists are basically anthropocentric, believing that the proper human purpose is to control and consume the resources of nature as wisely and safely—but as fully—as possible. They have yet to learn the ecocentric truth that nature and all its species have an intrinsic worth apart from any human designs.* . . .

The indictment is put in a characteristically dramatic way by Dave Foreman, a founder of Earth First! and editor of its rambunctious journal. "The grizzly has a right to live for her own sake," he says, "not for any real or imagined value she may have for human beings. The spotted owl, the wolverine, Brewer's spruce, the fungal web on the forest floor have a nature-given right to follow their own intertwined evolutionary destinies without being meaningless pawns in the arrogant games of industrial humans. What right does a man with a life span of seventy years have to destroy a two-thousand-year-old redwood to make picnic tables?"

3. *Environmentalists have become co-opted into the world of Washington politics, playing the bureaucratic game like any other lobby, turning their backs on the grass roots support and idealism that gave the movement its initial momentum.*

David Brower, who has twice done battle with this sort of mentality—first with the Sierra Club and then with Friends of the Earth—is particularly scathing about "business people" taking over. "There is too much movement now away from the ideals and too much emphasis on bottom lines. The MBAs are taking over from the people who have the dreams. Do MBAs dream?"

In one sense, of course, the environmentalists are victims of their own success—with the passage of the air- and water-quality acts in the 1970s and the formation of the Environmental Protection Agency, it was inevitable that watchdog organizations would be set up in Washington to see that the laws were properly carried out, that citizens groups would be formed to maintain the political pressures. Bill passing becomes all-important, as do horse-trading and good relations with the "right" people, especially committee and subcommittee chairs.

4. *Environmentalists, finally, are not successful even on their own terms in protecting the wilderness, in stopping the onrush of industrial devastation. They are so caught up in compromise that they're actually going backward.*

This line of criticism can be heard right across the continent these days, from organizers trying to save the Tongass National Forest in

Alaska to members of the Cumberland Green Council in the mid-South. . . .

Environmentalists, of course, maintain that *they* don't compromise; the system does. Geoff Webb, acting executive director of Friends of the Earth in Washington, admits that "it's often a matter of one step forward and two steps back. But," he points out, "if we *weren't* here, it'd be zero steps forward and six steps back." . . .

Dave Foreman, who fought battles like that both in the Southwest and in Washington for the Wilderness Society, now faults that approach. "Environmentalists, as reasonable advocates within the mainstream of modern society, have gone out of their way to appear to be moderate and willing to compromise. We have acquiesced in the clear-cutting of old-growth forests, massive road-building schemes on our public lands, mineral and energy development in the pristine areas, and the destruction of 'problem' bears. We have accepted that some wild lands will be, and should be, developed." . . .

Now, however, "it is time to have vision, to dream of the world the way it should be." . . . Which is why Foreman helped start Earth First!, and why Earth First! takes as its rallying cry, "No compromise in defense of Mother Earth!"

Beyond the distinctions embodied in the four-point indictment, it may be possible to distinguish the new breed of ecologists in other ways, even admitting that their attitudes sometimes seem as diverse as species in a rain forest. Michael McCloskey, for example, suggests that the New Ecologists generally have different priorities from traditional "reform" environmentalists. . . .

. . . [T]he distinction revolves around questions not of philosophy but of action: "It turns not on the fuzzy prescriptions of Deep Ecology nor on limited disagreements over growth, nor does it assume a split over the dominant social paradigm. Rather, it turns on whether it is wise to work within the context of the basic social, political, and economic institutions to achieve step-wise progress, or whether prime energies must be directed at changing those institutions." . . .

There is something in [the] . . . purity—or, as some would say, extremism—in the New Ecology viewpoint that grates on the sensibilities of the mainstream environmentalists. "They're just utopians," says Michael McCloskey, with some scorn. "We may be 'reformist' and all, but we know how to work within the context of the basic institutions of the society—and they're just blowing smoke." . . .

. . . [The] complaint [is] . . . dismissed, usually more in sorrow than in anger, by the . . . New Ecologists. . . . they say, it is the so-called real world, the world of industrial society, that is living in a fantasy. . . .

It is only with some sort of ecological balance . . . that any society can ever hope to achieve parity and basic sustenance for all, and this will require a deep understanding of the *limits* of human acquisition and intervention. As one Deep Ecology slogan has it, "Simple in means, rich in ends." . . .

What indeed are they doing? What alternatives do they offer? Let's look at two prominent national groups that more or less represent the New Ecology perspective. Earth First! was started by people dissatisfied with the tame responses of traditional organizations to federal encroachments onto national park and forest lands in the Carter era. Now, particularly in the West, it is actively confronting both private and governmental projects that threaten wilderness and its species. Greenpeace has become famous for the *Rainbow Warrior* tragedy and its nuclear test-site interventions, but the organization has also earned a reputation in the past decade as a practitioner of direct action and nonviolent protests over animal rights, toxic dumping, and environmental despoliation. Neither of these groups could be accused of bureaucratization—something more in the opposite direction would be nearer the mark—and neither seems likely to be seduced by establishmentarian wiles.

As to political tactics, the New Ecologists tend to be more confrontational than the traditional environmentalists, and direct action and civil disobedience are second nature to them. Many had their initial political experience in the 1960s, the heyday of confrontation, and others have come from the antinuclear protests of the 1970s that proved the merits of direct action. Greenpeace, in particular, has been boldly confrontational, claiming that "our greatest strength must be life itself, and the commitment to direct our own lives to protect others." It started sailing its ships into nuclear test-site zones in 1971, and since then it has directly intervened against the whaling ships of six nations, against seal hunters in four, and against toxic-waste dumpers all over the world.

There has even grown up among some New Ecology groups an "ecodefender" strategy that takes confrontation to its limits. The Earth First!ers take the lead here: "Lobbying, lawsuits, and research papers are fine," says one of their handouts, "but they are not enough. [We] also use confrontation, direct action, and civil disobedience to fight for wild places." And though they don't publicly approve of violence, what this fight has come down to in recent years has involved some no-holds-barred "ecotage": the spiking of trees to destroy chain-saw blades, tearing down billboards, cutting ranchers' fences that inhibit natural migration patterns, "decommissioning" bulldozers and heavy equipment used by clear-cutters and road builders, and a plan to plant glass shards and spikes against the tires of off-road vehicles. For Dave Foreman, who has written a book called *Ecodefense: A Guide to Strategic Monkeywrenching,** "these things say, Stay out of this place."

Finally, the New Ecologists may differ from the environmental establishment most profoundly in their sense of direction, of purpose. Perhaps George Sessions says it best: "The reform environmentalists have no program—where are they headed? Have they given us any vision of what they want the world to look like 10 or 20 or 30 years from now? No. There's no vision there. They're about on the level of the penal establishment. Deep ecology, bioregionalism, the rest—*they* have a vision of where we need to go, what is desirable, what's possible."

Whether it really is possible, of course, is difficult to say. But there is no question that the movement seeking to make it happen, for all that it is diverse and local and utopian, definitely exists and is definitely growing—behind dozens of labels, under dozens of different banners. And it shows every sign of being there for some time to come—not only because the need is so great and the crises to which it responds so persistent, but because its message seems to be touching a chord deep in the American soul.

*See Selection 45.

45

Shortcomings of Environmentalism

Murray Bookchin (1980)

Long before "deep ecology" (see Selection 47), gained a following, social critic Murray Bookchin identified the reason for the abuse of both people and nature as the human appetite for power and domination. As early as the 1950s he claimed that environmentalism would have little permanent effect unless it challenged human-nature dualism and anthropocentrism. He believed that community consciousness must replace hierarchy.

The following "open letter" to environmentalists criticizes many parts of the movement as superficial in its focus on symptoms rather than basic causes. What Bookchin favors is a wholesale revolution against most modern political, social, and economic institutions. Although few environmentalists went as far in their call for reform, Bookchin defined one end of the spectrum of possible responses to environmental abuse.

With the opening of the eighties, the ecology movement in both the United States and Europe is faced with a serious crisis. This crisis is literally one of its identity and goals, a crisis that painfully challenges the movement's capacity to fulfill its rich promise of advancing alternatives to the domineering sensibility, the hierarchical political and economic institutions, and the manipulative strategies for social change that have produced the catastrophic split between humanity and nature.

To speak bluntly: the coming decade may well determine whether the ecology movement will be reduced to a decorative appendage of an inherently diseased anti-ecological society, a society riddled by an unbridled need for control, domination and exploitation of humanity and nature—or, hopefully, whether the ecology movement will become the growing educational arena for a new ecological society

Murray Bookchin, *Toward an Ecological Society* (Montreal: Black Rose, 1980), 75–83.

based on mutual aid, decentralized communities, a people's technology, and non-hierarchical, libertarian relations that will yield not only a new harmony between human and human, but between humanity and nature. . . .

. . . For nearly thirty years I have written extensively on . . . the toxic social causes, values, and inhuman relations that have created a planet which is already vastly poisoned.

Ecology, in my view, has always meant *social* ecology: the conviction that the very concept of dominating nature stems from the domination of human by human, indeed, of women by men, of the young by their elders, of one ethnic group by another, of society by the state, of the individual by bureaucracy, as well as of one economic class by another or a colonized people by a colonial power. To my thinking, social ecology has to begin its quest for freedom not only in the factory but also in the family, not only in the economy but also in the psyche, not only in the material conditions of life but also in the spiritual ones. Without changing the most molecular relationships in society—notably, those between men and women, adults and children, whites and other ethnic groups, heterosexuals and gays (the list, in fact, is considerable)—society will be riddled by domination even in a socialistic "classless" and "nonexploitative" form. It would be infused by hierarchy even as it celebrated the dubious virtues of "people's democracies," "socialism" and the "public ownership" of "natural resources." And as long as hierarchy persists, as long as domination organizes humanity around a system of elites, the project of dominating nature will continue to exist and inevitably lead our planet to ecological extinction.

The emergence of the women's movement, even more so than the counterculture, the "appropriate" technology crusade and the anti-nuke alliances (I will omit the clean-up escapades of "Earth Day"), points to the very heart of the hierarchical domination that underpins our ecological crisis. Only insofar as a counterculture, an alternate technology or anti-nuke movement rests on the non-hierarchical sensibilities and structures that are most evident in the truly radical tendencies in feminism can the ecology movement realize its rich potential for basic changes in our prevailing anti-ecological society and its values. Only insofar as the ecology movement *consciously* cultivates an anti-hierarchical and a non-domineering sensibility, structure, and strategy for social change can it retain its very *identity* as the voice for a new balance between humanity and nature and its *goal* for a truly ecological society.

This identity and this goal is now faced with serious erosion. Ecology is now fashionable, indeed, faddish—and with this sleazy popularity has emerged a new type of environmentalist hype. From an outlook and movement that at least held the promise of challenging hierarchy and domination have emerged a form of *environmentalism* that is based more on tinkering with existing institutions, social relations, technologies, and values than on changing them. I use the word "environmentalism" to contrast it with ecology, specifically with social ecology. Where social ecology, in my view, seeks to eliminate the concept of the domination of nature by humanity by eliminating the domination of human by human, environmentalism reflects an "instrumentalist" or technical sensibility in which nature is viewed merely as a passive habitat, an agglomeration of external objects and forces, that must be made more "serviceable" for human use, irrespective of what these uses may be. Environmentalism, in fact, is merely environmental engineering. It does not bring into question the underlying notions of the present society, notably that man must dominate nature. On the contrary, it seeks to facilitate that domination by developing techniques for diminishing the hazards caused by domination. . . .

Nathan Glazer's "ecological" 24-square-mile solar satellite . . . and the DOE's* giant "ecological" windmills, to cite the more blatant examples of this environmentalistic mentality, are no more "ecological" than nuclear power plants or agribusiness. If anything, their "ecological" pretensions are all the more dangerous because they are more deceptive and disorienting to the general public. The hoopla about a new "Earth Day" or future "Sun Days" or "Wind Days," like the pious rhetoric of fast-talking solar contractors and patent-hungry "ecological" inventors, conceal the all-important fact that solar energy, wind power, organic agriculture, holistic health, and "voluntary simplicity" will alter very little in our grotesque imbalance with nature if they leave the patriarchal family, the multinational corporation, the bureaucratic and centralized political structure, the property system, and the prevailing technocratic rationality untouched. . . .

As an individual who has been deeply involved in ecological issues for decades, I am trying to alert well-intentioned ecologically oriented people to a profoundly serious problem in our movement. To put my concerns in the most direct form possible: I am disturbed by

---

*The U.S. Department of Energy. [Ed.]

a widespread technocratic mentality and political opportunism that threatens to replace social ecology by a new form of social engineering. For a time it seemed that the ecology movement might well fulfill its libertarian potential as a movement for a non-hierarchical society. Reinforced by the most advanced tendencies in the feminist, gay, community and socially radical movements, it seemed that the ecology movement might well begin to focus its efforts on changing the basic structure of our anti-ecological society, not merely on providing more palatable techniques for perpetuating it or institutional cosmetics for concealing its irremediable diseases. The rise of the anti-nuke alliances based on a decentralized network of affinity groups, on a directly democratic decision-making process, and on direct action seemed to support this hope. . . .

. . . [But] the opening of the eighties, so rich in its promise of sweeping changes in values and consciousness, has also seen the emergence of a new opportunism, one that threatens to reduce the ecology movement to a mere cosmetic for the present society. . . .

. . . [T]he radical implications of a decentralized society based on alternate technologies and closely knit communities are shrewdly placed in the service of a technocratic sensibility, of "managerial radicals," and opportunistic careerists. The grave danger here lies in the failure of many idealistic individuals to deal with major social issues on their own terms—to recognize the blatant incompatibilities of goals that remain in deep-seated conflict with each other, goals that cannot possibly coexist without delivering the ecology movement to its worst enemies. More often than not, these enemies are its "leaders" and "founders" who have tried to manipulate it to conform with the very system and ideologies that block . . . an ecological society.

Ecology is being used against an ecological sensibility, ecological forms of organization, and ecological practices to "win" large constituencies, *not to educate them.* The fear of "isolation," of "futility," of "ineffectiveness" yields a new kind of isolation, futility and ineffectiveness, namely, a complete surrender of one's most basic ideals and goals. "Power" is gained at the cost of losing the only power we really have that can change this insane society—our moral integrity, our ideals, and our principles. This may be a festive occasion for careerists who have used the ecology issue to advance their stardom and personal fortunes; it would become the obituary of a movement that has, latent within itself, the ideals of a new world in which masses become individuals and natural resources become nature, both to be respected for their uniqueness and spirituality.

An ecologically oriented feminist movement is now emerging and the contours of the libertarian anti-nuke alliances still exist. The fusing of the two together with new movements that are likely to emerge from the varied crises of our times may open one of the most exciting and liberating decades of our century. Neither sexism, ageism, ethnic oppression, the "energy crisis," corporate power, conventional medicine, bureaucratic manipulation, conscription, militarism, urban devastation or political centralism can be separated from the ecological issue. All of these issues turn around hierarchy and domination, the root conceptions of a radical social ecology.

It is necessary, I believe, for everyone in the ecology movement to make a crucial decision: will the eighties retain the visionary concept of an ecological future based on a libertarian commitment to decentralization, alternative technology, and a libertarian practice based on affinity groups, direct democracy, and direct action? Or will the decade be marked by a dismal retreat into ideological obscurantism and a "mainstream politics" that acquires "power" and "effectiveness" by following the very "stream" it should seek to divert? . . . In any case, the choice must be made now, before the ecology movement becomes institutionalized into a mere appendage of the very system whose structure and methods it professes to oppose. It must be made consciously and decisively—or the century itself, not only the decade, will be lost to us forever.

46

Monkeywrenching

Edward Abbey and Dave Foreman (1987)

In 1975, Edward Abbey wrote a novel about a group of radical environmentalists whose anger at the destruction of the wilderness qualities of the southwest led them to acts of sabotage against developers. His book The Monkey Wrench Gang *attracted those who felt that conventional defense of the environment—petitions, laws, and lawsuits—was slow and ineffective. One of those who responded to Abbey's message was Dave Foreman. In 1980, Foreman resigned his position with a conservation group he considered too moderate and organized Earth First! The name, complete with exclamation mark, expressed the conviction of Foreman and his colleagues that in any environmental decision, the welfare of the ecosystem must be considered ahead of economics, ahead of progress, indeed ahead of any human interest. The slogan the Earth First!ers adopted, "No Compromise in Defense of Mother Earth," was reminiscent of that of an early group of radical American reformers, the abolitionists who shouted, "No Compromise with Slavery!" Land slavery, Foreman and his friends pointed out, was just as immoral as human slavery.* Environmental *ethics had added a whole new dimension to moral philosophy. It also persuaded Earth First! to encourage its members to act illegally when the law in question sanctioned abuse of the environment. "Monkeywrenching," the Abbey-inspired term for direct defense of the earth, ranged from human blockades reminiscent of the civil rights campaign, to "spiking" trees in the hope of destroying lumbermen's saws, to the mock cracking of Glen Canyon Dam on the Colorado. Earth First!'s tactics came under heavy critical fire, even from other environmentalists, but by 1989 it counted 12,000 members and had local chapters in many states.*

Aldo Leopold's land ethic (Selection 27) inspired Earth First! and so did the philosophy of deep ecology (Selection 47). The following statements, first Abbey's and then Foreman's, appeared in a guidebook Earth First! issued for persons interested in uncompromising defense of the environment.

"Forward!" by Edward Abbey and "Strategic Monkeywrenching" by Dave Foreman, in *Ecodefense: A Field Guide to Monkeywrenching* (Tucson, AZ: Ned Ludd, 1987), 7–9, 10–17. Copyright by Ned Ludd Books, POB 5871, Tucson, AZ, 85703.

FORWARD!

If a stranger batters your door down with an axe, threatens your family and yourself with deadly weapons, and proceeds to loot your home of whatever he wants, he is committing what is universally recognized—by law and morality—as a crime. In such a situation the householder has both the right and the obligation to defend himself, his family, and his property by whatever means are necessary. This right and this obligation is universally recognized, justified and even praised by all civilized human communities. Self-defense against attack is one of the basic laws not only of human society but of life itself, not only of human life but of all life.

The American wilderness, what little remains, is now undergoing exactly such an assault. Dave Foreman has summarized the character and scale of the assault in the first chapter of this excellent and essential book. With bulldozer, earth mover, chainsaw and dynamite the international timber, mining and beef industries are invading our public lands—property of all Americans—bashing their way into our forests, mountains and rangelands and looting them for everything they can get away with. This for the sake of short-term profits in the corporate sector and multi-million dollar annual salaries for the three-piece-suited gangsters (M.B.A., Harvard, Yale, University of Tokyo, *et alia*) who control and manage these bandit enterprises. Cheered on, naturally, by *Time, Newsweek* and the *Wall Street Journal,* actively encouraged by those jellyfish Government agencies which are supposed to protect the public lands, and as always aided and abetted in every way possible by the quisling politicians of our Western states (such as Babbitt, DeConcini, Goldwater, Hatch, Garn, Symms, Hansen, Wallop, Domenici—to name but a few) who would sell the graves of their own mothers if there's a quick buck in the deal, over or under the table, what do they care.

Representative democracy in the United States has broken down. Our legislators do not represent those who elected them but rather the minority who finance their political campaigns and who control the organs of communication—the Tee Vee, the newspapers, the billboards, the radio—that have made politics a game for the rich only. Representative government in the USA represents money not people and therefore has forfeited our allegiance and moral support. We owe it nothing but the taxation it extorts from us under threats of seizure of property, or prison, or in some cases already, when resisted, a sudden and violent death by gunfire.

Such is the nature and structure of the industrial megamachine (in Lewis Mumford's term) which is now attacking the American wilderness. That wilderness is our ancestral home, the primordial homeland of all living creatures including the human, and the present final dwelling place of such noble beings as the grizzly bear, the mountain lion, the eagle and the condor, the moose and the elk and the pronghorn antelope, the redwood tree, the yellowpine, the bristlecone pine, even the aspen, and yes, why not say it?, the streams, waterfalls, rivers, the very bedrock itself of our hills, canyons, deserts, mountains.

For many of us, perhaps for most of us, the wilderness is as much our home, or a lot more so, than the wretched little stucco boxes, plywood apartments, and wallboard condominiums in which we are mostly confined by the insatiable demands of an overcrowded and ever-expanding industrial culture. And if the wilderness is our true home, and if it is threatened with invasion, pillage and destruction—as it certainly is—then we have the right to defend that home, as we would our private rooms, by whatever means are necessary. (An Englishman's home is his castle; an American's home is his favorite fishing stream, his favorite mountain range, his favorite desert canyon, his favorite swamp or patch of woods or God-created lake.)

The majority of the American people have demonstrated on every possible occasion that they support the ideal of wilderness preservation; even our politicians are forced by popular opinion to *pretend* to support the idea; as they have learned, a vote against wilderness is a vote against their own re-election. We are justified in defending our homes—our private home and public home—not only by common law and common morality but also by common belief. We are the majority; they—the greedy and powerful—are the minority.

How best defend our wilderness home? Well, that is a matter of strategy, tactics and technique, which is what this little book is about. Dave Foreman explains the principles of ecological defense in the complete, compact, and conclusive pages of his chapter on strategy. I can think of nothing I could add nor of anything I would subtract; he says exactly what needs to be said, no more and no less.

I am happy to endorse the publication of *Ecodefense.* Never was such a book so needed, by so many, for such good reason, as here and now. Tomorrow might well be too late. This is a book that will fit handily in any saddlebag, in any creel, in any backpack, in any river runner's ammo can—and in any picnicker's picnic basket. No good American should ever go into the woods again without this book and, for example, a hammer and a few pounds of 60-penny nails. Spike a few trees now and then whenever you enter an area condemned to chainsaw massacre by Louisiana Pacific and its affiliated subsidiary the U.S. Forest Service. You won't hurt the trees; they'll be grateful for the protection; and you may save the forest. My Aunt Emma back in West Virginia has been enjoying this pleasant exercise for years. She swears by it. It's good for the trees, it's good for the woods, it's good for the earth, and it's good for the human soul. Spread the word—and *carry on!*

STRATEGIC MONKEYWRENCHING

. . . Only one hundred and fifty years ago, the Great Plains were a vast, waving sea of grass stretching from the Chihuahuan Desert of Mexico to the boreal forest of Canada, from the oak-hickory forests of the Ozarks to the Rocky Mountains. Bison blanketed the plains—it has been estimated that 60 million of the huge, shaggy beasts moved across the grass. Great herds of pronghorn and elk also filled this Pleistocene landscape. Packs of wolves and numerous grizzly bears followed the immense herds.

One hundred and fifty years ago, John James Audubon estimated that there were several *billion* birds in a flock of passenger pigeons that flew past him for several days on the Ohio River. It has been said that a squirrel could travel from the Atlantic seaboard to the Mississippi River without touching the ground, so dense was the deciduous forest of the East.

At the time of the Lewis and Clark Expedition, an estimated 100,000 grizzlies roamed the western half of what is now the United States. The howl of the wolf was ubiquitous. The condor dominated the sky from the Pacific Coast to the Great Plains. Salmon and sturgeon filled the rivers. Ocelots, jaguars, margay cats and jaguarundis roamed the Texas brush and Southwestern deserts and mesas. Bighorn sheep in great numbers ranged the mountains of the Rockies, Great Basin, Southwest and Pacific Coast. Ivory-billed woodpeckers and Carolina parakeets filled the steamy forests of the Deep South. The land was alive.

East of the Mississippi, giant tulip poplars, chestnuts, oaks, hickories and other trees formed the most diverse temperate deciduous forest in the world. On the Pacific Coast, redwood, hemlock, Douglas fir, spruce, cedar, fir and pine formed the grandest forest on Earth.

In the space of a few generations we have laid waste to paradise. The tall grass prairie has been transformed into a corn factory where wildlife means the exotic pheasant. The short grass prairie is a grid of carefully fenced cow pastures and wheat fields. The passenger pigeon is no more. The last died in the Cincinnati Zoo in 1914. The endless forests of the East are tame woodlots. The only virgin deciduous forest there is in tiny museum pieces of hundreds of acres. Six hundred grizzlies remain and they are going fast. There are only three condors left in the wild and they are scheduled for capture and imprisonment in the Los Angeles Zoo. Except in northern Minnesota and Isle Royale, wolves are known merely as scattered individuals drifting across the Canadian and Mexican borders (a pack has recently formed in Glacier National Park). Four percent of the peerless Redwood Forest remains and the monumental old growth forest cathedrals of Oregon are all but gone. The tropical cats have been shot and poisoned from our southwestern borderlands. The subtropical Eden of Florida has been transformed into hotels and citrus orchards. Domestic cattle have grazed bare and radically altered the composition of the grassland communities of the West, displacing elk, moose, bighorn sheep and pronghorn and leading to the virtual extermination of grizzly, wolf, cougar, bobcat and other "varmints." Dams choke the rivers and streams of the land.

Nonetheless, wildness and natural diversity remain. There are a few scattered grasslands ungrazed, stretches of free-flowing river undammed and undiverted, thousand-year-old forests, Eastern woodlands growing back to forest and reclaiming past roads, grizzlies and wolves and lions and wolverines and bighorn and moose roaming the backcountry; hundreds of square miles that have never known the imprint of a tire, the bite of a drill, the rip of a 'dozer, the cut of a saw, the smell of gasoline.

These are the places that hold North America together, that contain the genetic information of life, that represent sanity in a whirlwind of madness.

In January of 1979, the Forest Service announced the results of RARE II [its Roadless Area Review and Evaluation]: of the 80 million acres of undeveloped lands on the National Forests, only 15 million acres were recommended for protection against logging, road building and other "developments." In the big tree state of Oregon, for example, only 370,000 acres were proposed for Wilderness protection out of 4.5 million acres of roadless, uncut forest lands. Of the areas nationally slated for protection, most were too high, too dry, too cold, too steep to offer much in the way of "resources" to the loggers, miners and graziers. Those roadless areas with critical old growth forest values were allocated for the sawmill. Important grizzly habitat in the Northern Rockies was tossed to the oil industry and the loggers. Off-road-vehicle fanatics and the landed gentry of the livestock industry won out in the Southwest and Great Basin. . . .

The BLM [Bureau of Land Management] wilderness review has been a similar process of attrition. It is unlikely that more than 9 million acres will be recommended for Wilderness out of the 60 million with which the review began. Again, it is the more spectacular but biologically less rich areas that will be proposed for protection.

During 1984, Congress passed legislation designating minimal National Forest Wilderness acreages for most states (generally only slightly larger than the pitiful RARE II recommendations and concentrating on "rocks and ice" instead of crucial forested lands). In the next few years, similar picayune legislation for National Forest Wilderness in the remaining states and for BLM Wilderness will probably be enacted. The other roadless areas will be eliminated from consideration. National Forest Management Plans emphasizing industrial logging, grazing, mineral and energy development, road building, and motorized recreation will be implemented. Conventional means of protecting these millions of acres of wild country will largely dissipate. Judicial and administrative appeals for their protection will be closed off. Congress will turn a deaf ear to requests for additional Wildernesses so soon after disposing of the thorny issue. The effectiveness of conventional political lobbying by conservation groups to protect endangered wild lands will evaporate. And in half a decade, the saw, 'dozer and drill will devastate most of what is unprotected. The battle for wilderness will be over. Perhaps 3% of the United States will be more or less protected and it will be open season on the rest. Unless. . . .

Many of the projects that will destroy roadless areas are economically marginal. It is costly for the Forest Service, BLM, timber companies, oil companies, mining companies and others to scratch out the "resources" in these last wild areas. It is expensive to maintain the necessary infrastructure of roads for the exploitation of wild lands. The cost of repairs, the hassle, the delay, the down-time may just be too much for the bureaucrats and exploiters to accept if there is a widely-dispersed, unorganized, *strategic* movement of resistance across the land.

It is time for women and men, individually and in small groups, to act heroically and admittedly illegally in defense of the wild, to put a monkeywrench into the gears of the machine destroying natural diversity. This strategic monkey wrenching can be safe, it can be easy, it can be fun, and—most importantly—it can be effective in stopping timber cutting, road building, overgrazing, oil & gas exploration, mining, dam building, powerline construction, off-road-vehicle use, trapping, ski area development and other forms of destruction of the wilderness, as well as cancerous suburban sprawl.

But it must.be strategic, it must be thoughtful, it must be deliberate in order to succeed. Such a campaign of resistance would follow these principles:

Monkeywrenching Is Non-violent

Monkeywrenching is non-violent resistance to the destruction of natural diversity and wilderness. It is not directed toward harming human beings or other forms of life. It is aimed at inanimate machines and tools. Care is always taken to minimize any possible threat to other people (and to the monkeywrenchers themselves).

Monkeywrenching Is Not Organized

There can be no central direction or organization to monkeywrenching. Any type of network would invite infiltration, *agents provocateurs* and repression. It is truly individual action. Because of this, communication among monkeywrenchers is difficult and dangerous. Anonymous discussion through this book and its future editions, and through the dear Ned Ludd section of the *Earth First! Journal,* seems to be the safest avenue of communication to refine techniques, security procedures and strategy.

Monkeywrenching Is Individual

Monkeywrenching is done by individuals or very small groups of people who have known each other for years. There is trust and a good working relationship in such groups. The more people involved, the greater are the dangers of infiltration or a loose mouth. Earth defenders avoid working with people they haven't known for a long time, those who can't keep their mouths closed, and those with grandiose or violent ideas (they may be police agents or dangerous crackpots).

Monkeywrenching Is Targeted

Ecodefenders pick their targets. Mindless, erratic vandalism is counterproductive. Monkeywrenchers know that they do not stop a specific logging sale by destroying any piece of logging equipment which they come across. They make sure it belongs to the proper culprit. They ask themselves what is the most vulnerable point of a wilderness-destroying project and strike there. Senseless vandalism leads to loss of popular sympathy.

Monkeywrenching Is Timely

There is a proper time and place for monkeywrenching. There are also times when monkeywrenching may be counterproductive. Monkeywrenchers generally should not act when there is a non-violent civil disobedience action (a blockade, etc.) taking place against the opposed project. Monkeywrenching may cloud the issue of direct action and the blockaders could be blamed for the ecotage and be put in danger from the work crew or police. Blockades and monkeywrenching usually do not mix. Monkeywrenching may also not be appropriate when delicate political negotiations are taking place for the protection of a certain area. There are, of course, exceptions to this rule. The Earth warrior always thinks: Will monkeywrenching help or hinder the protection of this place?

Monkeywrenching Is Dispersed

Monkeywrenching is a wide-spread movement across the United States. Government agencies and wilderness despoilers from Maine to Hawaii know that their destruction of natural diversity may be met with resistance. Nation-wide monkeywrenching is what will hasten overall industrial retreat from wild areas.

Monkeywrenching Is Diverse

All kinds of people in all kinds of situations can be monkeywrenchers. Some pick a large area of wild country, declare it wilderness in their own minds, and resist any intrusion against it. Others specialize against logging or ORV's [off road vehicles] in a variety of areas. Certain monkeywrenchers may target a specific project, such as a giant powerline, construction of a road, or an oil operation. Some operate in their backyards, others lie low at home and plan their ecotage a thousand miles away. Some are loners, others operate in small groups.

Monkeywrenching Is Fun

Although it is serious and potentially dangerous activity, monkeywrenching is also fun. There is a rush of excitement, a sense of accomplishment, and unparalleled camaraderie from creeping about in the night resisting those "alien forces from Houston, Tokyo, Washington, DC, and the Pentagon." As Ed Abbey says, "Enjoy, shipmates, enjoy."

Monkeywrenching Is Not Revolutionary

It does *not* aim to overthrow any social, political or economic system. It is merely non-violent self-defense of the wild. It is aimed at keeping industrial "civilization" out of natural areas and causing its retreat from areas that should be wild. It is not major industrial sabotage. Explosives, firearms and other dangerous tools are usually avoided. They invite greater scrutiny from law enforcement agencies, repression and loss of public support. (The Direct Action group in Canada is a good example of what monkeywrenching is *not.*) Even Republicans monkeywrench.

Monkeywrenching Is Simple

The simplest possible tool is used. The safest tactic is employed. Except when necessary, elaborate commando operations are avoided. The most effective means for stopping the destruction of the wild are generally the simplest: spiking trees and spiking roads. There are obviously times when more detailed and complicated operations are called for. But the monkeywrencher thinks: What is the simplest way to do this?

Monkeywrenching Is Deliberate and Ethical

Monkeywrenching is not something to do cavalierly. Monkeywrenchers are very conscious of the gravity of what they do. They are deliberate about taking such a serious step. They are thoughtful. Monkeywrenchers—although non-violent—are warriors. They are exposing themselves to possible arrest or injury. It is not a casual or flippant affair. They keep a pure heart and mind about it. They remember that they are engaged in the most moral of all actions: protecting life, defending the Earth.

A movement based on these principles could protect millions of acres of wilderness more stringently than any Congressional act, could insure the propagation of the grizzly and other threatened life forms better than an army of game wardens, and could lead to the retreat of industrial civilization from large areas of forest, mountain, desert, plain, seashore, swamp, tundra and woodland that are better suited to the maintenance of natural diversity than to the production of raw materials for overconsumptive technological human society.

If loggers know that a timber sale is spiked, they won't bid on the timber. If a Forest Supervisor knows that a road will be continually destroyed, he won't try to build it. If seismographers know that they will be constantly harassed in an area, they'll go elsewhere. If ORVers know that they'll get flat tires miles from nowhere, they won't drive in such areas.

John Muir said that if it ever came to a war between the races, he would side with the bears. That day has arrived.

47

Deep Ecology

George Sessions and Bill Devall (1985)

The philosophy of deep ecology was one of the factors splitting modern American environmentalism (see Selection 44) and motivating radical stances such as that of Earth First! (Selection 46). Deep ecologists contrast their viewpoint to "shallow" ecology which, they contend, has guided the American conservation movement for most of its history. The shallow position justifies the protection of nature in terms of human welfare. Its practitioners might protect certain parts of the environment like scenic landscapes and valuable natural resources, but they have no respect for the rights of all of nature above and beyond any human interest. Deep ecologists feel that traditional conservation and even environmentalism is piecemeal and anthropocentric and can never be effective in the long run.

Professional philosophers in Norway, Australia, and the United States conceived of and refined deep ecology. George Sessions and Bill Devall are its leading American exponents.

The term *deep ecology* was coined by Arne Naess in his 1973 article, "The Shallow and the Deep, Long-Range Ecology Movements." Naess was attempting to describe the deeper, more spiritual approach to Nature exemplified in the writings of Aldo Leopold and Rachel Carson. He thought that this deeper approach resulted from a more sensitive openness to ourselves and nonhuman life around us. The essence of deep ecology is to keep asking more searching questions about human life, society, and Nature as in the Western philosophical tradition of Socrates. As examples of this deep questioning, Naess points out "that we ask why and how, where others do not. For instance, ecology as a science does not ask what kind of a society would be the best for

George Sessions and Bill Devall, *Deep Ecology* (Layton, UT: Peregrine Smith, 1985), 65–70. Published by Gibbs Smith, Inc. Reprinted with permission. Footnotes in the original have been omitted.

maintaining a particular ecosystem—that is considered a question for value theory, for politics, for ethics." Thus deep ecology goes beyond the so-called factual scientific level to the level of self and Earth wisdom.

Deep ecology goes beyond a limited piecemeal shallow approach to environmental problems and attempts to articulate a comprehensive religious and philosophical worldview. The foundations of deep ecology are the basic intuitions and experiencing of ourselves and Nature which comprise ecological consciousness. Certain outlooks on politics and public policy flow naturally from this consciousness. And in the context of this book, we discuss the minority tradition as the type of community most conductive both to cultivating ecological conscioueness and to asking the basic questions of values and ethics addressed in these pages.

Many of these questions are perennial philosophical and religious questions faced by humans in all cultures over the ages. What does it mean to be a unique human individual? How can the individual self maintain and increase its uniqueness while also being an inseparable aspect of the whole system wherein there are no sharp breaks between self and the *other?* An ecological perspective, in this deeper sense, results in what Theodore Roszak calls "an awakening of wholes greater than the sum of their parts. In spirit, the discipline is contemplative and therapeutic."

Ecological consciousness and deep ecology are in sharp contrast with the dominant worldview of technocratic-industrial societies which regards humans as isolated and fundamentally separate from the rest of Nature, as superior to, and in charge of, the rest of creation. But the view of humans as separate and superior to the rest of Nature is only part of larger cultural patterns. For thousands of years, Western culture has become increasingly obsessed with the idea of *dominance:* with dominance of humans over nonhuman Nature, masculine over the feminine, wealthy and powerful over the poor, with the dominance of the West over non-Western cultures. Deep ecological consciousness allows us to see through these erroneous and dangerous illusions.

For deep ecology, the study of our place in the Earth household includes the study of ourselves as part of the organic whole. Going beyond a narrowly materialist scientific understanding of reality, the spiritual and the material aspects of reality fuse together. While the leading intellectuals of the dominant worldview have tended to view religion as "just superstition," and have looked upon ancient spiritual practice and enlightenment, such as found in Zen Buddhism, as essentially subjective, the search for deep ecological consciousness is the search for a more objective consciousness and state of being through an active deep questioning and meditative process and way of life.

Many people have asked these deeper questions and cultivated ecological consciousness within the context of different spiritual traditions—Christianity, Taoism, Buddhism, and Native American rituals, for example. While differing greatly in other regards, many in these traditions agree with the basic principles of deep ecology.

Warwick Fox, an Australian philosopher, has succinctly expressed the central intuition of deep ecology: "It is the idea that we can make no firm ontological divide in the field of existence: That there is no bifurcation in reality between the human and the non-human realms . . . to the extent that we perceive boundaries, we fall short of deep ecological consciousness."

From this most basic insight or characteristic of deep ecological consciousness, Arne Naess has developed two *ultimate norms* or intuitions which are themselves not deliverable from other principles or intuitions. They are arrived at by the deep questioning process and reveal the importance of moving to the philosophical and religious level of wisdom. They cannot be validated, of course, by the methodology of modern science based on its usual mechanistic assumptions and its very narrow definition of data. These ultimate norms are *self-realization* and *biocentric equality*.

I. SELF-REALIZATION

In keeping with the spiritual traditions of many of the world's religions, the deep ecology norm of self-realization goes beyond the modern Western *self* which is defined as an isolated ego striving primarily for hedonistic gratification or for a narrow sense of individual salvation in this life or the next. This socially programmed sense of the narrow self or social self dislocates us, and leaves us prey to whatever fad or fashion is prevalent in our society or social reference group. We are thus robbed of beginning the search for our unique spiritual/biological personhood. Spiritual growth, or unfolding, begins when we cease to understand or see ourselves as isolated and narrow competing egos and begin to identify with other humans from our family and friends to, eventually, our species. But the deep ecology sense of self requires a further maturity and growth, an identification which goes beyond humanity to include the nonhuman world. We must see beyond our narrow contemporary cultural assumptions and values, and the conventional wisdom of our time and place, and this is best achieved by the meditative deep questioning process. Only in this way can we hope to attain full mature personhood and uniqueness.

A nurturing nondominating society can help in the "real work" of becoming a whole person. The "real work" can be summarized symbolically as the realization of "self-in-Self" where "Self" stands for organic wholeness. This process of the full unfolding of the self can also be summarized by the phrase, "No one is saved until we are all saved," where the phrase "one" includes not only me, an individual human, but all humans, whales, grizzly bears, whole rain forest ecosystems, mountains and rivers, the tiniest microbes in the soil, and so on.

II. BIOCENTRIC EQUALITY

The intuition of biocentric equality is that all things in the biosphere have an equal right to live and blossom and to reach their own individual forms of unfolding and self-realization within the larger Self-realization. This basic intuition is that all organisms and entities in the ecosphere, as parts of the interrelated whole, are equal in intrinsic worth. Naess suggests that biocentric equality as an intuition is true in principle, although in the process of living, all species use each other as food, shelter, etc. Mutual predation is a biological fact of life, and many of the world's religions have struggled with the spiritual implications of this. Some animal liberationists who attempt to side-step this problem by advocating vegetarianism are forced to say that the entire plant kingdom including rain forests have no right to their own existence. This evasion flies in the face of the basic intuition of equality. Aldo Leopold expressed this intuition when he said humans are "plain citizens" of the biotic community, not lord and master over all other species.

Biocentric equality is intimately related to the all-inclusive Self-realization in the sense that if we harm the rest of Nature then we are harming ourselves. There are no boundaries and everything is interrelated. But insofar as we perceive things as individual organisms or entities, the insight draws us to respect all human and non-human individuals in their own right as parts of the whole without feeling the need to set up hierarchies of species with humans at the top.

The practical implications of this intuition or norm suggest that we should live with minimum rather than maximum impact on other species and on the Earth in general. Thus we see another aspect of our guiding principle: "simple in means, rich in ends." Further practical implications of these norms are discussed at length in chapters seven and eight.

A fuller discussion of the biocentric norm as it unfolds itself in practice begins with the realization that we, as individual humans, and as communities of humans, have vital needs which go beyond such basics as food, water, and shelter to include love, play, creative expression, intimate relationships with a particular landscape (or Nature taken in its entirety) as well as intimate relationships with other humans, and the vital need for spiritual growth, for becoming a mature human being.

Our vital material needs are probably more simple than many realize. In technocratic-industrial societies there is overwhelming propaganda and advertising which encourages false needs and destructive desires designed to foster increased production and consumption of goods. Most of this actually diverts us from facing reality in an objective way and from beginning the "real work" of spiritual growth and maturity.

Many people who do not see themselves as supporters of deep ecology nevertheless recognize an overriding vital human need for a healthy and high-quality natural environment for humans, if not for all life, with minimum intrusion of toxic waste, nuclear radiation from human enterprises, minimum acid rain and smog, and enough free flowing wilderness so humans can get in touch with their sources, the natural rhythms and the flow of time and place.

Drawing from the minority tradition and from the wisdom of many who have offered the insight of interconnectedness, we recognize that deep ecologists can offer suggestions for gaining maturity and encouraging the processes of harmony with Nature, but that there is no grand solution which is guaranteed to save us from ourselves.

The ultimate norms of deep ecology suggest a view of the nature of reality and our place as an individual (many in the one) in the larger scheme of things. They cannot be fully grasped intellectually but are ultimately experiential. . . .

. . . [The following figure] summarizes the contrast between the dominant worldview and deep ecology.

Dominant Worldview	Deep Ecology
Dominance over Nature	Harmony with Nature
Natural environment as resource for humans	All nature has intrinsic worth/biospecies equality
Material/economic growth for growing human population	Elegantly simple material needs (material goals serving the larger goal of self-realization)
Belief in ample resource reserves	Earth "supplies" limited
High technological progress and solutions	Appropriate technology; nondominating science
Consumerism	Doing with enough/recycling
National/centralized community	Minority tradition/bioregion

III. BASIC PRINCIPLES OF DEEP ECOLOGY

In April 1984, during the advent of spring and John Muir's birthday, George Sessions and Arne Naess summarized fifteen years of thinking on the principles of deep ecology while camping in Death Valley, California. In this great and special place, they articulated these principles in a literal, somewhat neutral way, hoping that they would be understood and accepted by persons coming from different philosophical and religious positions.

Readers are encouraged to elaborate their own versions of deep ecology, clarify key concepts and think through the consequences of acting from these principles.

Basic Principles

1. The well-being and flourishing of human and nonhuman life on Earth have value in themselves (synonyms: intrinsic value, inherent value). These values are independent of the usefulness of the nonhuman world for human purposes.

2. Richness and diversity of life forms contribute to the realization of these values and are also values in themselves.

3. Humans have no right to reduce this richness and diversity except to satisfy *vital* needs.

4. The flourishing of human life and cultures is compatible with a substantial decrease of the human population. The flourishing of nonhuman life requires such a decrease.

5. Present human interference with the nonhuman world is excessive, and the situation is rapidly worsening.

6. Policies must therefore be changed. These policies affect basic economic, technological, and ideological structures. The resulting state of affairs will be deeply different from the present.

7. The ideological change is mainly that of appreciating *life quality* (dwelling in situations of inherent value) rather than adhering to an increasingly higher standard of living. There will be a profound awareness of the difference between big and great.

8. Those who subscribe to the foregoing points have an obligation directly or indirectly to try to implement the necessary changes.

48

Species Extinction

Edward O. Wilson (1984)

The protection of endangered species is one of the focal points of the new environmentalism. It could be defended both in terms of human interest and on ethical, deep ecological grounds (see Selection 47). Of course, certain celebrated species—buffalo, passenger pigeons, whooping cranes—had long been of concern to conservationists. The new emphasis was not on individual species so much as on biological diversity in general and in a global context. Small and humble life forms, some of them even unknown to science, began to receive attention. The 1973 Endangered Species Act was unprecedented in the protection it afforded to any organism regardless of its usefulness to mankind. But in other parts of the earth, particularly the tropics, species extinction proceeded at an alarming rate. Edward O. Wilson, a Harvard expert on tropical insects, was among the most eloquent dramatizers of the assault civilization was making on the wild habitats necessary for biological diversity. A utilitarian argument is evident in his essay as well as an ethical one stemming from Aldo Leopold's concept of "biotic right" (Selection 27).

They are best seen not on foot or from outer space but through the window of an airplane: the newly cleared lands, the expanding web of roads and settlements, the inexplicable plumes of smoke, and the shrinking enclaves of natural habitat. In a glance we are reminded that the once mighty wilderness has shriveled into timber leases and threatened nature reserves. We measure it in hectares and count the species it contains, knowing that each day something vital is slipping another notch down the ratchet, a million year history is fading from sight. . . .

. . . Now we are near the end. The inner voice murmurs *you went*

Edward O. Wilson, "Million-Year Histories: Species Diversity as an Ethical Goal," *Wilderness*, **47** (Summer 1984), 12–15, 17. Reprinted by permission of the Wilderness Society.

too far and disturbed the world and gave away too much for your control of nature. Perhaps Hobbes' definition is correct and this will be the hell we earned for realizing truth too late.

But it is not too late: the actors have not yet left the stage of this particular tragedy. The course of the future can be changed with sufficient knowledge and a strong enough commitment shared by enough people. Like many scientists concerned with the problem, I have emphasized two aspects I consider vital to the development of a better conservation ethic: the appreciation of the vastness of the species diversity that is endangered by the loss of wilderness and the lesser natural reserves, and a fuller understanding of the dependence people feel on other forms of life. Let us begin with the first.

Think of scooping up a handful of soil and leaf litter and spreading it out on a white ground cloth, in the manner of the field biologist, for close examination. This unprepossessing lump contains more order and richness of structure, and particularity of history, than the entire surface of all the other planets combined. It is a miniature wilderness that can take almost forever to explore.

Tease apart the adhesive grains with the aid of forceps, and you will expose the tangled rootlets of a flowering plant, curling around the rotting veins of humus, and perhaps some larger object such as the boat-shaped husk of a seed. Almost certainly among them will be a scattering of creatures that measure the world in millimeters and treat this soil sample as traversable: ants, spiders, springtails, armored oribatid mites, enchytraeid worms, millipedes. With the aid of a dissecting microscope now proceed on down the size scale to the roundworms, a world of scavengers and fanged predators feeding on them. In the hand-held microcosm all of these creatures are still giants in a relative sense. The organisms of greatest diversity and numbers are invisible or nearly so. When the soil-and-litter clump is progressively magnified, first with a compound light microscope and then with scanning electron micrographs, specks of dead leaf expand into mountain ranges and canyons, and soil particles become heaps of boulders. A droplet of moisture trapped between root hairs grows into an underground lake, surrounded by a three-dimensional swamp of moistened humus. The niches are defined by both topography and nuances in chemistry, light, and temperature shifting across fractions of a millimeter. Organisms for which the soil sample is a complete world, now come into view. . . .

Still smaller than the parasitic fungi are the bacteria [and] . . . specialized predators that consume other bacteria. All around them live rich mixtures of rods, cocci, coryneforms, and slime azotobacteria. Together these microorganisms metabolize the entire spectrum of live and dead tissue. At the moment of discovery some are actively growing and fissioning, while others lie dormant in wait for the right combination of nutrient chemicals. Each species is kept at equilibrium by the harshness of the environment. Any one, if allowed to expand without restriction for a few weeks, would multiply exponentially, faster and faster, until it weighed more than the entire earth. . . .

In other words, biologists have begun a reconnaissance into a land of magical names. In exploring life they have commenced a pioneering adventure with no imaginable end. The abundance of organisms increases downward by level, like layers in a pyramid. The handful of soil and litter is home for hundreds of insects, nematode worms, and other larger creatures, about 1 million fungi, and 10 billion bacteria. Each of the species of these organisms has a distinct life cycle fitted to the portion of the microenvironment in which it thrives and reproduces. . . .

The amount of information in the sequence can be measured in bits in the following way. One bit is the information required to determine which of two equally likely alternatives is chosen, such as heads or tails in a coin toss. The English language averages two bits per letter. A single bacterium possesses about 10 million bits of genetic information, a fungus 1 billion, and an insect from 1 to 10 billion bits according to species. If the information in just one insect—say an ant or beetle—were to be translated into a code of English words and printed in letters of standard size, the string would stretch over 1,000 miles. The lump of earth contains information that would fill all fifteen editions of the Encyclopaedia Britannica.

I invite you now to try to visualize the loss in biological diversity due to the reduction of natural habitats. If so much complexity of information can be held in the cupped hands, think of how much more exists in an entire habitat. Consider the loss, mostly invisible to us today but destined to be painfully obvious to our descendants, that occurs when an entire wilderness area is degraded or destroyed.

It is an issue that turns otherwise cautious scientists into outspoken activists. On a worldwide basis, extinction is accelerating and could reach ruinous proportions during the next twenty years. Not just birds and mammals are vanishing but such smaller forms as mosses, insects, and minnows. A conservative estimate of the current extinction rate is 1,000 species a year, mostly because of the destruction of forests and other key habitats in the tropics. By the 1990s, the figure is expected to rise past 10,000 species a year (one species per hour). During the next thirty years, fully 1 million species could be erased. . . .

. . . In our own brief lifetime humanity will suffer an incomparable loss in aesthetic value, practical benefits from biological research, and worldwide biological stability. Deep mines of biological diversity will have been dug out and carelessly discarded in the course of environmental exploitation, without our even knowing fully what they contained.

These calculations lend great importance to the National Wilderness Preservation System in our own country and underscore the need to both enlarge and strengthen it. The 1964 Wilderness Act that created the program is sound in philosophy, but its implementation thus far falls grievously short of protecting the American heritage of living diversity. Of the 233 distinct ecosystems recognized by the Forest Service in the United States and Puerto Rico, only 81 are represented in the National Wilderness Preservation System. Another 102 ecosystems could be set aside within the domain of federally owned undeveloped lands.

In the end, the problem of wilderness preservation is a moral issue, for us and for our descendants. It is a curious fact that when very little is known about a subject, the important questions people raise are ethical. Then as knowledge grows, they become more concerned with information than with morality, in other words more narrowly intellectual. Finally, as understanding becomes sufficiently complete, the questions turn ethical again. Environmentalism is now passing from the first to the second phase, and there is reason to hope that it will proceed directly on to the third.

The future of the conservation movement depends on such an advance in moral reasoning. . . . The goal is to join emotion with the rational analysis of emotion in order to create a deeper and more enduring conservation ethic.

Aldo Leopold, the pioneer ecologist and author of *A Sand County Almanac,* defined an ethic as a set of rules invented to meet circumstances so new or intricate, or else encompassing responses so far in the future, that the average person cannot foresee the final outcome. What is good for you and me at this moment might easily sour within ten years, and what seems ideal for the next few decades could ruin future generations. That is why any ethic worthy of the name has to encompass the distant future. . . .

Why then should the human race protect biological diversity? Let me count the ways. The first is that we are part of life on earth, share its history, and hence should hesitate before degrading and destroying it. The acceptance of this principle does not diminish humanity but raises the status of nonhuman creatures. We should at least pause and give reason before treating them as disposable matter. Peter Singer, a philosopher and animal liberationist, has gone so far as to propose that the circle of altruism be expanded beyond the limits of our own species to animals with the capacity to feel and suffer, just as we have extended the label of brotherhood steadily until most people now feel comfortable with an all-inclusive phrase, the family of man. . . .

. . . Yet to force the argument entirely within the flat framework of kinship and legal rights is to trivialize the case favoring conservation, to justify one set of ethical beliefs (conservation, animal rights) on the basis of another (kinship, human rights). It is also very risky. Human beings, for all their professed righteousness and brotherhood, easily discriminate against strangers and are content to kill them during wars declared for relatively frivolous causes. How much easier it is to find an excuse to exterminate another species. A stiffer dose of biological realism appears to be in order. We need to apply the first law of human altruism, ably put by Garrett Hardin: never ask people to do anything they consider contrary to their own best interests. The only way to make a conservation ethic work is to ground it in ultimately selfish reasoning—but the premises must be of a new and more potent kind.

An essential component of this formula is the principle that people will conserve land and species fiercely if they foresee a material gain for themselves, their kin, and their tribe. By this economic measure alone the diversity of species is one of the earth's most important resources. It is also the least utilized. We have come to depend completely on less than 1 percent of living species for our existence, with the remainder waiting untested and fallow. In the course of history, according to estimates recently made by Norman Myers, people have utilized about 7,000 kinds of plants for food, with emphasis on wheat, rye, maize, and about a dozen other highly domesticated species. Yet at least 75,000 exist that are edible, and many of these have traits superior to those of the crop plants in use. The strongest of all arguments from surface ethics is a logical conclusion about this unrealized potential: the more the living world is explored and utilized, the greater will be the efficiency and reliability of the particular species chosen for economic use. . . .

Even with limited programs of research, biologists have compiled

an impressive list of such candidate organisms in the technical literature. The vast majority of wild plants and animals are not known well
enough (almost certainly many have not even been discovered) even
to guess at those with the greatest economic potential. Nor is it possible to imagine all the uses to which each species can be put. Consider
the case of the natural food sweeteners. Several species of plants have
been identified whose chemical products can replace conventional
sugar with negligible calories and no known side effects. The katemfe
. . . of the West African forests contains two proteins that are 1,600
times sweeter than sucrose and are now widely marketed in Great
Britain and Japan. . . .

Natural products have been called the sleeping giants of the phar-
maceutical industry. One in every ten plant species contains compounds with some anticancer activity. Among the leading successes
from the screening conducted thus far is the rosy periwinkle, a native
of the West Indies. It is the very paradigm of a previously minor
species, with pretty five-petaled blossoms but otherwise rather ordinary in appearance, a roadside casual, the kind of inconspicuous flowering plant that might otherwise have been unknowingly consigned to
extinction by the growth of sugarcane plantations and parking lots.
But it also happens to produce two alkaloids . . . that achieve 80 percent
remission from Hodgkins' disease, a cancer of the lymphatic system,
as well as 99 percent remission from acute lymphocytic leukemia.
Annual sales of the two drugs reached $100 million in 1980. . . .

Finally, beyond such practical concerns and far more difficult to
put into words, is what biological diversity means to the human spirit.
This is what can be called the deep ethic as opposed to the surface ethic
of conservation. It is ultimately more convincing and durable and takes
approximately the following form. We are human in good part because
of the particular way we affiliate with organisms. They are the matrix
in which the human mind originated and is permanently rooted, and
they offer the virtually endless challenge and freedom innately sought.
The scientist is perhaps for the moment more aware than most of the
opportunities for discovery and the unending sense of wonder that the
living world offers—bear in mind the 1,000 miles of mostly new information in each handful of soil. To the extent that each person can feel
as a naturalist, the old excitement of the untrammeled world will be
regained. I offer this then as a formula of reenchantment to reinforce
poetry and myth: mysterious and little known organisms still live
within reach of where you sit. Splendor awaits in minute proportions.

The counterargument to a conservation ethic of any kind is that people come first. After their problems have been solved we can enjoy the natural environment as a luxury. If that is indeed the answer, the wrong question was asked. The question of importance concerns purpose. Solving practical problems is the means, not the purpose. Let us assume that human genius has the power to thread the needles of technology and politics. Let us imagine that we can avert nuclear war, feed a stabilized population, and generate a permanent supply of energy—what then? The answer is the same all around the world: individuals will strive toward personal fulfillment and at least realize their potential. But what is fulfillment, and for what purpose did human potential evolve?

The truth is that we never conquered the world, we never understood it; we only thought we had taken control. We do not even know why we respond in a certain way to other organisms and need them in diverse ways so deeply. The prevailing myths concerning our predatory actions toward each other and the environment are obsolete, unreliable, and destructive. The more the mind is fathomed in its own right, as an organ of survival, the greater will be the reverence for life for purely rational reasons.

Science and natural philosophy have brought into clear relief the following paradox of human existence. The drive toward perpetual expansion—or if you prefer, personal freedom—is basic to the human spirit. But to sustain it we need the most delicate, knowing stewardship of the living world that can be devised. Expansion and stewardship may appear at first to be conflicting goals, but they are not. The depth of the conservation ethic will be measured by the extent to which each of the two approaches to nature is used to reshape and reinforce the other. The paradox can be resolved by changing its premises into forms more suited to ultimate survival, by which I mean protection of the human spirit.

49

Sustainability

Lester R. Brown and Sandra L. Postel (1987)

The Worldwatch Institute of Washington, D.C., is one of a handful of organizations carrying on the study of the global environmental change that William Vogt (Selection 26) noted as critically important forty years earlier. Here two Worldwatch officers point to problems that threaten one of the primary goals of the new environmentalism: the long-term sustainability of natural systems on which human life and all life depend. Characteristic of these problems is a global dimension and the fact that they cannot be easily addressed, or even understood, by individuals and their conservation groups. Protecting a national park, for example, is a feasible task; halting the depletion of ozone in the stratosphere boggles the average mind. One prerequisite for addressing the big-picture problems is the monitoring of environmental trends on a global level. The science and technology necessary for this task, such as remote sensing, are becoming key ingredients of global environmentalism.

Daily news events remind us that our relationship with the earth and its natural systems is changing, often in ways we do not understand.

In May 1985, a British research team reported findings of a sharp decline in the level of atmospheric ozone over Antarctica. This "hole" in the earth's protective shield of ozone sent waves of concern throughout the international scientific community. In late July 1986, scientists studying the effect of rising atmospheric levels of carbon dioxide and other "greenhouse gases" published evidence that the predicted global warming has begun. And recently, biologists at a forum on biodiversity warned of a forthcoming wave of mass extinction driven by human activities—one that would approach the magnitude of that which wiped out the dinosaurs and half of all other extant species some 65 million years ago.

These changes in atmospheric chemistry, global temperature, and the abundance of living species reflect the crossing of key thresholds in natural systems, crossings that may impair the earth's capacity to sustain an ever-growing human population. A frustrating paradox is emerging. Efforts to improve living standards are themselves beginning to threaten the health of the global economy. The very notion of progress begs for redefinition in light of the intolerable consequences unfolding as a result of its pursuit.

The breaching of many thresholds has occurred inadvertently from advances in technology and growth in human numbers. Corporations manufacturing the family of chemicals known as chlorofluorocarbons, for example, surely did not intend for these compounds to deplete the ozone layer. Their goal was to produce efficient refrigerants, a practical propellant for aerosol spray cans, and a chemical agent for making foam products. Nonetheless, the accumulation of chlorofluorocarbons in the atmosphere threatens to subject all forms of life to damaging doses of ultraviolet radiation, a threat that will take on new urgency if scientists determine that chlorofluorocarbons play a role in the periodic depletion of the ozone layer over Antarctica.

Other trends of the mid-1980s also call into question the viability of our path toward economic progress. World agriculture is producing surpluses, but for the wrong reasons. A portion of today's surplus is being produced only by diminishing the agricultural resource base—for example, by plowing highly erodible land and overdrafting underground water supplies.

Burgeoning populations in many urban areas are overtaxing local water sources, fuel supplies, and waste-disposal capacities, crossing natural thresholds and translating directly into economic costs. Resource demands in numerous cities already exceed the limits of local supplies, whether it be water in Tucson and Mexico City or firewood in Hyderabad. . . .

A sustainable society satisfies its needs without diminishing the prospects of the next generation. By many measures, contemporary society fails to meet this criterion. Questions of ecological sustainability are arising on every continent. The scale of human activities has begun to threaten the habitability of the earth itself. Nothing short of fundamental adjustments in population and energy policies will stave off the host of costly changes now unfolding, changes that could overwhelm our long-standing efforts to improve the human condition. . . .

Though impressive by historical standards, this growth was

dwarfed by what followed. Between 1950 and 1986, human numbers doubled to nearly 5 billion, expanding as much during these 36 years as during the preceding few million. Per capita income also roughly doubled, pushing the gross world product to over $13 trillion. Within a generation, the global output of goods and services quadrupled. A variety of technological advances aided this expansion, but none compares with the growth in fossil-fuel use. Between 1950 and 1986, world fossil-fuel consumption also increased fourfold, paralleling the growth in the global economy. . . .

While the global economy has expanded continuously, the natural systems that support it have not. . . . As currently pursued, economic activity could be approaching a level where further growth in the gross world product costs more than it is worth.

The negative side effects of this century's twentyfold expansion of economic activity are now becoming inescapable. Whether through spreading forest damage, a changing climate, or eroding soils, the pursuit of short-term economic growth at the environment's expense will exact a price. As the natural systems that underpin economies deteriorate, actions that make good sense environmentally will begin to converge with those that make good sense economically. But will that convergence occur before irreversible changes unfold? . . .

Sometimes a natural threshold can be defined fairly precisely, and the consequences of breaching that threshold can be known with a reasonable degree of certainty. If wood harvesting exceeds annual forest growth, for example, the volume of standing timber will diminish, and it will do so at a rate directly tied to how much the sustainable yield has been exceeded. Similarly, in a fishery, if the annual fish catch exceeds the rate of replacement, the stock of fish will gradually dwindle.

With many of the natural systems now at risk, however, thresholds are not well defined. Exactly how systems respond to threshold crossings is not well understood, so the consequences of crossing a threshold are largely incalculable. Moreover, threshold effects are now appearing in systems of continental and global scale. . . .

The world is now uncomfortably close to what may be the most economically costly threshold of all. For at least a century, the annual release of carbon into the atmosphere from human activities—mainly fossil-fuel combustion and deforestation—has exceeded the uptake of carbon by terrestrial vegetation and the oceans. As a result, carbon dioxide has been building up in the atmosphere. Analyses of air trapped in glaciers indicate that the atmospheric carbon dioxide level in 1860 was about 260 parts per million (ppm). Today, CO_2 measures 346 ppm, a 30% increase. Since just 1958, when scientists began routinely monitoring CO_2, the concentration has risen 9%.

Climate modelers warn that if the CO_2 concentration approaches double preindustrial levels, a dramatic change in climate will result. By pushing the release of CO_2 into the atmosphere above the rate at which it could be assimilated by natural systems, we have crossed one threshold. But we can still avoid crossing a second threshold: the level of atmospheric CO_2 that will cause an unprecedented and irreversible change in climate.

One of the most feared consequences of the projected global warming is the rise in sea level that will result from the melting of glaciers and polar ice caps. A 1°C increase in the temperature of the ocean would raise the sea level an estimated 60 centimeters, or roughly two feet. . . .

As the human population continues to expand, the ability of the earth's biological systems to support it adequately is diminishing.

An increasing share of the earth's net primary productivity—the total amount of solar energy fixed biologically through photosynthesis minus the amount of energy respired by plants—is being spent on meeting human demands. Stanford University biologist Peter M. Vitousek and his colleagues estimate that nearly 40% of the potential net primary productivity on land is now used directly or indirectly by human populations—mostly for food production but also for fiber, lumber, and fuel—or is lost as a result of human activities. The portion remaining to sustain all other species, and to maintain the integrity of natural systems, gets smaller and smaller as the size and demands of the human population mount. Deprived of needed energy, natural support systems could begin to deteriorate on a large scale. . . .

THREATS TO OUR CIVILIZATION

In the modern world, the aura of high technology, sophisticated industrial processes, and a century of unprecedented growth might easily lead us to think that we are immune from the kinds of stresses that could cause a civilization to collapse. Yet the citizens of flourishing societies from the past would probably never have believed that their cultures could deteriorate so rapidly. . . .

As we near the end of the twentieth century, we are entering uncharted territory. Localized changes in natural systems are now being overlaid with continental and global ones, some of which may be irreversible. Everyday human activities, such as driving automobiles, generating electricity, and producing food, may collectively cause changes of geological proportions within a matter of decades.

A human population of 5 billion, expanding at 83 million per year, has combined with the power of industrial technologies to create unprecedented momentum toward human-induced environmental change. We have inadvertently set in motion grand ecological experiments involving the entire earth without yet having the means to systematically monitor the results.

Pollution-induced forest damage and the potential depletion of the earth's ozone layer are relatively recent discoveries. Yet the activities believed to have brought about these threats—fossil-fuel pollutants and the release of chlorofluorocarbons—have been under way for decades. Taken further by surprise, industrial societies may trap themselves into costly and dubious tasks of planetary maintenance—perhaps seeding clouds in attempts to trigger rainfall where it has diminished with climatic change, or seeking means of protection from increased exposure to ultraviolet radiation, or liming vast areas of land sterilized by acidification.

The existence of thresholds beyond which change occurs rapidly and unpredictably creates an urgent need for early warning systems and mechanisms for averting disastrous effects. Despite impressive progress, the scientific groundwork has yet to be laid for monitoring the pulse of the earth's life-support systems. Meanwhile, the pace of change quickens.

We have crossed many natural thresholds in a short period of time. No one knows how the affected natural systems will respond, much less how changes in natural systems will in turn affect economic and political systems. We can be reasonably certain that deforestation will disrupt hydrologic cycles and that ozone depletion will induce more skin cancer. But beyond these first-order effects, scientists can provide little detail.

Any system pushed out of equilibrium behaves in unpredictable ways. Small external pressures may be sufficient to cause dramatic changes. Stresses may become self-reinforcing, rapidly increasing the system's instability. . . .

Never have so many systems vital to the earth's habitability been out of equilibrium simultaneously. New environmental problems also span time periods and geographic areas that stretch beyond the authority of existing political and social institutions. No single nation can stabilize the earth's climate, protect the ozone layer, or preserve the planet's mantle of forests and soils. Only a sustained, international commitment will suffice.

Matters of the global environment now warrant the kind of high-level attention and concern that the global economy receives. World leaders historically have cooperated to preserve economic stability, even to the point of completely overhauling the international monetary system at the 1944 conference in Bretton Woods. Summit meetings are held periodically to attempt to iron out international economic problems. Policy makers carefully track economic indicators to determine when adjustments—national or international—are required. Similar efforts are needed to delineate the bounds of environmental stability, along with mechanisms for making prompt adjustments when these bounds draw near.

50

A Troubled Future

Gerald O. Barney (1980)

The debate over planetary carrying capacity launched after World War II by William Vogt (Selection 26) and in the 1960s by Paul Ehrlich (Selection 32) continued in 1972 with the Club of Rome's The Limits to Growth *(see Selection 37). In 1980 a team appointed three years earlier by President Jimmy Carter released* The Global 2000 Report. *Using computer modeling techniques to make projections of future population levels and demands for resources, the report predicted severe environmental deterioration and stress on civilization. However,* Global 2000 *remained guardedly optimistic provided policies could be changed in an atmosphere of international cooperation. The United States, it concluded, should be prepared to take a leadership role in this process, but the lack of enthusiasm for* Global 2000 *by the Reagan administration was not encouraging.*

If present trends continue, the world in 2000 will be more crowded, more polluted, less stable ecologically, and more vulnerable to disruption than the world we live in now. Serious stresses involving population, resources, and environment are clearly visible ahead. Despite greater material output, the world's people will be poorer in many ways than they are today.

For hundreds of millions of the desperately poor, the outlook for food and other necessities of life will be no better. For many it will be worse. Barring revolutionary advances in technology, life for most people on earth will be more precarious in 2000 than it is now—unless the nations of the world act decisively to alter current trends.

This, in essence, is the picture emerging from the U.S. Government's projections of probable changes in world population, resources, and environment by the end of the century, as presented in the Global

Gerald O. Barney, ed., *The Global 2000 Report to the President* (New York: Penguin Books, 1982), 1–5, 41–42. Footnotes in the original have been omitted.

2000 Study. They do not predict what will occur. Rather, they depict conditions that are likely to develop if there are no changes in public policies, institutions, or rates of technological advance, and if there are no wars or other major disruptions. A keener awareness of the nature of the current trends, however, may induce changes that will alter these trends and the projected outcome.

PRINCIPAL FINDINGS

Rapid growth in world population will hardly have altered by 2000. The world's population will grow from 4 billion in 1975 to 6.35 billion in 2000, an increase of more than 50 percent. The rate of growth will slow only marginally, from 1.8 percent a year to 1.7 percent. In terms of sheer numbers, population will be growing faster in 2000 than it is today, with 100 million people added each year compared with 75 million in 1975. Ninety percent of this growth will occur in the poorest countries.

While the economies of the less developed countries (LDCs) are expected to grow at faster rates than those of the industrialized nations, the gross national product per capita in most LDCs remains low. The average gross national product per capita is projected to rise substantially in some LDCs (especially in Latin America), but in the great populous nations of South Asia it remains below $200 a year (in 1975 dollars). The large existing gap between the rich and poor nations widens.

World food production is projected to increase 90 percent over the 30 years from 1970 to 2000. This translates into a global per capita increase of less than 15 percent over the same period. The bulk of that increase goes to countries that already have relatively high per capita food consumption. Meanwhile per capita consumption in South Asia, the Middle East, and the LDCs of Africa will scarcely improve or will actually decline below present inadequate levels. At the same time, real prices for food are expected to double.

Arable land will increase only 4 percent by 2000, so that most of the increased output of food will have to come from higher yields. Most of the elements that now contribute to higher yields—fertilizer, pesticides, power for irrigation, and fuel for machinery—depend heavily on oil and gas.

During the 1990s world oil production will approach geological estimates of maximum production capacity, even with rapidly increasing petroleum prices. The Study projects that the richer industrialized nations will be able to command enough oil and other commercial energy supplies to meet rising demands through 1990. With the expected price increases, many less developed countries will have increasing difficulties meeting energy needs. For the one-quarter of humankind that depends primarily on wood for fuel, the outlook is bleak. Needs for fuelwood will exceed available supplies by about 25 percent before the turn of the century.

While the world's finite fuel resources—coal, oil, gas, oil shale, tar sands, and uranium—are theoretically sufficient for centuries, they are not evenly distributed; they pose difficult economic and environmental problems; and they vary greatly in their amenability to exploitation and use.

Nonfuel mineral resources generally appear sufficient to meet projected demands through 2000, but further discoveries and investments will be needed to maintain reserves. In addition, production costs will increase with energy prices and may make some nonfuel mineral resources uneconomic. The quarter of the world's population that inhabits industrial countries will continue to absorb three-fourths of the world's mineral production.

Regional water shortages will become more severe. In the 1970–2000 period population growth alone will cause requirements for water to double in nearly half the world. Still greater increases would be needed to improve standards of living. In many LDCs, water supplies will become increasingly erratic by 2000 as a result of extensive deforestation. Development of new water supplies will become more costly virtually everywhere.

Significant losses of world forests will continue over the next 20 years as demand for forest products and fuelwood increases. Growing stocks of commercial-size timber are projected to decline 50 percent per capita. The world's forests are now disappearing at the rate of 18–20 million hectares a year (an area half the size of California), with most of the loss occurring in the humid tropical forests of Africa, Asia, and South America. The projections indicate that by 2000 some 40 percent of the remaining forest cover in LDCs will be gone.

Serious deterioration of agricultural soils will occur worldwide, due to erosion, loss of organic matter, desertification, salinization, alkalinization, and waterlogging. Already, an area of cropland and grassland approximately the size of Maine is becoming barren wasteland each year, and the spread of desert-like conditions is likely to accelerate.

Atmospheric concentrations of carbon dioxide and ozone-depleting chemicals are expected to increase at rates that could alter the world's climate and upper atmosphere significantly by 2050. Acid rain from increased combustion of fossil fuels (especially coal) threatens damage to lakes, soils, and crops. Radioactive and other hazardous materials present health and safety problems in increasing numbers of countries.

Extinctions of plant and animal species will increase dramatically. Hundreds of thousands of species—perhaps as many as 20 percent of all species on earth—will be irretrievably lost as their habitats vanish, especially in tropical forests.

The future depicted by the U.S. Government projections, briefly outlined above, may actually understate the impending problems. . . . More consistent, better-integrated projections would produce a still more emphatic picture of intensifying stresses, as the world enters the twenty-first century.

CONCLUSIONS

At present and projected growth rates, the world's population would reach 10 billion by 2030 and would approach 30 billion by the end of the twenty-first century. . . . Already the populations in sub-Saharan Africa and in the Himalayan hills of Asia have exceeded the carrying capacity of the immediate area, triggering an erosion of the land's capacity to support life. The resulting poverty and ill health have further complicated efforts to reduce fertility. Unless this circle of interlinked problems is broken soon, population growth in such areas will unfortunately be slowed for reasons other than declining birth rates. Hunger and disease will claim more babies and young children, and more of those surviving will be mentally and physically handicapped by childhood malnutrition.

Indeed, the problems of preserving the carrying capacity of the earth and sustaining the possibility of a decent life for the human beings that inhabit it are enormous and close upon us. Yet there is reason for hope. It must be emphasized that the Global 2000 Study's projections are based on the assumption that national policies regarding population stabilization, resource conservation, and environmental protection will remain essentially unchanged through the end of the century. But in fact, policies are beginning to change. In some areas, forests are being replanted after cutting. Some nations are taking steps to reduce soil losses and desertification. Interest in energy conservation is growing, and large sums are being invested in exploring alternatives to petroleum dependence. The need for family planning is slowly becoming better understood. Water supplies are being improved and waste treatment systems built. High-yield seeds are widely available and seed banks are being expanded. Some wildlands with their genetic resources are being protected. Natural predators and selective pesticides are being substituted for persistent and destructive pesticides.

Encouraging as these developments are, they are far from adequate to meet the global challenges projected in this Study. Vigorous, determined new initiatives are needed if worsening poverty and human suffering, environmental degradation, and international tension and conflicts are to be prevented. There are no quick fixes. The only solutions to the problems of population, resources, and environment are complex and long-term. These problems are inextricably linked to some of the most perplexing and persistent problems in the world—poverty, injustice, and social conflict. New and imaginative ideas—and a willingness to act on them—are essential.

The needed changes go far beyond the capability and responsibility of this or any other single nation. An era of unprecedented cooperation and commitment is essential. Yet there are opportunities—and a strong rationale—for the United States to provide leadership among nations. A high priority for this Nation must be a thorough assessment of its foreign and domestic policies relating to population, resources, and environment. The United States, possessing the world's largest economy, can expect its policies to have a significant influence on global trends. An equally important priority for the United States is to cooperate generously and justly with other nations—particularly in the areas of trade, investment, and assistance—in seeking solutions to the many problems that extend beyond our national boundaries. There are many unfulfilled opportunities to cooperate with other nations in efforts to relieve poverty and hunger, stabilize population, and enhance economic and environmental productivity. Further cooperation among nations is also needed to strengthen international mechanisms for protecting and utilizing the "global commons"—the oceans and atmosphere. . . .

With its limitations and rough approximations, the Global 2000 Study may be seen as no more than a reconnaissance of the future; nonetheless its conclusions are reinforced by similar findings of other recent global studies that were examined in the course of the Global 2000 Study. . . . All these studies are in general agreement on the nature of the problems and on the threats they pose to the future welfare of humankind. The available evidence leaves no doubt that the world—including this Nation—faces enormous, urgent, and complex problems in the decades immediately ahead. Prompt and vigorous changes in public policy around the world are needed to avoid or minimize these problems before they become unmanageable. Long lead times are required for effective action. If decisions are delayed until the problems become worse, options for effective action will be severely reduced. . . .

There are no quick or easy solutions, particularly in those regions where population pressure is already leading to a reduction of the carrying capacity of the land. In such regions a complex of social and economic factors (including very low incomes, inequitable land tenure, limited or no educational opportunities, a lack of nonagricultural jobs, and economic pressures toward higher fertility) underlines the decline in the land's carrying capacity. Furthermore, it is generally believed that social and economic conditions must improve before fertility levels will decline to replacement levels. Thus a vicious circle of causality may be at work. Environmental deterioration caused by large populations creates living conditions that make reductions in fertility difficult to achieve; all the while, continuing population growth increases further the pressures on the environment and land.

The declines in carrying capacity already being observed in scattered areas around the world point to a phenomenon that could easily be much more widespread by 2000. In fact, the best evidence now available—even allowing for the many beneficial effects of technological developments and adoptions—suggests that by 2000 the world's human population may be within only a few generations of reaching the entire planet's carrying capacity.

The Global 2000 Study does not estimate the earth's carrying capacity, but it does provide a basis for evaluating an earlier estimate published in the U.S. National Academy of Sciences' report, *Resources and Man*. In this 1969 report, the Academy concluded that a world population of 10 billion "is close to (if not above) the maximum that an *intensively managed* world might hope to support with some degree of comfort and individual choice." The Academy also concluded that even with the sacrifice of individual freedom and choice, and even with chronic near starvation for the great majority, the human population of the world is unlikely to ever exceed 30 billion.

Nothing in the Global 2000 Study counters the Academy's conclusions. If anything, data gathered over the past decade suggest the

Academy may have underestimated the extent of some problems, especially deforestation and the loss and deterioration of soils.

At present and projected growth rates, the world's population would rapidly approach the Academy's figures. If the fertility and mortality rates projected for 2000 were to continue unchanged into the twenty-first century, the world's population would reach 10 billion by 2030. Thus anyone with a present life expectancy of an additional 50 years could expect to see the world population reach 10 billion. This same rate of growth would produce a population of nearly 30 billion before the end of the twenty-first century.

Here it must be emphasized that, unlike most of the Global 2000 Study projections, the population projections assume extensive policy changes and developments to reduce fertility rates. Without the assumed policy changes, the projected rate of population growth would be still more rapid.

Unfortunately population growth may be slowed for reasons other than declining birth rates. As the world's populations exceed and reduce the land's carrying capacity in widening areas, the trends of the last century or two toward improved health and longer life may come to a halt. Hunger and disease may claim more lives—especially lives of babies and young children. More of those surviving infancy may be mentally and physically handicapped by childhood malnutrition.

The time for action to prevent this outcome is running out. Unless nations collectively and individually take bold and imaginative steps toward improved social and economic conditions, reduced fertility, better management of resources, and protection of the environment, the world must expect a troubled entry into the twenty-first century.

51

Future Environmental Challenges

John H. Adams, Robert Cahn, et al. (1985)

In the mid-1980s the leaders of the ten most important conservation organizations in the private sector in the United States collaborated on an analysis of the most severe environmental problems facing the nation. This document reviews environmental history; then it presents eleven issues. Few could disagree that these will be the focal points of future environmental concern.

For more than a century Americans, as individuals and as part of what has grown into a nationwide conservation movement, have been a motivating force behind the formulation and implementation of public conservation policies. In the early days it was a small group of wilderness-loving citizens who decided that the Yellowstone area should be preserved for posterity, and succeeded in having Congress establish it as the world's first national park in 1872 "for the benefit and enjoyment of the people." To achieve their objectives, hunters, fishermen, and outdoorsmen, forest conservators, bird protectors, and wilderness advocates formed organizations, each with a particular motivation for saving the nation's natural resources and scenic beauty. Thus were the roots of the conservation movement formed in the 19th and early 20th centuries.

By the 1950s the challenges had changed and multiplied. The pressures of a burgeoning population led to a passion for acquisition and development of land and resources that overtook the nation. Decades of overuse and inappropriate use had contaminated lakes, rivers, and streams; city air was heavy with pollution; sewage and solid waste were fouling population centers; and many of the nation's last remaining wilderness areas were threatened by exploitation. DDT,

John H. Adams, Robert Cahn, et al., *An Environmental Agenda for the Future* (Washington, DC: Island Press, 1985), 2–23.

originally hailed as a great benefactor, was discovered to have dangerous side effects as it worked its way through the food chain, weakening and killing wildlife, and posing serious threats to human health.
Within a few years hundreds of other substances were found to be
detrimental to human health.

In the face of these and other threats, the conservation movement
had to redefine its purposes. The old concept of conservation as the
"wise use" of natural resources—rivers to be dammed for irrigation
and hydropower or forests used primarily as sources of timber—were
not sufficient for the needs of the times. The old priorities had to be
reconsidered in line with other factors such as the intrinsic value of the
rivers, oceans, and forests, the land and the atmosphere, habitat for the
wildlife, sustainable ecological systems, and places for harmonious
living, recreation, and aesthetic opportunity.

In the 1960s and 1970s, these new concerns coalesced into an
environmental revolution. By Earth Day 1970, the stalwarts of the
conservation community were joined by millions of people acutely
aware of the state of their environment and its potential effects on the
health and well-being of their families and neighbors. They were
women and men, young and old, poor and wealthy—homemakers,
students, people from the professions, business, and labor, all reacting
to what they saw happening to the air, the water, and the land. Political leaders who had not shown much concern for environmental affairs
suddenly responded to the will of the people. At the start of the '70s,
a President sent to Congress three consecutive annual environmental
messages outlining the legislation being demanded by the American
public. Congress enacted laws for stricter regulations on air and water
pollution, to reduce solid waste, prevent ocean dumping, restrict
harmful pesticides, require reclamation of lands stripmined for coal,
and control toxic wastes, to add wilderness, wildlife refuges, and national parks, protect wetlands, coastal areas, and endangered species,
and to assist in providing more urban and state parks and outdoor
recreation. And at the end of the decade, Congress acted to protect for
the entire nation and future generations most of the still pristine
Alaska federal lands.

The agenda of the '70s was reactive to a newly perceived crisis.
The laws and regulations met with resistance, however, and compliance had to be won through citizen vigilance and court actions. The
National Environmental Policy Act of 1969 (NEPA) set forth a continuing policy for the federal government, as a trustee of the environment for succeeding generations, to "attain the widest range

of beneficial uses of the environment without degradation, risk to health or safety, or other undesirable and unintended consequences" and to "achieve a balance between population and resource use which will permit high standards of living and a wide sharing of life's amenities." To implement this policy, the law required all agencies of the federal government to prepare environmental impact statements before making any proposal for legislation and other major federal action that could significantly affect the quality of the human environment. . . .

Marked progress has been made in the 16 years since passage of NEPA, but many of the problems it was meant to solve still remain. Congress has passed a multitude of laws, and the courts have in many instances upheld the lawsuits brought by citizens to force compliance by some recalcitrant elements in industry and government agencies. But compliance and enforcement are still spotty and not adequately achieving the purposes of the laws. And because the laws and regulations often have not dealt with root causes, they have been inadequate to cope with added problems that have arisen, partly from new technologies.

Many of today's problems are global in scope and make local, regional, or even national solutions difficult. These problems include human population growth that is exceeding the capacity of some countries to feed and sustain their burgeoning numbers; toxic chemicals, developed with the intent of benefiting humankind, that turn out to be serious threats to health with side effects that kill and maim; the greatly increased burning of fossil fuels, producing atmospheric effects that could melt icecaps and flood coastal cities. Looming over all is the specter of nuclear war with its massive immediate death and destruction, which could be followed by the cold and dark of nuclear winter spreading climatic change throughout the world, destroying the life support systems, eliminating many species of plants and animals, and even threatening the survival of the human species.

These and other global problems call for pragmatic approaches and an agenda that can help the nation look toward ways of meeting the environmental challenges of the next 15 years and on into the new century. Building upon the strategies that have brought results in the past two decades, citizens, working with government, must continue to find new ways to achieve solutions. . . .

The increased visibility of citizen and governmental efforts to meet environmental challenges in the past two decades has stimulated debate about how concern for the environment affects other important national objectives, particularly economic ones. When there is conflict over objectives, various interests predictably bring different perspectives to the role environmental concerns have in shaping other important national goals. Some public officials and business executives have suggested that environmental regulations are strangling business and industry and have sought to weaken or abolish the environmental protection laws enacted in the 1960s and 1970s.

The public and many economists, however, do not give credence to that argument. When a recent Gallup poll asked citizens what they would do if they had to choose between economic growth or environmental protection, the citizens, two-to-one, favored protecting the environment. Numerous economic analyses have shown that such a choice does not need to be made because no inevitable significant conflict exists between economic strength and environmental protection.

Concern for the environment at a deeply personal level has joined with concern for economic well-being and the two have become integrated into a quality-of-life goal shared by Americans from all regions and in all economic groups. This strong public support is founded on the rejection of policies that would require fundamental tradeoffs of environmental quality for economic opportunity, because the majority of citizens and economists perceive that such tradeoffs are not necessary and are not likely to happen on any scale that would negatively impact on the economy. Whenever a region, an industry, or an enterprise is required to pay the cost of preventing or repairing environmental damage, or to forgo the profit of developing a resource, some kinds of economic activity may become less rewarding. At the same time, new or modified enterprises may become more profitable. Americans as a people have prospered from economic change, are proud of turning challenges into rewarding opportunities, and believe that American ingenuity can solve most difficult problems. Their willingness to pay for protecting the environment is based on the assumption that the price is worth paying and will be balanced by gains in environmental quality.

More and more businesses have come to accept the fact that concern for the environment should be integrated into the planning of every resource-using enterprise. There will continue to be debate about how best to manage the nation's resources and protect the environment, but many leaders of U.S. business, industry, and labor are working creatively toward environmentally sound practices. Further, American industry has demonstrated that technological or process changes designed to protect resources can also represent sound business opportunities. For some electric utilities, investments in energy conservation and diverse, small-scale energy technologies have become attractive alternatives to traditional central-station power generation. Redesign of industrial processes and products to save energy has also saved money for producers and consumers. Integrated pest management and better irrigation technologies are saving money for many farmers. Increasingly, environmentally sound practices are being seen as good for business.

As more is learned about what must be done to protect public health and the environment, as various non-environmental factors make some industries vulnerable to added costs, and as economic and social changes make some former practices in the use of resources unacceptable, a few communities suffer economic disruption. Companies that were only marginally profitable for reasons other than pollution may be forced to close because they cannot afford to comply with pollution control laws. But poisoning the air and water, ruining land, damaging the health and safety of workers and nearby communities, or destroying wildlife and natural areas would make *sustainable* development impossible. The public's faith in society's ability to reconcile environmental and economic goals requires those working for sound resource management to be sensitive to the local or temporary negative economic implications that can result from some environmental policy choices. In those instances when the national interest requires environmental protection measures that do result in some degree of local or regional economic dislocation, industry and government working together should provide help for affected communities and families.

There is ample evidence that sound resource management and careful protection of the environment are necessary to American society and of value to the economy. From the human tragedy of the 1930s dustbowl, when the rural U.S. heartland paid for years of abusive soil management, to more recent examples of fisheries closed in Virginia's James River because of Kepone, or communities abandoned in Love Canal, New York, and Times Beach, Missouri because of irresponsible hazardous waste management, failure to protect the environment has disrupted lives and cost billions of dollars. . . .

Economists and most business executives recognize that prevention is cheaper in the long run than the costs of cleaning up pollution. The economic benefits accruing from laws or regulations established to prevent or avoid environmental harm are sometimes difficult to quantify. These benefits include fewer medical bills, less time off work due to illness, reduced property damage, and increased crop yields. Also the necessity of preventing pollution or cleaning it up has led to development of new industrial processes and served to increase economic efficiency.

Continued economic growth is essential. Past environmental gains will be maintained and new ones made more easily in a healthy economy than in a stagnant one with continued high unemployment. Subsidies that stimulate harm to the environment should be removed and the government should charge realistic prices for publicly owned natural resources. Laws and regulations adopted to protect the environment should be formulated, whenever possible, so as to give manufacturers a continuing incentive to protect the environment as part of making a profit. Competitive pressures will, however, lead businesses to develop more efficient and less costly processes that prevent environmental harm.

One of the problems in relating economic health and environmental health is that the nation has not developed a quality of life index that measures both. Environmental health factors such as morbidity and mortality, crop and forest damage, soil erosion, air and water pollution, and aesthetic degradation are given little attention compared to such economic health factors as Gross National Product (GNP) and unemployment. Much work needs to be done to develop and use more comprehensive measurements of quality of life.

The relationship between economic prosperity and environmental health extends far beyond U.S. borders. In a global economy, the United States has a direct economic interest in the environmental quality and resource management practices of the rest of the world, and vice versa. Apart from all countries' obvious common concern about the oceans and the atmosphere and the imperative need to prevent the ultimate human and environmental tragedy of nuclear war, it is becoming ever more apparent that the United States will not prosper if global biological systems become more abused. The economic consequences of desertification in Mexico or Africa are felt in the United States. Manufacture of American goods overseas in areas requiring minimal pollution control or safety measures costs Americans jobs. And when this practice leads to the perception of American responsibility for lost lives, damaged health, or degraded communities, the direct and indirect costs can be severe. American economic relations with other nations should include encouragement of sound resource management and environmental protection, with emphasis on restoration of fisheries, soils, and forests. . . .

THE ISSUES IN BRIEF

Nuclear Issues

Mankind has the power to destroy all life on earth. That power may be released at any time, for it is harnessed only by fallible humans, and, increasingly, by fallible machines. As knowledge and anxiety about nuclear risks increase, however, the situation becomes impossible to ignore and difficult to tolerate. Recent scientific study has revealed that our planet is even more fragile and our "security" systems much more deadly than previously thought. Scientific findings indicate that the detonation of even a small fraction of the weapons in the world's nuclear arsenals could send enough dust and soot into the atmosphere to trigger major climatic disruptions and create a deadly, global "nuclear winter." The consequent disruptions of ecosystems could cause the extinction of many forms of life, and, some scientists believe, the extinction of the human species.

The nuclear winter studies have underscored the catastrophic consequences of nuclear war to all forms of life on earth, and have confirmed in a compelling and unavoidable way that nuclear war is the ultimate environmental threat. . . .

Human Population Growth

The 4.8 billion humans who now people the earth are overtaxing the capacities of some of the world's biological systems to support them, and are in fact reducing the earth's productive resource base at the very time when still more resources will be required to take care of the growing population. At the present rate of growth, more than six billion people will be living on earth by the year 2000. . . .

U.S. population growth results in pressures on water supplies, more air and water pollution, and destruction of wetlands and farmlands for development, and leads to overintensive farming with its resultant soil erosion. . . .

The United States and other affluent countries, which use a disproportionate share of the world's raw materials, must learn to use natural resources far more efficiently, and the United States must move rapidly to stabilize its own population as an essential step in bringing the world's people and resources into equilibrium. . . .

Energy Strategies

The best solution to U.S. and world energy problems relies predominantly on a variety of energy efficiency improvements in all sectors of the world economy. This strategy, sometimes called the soft energy path, affords significant economic, social, health, and environmental advantages over any other approach. . . .

As supplies of non-renewable resources dwindle in the future, competitive costs of providing them will increase and environmental damage from the development of new sources will grow. The development of renewable energy sources, including all forms of solar energy such as direct solar, biomass, and wind, can break the cycle of an increasingly limited fuel supply and its accompanying increase in costs.

Water Resources

Just as the best energy strategy for the nation is the pursuit of efficiency improvements in all sectors, so the best water resources strategy is to improve management of existing water projects and increase the efficiency of water use in the residential, agricultural, and industrial segments of the country. . . .

. . . In contrast, the typical water development scenario of dams and channels favored by many politicians and well-entrenched water-use lobbies is a high cost path with many serious environmental and social impacts. The major challenge of the next 15 years will be to redirect institutions and redesign procedures to bring about the necessary shift to the efficiency path as smoothly and swiftly as possible.

Requiring users of water projects to pay the full costs of construction, operation, and maintenance . . . will encourage a shift toward efficient use of water. . . .

Toxics and Pollution Control

Despite much progress over the past two decades, when landmark pollution control legislation was enacted, most forms of pollution are not yet under control and many new problems exist. More than half of the U.S. population lives in areas where air pollutants still exceed health standards some of the time. The nation annually produces more than one ton per person of hazardous wastes. Eight years after Congress passed legislation to control the treatment, storage and disposal of hazardous waste, less than ten percent of the facilities currently handling wastes have been licensed. Five years after passage of the 1980 Superfund legislation to clean up dangerous, abandoned waste dumps, less than one percent of the known dumps have been cleaned up. Groundwater has been contaminated in areas throughout the nation, and tens of thousands of wells have been closed. The Environmental Protection Agency (EPA) has not adequately regulated pesticides.

More than 65,000 commercial chemicals identified by the National Academy of Sciences are currently being marketed, yet little or no data has been compiled on the potential many of them have to cause cancer, birth defects, or chronic diseases. Pesticides and toxic substances banned for use in the United States are allowed to be exported overseas or produced by U.S. companies in developing nations without full examination of the danger of accident or understanding of potential impacts on residents near manufacturing sites. Half of the water pollution that affects lakes and streams comes from non-point sources, particularly unregulated storm water runoff from city streets and runoff from agricultural lands. The amount of carbon dioxide and methane released into the atmosphere continues to increase rapidly, creating a threat of profound climate change in the future. . . .

Wild Living Resources

The planet today faces the immediate threat of a staggering loss of wild species, unequalled in history. The conservation of biological diversity—the immense variety and abundance of plant and animal life—and the maintenance or restoration of areas of natural habitat upon which species survival depends are of vital importance. This diversity of wild species forms the base from which future human needs may be met, ranging from genetic strains for improving agricultural products to new medicines.

Conserving biological diversity and maintaining or restoring natural plant and animal habitats are goals shared by people throughout the world. Since wild living organisms do not recognize national boundaries and since the areas of highest biological diversity, such as tropical forests which are critical to all of humanity, lie outside U.S. jurisdiction, extinction prevention and habitat protection must be addressed in international as well as domestic arenas. . . .

Private Lands and Agriculture

Difficult environmental and resource problems surround privately held farmlands, range, forests, wetlands, and valuable natural areas in the United States. A variety of corrective measures are urgently needed for stemming the conversion of fragile lands to crop production, preventing the soil erosion and off-farm site damage that result from poor land management practices; protecting private forest land to enhance its watershed capabilities and maintain its ability to supply forage and provide fish and wildlife habitat; protecting private lands from degradation and pollution from mining; and protecting from development private lands that have natural and cultural values. . . .

Significant amounts of agricultural land are lost to development and urbanization each year despite fluctuating but generally increasing demand for export of U.S. farm products. Eroded soil laden with chemical nutrients and pesticides costs the nation hundreds of millions of dollars a year as it fills up reservoirs, adds to flood damage, clogs navigation facilities and canals, affects drinking water supplies, destroys aquatic wildlife, and diminishes recreational potential. . . .

Private national, state, and local land-saving conservation organizations, as well as government agencies, will need to continue and increase their activities that have resulted in acquisition of millions of acres of natural lands. It will also be necessary to multiply efforts to educate all citizens regarding the ethical use of land—acceptance of individual responsibility for the health of the land and a full understanding of how people are linked to and depend upon the land. . . .

Protected Land Systems

The national park, wildlife refuge, wilderness preservation, wild and scenic river, marine sanctuary systems, and wildlands on the national forests protect some of the country's most important and outstanding natural resources and provide varied habitats necessary to support a rich and diverse wildlife heritage. At the same time they afford important outdoor recreational opportunities for the public and constitute a national heritage of scenic and cultural treasures. The existing federal sanctuaries, which have been established over the last century for the benefit of future generations, should be safeguarded from the increasing internal and external threats to their preservation. The most urgent need today is to add critical natural areas to existing systems before their unique values are lost to development or other factors, thus ensuring that suitable portions of all basic types of ecosystems receive appropriate protection. . . .

Public Lands

In dealing with the nation's public lands, which comprise one-third of the land in the United States, more legal checks and balances are needed to prevent overexploitation of forest, range, and mineral resources. Planning is needed to ensure truly balanced multiple use of the lands so that timber production, mining, oil, and coal exploitation and grazing do not overshadow conservation values. Modern techniques of analysis should be applied to the management of public lands, and fees and sale prices of land should reflect fair market value, and should cover administrative costs. Timber from national forests should not be sold at a loss. Methods should be developed to protect areas of special natural value such as sensitive seabed and coastal zones, areas of critical environmental concern, and areas with old-growth timber. Between 15 and 25 percent of the remaining old-growth timber on each national forest should remain uncut to assure necessary biological diversity. . . .

Urban Environment

America's cities, home to more than 70 million people and centers of employment, shopping, and culture for millions who live in suburban areas, are facing difficult environmental and health problems into the next century.

Air quality is worse in urban areas than elsewhere, due to many factors such as concentration of emissions from motor vehicles and industry. Conversion by trucks and buses to diesel engines, with their dangerous particulate emissions, poses a growing health hazard that will require stricter standards and better inspection programs. Indoor air pollutants such as toxic chemicals used in cleaning agents and pesticides, gas from unvented indoor combustion, or substances such as asbestos and formaldehyde cause serious problems.

The growing risks of contamination of urban water supplies and the uncertainty surrounding the ability of many cities to satisfy future water demands require cooperative action from federal, state, and local regulatory agencies. . . .

Garbage and other solid waste disposal problems will confront nearly every urban area over the next two decades. . . .

... Congress should eliminate tax breaks, investments, grants, and loans for programs that encourage development of urban sprawl.

Urban sprawl also heightens the need for adequate public transportation. With greatly increased automobile and truck traffic predicted for urban areas over the next 15 years, the failure to resolve the public transit crisis in most cities is a major social and environmental problem. Public transit systems are inadequate, older ones are starved for funds, and newer systems remain incomplete. To help alleviate the crisis, Congress should increase the motor vehicle gasoline tax five cents a gallon. This could generate $5 billion a year for the federal transit fund earmarked to finance capital projects.

The few recreational facilities available to city dwellers are inadequate and many are deteriorating. Congress should allocate to the states higher levels of funding from the Land and Water Conservation Fund, to be used for urban open space and recreation. . . .

International Responsibilities

The health and availability of natural resources and the quality of the environment can no longer be treated as only of national concern. The destruction of the natural environment resulting from population expansion, industrial demands, unplanned and unchecked urbanization, and inappropriate development have effects that reach beyond the individual nations. Their impacts are felt in neighboring nations and across oceans and hemispheres. Polluted air or acid rain spreads far beyond national boundaries and water pollution affects shared river basins and oceans. Destruction of tropical forests, desertification of vast areas, and the potential exploitation of the Antarctic are now of universal concern. The economic distress, degradation of environmental quality, and displacement of peoples in many countries throughout the world and the ultimate disaster of nuclear war and an accompanying nuclear winter confront the world with a precarious future. . . .

Conclusion

The key to the solution of most of the problems raised in this agenda for the future is public awareness of the issues and a recognition of the interconnections among population growth, natural resource availability, development, and environmental impacts. The general public and decision-makers need to understand the true costs of their own actions and those of government and the private sector and how to weigh the long-term, far-reaching benefits against the immediate, localized costs or risks. . . .

Carrying out the agenda will require the cooperation of individuals from all walks of life. The involvement and assistance of industry, labor, educators, scientists, lawyers, students, government workers, homemakers, and other elements of the society will be needed.

═ SELECTED BIBLIOGRAPHY

•

The literature noted here is the essential starting point for further investigation of the relationship of the American people with the environment and, in particular, the development of the conservation movement.

HISTORIOGRAPHY AND METHODOLOGY

BAILES, KENDALL. "Critical Issues in Environmental History," in Kendall Bailes, ed., *Environmental History: Critical Issues in Comparative Perspective* (Lanham, MD: University Press, 1985).

CROOK, LEONARD. "American Environmental History," *Environmental Education Report*, **2** (1974), 3–5, 13.

DAVIS, RICHARD C., ed. *Encyclopedia of American Forest and Conservation History*, 2 vols. (New York: Macmillan, 1983).

DODDS, GORDON B. "The Historiography of American Conservation: Past and Prospects," *Pacific Northwest Quarterly*, **56** (1965), 75–81.

FAHL, RONALD J. *North American Forest and Conservation History: A Bibliography* (Santa Barbara, CA: Clio, 1976).

LE DUC, THOMAS. "Historiography of Conservation," *Forest History*, **9** (1965), 23–28.

MELOSI, MARTIN V. "Urban Pollution: Historical Perspective Needed," *Environmental Review*, **3** (1979), 37–45.

NASH, RODERICK. "The State of Environmental History," in Herbert Bass, ed., *The State of American History* (Chicago: Quadrangle, 1970), 249–260.

———. "American Environmental History: A New Teaching Frontier," *Pacific Historical Review*, **41** (1972), 362–372.

OPIE, JOHN. "Environmental History: Pitfalls and Opportunities," *Environmental Review*, **7** (1983), 8–16.

PETULLA, JOSEPH M. "Environmental Values: The Problem of Method in Environmental History," in Kendall Bailes, ed., *Environmental History: Critical Issues in Comparative Perspective* (Lanham, MD: University Press, 1985).

RAKESTRAW, LAWRENCE. "Conservation Historiography: An Assessment," *Pacific Historical Review*, **41** (1972), 271–288.

STRONG, DOUGLAS. "Teaching American Environmental History," *The Social Studies*, **65** (1974), 196–200.

TUAN, YI-FU. *Space and Place: The Perspective of Experience* (Minneapolis: University of Minnesota Press, 1977).

WHITE, RICHARD. "Historiographical Essay—American Environmental History: The Development of a New Historical Field," *Pacific Historical Review,* **54** (1985), 297–335.

WORSTER, DONALD. "History as Natural History: An Essay on Theory and Method," *Pacific Historical Review,* **53** (1984) 1–19.

———. "World Without Borders: The Internationalizing of Environmental History," in Kendall Bailes, ed., *Environmental History: Critical Issues in Comparative Perspective* (Lanham, MD: University Press, 1985).

AMERICANS AND NATURE

BROOKS, PAUL. *Speaking for Nature: How Literary Naturalists from Henry Thoreau to Rachel Carson Have Shaped America* (Boston: Houghton Mifflin, 1980).

CARROLL, PETER N. *Puritanism and the Wilderness: The Intellectual Significance of the New England Frontier, 1629–1700* (New York: Columbia University Press, 1969).

CLOUGH, WILSON O. *The Necessary Earth: Nature and Solitude in American Literature* (Austin: University of Texas Press, 1964).

CRONON, WILLIAM. *Changes in the Land: Indians, Colonists and the Ecology of New England* (New York: Hill and Wang, 1983).

CROSBY, ALFRED W. *The Columbian Exchange: Biological and Cultural Consequences of 1492* (Westport, CT: Greenwood, 1972).

———. *Ecological Imperialism: The Biological Expansion of Europe, 900–1900* (Cambridge: Cambridge University Press, 1986).

CULMSEE, CARLTON. *Malign Nature and the Frontier* (Logan: Utah State University Press, 1959).

DETWEILER, ROBERT, JON N. SUTHERLAND, and MICHAEL S. WERTHMANX, eds. *Environmental Decay in its Historical Context* (Glenview, IL: Scott Foresman, 1973).

DUKE, FREDERICK, WILLIAM L. HOWENSTINE, and JUNE SOCHEN, eds. *Destroy to Create: Interaction with the Natural Environment in the Building of America* (Hinsdale, IL: Dryden, 1972).

EKIRCH, ARTHUR, JR. *Man and Nature in America* (New York: Columbia University Press, 1963).

FLEXNER, JAMES THOMAS. *That Wilder Image: The Painting of America's Native School from Thomas Cole to Winslow Homer* (Boston: Little Brown, 1962).

FOERSTER, NORMAN. *Nature in American Literature* (New York: Macmillan, 1927).

FUSSELL, EDWIN. *Frontier: American Literature and the American West* (Princeton, NJ: Princeton University Press, 1965).

GLACKEN, CLARENCE. *Traces on the Rhodian Shore: Nature and Culture in Western Thought from Ancient Times to the End of the Eighteenth Century* (Berkeley: University of California Press, 1967).

GRABER, LINDA H. *Wilderness as Sacred Space* (Association of American Geographers, Washington, DC, 1976).

HUGHES, J. DONALD. *American Indian Ecology* (El Paso: Texas Western University Press, 1983).

HUTH, HANS. *Nature and the American: Three Centuries of Changing Attitudes* (Berkeley: University of California Press, 1957).

JONES, HOWARD MUMFORD. *Strange New World* (New York: Viking, 1964).

KOLODNY, ANNETTE. *The Land Before Her: Fantasy and Experience of the American Frontiers, 1630–1860* (Chapel Hill: North Carolina University Press, 1984).

LEISS, WILLIAM. *The Domination of Nature* (New York: Braziller, 1972).

LOWENTHAL, DAVID and MARTYN J. BOWDEN, eds. *Geographies of the Mind: Essays in Historical Geography in Honor of John Kirtland Wright* (New York: Oxford University Press, 1976).

MARTIN, CALVIN. *Keepers of the Game: Indian Animal Relationships in the Fur Trade* (Berkeley: University of California Press, 1978).

MARX, LEO. *The Machine in the Garden: Technology and the Pastoral Ideal in America* (New York: Oxford University Press, 1964).

MERCHANT, CAROLYN. *The Death of Nature: Women, Ecology and the Scientific Revolution* (San Francisco: Harper & Row, 1980).

MILLER, CHARLES A. *Jefferson and Nature: An Interpretation* (Baltimore, MD: Johns Hopkins University Press, 1988).

MILLER, PERRY. *Errand into the Wilderness* (Cambridge, MA: Harvard University Press, 1956).

———. *Nature's Nation* (Cambridge, MA: Harvard University Press, 1967).

MITCHELL, LEE CLARK. *Witness to a Vanishing America: The Nineteenth-Century Response* (Princeton, NJ: Princeton University Press, 1981).

MOORE, ARTHUR K. *The Frontier Mind: A Cultural Analysis of the Kentucky Frontiersman* (Lexington: University of Kentucky Press, 1957).

NAEF, WESTON J. *Era of Exploration: The Rise of Landscape Photography in the American West, 1860–1885* (Boston: New York Graphic Society, 1975).

NASH, RODERICK, ed. *Environment and Americans: The Problem of Priorities* (New York: Holt Dryden, 1972).

———. *Wilderness and the American Mind,* third, revised edition (New Haven, CT: Yale University Press, 1982).

NOVAK, BARBARA. *Nature and Culture: American Landscape and Painting, 1825–1875* (New York: Oxford University Press, 1980).

O'BRIEN, RAYMOND J. *American Sublime: Landscape and Scenery of the Lower Hudson Valley* (New York: Columbia University Press, 1981).

PEARCE, ROY HARVEY. *The Savages of America: A Study of the Indian and the Idea of Civilization,* revised edition (Baltimore, MD: Johns Hopkins University Press, 1965).

PYNE, STEPHEN J. *Fire in America: A Cultural History of Wildland and Rural Fire* (Princeton, NJ: Princeton University Press, 1982).

RENO, PHILIP. *Mother Earth, Father Sky, and Economic Development: Navahoe Resources and Their Use* (Albuquerque: University of New Mexico Press, 1981).

ROSENKRANTZ, BARBARA GUTMANN and WILLIAM A. KOELSCH, eds. *American Habitat: A Historical Perspective* (New York: Free Press, 1973).

SANFORD, CHARLES L. *The Quest for Paradise* (Urbana: University of Illinois Press, 1961).

SCHMITT, PETER J. *Back to Nature: The Arcadian Myth in Urban America* (New York: Oxford University Press, 1969).

SHEPARD, PAUL. *Man in the Landscape: A Historic View of the Esthetics of Nature* (New York: Knopf, 1967).

SLOTKIN, RICHARD. *Regeneration through Violence: The Mythology of the American Frontier, 1600–1860* (Middletown, CT: Wesleyan University Press, 1973).

———. *The Fatal Environment: The Myth of the Frontier in the Age of Industrialization* (New York: Atheneum, 1985).

SMALLWOOD, WILLIAM MARTIN. *Natural History and the American Mind* (New York: Columbia University Press, 1941).

SMITH, HENRY NASH. *Virgin Land: The American West as Symbol and Myth* (Cambridge: Harvard University Press, 1950).

STILGOE, JOHN. *Common Landscape of America, 1580 to 1845* (New Haven, CT: Yale University Press, 1982).

TUAN, YI-FU. *Topophilia: A Study of Environmental Perceptions, Attitudes and Values* (Englewood Cliffs, NJ: Prentice-Hall, 1974).

TURNER, FREDERICK. *Beyond Geography: The Western Spirit Against the Wilderness* (New York: Viking, 1980).

TURNER, FREDERICK JACKSON. *The Frontier in American History* (New York: Holt, Rinehart and Winston, 1962, originally 1920).

VECSEY, CHRISTOPHER and ROBERT W. VENABLES, eds. *American Indian Environments: Ecological Issues in Native American History* (Syracuse, NY: Syracuse University Press, 1980).

WHITE, EDWARD. *The Eastern Establishment and the Western Experience: The West of Frederick Remington, Theodore Roosevelt and Owen Wister* (New Haven, CT: Yale University Press, 1968).

WILLIAMS, GEORGE H. *Wilderness and Paradise in Christian Thought* (New York: Harper, 1962).

WORSTER, DONALD. *Nature's Economy: The Roots of Ecology* (San Francisco: Sierra Club, 1977).

THE CONSERVATION/ENVIRONMENT MOVEMENT

BATES, J. LEONARD. *The Origins of Teapot Dome: Progressives, Parties and Petroleum, 1909–1921* (Urbana: University of Illinois Press, 1963).

CLEPPER, HENRY, ed. *Origins of American Conservation* (New York: Ronald, 1966).

COHEN, MICHAEL P. *History of the Sierra Club, 1892–1970* (San Francisco: Sierra Club, 1988).

COOLEY, RICHARD A. and GEOFFREY WANDESFORDE-SMITH, eds. *Congress and the Environment* (Seattle: University of Washington Press, 1970).

COYLE, DAVID CUSHMAN. *Conservation: An American Story of Conflict and Accomplishment* (New Brunswick, NJ: Rutgers University Press, 1957).

DUNLAP, THOMAS R. *DDT: Scientists, Citizens and Public Policy* (Princeton, NJ: Princeton University Press, 1981).

DUPREE, A. HUNTER. *Science in the Federal Government: A History of Policies and Activities to 1940* (Cambridge, MA: Harvard University Press, 1957).

FLEMING, DONALD. "Roots of the New Conservation Movement," *Perspectives in American History*, **6** (1972), 7–91.

FOX, STEPHEN. *John Muir and His Legacy: The American Conservation Movement* (Boston: Little Brown, 1981).

FRIENDS OF THE EARTH et al. *Ronald Reagan and the American Environment: An Indictment* (Andover, MA: Brick House, 1982).

GRAHAM, FRANK, JR. *Since Silent Spring* (Boston: Houghton Mifflin, 1970).

———. *Man's Dominion: The Story of Conservation in America* (New York: Lippincott, 1971).

HAYS, SAMUEL P. *Conservation and the Gospel of Efficiency: The Progressive Conservation Movement, 1890–1920* (Cambridge, MA: Harvard University Press, 1959).

———. *Beauty, Health and Permanence: Environmental Politics in the United States, 1955–1985* (Cambridge: Cambridge University Press, 1987).

JARRETT, HENRY, ed. *Perspectives on Conservation: Essays on America's Natural Resources* (Baltimore, MD: Johns Hopkins University Press, 1958).

KING, JUDSON. *The Conservation Fight: From Theodore Roosevelt to the Tennessee Valley Authority* (Washington, DC: Public Affairs, 1959).

LASH, JONATHAN. *A Season of Spoils: The Story of the Reagan Administration's Attack on the Environment* (New York: Pantheon, 1984).

MARTIN, DANIEL. *Three Mile Island: Prologue or Epilogue?* (Cambridge, MA: Ballinger, 1980).

MCCARTHY, MICHAEL. *Hour of Trial: The Conservation Conflict in Colorado and the West, 1891–1907* (Norman: University of Oklahoma Press, 1977).

MCCONNELL, GRANT. "The Conservation Movement: Past and Present," *Western Political Quarterly*, **7** (1954), 463–478.

MCHENRY, ROBERT, ed. *A Documentary History of Conservation in America* (Praeger, New York, 1972).

MELOSI, MARTIN. *Pollution and Reform in American Cities, 1870–1930* (Austin: University of Texas Press, 1980).

————. *Garbage in the Cities: Refuse, Reform and the Environment, 1880–1980* (College Station: Texas A&M University Press, 1981).

MILBRATH, LESTER. *Environmentalists: Vanguard of a New Society* (Albany: State University of New York Press, 1984).

NASH, RODERICK. *The American Conservation Movement* (St. Charles, MO: Forum, 1974).

NICHOLSON, E. M. *The Environmental Revolution: A Guide for the New Masters of the World* (New York: McGraw-Hill, 1970).

NOGGLE, BURL. *Teapot Dome: Oil and Politics in the 1920s* (Baton Rouge: Louisiana State University Press, 1962).

ODELL, RICE. *Environmental Awakening: The New Revolution to Protect the Earth* (Cambridge, MA: Ballinger, 1980).

OPIE, JOHN, ed. *Americans and Environment: The Controversy over Ecology* (Lexington, KY: Heath, 1971).

PENICK, JAMES. *Progressive Politics and Conservation: The Ballinger-Pinchot Affair* (Chicago: Loyola University Press, 1968).

PEPPER, D. M. *The Roots of Modern Environmentalism* (Dover, NH: Croom Helm, 1984).

PETULLA, JOSEPH M. *American Environmental History: The Exploitation and Conservation of Natural Resources* (San Francisco: Boyd and Fraser, 1977).

————. *American Environmentalism: Values, Tactics, Priorities* (College Station: Texas A&M University Press, 1980).

————. *Environmental Protection in the United States* (San Francisco: San Francisco Study Center, 1987).

PURSELL, CARROLL, ed. *From Conservation to Ecology* (New York: Cromwell, 1979).

REIGER, JOHN F. *American Sportsmen and the Origins of Conservation* (Norman: University of Oklahoma Press, 1986).

RICHARDSON, ELMO R. *The Politics of Conservation: Crusades and Controversies, 1897–1913* (Berkeley: University of California Press, 1962).

————. *Dams, Parks and Politics: Resource Development and Preservation in the Truman-Eisenhower Era* (Lexington: University of Kentucky Press, 1973).

RIESCH-OWEN, A. L. *Conservation Under FDR* (New York: Praeger, 1983).

ROSENBAUM, WALTER A. *The Politics of Environmental Concern* (New York: Praeger, 1977).

RUDD, ROBERT L. *Pesticides and the Living Landscape* (Madison: University of Wisconsin Press, 1964).

SALMOND, JOHN A. *The Civilian Conservation Corps, 1933–1942: A New Deal Case Study* (Durham, NC: Duke University Press, 1967).

SAX, JOSEPH. *Defending the Environment* (New York: Knopf, 1971).

SIRY, JOSEPH V. *Marshes of the Ocean Shore: Development of an Ecological Ethic* (College Station: Texas A&M University Press, 1984).

SMITH, FRANK, ed. *Conservation in the United States: A Documentary History,* 5 vols. (New York: Chelsea, 1971).

STRONG, DOUGLAS H. *The Conservationists* (Menlo Park, CA: Addison Wesley, 1971).

STROUD, RICHARD, ed. *National Leaders of American Conservation* (Washington, DC: Smithsonian Institution, 1985).

SWAIN, DONALD C. *Federal Conservation Policy, 1921–1933* (Berkeley: University of California Press, 1963).

TALBOT, ALAN R. *Power Along the Hudson: The Storm King Case and the Birth of Environmentalism* (New York: Dutton, 1972).

TUCKER, WILLIAM. *Progress and Privilege* (New York: Anchor/Doubleday, 1982).

UDALL, STEWART. *The Quiet Crisis* (New York: Holt, Rinehart and Winston, 1963).

———. *The Quiet Crisis and the Next Ge..eration* (Salt Lake City, UT: Peregrine Smith, 1988).

WENGERT, NORMAN. *Natural Resources and the Political Struggle* (Garden City, NY: Doubleday, 1955).

WHISENHUNT, DONALD W. *The Environment and the American Experience: A Historian Looks at the Ecological Crisis* (Port Washington, NY: Kennikat, 1974).

WHITAKER, JOHN. *Striking a Balance: Environment and Natural Resource Policy in the Nixon-Ford Years* (Washington, DC: American Enterprise Institute for Public Policy Research, 1976).

WHORTON, JAMES. *Before Silent Spring: Pesticides and Public Health in Pre-DDT America* (Princeton, NJ: Princeton University Press, 1974).

WILD, PETER. *Pioneer Conservationists of Western America* (Missoula, MT: Mountain, 1979).

WORSTER, DONALD, ed. *American Environmentalism: The Formative Period, 1860–1915* (New York: Wiley, 1973).

REGIONAL STUDIES

ATKINSON, BROOKS J. and W. KENT OLSON. *New England's White Mountains: At Home in the Wild* (San Francisco: Sierra Club, 1978).

BLAKE, NELSON M. *Land Into Water—Water Into Land: A History of Water Management in Florida* (Tallahassee: University Presses of Florida, 1980).

BLOUET, BRIAN W. and FREDERICK C. LUEBKE, eds. *The Great Plains: Environment and Culture* (Lincoln: University of Nebraska Press, 1979).

CLARK, THOMAS D. *The Greening of the South: The Recovery of Land and Forest* (Lexington: University of Kentucky Press, 1984).

COOLEY, RICHARD. *Alaska: A Challenge in Conservation* (Madison: University of Wisconsin Press, 1966).

COWDREY, ALBERT E. *This Land, This South: An Environmental History* (Lexington: University of Kentucky Press, 1983).

DASMANN, RAYMOND. *The Destruction of California* (New York: Macmillan, 1965).

————. *California's Changing Environment* (San Francisco: Boyd and Fraser, 1981).

ENGLE, J. RONALD. *Sacred Sands: The Struggle for Community in the Indiana Dunes* (Middletown, CT: Wesleyan, 1983).

EVERS, ALF. *The Catskills: From Wilderness to Woodstock* (Garden City, NY: Doubleday, 1972).

FARQUHAR, FRANCIS P. *History of the Sierra Nevada* (Berkeley: University of California Press, 1965).

FLADER, SUSAN, ed. *The Great Lakes Forest: An Environmental and Social History* (Minneapolis: University of Minnesota Press, 1982).

FRANKLIN, KAY and NORMAN SCHAEFFER. *Duel for the Dunes: Land Use Conflict on the Shores of Lake Michigan* (Urbana: University of Illinois Press, 1983).

FROME, MICHAEL. *Strangers in High Places: The Story of the Great Smokey Mountains* (Garden City, NY: Doubleday, 1966).

JAKLE, JOHN A. *Images of the Ohio River Valley; A Historical Geography of Travel, 1740–1860* (New York: Oxford University Press, 1977).

MALIN, JAMES C. *The Grassland of North America: Prolegomena to its History* (Lawrence: University of Kansas Press, 1947).

———— In Robert P. Swierenga, ed. *History and Ecology: Studies of the Grassland* (Lincoln: University of Nebraska Press, 1984).

MCKINLEY, CHARLES. *Uncle Sam in the Pacific Northwest: Federal Management of Natural Resources in the Columbia River Valley* (Berkeley: University of California Press, 1952).

PRESTON, WILLIAM L. *Vanishing Landscapes: Land and Life in the Tulare Lake Basin* (Berkeley: University of California Press, 1981).

SCARPINO, PHILLIP V. *Great River: An Environmental History of the Upper Mississippi, 1890–1950* (Columbia: University of Missouri Press, 1985).

SEARLE, R. NEWTON. *Saving Quetico-Superior: A Land Set Apart* (St. Paul: Minnesota Historical Society, 1977).

STRONG, DOUGLAS H. *Tahoe, An Environmental History* (Lincoln: University of Nebraska Press, 1984).

TRENTON, PATRICIA and PETER H. HASSRICK. *The Rocky Mountains: A Vision for Artists in the Nineteenth Century* (Norman: University of Oklahoma Press, 1983).

WEBB, WALTER PRESCOTT. *The Great Plains* (Boston: Ginn, 1931).

WEIGOLD, MARILYN E. *The American Mediterranean: An Environmental, Economic and Social History of Long Island Sound* (Lincoln: University of Nebraska Press, 1979).

WHITE, RICHARD. *Land Use, Environment and Social Changes: The Shaping of Island County, Washington* (Seattle: University of Washington Press, 1980).

WHITE, WILLIAM C. *Adirondack Country* (New York: Duell, Sloan and Pearce, 1954).

WORSTER, DONALD. *Dust Bowl: The Southern Plains in the 1930s* (New York: Oxford University Press, 1979).

WILDLIFE

BEAN, MICHAEL. *The Evolution of National Wildlife Law,* revised edition (New York: Praeger, 1983).

BERLANGER, DIAN OLSON. *Managing American Wildlife: A History of the International Association of Fish and Wildlife Agencies* (Amherst: University of Massachusetts Press, 1988).

DOUGHTY, ROBIN W. *Wildlife and Man in Texas: Environmental Change and Conservation* (Texas A&M University Press, College Station, 1983).

DUNLAP, THOMAS P. *Saving America's Wildlife* (Princeton, NJ: Princeton University Press, 1988).

GRAHAM, EDWARD H. *The Land and Wildlife* (New York: Oxford University Press, 1947).

KELLERT, STEPHEN R. *Public Attitudes Toward Critical Wildlife and Natural Habitat Issues* (Washington, DC: U.S. Government Printing Office, 1980).

LUND, THOMAS A. *American Wildlife Law* (Berkeley: University of California Press, 1980).

REED, NATHANIEL P. and DENNIS DRABELLE. *The United States Fish and Wildlife Service* (Boulder, CO: Westview, 1984).

REIGER, JOHN F. *American Sportsmen and the Origins of Conservation* (Norman: University of Oklahoma Press, 1986).

SHERWOOD, MORGAN. *Big Game in Alaska: A History of Wildlife and People* (New Haven CT: Yale University Press, 1981).

SHOEMAKER, CARL D. *The Stories Behind the Organization of the National Wildlife Federation* (Washington, DC: National Wildlife Federation, 1960).

TOBER, JAMES A. *Who Owns the Wildlife?: The Political Economy of Conservation in Nineteenth-Century America* (Westport, CT: Greenwood, 1981).

TREFETHEN, JAMES B. *Crusade for Wildlife* (New York: Winchester, 1975).

WELKER, HENRY. *Birds and Men: American Birds in Science, Art, Literature and Conservation* (Cambridge, MA: Harvard University Press, 1955).

YAFFEE, STEVEN L. *Prohibitive Policy: Implementing the Federal Endangered Species Act* (Cambridge, MA: MIT Press, 1982).

FORESTS

CARHART, ARTHUR H. *The National Forest* (New York: Knopf, 1959).

CLARY, DAVID A. *Timber and the Forest Service* (Lawrence: University of Kansas Press, 1986).

CLEPPER, HENRY E. *Crusade for Conservation: The Centennial History of the American Forestry Association* (Washington, DC: American Forestry Association, 1975).

CLEPPER, HENRY and ARTHUR B. MEYER, eds. *American Forestry: Six Decades of Growth* (Washington, DC: Society of American Forestry, 1960).

COX, THOMAS R., ROBERT S. MAXWELL, PHILLIP DRENNON THOMAS, and JOSEPH J. MALONE.

This Well-Wooded Land: Americans and Their Forests From Colonial Times to the Present (Lincoln: University of Nebraska Press, 1985).

DANA, SAMUEL T. *Forest and Range Policy: Its Development in the United States* (New York: McGraw-Hill, 1956).

FROME, MICHAEL. *Whose Woods These Are: The Story of the National Forests* (Garden City, NY: Doubleday, 1962).

———. *The Forest Service* (New York: Praeger, 1971).

———. *The Forest Service,* second, revised edition (Boulder, CO: Westview, 1984).

GREELEY, WILLIAM B. *Forests and Men* (Garden City, NY: Doubleday, 1951).

LILLARD, RICHARD G. *The Great Forest* (New York: Knopf, 1947).

LOCKMANN, RONALD F. *Guarding the Forests of Southern California: Evolving Attitudes Toward Conservation of Watershed, Woodlands and Wilderness* (Glendale, CA: Clark, 1981).

PLATT, RUTHERFORD. *The Great American Forest* (Englewood Cliffs, NJ: Prentice-Hall, 1965).

RAKESTRAW, LAWRENCE W. *A History of the United States Forest Service in Alaska* (Anchorage: Alaska Historical Commission, 1981).

ROBINSON, GLEN O. *The Forest Service: A Study in Public Land Management* (Baltimore, MD: Johns Hopkins University Press, 1975).

SCHREPFER, SUSAN R. *The Fight to Save the Redwoods: A History of Environmental Reform, 1917–1978* (Madison: University of Wisconsin Press, 1983).

STEEN, HOWARD K. *The U.S. Forest Service: A History* (Seattle: University of Washington Press, 1976).

SOIL, MINERALS, AND THE PUBLIC DOMAIN

BUCKLEY, STUART E., ed. *Petroleum Conservation* (New York: American Institute of Mining and Metallurgical Engineers, 1951).

CARSTENSEN, VERNON, ed. *The Public Lands: Studies in the History of the Public Domain* (Madison: University of Wisconsin Press, 1963).

CLARK, J. STANLEY. *The Oil Century: From Drake Well to the Conservation Era* (Norman: University of Oklahoma Press, 1958).

CLAWSON, MARION. *Man and Land in the United States* (Lincoln: University of Nebraska Press, 1964).

———. *The Bureau of Land Management* (New York: Praeger, 1971).

——— and BERNELL HELD. *The Federal Lands: Their Use and Management* (Baltimore, MD: Johns Hopkins University Press, 1957).

CULHANE, PAUL J. *Public Lands Politics: Interest Group Influence on the Forest Service and the Bureau of Land Management* (Baltimore, MD: Johns Hopkins University Press, 1981).

EASTON, ROBERT. *Black Tide* (New York: Delacorte, 1972) (a history of the Santa Barbara oil spill in 1969).

FRANCIS, JOHN G. and RICHARD GANZELL, eds. *Western Public Lands: The Management of Natural Resources in a Time of Declining Federalism* (Totowa, NJ: Rowman and Allanheld, 1984).

FOSS, PHILLIP O. *Politics and Grass: The Administration of Grazing on the Public Domain* (Seattle: University of Washington Press, 1960).

HELD, R. BURNELL and MARION CLAWSON. *Soil Conservation in Perspective* (Baltimore, MD: Johns Hopkins University Press, 1965).

HIBBARD, BENJAMIN H. *A History of Public Land Policies* (New York: Macmillan, 1924).

HURT, DOUGLAS. *The Dust Bowl: An Agricultural and Social History* (Chicago: Nelson-Hall, 1981).

ISE, JOHN. *The United States Oil Policy* (New Haven, CT: Yale University Press, 1926).

JACKS, GRAHAM V. and ROBERT O. WHYTE. *Vanishing Lands: A World Survey of Soil Erosion* (Doran, NY: Doubleday, 1939).

KELLEY, ROBERT L. *Gold vs. Grain: The Hydraulic Mining Controversy in California's Sacramento Valley* (Glendale, CA: Clark, 1959).

KINNEY, JAY P. *Indian Forest and Range: A History of the Administration and Conservation of the Redman's Heritage* (Washington, DC: Forestry Enterprises, 1951).

MCDONALD, ANGUS. *Early American Soil Conservationists* (Washington, DC: U.S. Government Printing Office, 1941).

MORGAN, ROBERT J. *Governing Soil Conservation: Thirty Years of the New Decentralization* (Baltimore, MD: Johns Hopkins University Press, 1966).

PARSONS, A. B., ed. *Seventy-Five Years Progress in the Mineral Industry, 1871–1946* (New York: American Institute of Mining and Metallurgical Engineers, 1947).

PEFFER, E. LOUISE. *The Closing of the Public Domain: Disposal and Reservation Policies, 1900–1950* (Stanford, CA: Stanford University Press, 1951).

RICKARD, THOMAS A. *History of American Mining* (New York: McGraw-Hill, 1932).

ROBBINS, ROY M. *Our Landed Heritage: The Public Domain, 1776–1936* (Princeton, NJ: Princeton University Press, 1942).

SMITH, DUANE A. *Mining America: The Industry and the Environment* (Lawrence: University of Kansas Press, 1987).

VIETOR, RICHARD H. K. *Environmental Politics and the Coal Coalition* (College Station: Texas A&M University Press, 1980).

VOIGHT, WILLIAM, JR. *Public Grazing Lands: Use and Misuse by Industry and the Government* (New Brunswick, NJ: Rutgers University Press, 1976).

WORSTER, DONALD. *Dust Bowl: the Southern Plains in the 1930s* (New York: Oxford University Press, 1979).

WYANT, WILLIAM K. *Westward in Eden: The Public Lands and the Conservation Movement* (Berkeley: University of California Press, 1982).

ZIMMERMANN, ERICH W. *Conservation in the Production of Petroleum: A Study in Industrial Control* (New Haven, CT: Yale University Press, 1957).

PARKS AND WILDERNESS

ALBRIGHT, HORACE and ROBERT CAHN. *The Birth of the National Park Service: The Founding Years* (Salt Lake City, UT: Howe, 1985).

ALLIN, CRAIG W. *The Politics of Wilderness Preservation* (Westport, CT: Greenwood, 1982).

BALDWIN, DONALD NICHOLAS. *The Quiet Revolution: The Grass Roots of Today's Wilderness Preservation Movement* (Boulder, CO: Pruett, 1972).

BARTLETT, RICHARD. *Nature's Yellowstone* (Albuquerque: University of New Mexico Press, 1974).

――――. *Yellowstone: A Wilderness Besieged* (Tucson: University of Arizona Press, 1985).

BUCHHOLTZ, C. W. *Rocky Mountain National Park: A History* (Boulder: Colorado Associated University Press, 1983).

CHASE, ALSTON. *Playing God in Yellowstone: The Destruction of America's First National Park* (Boston: Atlantic Monthly, 1986).

EVERHART, WILLIAM C. *The National Park Service* (New York: Praeger, 1972).

FORESTA, RONALD A. *America's National Parks and Their Keepers* (Washington, DC: Resources for the Future, 1984).

FOX, TOM, IAN KOEPPEL, and SUSAN KELLAM. *Struggle for Space: The Greening of New York City, 1970–1984* (New York: Neighborhood Open Space Coalition, 1985).

FROME, MICHAEL. *Battle for the Wilderness* (New York: Praeger, 1974).

GRAHAM, FRANK, JR. *The Adirondack Park: A Political History* (New York: Knopf, 1978).

HAINES, AUBREY. *The Yellowstone Story: A History of Our First National Park,* 2 vols. (Yellowstone, WY: Yellowstone Library and Museum Association, 1977).

HENDEE, JOHN, GEORGE H. STONKAY, and ROBERT C. LUCAS. *Wilderness Management* (Washington, DC: U.S. Government Printing Office, 1978).

HUTH, HANS. "Yosemite: The Story of an Idea," *Sierra Club Bulletin,* **33** (1948), 47–78.

ISE, JOHN. *Our National Park Policy: A Critical History* (Baltimore, MD: Johns Hopkins University Press, 1961).

JONES, HOLWAY R. *John Muir and the Sierra Club: The Battle for Yosemite* (San Francisco: Sierra Club, 1965).

KELLER, JANE EBLEN. *Adirondack Wilderness: A Story of Man and Nature* (Syracuse, NY: Syracuse University Press, 1980).

NASH, RODERICK. "Tourism, Parks and the Wilderness Idea in the History of Alaska," *Alaska in Perspective,* **4** (1981), 1–27.

――――. *Wilderness and the American Mind,* third, revised edition (New Haven, CT: Yale University Press, 1982).

RIGHTER, ROBERT W. *Crucible for Conservation: The Creation of Grand Teton National Park* (Boulder: Colorado Associated University Press, 1982).

ROBERTSON, DAVID. *West of Eden: A History of the Art and Literature of Yosemite* (Berkeley, CA: Yosemite Natural History Association, 1984).

ROTH, DENNIS M. *The Wilderness Movement and the National Forests, 1964–1980* (Washington, DC: U.S. Government Printing Office, 1984).

RUNTE, ALFRED. *National Parks: The American Experience,* second, revised edition (Lincoln: University of Nebraska Press, 1982).

RUSSELL, CARL P. *One Hundred Years in Yosemite: The Story of a Great Park and Its Friends* (Berkeley: University of California Press, 1947).

SAX, JOSEPH. *Mountains Without Handrails: Reflections on the National Parks* (Ann Arbor: University of Michigan Press, 1980).

STRONG, DOUGLAS. *Trees or Timber?: The Story of Sequoia and Kings Canyon National Parks* (Three Rivers, CA: Sequoia Natural History Association, 1968).

TERRIE, PHILIP. *Forever Wild: Environmental Aesthetics and the Adirondack Forest Preserve* (Philadelphia: Temple University Press, 1985).

TILDEN, FREEMAN. *State Parks* (New York: Knopf, 1962).

TWIGHT, BEN. *Organization Values and Political Power: The Forest Service Versus Olympic National Park* (University Park: Pennsylvania State University Press, 1983).

ZASLOWSKY, DYAN. *These American Lands: Parks, Wilderness and the Public Lands* (New York: Holt, 1986).

WATER

CLAPP, GORDON R. *The TVA: An Approach to the Development of a Region* (Chicago: University of Chicago Press, 1955).

FRADKIN, PHILIP L. *A River No More: The Colorado River and the West* (New York: Knopf, 1981).

FRANK, ARTHUR DEWITT. *The Development of the Federal Program of Flood Control on the Mississippi River* (New York: Columbia University Press, 1930).

FRANK, BERNARD AND ANTHONY NETBOY. *Water, Land and People* (New York: Knopf, 1950).

HARDING, SIDNEY T. *Water in California* (Palo Alto, CA: N-P Publications, 1960).

HART, HENRY. *The Dark Missouri* (Madison: University of Wisconsin Press, 1957).

High Country News and ED MARSTON. *Western Water Made Simple* (Washington, DC: Island, 1987).

HOFFMAN, ABRAHAM. *Vision or Villainy: Origins of the Owens Valley–Los Angeles Water Controversy* (College Station: Texas A&M University Press, 1981).

HUBBARD, PRESTON. *Origins of TVA: The Muscle Shoals Controversy, 1920–1932* (Nashville, TN: Vanderbilt, 1961).

HUFFMAN, ROY E. *Irrigation Development and Public Water Policy* (New York: Ronald, 1953).

HUNDLEY, NORRIS, JR. *Water and the West: The Colorado River Compact and the Politics of Water in the American West* (Berkeley: University of California Press, 1975).

JAMES, GEORGE WHARTON. *Reclaiming the Arid West: The Story of the United States Reclamation Service* (New York: Dodd and Mead, 1917).

KAHRL, WILLIAM. *Water and Power: The Conflict over Los Angeles' Water Supply in the Owens Valley* (Berkeley: University of California Press, 1982).

⌐CHTENBURG, WILLIAM E. *Flood Control Politics: The Connecticut River Valley Problem, 1927–1950* (Cambridge, MA: Harvard University Press, 1953).

MAASS, ARTHUR. *Muddy Waters: The Army Engineers and the Nation's Rivers* (Cambridge, MA: Harvard University Press, 1951).

MORGAN, MURRAY C. *The Columbia: Powerhouse of the West* (Seattle: Superior, 1949).

MURPHY, EARL FINBAR. *Water Purity: A Study in Legal Control of Natural Resources* (Madison: University of Wisconsin Press, 1961).

NADEAU, REMI A. *The Water Seeker* (New York: Doubleday, 1950).

PALMER, TIM. *Endangered Rivers and The Conservation Movement* (Berkeley: University of California Press, 1986).

PISANI, DONALD J. *From the Family Farm to Agribusiness: The Irrigation Crusade in California and the West, 1850–1931* (Berkeley: University of California Press, 1984).

REISNER, MARC. *Cadillac Desert: The American West and Its Disappearing Water* (New York: Viking, 1986).

SUNDBORG, GEORGE. *Hail Columbia: The Thirty-Year Struggle for Grand Coulee Dam* (New York: Macmillan, 1954).

WHEELER, BRUCE. *TVA and the Tellico Dam, 1936–1979* (Knoxville: University of Tennessee Press, 1986).

WORSTER, DONALD. *Rivers of Empire: Water, Aridity and the Growth of the American West* (New York: Pantheon, 1985).

ENVIRONMENTAL ETHICS

ALTFIELD, ROBIN. *The Ethics of Environmental Concern* (New York: Columbia University Press, 1983).

BARBOUR, IAN, ed. *Western Man and Environmental Ethics* (Reading, MA: Addison-Wesley, 1973).

BLACKSTONE, WILLIAM T., ed. *Philosophy and the Environmental Crisis* (Athens: University of Georgia Press, 1974).

CAHN, ROBERT. *Footprints on the Planet: A Search for An Environmental Ethic* (New York: Universe, 1978).

DEVALL, BILL and GEORGE SESSIONS. *Deep Ecology: Living as if Nature Mattered* (Salt Lake City, UT: Peregrine Smith, 1985).

FOX, MICHAEL ALLEN and LEO GROARKE, eds. *Nuclear War: Philosophical Perspectives* (New York: Lang, 1985).

HARGROVE, EUGENE, ed. *Beyond Spaceship Earth: Environmental Ethics and the Solar System* (San Francisco: Sierra Club, 1986).

———, ed. *Religion and Environmental Crisis* (Athens: University of Georgia Press, 1986).

———. *Foundations of Environmental Ethics* (New York: Prentice-Hall, 1988).

NASH, RODERICK. *The Rights of Nature: A History of Environmental Ethics* (Madison: University of Wisconsin Press, 1988).

NORTON, BRYON G. *Why Preserve Natural Variety?* (Princeton, NJ: Princeton University Press, 1988).

PASSMORE, JOHN. *Man's Responsibility for Nature: Ecological Problems and Western Traditions* (London: Duckworth, 1974).

RALSTON, HOLMES. *Philosophy Gone Wild: Essays in Environmental Ethics* (Buffalo: NY, Prometheus, 1986).

REGAN, TOM, ed. *Earthbound: New Introductory Essays in Environmental Ethics* (New York: Random House, 1984).

ROLSTON, HOLMES. *Environmental Ethics: Duties to and Value in the Natural World* (Philadelphia: Temple University Press, 1988).

SALE, KIRKPATRICK. *Dwellers in the Land: The Bioregional Vision* (San Francisco: Sierra Club, 1981).

SCHERER, DONALD and THOMAS ATLIG, eds. *Ethics and the Environment* (Englewood Cliffs, NJ: Prentice-Hall, 1983).

TOBIAS, MICHAEL, ed. *Deep Ecology* (San Diego, CA: Avant, 1985).

BIOGRAPHY

BRINK, WELLINGTON. *Big Hugh: The Father of Soil Conservation* (New York: Macmillan, 1951) (concerns Hugh Hammond Bennett).

CALLICOTT, BAIRD, ed. *Companion to a Sand County Almanac* (Madison: University of Wisconsin Press, 1987).

COHEN, MICHAEL P. *The Pathless Way: John Muir and American Wilderness* (Madison: University of Wisconsin Press, 1984).

CUTRIGHT, PAUL RUSSELL. *Theodore Roosevelt: The Making of a Conservationist* (Champaign: University of Illinois Press, 1985).

DARRAH, WILLIAM CULP. *Powell of the Colorado* (Princeton, NJ: Princeton University Press, 1954).

FAUSOLD, MARTIN L. *Gifford Pinchot, Bull Moose Progressive* (Syracuse, NY: Syracuse University Press, 1961).

FLADER, SUSAN L. *Thinking Like A Mountain: Aldo Leopold and the Evolution of an Ecological Attitude Toward Deer, Wolves and Forests* (Columbia, MO: University of Missouri Press, 1974).

FOX, STEPHEN. *John Muir and His Legacy: The American Conservation Movement* (Boston: Little Brown, 1981).

GARTNER, CAROL B. *Rachel Carson* (New York: Ungar, 1983).

GLOVER, JAMES. *A Wilderness Original: The Life of Bob Marshall* (Seattle, WA: Mountaineers, 1986).

HALES, PETER B. *William Henry Jackson and the Transformation of The American Landscape* (Philadelphia: Temple University Press, 1988).

HUNTINGTON, DAVID C. *The Landscapes of Frederic Edwin Church* (New York: Braziller, 1966).

LENDT, DAVID L. *Ding: The Life of Jay Norwood Darling* (Ames: Iowa State University Press, 1979).

LOWENTHAL, DAVID. *George Perkins Marsh: Versatile Vermonter* (New York: Columbia University Press, 1958).

MARGOLIS, JOHN D. *Joseph Wood Krutch: A Writer's Life* (Knoxville: University of Tennessee Press, 1980).

MCCRACKEN, HAROLD. *George Catlin and the Old Frontier* (New York: Dial, 1959).

MCGEARY, M. NELSON. *Gifford Pinchot: Forester-Politician* (Princeton, NJ: Princeton University Press, 1960).

MCPHEE, JOHN. *Encounters with the Archdruid* (New York: Farrar, Straus and Giroux, 1971) (biographical treatment of David R. Brower).

MEINE, CURT. *Aldo Leopold: His Life and Work* (Madison: University of Wisconsin Press, 1988).

MORGAN, GEORGE T. JR. *William B. Greeley, a Practical Forester, 1879–1955* (St. Paul, MN: Forest History Society, 1961).

PAUL, SHERMAN. *The Shores of America: Thoreau's Inward Exploration* (Urbana: University of Illinois Press, 1959).

PINKETT, HAROLD T. *Gifford Pinchot: Private and Public Forester* (Urbana: University of Illinois Press, 1970).

RICHARDSON, ROBERT D. *Henry Thoreau: A Life of the Mind* (Berkeley: University of California Press, 1986).

RODGERS, ANDREW DENNEY. *Bernhard Eduard Fernow: A Story of North American Forestry* (Princeton, NJ: Princeton University Press, 1951).

SHANKLAND, ROBERT. *Steve Mather of the National Parks,* second, revised edition (New York: Knopf, 1954).

STEGNER, WALLACE. *Beyond the Hundredth Meridian: John Wesley Powell and the Second Opening of the West* (Boston: Houghton Mifflin, 1954).

SWAIN, DONALD C. *Wilderness Defender: Horace M. Albright and Conservation* (Chicago: University of Chicago Press, 1970).

TANNER, THOMAS, ed. *Aldo Leopold: The Man and His Legacy* (Ankeny, IA: Soil Conservation Society, 1987).

TURNER, FREDERICK. *Rediscovering America: John Muir in His Time and Ours* (New York: Viking, 1985).

WADLAND, JOHN HENRY. *Ernest Thompson Seton: Man and Nature in the Progressive Era, 1880–1915* (New York: Arno, 1978).

WHITE, GRAHAM and JOHN MAZE. *Harold Ickes of the New Deal: His Private Life and Public Career* (Cambridge, MA: Harvard University Press, 1985).

WILKINS, THURMAN. *Thomas Moran: Artist of the Mountains* (Norman: University of Oklahoma Press, 1966).

WOLFE, LINNIE MARSH. *Son of the Wilderness: The Life of John Muir* (New York: Knopf, 1945).

ZUCKER, NORMAN. *George W. Norris* (Urbana: University of Illinois Press, 1966).